Reshaping Blended Learning Environments With AI

Shafiq Ul Rehman
Kingdom University, Bahrain

IGI Global
Scientific Publishing
Publishing Tomorrow's Research Today

Vice President of Editorial — Melissa Wagner
Director of Acquisitions — Mikaela Felty
Director of Book Development — Jocelynn Hessler
Production Manager — Mike Brehm
Cover Design — Jose Rosado

Published in the United States of America by
IGI Global Scientific Publishing
701 East Chocolate Avenue
Hershey, PA, 17033, USA
Tel: 717-533-8845 | Fax: 717-533-7115
Website: https://www.igi-global.com E-mail: cust@igi-global.com

Copyright © 2026 by IGI Global Scientific Publishing. All rights reserved. No part of this publication may be reproduced, stored or distributed in any form or by any means, electronic or mechanical, including photocopying, without written permission from the publisher. Use of this publication to train generative artificial intelligence (AI) technologies is expressly prohibited. The publisher reserves all rights to license its use for generative AI training and machine learning model development.

Product or company names used in this set are for identification purposes only. Inclusion of the names of the products or companies does not indicate a claim of ownership by IGI Global Scientific Publishing of the trademark or registered trademark.

Library of Congress Cataloging-in-Publication Data

Names: Ul Rehman, Shafiq, 1981- editor
http://id.loc.gov/authorities/names/n2025007696
http://id.loc.gov/rwo/agents/n2025007696
Title: Reshaping blended learning environments with AI / [edited by] Shafiq Ul Rehman.
Description: Hershey, PA : IGI Global Scienitfic Publishing, [2026] | Includes bibliographical references and index. | Summary: "This book aims to provide practical insights, real-world applications, and case studies demonstrating the role of AI in personalizing learning, automating administrative tasks, and improving student engagement"-- Provided by publisher.
Identifiers: LCCN 2025021002 (print) | LCCN 2025021003 (ebook) | ISBN 9798337338156 hardcover | ISBN 9798337338163 paperback | ISBN 9798337338170 ebook
Subjects: LCSH: Blended learning--Technological innovations | Artificial intelligence--Educational applications
http://id.loc.gov/authorities/subjects/sh87006783
Classification: LCC LB1028.5 .R4284 2026 (print) | LCC LB1028.5 (ebook) | DDC 371.33/463--dc23/eng/20250621
LC record available at https://lccn.loc.gov/2025021002
LC ebook record available at https://lccn.loc.gov/2025021003

British Cataloguing in Publication Data
A Cataloguing in Publication record for this book is available from the British Library.

All work contributed to this book is new, previously-unpublished material.
The views expressed in this book are those of the authors, but not necessarily of the publisher.
This book contains information sourced from authentic and highly regarded references, with reasonable efforts made to ensure the reliability of the data and information presented. The authors, editors, and publisher believe the information in this book to be accurate and true as of the date of publication. Every effort has been made to trace and credit the copyright holders of all materials included. However, the authors, editors, and publisher cannot assume responsibility for the validity of all materials or the consequences of their use. Should any copyright material be found unacknowledged, please inform the publisher so that corrections may be made in future reprints.

Table of Contents

Detailed Table of Contents

Blended learning has emerged as a transformative educational model, combining digital instruction with conventional classrooms. As academic institutions try to answer the growing demands of learners, AI-aided adaptive learning algorithms become a tool for personalized data-driven means of instruction. The chapter explores adaptive learning algorithms for maximizing effective use of a blended learning environment by tailoring content, pace, and feedback to a student's needs in real-time. Focusing on the architecture and application of adaptive systems in various learning platforms, and discusses how AI models evolve continually on the basis of learner's behavior and performance. Real-world case studies provide the chapter with examples of adaptive algorithms in practice across disciplines. Issues of ethics like data privacy and biases in algorithmic decisions, are also critically analyzed. This chapter extends promising recommendations to instructors, instructional designers, and policymakers to develop an inclusive, efficient, and effective mode of AI-based education.

This chapter explores the role of artificial intelligence (AI) and summative assessment in blended learning environments, beginning with the historical evolution of assessment systems. It highlights the limitations of traditional methods in objectivity, validity, inclusiveness, and feedback. AI technologies address these issues through functions such as personalised learning, real-time feedback, automated scoring, and enhanced test security. AI not only reduces teachers' workload but also enriches students' learning through data-driven insights. While formative assessment guides learning based on immediate performance data, summative assessment evaluates outcomes effectively. These AI-supported approaches transform assessment into a continuous, integrated component of the learning process. The chapter also addresses ethical concerns, such as data privacy and algorithmic fairness, stressing the importance of teacher competence and secure data handling. In conclusion, AI-

Preface

The rapid advancement of Artificial Intelligence (AI) has brought profound shifts across nearly every facet of society, but nowhere is its transformative potential more visible than in the realm of education. As traditional teaching models increasingly give way to flexible, data-driven, and student-centered approaches, the integration of AI into blended learning environments has emerged not just as a possibility, but as a necessity.

Reshaping Blended Learning Environments with AI presents a comprehensive exploration of how AI is reshaping educational landscapes, offering new models for personalization, engagement, assessment, support, and governance in both physical and digital classrooms. This edited volume brings together diverse voices from across academic disciplines and geographic regions to unpack the multifaceted relationship between AI technologies and blended learning pedagogies.

The book addresses a central question: How can educators, institutions, and policymakers leverage AI to make learning more inclusive, effective, and future-ready, while navigating the ethical, technical, and systemic challenges it brings?

What emerges is a dynamic collection of chapters that not only examine AI's technical capabilities but also reflect deeply on its pedagogical, social, and ethical dimensions. Together, they form a blueprint for designing, implementing, and governing AI-enhanced blended learning systems in ways that are humane, adaptive, and sustainable.

CHAPTER OVERVIEW

Chapter 1: Tracing the Intellectual Landscape of Learning Design and Technology: Four Decades of Insights and Emerging Trends

The opening chapter offers a rich historical and theoretical foundation for understanding how learning design has evolved over four decades. It maps the shift from traditional instructional models to AI-driven, learner-centered digital frameworks, and sets the stage for understanding the interplay between pedagogy and technology.

Chapter 2: Blended Learning in the Age of Artificial Intelligence: Transforming Education through Innovation

This chapter delves into how AI is transforming education through personalized learning, predictive analytics, and intelligent automation. It balances innovation with caution, addressing the ethical implications and policy needs for AI's responsible adoption in blended education.

Chapter 3: AI-Enhanced Network Learning Theory Transforming Education Through Personalized, Inclusive, and Ethical Artificial Intelligence

A theoretical contribution, this chapter introduces AI-Enhanced Network Learning Theory (AI-NLT), framing learning as the product of human-AI-network collaboration. The chapter outlines a model for ethical and inclusive AI-based learning systems, backed by a case study on human-AI co-creation.

Chapter 4: AI-Powered Personalization: Redefining Learner Pathways in Blended Classrooms

Focusing on the philosophical and pedagogical shifts brought by AI, this chapter reimagines personalization not just as algorithmic adaptation but as a redefinition of learning agency, equity, and engagement within the blended classroom.

Chapter 5: From One-Size-Fits-All to Just-for-Me, Adaptive Learning Algorithms Transforming Blended Education

This practical chapter explores the architecture and implementation of adaptive learning systems, providing real-world examples of how AI can dynamically tailor content and feedback. It also critically addresses concerns around bias, data ethics, and equitable access.

Chapter 6: Artificial Intelligence Supported Formative and Summative Assessment Approaches in Blended Learning Environments

Here, the authors investigate how AI transforms assessment into a continuous, feedback-rich process. By improving objectivity and providing real-time insights, AI reshapes how learning is measured—though ethical concerns around surveillance and fairness remain pivotal.

Chapter 7: How AI Chatbots Enhance Student Support in Higher education? Exploring the Opportunities and Challenges

This chapter examines the growing role of AI-powered chatbots in enhancing student services. It evaluates both the opportunities (24/7 support, administrative automation, personalized guidance) and the challenges (data ethics, engagement quality, contextual adaptation).

Chapter 8: Integration of Artificial Intelligence in Blended Business Education: Fostering Critical Thinking and Student Engagement

By focusing on business schools, this chapter presents a framework for using AI to foster critical thinking and student engagement in blended environments. It warns against the risk of surface learning while advocating for AI's strategic alignment with cognitive outcomes.

Chapter 9: From Passive Learning to Experiential Engagement the Role of AI and Immersive Technologies in: Tourism Education

Tourism education demands contextual, experiential learning. This chapter highlights how AI and immersive technologies like VR/AR are enriching blended tourism pedagogy by creating engaging, real-world simulations that enhance motivation and learning outcomes.

Chapter 10: Exploring the Integration of AI and Metaverse in Education- Opportunities, Challenges, and Future Directions

Exploring a frontier domain, this conceptual chapter discusses the convergence of AI and the metaverse. It proposes a comprehensive framework for integrating immersive, intelligent systems into education while addressing access, ethics, and governance.

Chapter 11: Crafting Education Policies and Governance: Factoring the Eclipse of Artificial Intelligence

The final chapter emphasizes the critical need for responsive, context-sensitive policy frameworks that guide AI integration. Drawing on global examples, it outlines a governance model that balances AI's promise with its ethical and infrastructural risks.

As the chapters collectively demonstrate, AI is a transformative force that compels educators, designers, and policymakers to reimagine what learning means in the 21st century. From algorithmic personalization to immersive metaverse experiences, from adaptive assessments to intelligent support systems, this volume invites readers to engage critically and creatively with the question: How can we shape AI-enhanced blended learning environments that are smart, just, inclusive, and human-centered?

It is our hope that this book serves as a resource, a provocation, and a collaborative guide for all those who are committed to reshaping education for a more intelligent and equitable future.

Shafiq Ul Rehman
Kingdom University, Bahrain

Chapter 1

Tracing the Intellectual Landscape of Learning Design and Technology: Four Decades of Insights and Emerging Trends

Shikha Mann
https://orcid.org/0000-0003-0395-9164
School of Business, Indira University, Pune, India

Sakshi Mann
https://orcid.org/0009-0002-8238-5268
School of Business, Indira University, Pune, India

Yogesh Mahajan
Symbiosis Centre for Management and Human Resource Development, Symbiosis International University, India

Tausif Mistry
https://orcid.org/0000-0003-2377-9371
School of Business, Indira University, Pune, India

ABSTRACT

The field of Learning Design and Technology is transforming education by integrating innovative instructional strategies with emerging technologies. This chapter explores key theories, models, and digital tools that enhance teaching effectiveness and learner engagement. It delves into instructional design frameworks, adaptive learning environments, and the role of artificial intelligence, gamification, and data analytics in personalizing education. Additionally, it examines best practices

DOI: 10.4018/979-8-3373-3815-6.ch001

…right © 2026, IGI Global Scientific Publishing. Copying or distributing in print or electronic forms without written permission of IGI Global Scientific Publishing is prohibited. Use of this chapter to …in generative artificial intelligence (AI) technologies is expressly prohibited. The publisher reserves all rights to license its use for generative AI training and machine learning model development.

for creating interactive, inclusive, and accessible learning experiences in diverse educational settings. By bridging pedagogy with technological advancements, this chapter provides educators, instructional designers, and institutions with insights into designing impactful, learner-centered digital education frameworks that cater to evolving academic and professional demands.

INTRODUCTION

Learning Design and Technology (LDT) refers to the practice of using sophisticated technology in combination with effective pedagogical interventions to improve learning (Morrison et al, 2019). LDT is also focused on the development of immersive and personalized learning programs that empower the learners with abilities to deal with the current digital environment (Goodyear & Retalis, 2010). The current education environment necessitates the employment of LDT due to an ever-changing technological environment on which we reside in our schools and colleges nowadays. There is an ongoing pressure from these schools and colleges to adopt new approaches that can help them integrate technology into their pedagogical interventions alongside an interest in maximizing their learners' learning achievements alongside experiences (Ertmer & Newby, 2013).

The new education system relies on the ability of LDT to enhance access and facilitate individualized learning alongside addressing diverse students' needs as claimed by Reigeluth et al. (2017).

The trend shows that the researchers are keen on knowing trends in research and contributions in LDT, and researchers have conducted various exploratory studies on various facets of LDT ranging from new technology used in teaching methods to research on how the technology changes trends used for learning (Johann et al, 2020).

The research area in LDT has been enriched greatly because of these efforts, which were conducted in 2019. To derive valuable insights into existing trends of LDT as well as to understand its limitation and guide towards future research direction it is imperative to conduct a bibliometric analysis (Zupic & Čater, 2015).

The discipline of Learning Design and Technology (LDT) has grown exponentially over the last few years; however, there is a lack as far as definitive analyses go in terms of the representative scholarly literature of its breadth as well as depth in this discipline as per Morrison et al., 2019 There is a broad spectrum of studies in the discipline of the LDT, which has been derived from diverging viewpoints researching disparate themes and geographies (Saçak et al, 2022) Researchers are likely to suffer from attempting to identify prevailing areas of research or even make constructive contributions if they lack a bird's eye view of the topic at hand.

One possible way of addressing the requirement is through bibliometric research, as a quantitative approach such as bibliometric analysis might be able to make astute observations about trends in journal literature that would otherwise be invisible (Zupic & Čater, 2015). A lot can be learned regarding LDT's research landscape if it is observed at a macroscopic scale - this includes notable information like most cited papers and top authors and an overview of common topics (Haustein, 2016).

Macroscopic view provided by Sugimoto & Larivière (2018) is a good means of shedding light on the broad trend of LDT research under which the decision-making of the stakeholders can be made in a well-informed manner.

Our purpose in this research essay is to investigate academic literature in Learning Design and Technology (LDT) using bibliometric analysis, which is especially useful in understanding an overview of the structural growth and evolution of a specific discipline in terms of systematic assessment and analysis of research trends (Zupic & Čater, 2015). In their recent publication of LDT research contributions (Park & Lee, 2022), it is suggested that such studies can potentially provide a big-picture statistical assessment on scholarship's contribution to this ever-evolving discipline.

From its identification of the most prominent research themes and trend authors in LDT this research is well-placed to make a valuable contribution. Secondly, from tracking the development of this field over the years researchers are able to discern future areas of research and contribute to future research directions (Haustein, 2016). Tracking the research agenda in LDTs allows educators and policymakers to make informed decisions that reflect their interest. Further, carrying out a bibliometrics study helps to integrate ideas and consolidate them in the LDT field and contribute to greater clarity and brevity. Intellectual orders in LDT research became apparent through this exercise by categorizing existing themes in an attempt to identify emerging trends and highlighting strong interdisciplinary relationships for future research (Bornmann & Mutz, 2015).

According to the above, the present study intends to achieve the following research objectives:

- To conduct a comprehensive bibliometric study of the scholarly literature in LDT.
- To identify and examine the main research topics, key papers, and main authors in the subject.
- To trace the evolution of LDT research over time and to identify emerging research frontiers.
- To inform future research directions and policy decisions in LDT.

These results from our bibliometric study hold considerable weight for numerous stakeholders operating within Learning Design and Technology (LDT) and the broad-ranging implications for further research that these thorough and numerical assessments of LDT literature provide are noteworthy. By revealing key recurring topics that researchers have examined in this area and uncovering key gaps or opportunities to explore new ideas further, we hope that these findings support future work conducted here. According to Zupic & Čater's (2015) study results, researchers may be assisted by it in devising their research schedules while motivating new strands of investigation. Policy makers can use these findings to create effective evidence-based strategies and programs for addressing the changing needs and challenges in LDT. Familiarity with key trends and trajectories helps policymakers to develop policies that promote excellence in the field with an emphasis on innovation (Haustein, 2016).

Becoming informed by these insights will not only enhance understanding of effective LDT practices but will also aid in making informed choices when it comes to integrating technology into their teaching strategies(Bhandari, 2022).

LITERATURE REVIEW

In order to enhance the process and results of education through technology, LDT applies knowledge and techniques creatively (Branch & Merrill, 2012), and looking at it historically reveals that LDT originates from the mid-twentieth century's programmed instruction and audiovisual education movements. During its formative years the field concentrated largely on using technology as a means to advance customary instructional methods. The initial technological breakthroughs in this area involved incorporating filmstrips and overhead projectors along with audio tapes to supplement classroom learning (Reiser, 2001), but with the passage of time the field embraced technological advancements and incorporated sophisticated design principles for better learning.

This development was greatly influenced by the rise of the digital era. Advancements in computing such as personal computers and mobile devices have paved the way for incorporating technology into learning experiences (Mishra & Koehler, 2006), considering technology as an indispensable part of education has resulted in a wide range of technology-enhanced learning spaces (Ertmer & Newby, 2013). Collaborative and tailored study sessions are facilitated through utilizing technology as a tool within the context of LDT. With its focus on integrating instructional design with learning theories as well as technological expertise (Goodyear & Retalis, 2010), it seeks to enhance the efficiency and effectiveness of studying.

In Learning Design and Technology (LDT) research it has been established that technology plays a crucial role in learning and instruction. The history of technologies used for education spans from simple audiovisual aids like filmstrips and overhead projectors to early computer systems. In light of the digital era we now have access to a more varied and advanced range of educational technologies. Flexible, personalized, and interactive learning environments are now possible thanks to digital technologies such as personal computers, internet, mobile devices, Multimedia Applications, and Learning Management Systems(Ertmer & Newby, 2013; Wu et al, 2012) cite advancements in artificial intelligence along with virtual reality and augmented reality as the main drivers widening LDT's horizon. These technologies have the potential to create immersive and authentic learning experiences while also providing support for adaptive and competency based-learning paradigms according to Johnson et al (2016).

While there are manifold benefits to using technology in the classroom, there are also obstacles to consider. Incorporating technology in education can lead to better learning outcomes by promoting collaborative activities for students while also allowing for formative assessments that build essential skills for the future (Roblyer & Doering, 2007).Although progress has been made towards integrating technology into education system some challenges persist like inadequate technical competencies among both teachers and pupils as well as unbalanced technological access across different areas (Ertmer, 2005), there is an increasing emphasis on addressing data security concerns as well as ethical questions regarding the use of technology in current debates (Marshall, 2018). To conclude our discussion on the critical topic of LDT research, technology plays a vital role in improving learning. However, it has its own set of complexities that must be analyzed. Learning theorists' insights are a crucial factor in the development of Learning Design and Technology (LDT) and there have been different learning theories that have informed instructional design and use of technology for learning.

Behaviorism, cognitivism, and constructivism have typically guided the development of LDT. However, it has been found that in computer-based training programs which apply reinforcement strategies for learning (Ertmer & Newby, 2013), the use of behaviorist principles is effective. Considering the limits of working memory falls under cognitivist principles and informs the design of multimedia learning environments (Mayer, 2011), while constructivist thinking has given rise to the creation of interactive problem-solving spaces for learners that help them in developing their understanding of a topic (Jonassen and Rohrer-Murphy, 1999).

Theories like socioculturalism and constructivism are gaining popularity lately as they reflect how digital tech affects learning. Collaborative digital teaching platforms enabled through web 2.0 technologies have been developed based on the principles laid out by Vygotsky's (1978) sociocultural theories with regards to the pivotal role played by social interaction and cultural tools in facilitating effective knowledge acquisition. In an era where information overflows abundantly every day around us, Connectivism becomes more relevant by highlighting the importance of both networked learning and knowledge management (Goldie, 2016).

Significant improvement in learning performance is achievable through the use of instructional design as a science of implementing theoretical principles. Enhanced understanding and memory gained via instruction well-crafted can be translated into enhanced learning performance as indicated by Morrison et al (2011). Use of multimedia learning principles of contiguity and modality reduction has been shown to facilitate one's ability to understand and remember learning material (Mayer & Moreno, 2003).

To sum up earlier comments made - acquiring knowledge about learning theories is a must while designing effective learning spaces. It's also crucial to realize that successful implementation of these based designs to a great extent relies on successful instructional design to bring forth positive learning outcomes. Emerging technologies shape the field of Learning Design and Technology (LDT) with the passage of time Artificial Intelligence(AI), Virtual Reality(VR),(AR) Augmented Reality and Learning Analytics overshadow other fields in importance in these changing issues. AI has revolutionized the manner in which we are conducting education by providing intelligent tutors for individualized instruction and grading essays and other assignments automatically while providing adaptive learning platforms for each student's need. By providing individualized instruction that adjusts itself according to learners' personal feedback and needs which results in better academic outcomes is the promise of AI. In the interest of ethics and privacy concerns about AI's data-based characterization measures need to be taken (Holmes et al, 2019). Teaching and learning can be revolutionized by employing VR and AR by creating experiential environments that enable better comprehension. In both medical and history educations, VR serves as an important tool respectively for surgical training and event recreation (Huang et al, 2019). By overlaying digital content over the real-world environment in just-in-time contexts AR allows for contextualized learning opportunities as discussed by Radu (2014).

Data collection through the use of Learning Analytics can help provide powerful insights that will aid in understanding and improving the methods of teaching(Siemens, 2013) Insights gained from this approach into student performance and engagement can inform instructional design for better personalized learning. Sharples et al (2016) predicts a shift towards decentralized educational systems using blockchain technology and increased utilization of neurotechnology to enhance cognitive capacity. Yet these hypothetical trends do raise key questions about how to ensure both fairness and privacy in handling information.

When exploring emerging technologies that may shape the future of education it is vitally important to address their pedagogical implications along with technical feasibility as well as ethical dimensions by carefully considering what will promote effective learning outcomes which remain fair-minded.

The Learning Design and Technology (LDT) discipline has benefited greatly from the important works of notable authors, including Mayer's (2011) extensive research on the cognitive theory of multimedia design and multimedia learning is considered instrumental in shaping technology-enhanced learning environments (Mayer, 2011), and as a result of his research on constructivist learning environments and problem-solving techniques (Jonassen and Rohrer-Murphy, 1999), David Jonassen has become an eminent scholar. George Siemens played a vital role in this matter through introducing Connectivism theory which strongly emphasizes on the role of networks and technology for successful learning outcomes (Siemens, 2004). LDT was greatly impacted by the revolutionary contributions of seminal works, and the design of multimedia instruction should incorporate principles that align with our knowledge about how the human brain operates. This is according to Mayer's 'Multimedia Learning' (2009) and according to Jonassen's 'Designing Constructivist Learning Environments' (1999), effective learning requires a genuine and contextual approach. By writing about 'Connectivism: A Learning Theory for the Digital Age', Siemens(2005) contributed significantly to improving educators' and researcher's knowledge of learning mechanisms in a digital age.

Numerous research findings in LDT hold theoretical as well as practical significance. Multimedia designers should take note from research into multimedia design principles that found aligned audio and visual content resulted in more effective learning outcomes thus contributing to advancements in both instructional practices and media tool development (Mayer & Moreno, 2003). Gaining insight into the scholarly scope of LDT by recognizing influential authors & works as well as comprehending key research findings would assist in informing the field's prospective avenues.

Analyzing the impact and influence of scholarly publications quantitatively through bibliometrics is crucial to gaining insight into research trends within LDT, and the structured approach presented by Zupic and Cater's (2015) allows us to gain insight into how the discipline has evolved having considered contributions from leading scholars.

To develop an integrated perception of LDT, which is dynamically changing at a high rate; conduct an advanced bibliometric analysis that fills knowledge gaps & proposes probable areas of research in the future.

Several analyses of publications under related topics provide useful findings, and the findings of a bibliometric study by Zawacki-Richter et al (2019) revealed how the emphasis has been on more networked and collaborative learning approaches compared to individual-based ones. Their study revealed leading authors while providing top academic journals and nations that contribute significantly to this specific field. Furthermore, educational technology researchers have been interested in leading themes such as blended learning and game-based learning based on

Tlili et al.'s (2022) bibliometric study had some limitations, however, as some of the newest themes in the LDT field might not have been covered by the otherwise useful studies. A bibliometric study conducted specifically for LDT will contribute to these efforts by providing a more focused study of scholarly output in this field. Using an analytical process, this tool is able to identify which authors have created useful work on a particular subject matter like their publications and leading research topics. Furthermore, this kind of study may contribute to revealing possible emerging areas and directions that need further research to benefit the course of LDT research and practice.

In short, Learning Design and Technology (LDT) has profound historical roots alongside new emerging trends that can be used to drive future innovative technology. These concepts date back decades to when Instructional Design Theory's core principles were the basis of what we still see today (Reigeluth, 1999). Adopting technology has brought about considerable benefits such as customized learning and enhanced outcomes although challenges still exist (Huang et al, 2010). Significant contribution towards the understanding of multimenda learning, constructivist environments, and networked learning brought by renowned personalities in LDT including Mayer, Jonnasen as well as Siemens (Mayor:2009; Jonnasen:1999; Siemans:2014).

New advances such as AI and VR indicate a fresh direction for the field through emerging technologies (Holmes et al, 2019; Huang et al, 2010). To fully comprehend emerging trends and scholarly contributions within LDT research community requires objectivity that can be achieved through the use of bibliometric analysis (Zupic & Čater 2015).

Even though there are existing bibliometric studies on relevant subjects (Zawacki-Richter et al, 2019). The aim of this current study is to overcome the gap by facilitating a detailed comprehension regarding LDT's development alongside its major players along with significant literature contributions and upcoming movements, thereby contributing to the already established body of knowledge. This provides valuable input into shaping future research direction as well as informing key aspects of education practice and public policies in this vital domain.

SCOPE AND METHODOLOGY

The keyword used for this study in scopus database are- "learning Design" and "Technology". On limiting the search to publications in the field of Business Management and Accounting and considering only research articles in journals and conference proceedings, 666 publications were received as csv output as on 20th June 2023. These 666 articles constitute the scope of this research paper. We made use of the bibliometrix package in R to analyze, scrutinize, use data visualization on this dataset which is a potent instrument developed specifically for exhaustive bibliometric analyses. This invaluable tool was fashioned by Aria and Cuccurullo (2017) primarily to help extract practical information from bibliographic data. Specifically created to handle the complex data structures characteristic of significant bibliographic datasets; it boasts a wide range of functions.

ANALYSIS

Data summary

Table 1 depicts the summary of the input data. A total of 666 documents published in period 1977 to 2023

Table 1. Data summary

Description	Results
Timespan	1977:2023
Sources (Journals, Books, etc)	266
Documents	666
Annual Growth Rate %	7.25
Document Average Age	6.86
Average citations per doc	18.76
References	28441
Keywords Plus (ID)	1117
Author's Keywords (DE)	1964
Authors	1615
Authors of single-authored docs	150
Single-authored docs	160
Co-Authors per Doc	2.79
International co-authorships %	16.37
article	666

(source: biblioshiny)

Figure 1. Annual scientific production

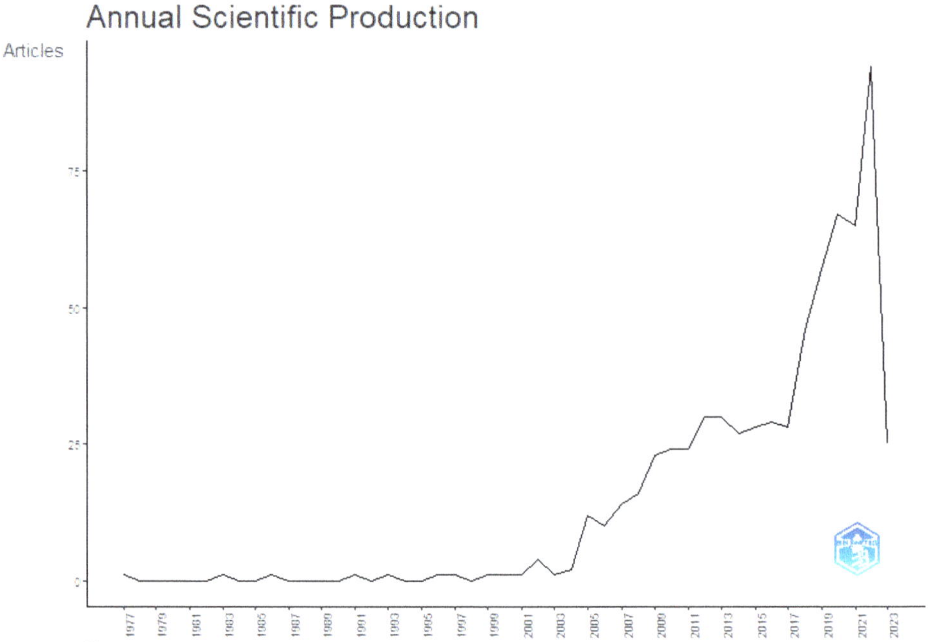

(source: Biblioshiny)

Figure 1 displays the annual scientific production by year. As depicted in graph, from 1977 to 2003, there has been steady rate of publications but from 2004 to 2016 there has been increase in documents published in the concerned subject area. After year 2005, the production in each year has been in double digits. From 2018 onwards, more than 40 documents have been published each year. Since this data is as on 20th May 2023, the year is yet not completed. In just about 5 months of 2023, 25 documents have already been published. These trends clearly establish the interest of researchers in the field of training design and technology.

Figure 2. Most relevant sources

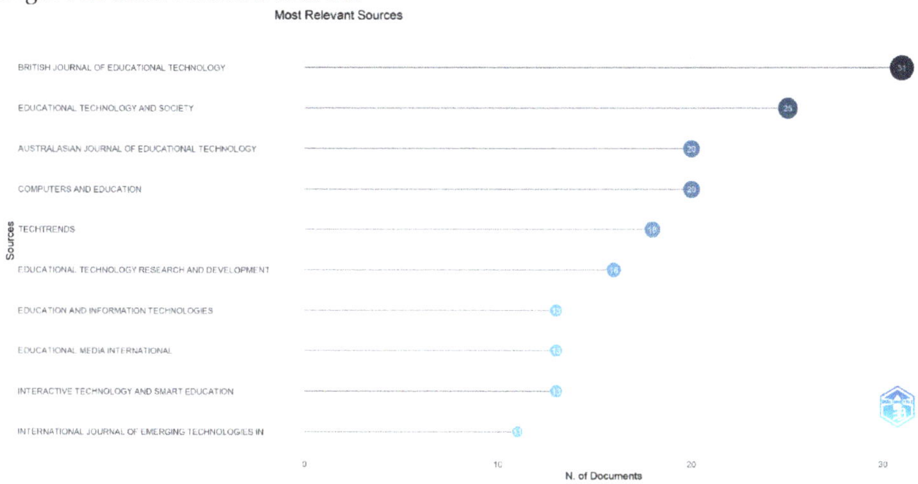

(Source: Biblioshiny)

Figure 2 depicts the most relevant sources by number of documents produced. The top two sources i.e. British Journal of Education Technology and Education technology and Society alone hold 31% of total publications (56/180).

Figure 3. Most relevant authors

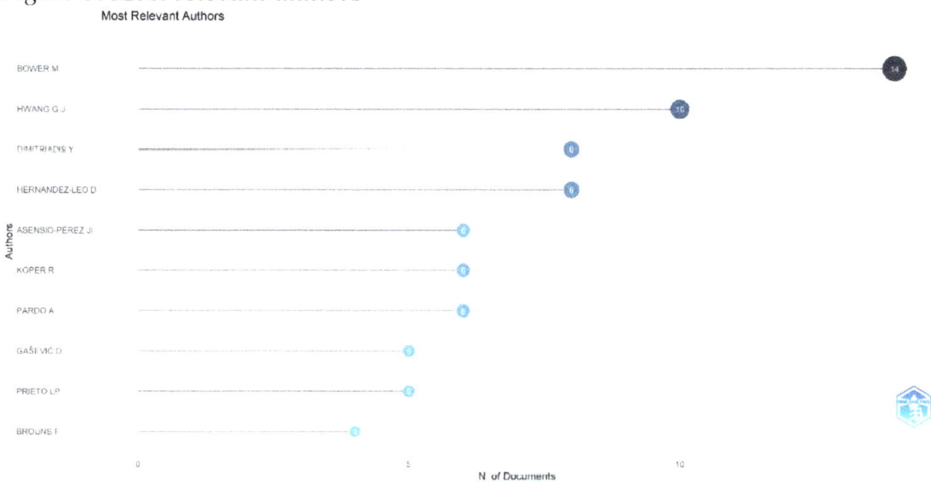

(Source: Biblioshiny)

As far as most relevant authors are concerned, Bower M (14 publications), Hwang G-J (10 publications), Dimitriadis and Hernandez (8 each publication) have highest number of publications thus their work can be studied by scholars interested in the field of learning, design and technology, to know more about this field.

Figure 4 depicts the most relevant keywords in the field of learning, design and technology. Teaching, students, e learning, education, learning designs, learning systems, engineering education, curriculum, design and learning are the most prominent keywords associated with concerned field of research. These keywords indicate the research trend.

Figure 4. Most relevant keywords

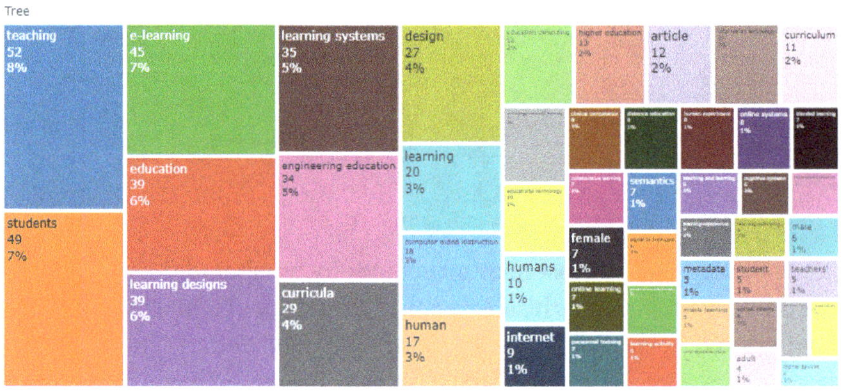

(source: Biblioshiny)

THEMATIC ANALYSIS

To analyse how the research has evolved over period of time, the entire research period has been segregated into 3 time zones: initial period from 1977-2014, developing period from 2015-2020 and advanced period from 2021-2023.

Figure 5. Alluvial diagram of thematic evolution

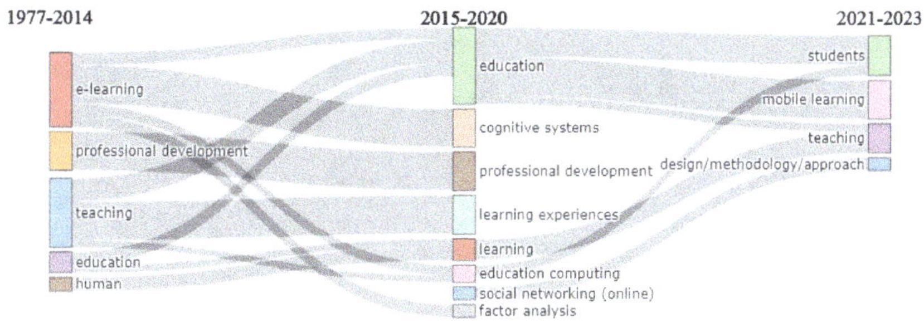

Thematic maps are one method for analysing and visualising the study areas of an academic discipline. It is a coordinate system made up of centrality (x axis) and density (y axis), and it was first put forth by Callon, Courtial, and Laville (1991). They claim that "centrality gauges the strength of a cluster's connections to other clusters. The stronger and more numerous the these connections are, the more this cluster considers a research problem as crucial by the research community" (p. 164), while "density characterises the strength of the connections binding the words in the cluster together. The more robust these relationships are, the associated research issues form a cohesive and integrated group.

Figure 6, 7, 8 represents the thematic maps of 3 phases.

Figure 6. Thematic map of Time slice 1 (1977-2014)

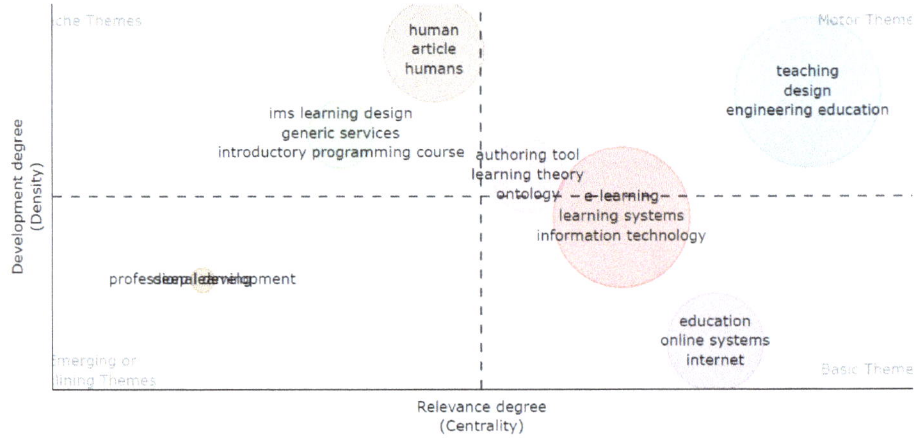

For the Time slice 1, initial period (1977-2014), the thematic analysis is as below

Major Motor Themes

Teaching, Design, Engineering Education:

Teaching and Design: This convergence highlights the importance of integrating design principles into educational methods. As instructional design gains prominence, this is the relevant trend.

Engineering Education: Engineering fields witnessed remarkable technological progress. Bridging engineering knowledge with teaching methods underscores the significance of engineering education.

Other Motor Themes

Authoring Tool: Throughout the 20th century's latter stages, digital tools were adopted to augment educational experiences. Since the introduction of authoring tools, teachers can produce new learning materials with relative simplicity.

Learning Theory: Through the incorporation of technological innovation and traditional teaching approaches, this theme significantly improves the learning process.

Group Work: Technology-supported collaboration is known to be one of the fundamental components of learning today, exemplified by the growing focus on group work.

Peripheral and Emerging Themes: Examining Human Relationships, LMS Learning Systems, and a First Programming Course

These are well-designed topics but not the central ones. The movement toward LMS adoption highlights the increasing importance of understanding learner needs and behaviors in educational technology design. The increase in programming courses is probably due to the recognition that these skills are essential.

Central and Underdeveloped Themes: E-learning, Learning Systems, Information Technology, Higher Education; Educational Systems, Web-Based Systems

The main themes are significant, but they are in a nascent stage in the sense that they are new subject matter. The advent of the internet witnessed e-learning and systems online being given a push but need time to develop.

Peripheral and Underdeveloped Theme: Professional Development, Deep Learning

Professional Development: The theme's inclusion indicates the growing importance of adapting to technological shifts through continuous learning and skill upgradation.

Deep Learning: As of 2014, deep learning was in its infancy stage regarding technology in education. The peripheral position of this domain is a reflection of its growth and experimentation.

In essence, the trends that have been uncovered highlight the shifting terrain of education and technology across four decades. The image depicts a field in the midst of rapid technological advancements, the internet's expansion, and the persistent pursuit of sound teaching methods.

Figure 7. Thematic map of Time slice 1 (2015-2020)

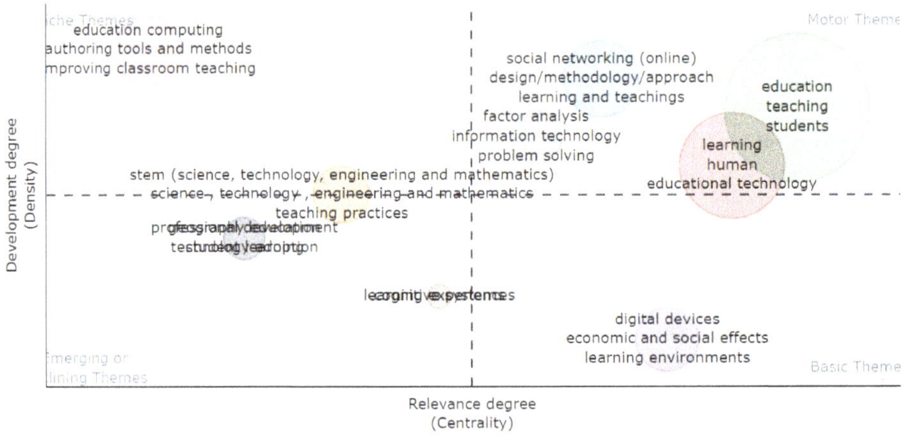

In time slice 1 (2015-2020), the themes and their probable background is as mentioned below-

Central and Developed Themes

Education, Teaching, Students

The primary emphasis continues to be placed on the fundamental principles of education. The rapid digitization of society created an urgent need to modify pedagogical approaches for a new breed of students.

Learning, Human, Education Technology, Internet, Curriculum

This period represented a fusion of traditional learning approaches with technological resources, indicating a transition phase. By emphasizing 'human', the importance of student-centric approach in tech adoption in education is underscored.

Social Networking, Social Media, Software, Design

This time frame witnessed a notable rise in the popularity of social media platforms for learning-related activities. These platforms' potential was realized by institutions, leading to their integration for information sharing, peer learning, and community building.

Information Technology, Problem Solving

The combination of these two elements suggests the growing priority of utilizing IT to bolster cognitive capabilities. With the incorporation of IT tools, students were better prepared to address real-world challenges via computational and critical thinking.

Central and Underdeveloped Themes

Digital Devices, Economic and Social Effects, Learning Environments

Despite being central to the conversation, these themes continued to develop. The advent of digital devices like tablets in classrooms marked a significant milestone, but their broader social and economic impact was yet to be evaluated. As with digital learning environments, there was a need to explore how to create them effectively.

Peripheral and Developed Themes

Education Computing, Authoring Tools and Methods, Improving Classroom Teaching

These themes, while not the main focus, carry substantial weight. The technology had advanced, enabling educational computing tools and platforms to mature. Both traditional and technologically-enhanced teaching methods were given equal importance, with an emphasis on refining classroom teaching methodologies.

STEM (Science, Technology, Engineering, and Mathematics)

In light of STEM's growing influence, a global focus on education has become more prominent. STEM's importance, though evident, remained in the background when compared to other themes like digital pedagogy or online learning.

Peripheral and Underdeveloped Themes

Geography Education, Technology Adoption

The relatively minor role geography education plays may result from its niche position in the educational sphere. Although this reference exists, it implies further examination of technological instruments.

The underdeveloped nature of technology adoption might indicate the challenges encountered by institutions while smoothly incorporating new technological tools into their curriculum.

In this period, educational institutions endeavored to incorporate and navigate the digital revolution. The study revealed mature and central themes alongside evolving ones, underscoring future research opportunities.

Figure 8. Thematic map of Time slice 2 (2021-23)

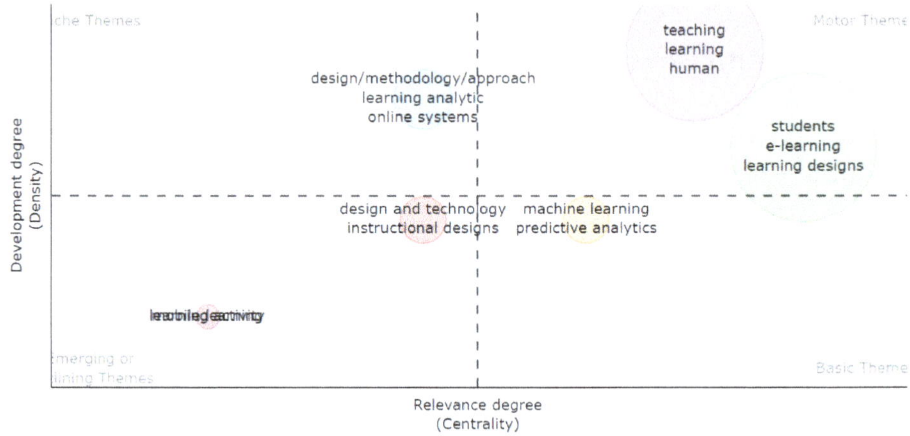

In time slice 3 (2021-2023), the themes and their probable background is as mentioned below-

Central and Developed Themes

Students, E-learning, Learning Designs, Learning Systems, Curricula, Designs

Post-pandemic Influence: The pandemic's impact significantly sped up the shift to e-learning, and by 2021, these platforms were widely used and at the core of global educational approaches.

Emphasis on Adaptive Curriculum: The multiple references to curriculum, learning designs, and systems highlight the significant attempt to transform traditional educational material for the innovative e-learning environment.

Teaching, Learning, Human Education, Students, Education, Distance

Normalization of Distance Learning: The pandemic's impact caused distance learning to transition from being a secondary option to a prominent method in contemporary education.

Human Element Remains: The continued relevance of the human factor in education, even with technological enhancements, underscores its enduring value.

Central and Underdeveloped Themes

Machine Learning, Predictive Analytics

AI's Growing Relevance: With the evolving technology, AI's role in education is actualized. At the core of their current position, their future relevance is highlighted.

Inception Stage: Currently, these technologies are in the inception stage of adoption, and therefore they are underdeveloped.

Peripheral and Developed Themes: Design/Methodology/ Approach, Learning Analytics, Online Systems

Refining Online Pedagogy: A more subtle appreciation of their importance, albeit not core, can be seen in these themes. Pedagogical approaches need to bc rcfincd in online education to get the best outcomes.

Data's Role: In highlighting the students' behavior, preferences, and performance, learning analytics truly uplifts online learning, but it is not at the core.

Peripheral and Underdeveloped Themes: Design and Technology, Instructional Designs

Emerging Integration: These topics, while secondary, point ahead to emerging research streams. With technology and instructional design increasingly entwining, institutions seek to discover the best ways of interweaving these threads in a harmonious manner.

Emerging Modality: The pervasiveness of cellular phones offers a fertile ground for learning activities. Although mobile learning has potential, the challenge of creating tailored learning experiences for smaller screens and on-the-go situations means it's still an undeveloped and marginal aspect of main discussions.

The education sector is undergoing a radical transformation, driven by the swift digitization that accelerated during the pandemic and subsequent worldwide occurrences. While honing e-learning modalities, institutions are simultaneously delving into the realm of AI. Concurrently, a more complex landscape of educational design and technology integration is developing, revealing varied paths for future inquiry and advancement.

Figure 9. Alluvial diagram of thematic evolution

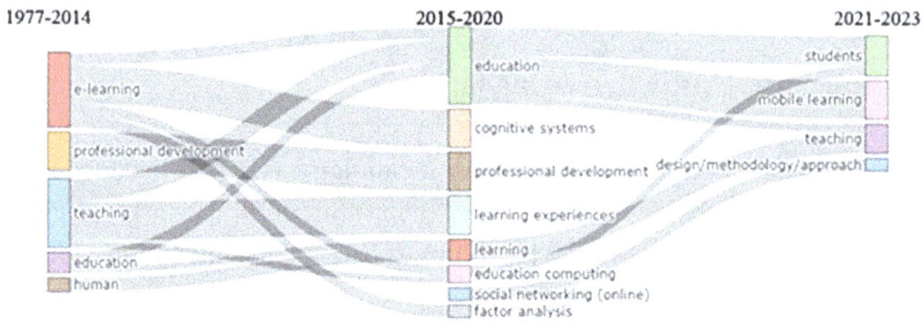

Figure 9 depicts the alluvial diagram of previously explained 3 time slices. It provides us a global view of the changes. Each of the nodes represents a cluster and is labeled by the first three words of the clusters, the edges are their temporal evolution track, generated by keyword co-occurrence of the topics between two time slices (Callon, Courtial and Laville, 1991). By examining the changes and developments in themes or topics through an alluvial diagram, valuable insights can be gained regarding the evolution of a given field.

1977-2014:

Clusters: The intersection of e-learning, professional development, teaching, education, and human resource is intricate.

E-Learning Emergence: The rapid growth of the internet and digital technology occurred during this timeframe. Institutions' growing recognition of the value of online platforms helped to establish e-learning as a prominent force.

Emphasis on Human Element: The significance of "human" lies in the fact that, despite technological progress, the essence of teaching remains focused on personalized, human-centered approaches.

Professional Development & Teaching: As digital education emerged, there was an increased focus on educators' training and development to excel in this innovative environment.

2015-2020:

Clusters: The interconnectedness of education, cognitive systems, professional development, and learning experiences is evident.

Cognitive Systems and Learning: As the digital age took hold, interest in the cognitive aspects of learning expanded. By combining cognitive science and pedagogy, we can improve digital learning experiences.

Social Networking's Role: With the increasing prevalence of these platforms, educators began examining how social networking could support education, create communities, and aid professional development.

Factor Analysis: This method sheds light on a more detailed comprehension of education. To uncover patterns, preferences, and influential factors, factor analysis likely played a crucial role in digital learning outcomes analysis.

Continued Professional Development: Even with advancements, continuous learning and teaching methodology improvements are necessary for educators.

2021-23:

Clusters: Students, mobile learning, teaching, design/methodology/approach

Student-Centric Approach: By placing the spotlight on "students," education takes on a more individualized, student-oriented form. The advanced nature of online platforms allows for the seamless personalization of educational experiences.

Mobile Learning: The omnipresence of these devices fueled a growing interest in mobile learning. Educational institutions researched how to deliver content in a way that is accessible and flexible via these devices.

Design/Methodology/Approach: With digital education's advancement, attention turned to refining methodologies and approaches. As educators, we focused on perfecting and streamlining digital instruction techniques.

From 1977 to 2023, the thematic evolution shows the progression from simple e-learning to a more advanced digital education method based on analytics. The continuous evolution of education is reflected in each period, which represents a phase in response to technological advancements and changing global circumstances.

CONCLUSION

The intersection of pedagogical change and technological innovation over the specified period of time has brought about an amazing transformation of the educational landscape. A rigorous thematic analysis of the educational landscape reveals its amazing resilience and responsiveness. Since its beginning, e-learning has embraced the importance of human interaction and is using technology to enable but not replace the natural passion for teaching and learning. In the mid-2010s, the intersection of cognitive systems, an enhanced focus on analytical approaches like factor analysis, and the impact of social networking brought about an education landscape that was open to adopting an extensive gamut of tools and techniques.

A reading of education subjects across two time periods reveals the intricate convergence of technological advance and the persistent pertinence of pedagogical approaches based on human necessity. Based on bibliometric evidence and thematic insight, this study provides an integrated perspective on the education process across nearly 50 years.

During the 1977-2014 decade, the early years of e-learning were followed by a concurrent growth in tandem with a sterling focus on the human factor of learning. The decade's professional development focus is a reflection of the education industry's concerted effort to utilize digital tools in a systematic, rather than replacement, fashion. As we navigated through the data, a more complex dance of themes unfolded between 2015-2020. The industry's necessity to balance digital learning environments with cognition and technology expertise was characterized by the injection of cognitive systems. The increasing importance of social networking and factor analysis brought in an analytical, data-driven philosophy, along with the recognition of communal learning's growing influence in the digital age. Through the decade (2021-2023), an unmistakable turn towards student-centricity was evident, characterized by mobile learning and improved methodologies. A synthesis of earlier wisdom and modern creativity, the decade is reflective of the education industry's search for balance. Gliding effortlessly across these varied thematic decades is a strand common to all, comprising an unshakeable focus on professional development, an interconnected integration of design and pedagogy, and an effort towards perfection in the symbiotic marriage of technological innovation and human-led pedagogy.

Looking back, this study is a reflection of the evolution of education, characterized by continuous adaptation and boundless aspiration for perfection. Trailblazing innovation, this thematic evolution is our way and lights the way forward. We ought, as a people, to understand the nature of education, calling for vibrant and integrated learning experiences in the light of technological advancements.

Future Research Direction

The learning theme evolution between 1977 and 2023 provides rich scope for minute examination in the years to come. The common thread of this trend is more focus on those pedagogies that are centered on those approaches that put the learner at the center of the school system. This calls for more scrutiny of how creating tailored learning experiences or adaptive learning packages might affect learners of diverse backgrounds. Meanwhile, technologies developing at breakneck speed—from the advent of artificial intelligence (AI), virtual reality (VR), augmented reality (AR)—call for investigation of their probable integration into pedagogy. This question hopes to explore their implications for experiential learning. The issue of ongoing professional development calls for renewed attention. More specifically, research studies must investigate the interfaces between learning new technology; pedagogy of teaching well; emotional intelligence teachers require in pandemic-reshuffled times. As digital platforms double at breakneck speeds, it is imperative to explore ethically managing heaps of learner data. Also pertinent is the challenge on possible discrimination by data-driven school systems. Sustained interest with STEM of past years presents the interesting possibility of inter-disciplinary knowledge particularly where technology converges with traditional school subjects. But as digital learning goes mass around the world it is crucial to explore access equity worldwide to derive equitable results. Contrast geographies with varied digital ecosystems could reflect any differences created by them which can be plugged. More mobile learning a rapidly emerging field offers rich terrain for researchers to explore long-term effects on cognition & acquiring complex tailor-made mobile learning experiences. Finally the way social media is used in education a key feature from 2015-2020 is another dynamic area of research. Further studies can reveal how various old & new platforms facilitate communal learning foster student interaction & support professional growth. In conclusion past themes not only chart out the course of digital learning developments but also light up the journey ahead cast upon societal needs technological progress & enduring educational fundamentals.

Research implications

This bibliometric study of learning design technology is essential for a broad audience in the industry. It gives to instructional designers and teachers alike a step-by-step walkthrough of history from e-learning to mobile learning that acts as a guide to their development in educational tools. Through the identification of key authors being highlighted in the research paper, a treasure trove of valuable information is given to all teachers to guide their teaching methodologies. The study also helps research scholars in academics by basing them on an existing scholarly foundation so they can identify gaps in existing studies which then give rise to new explorations in the field. The findings of the study give all the information required for edtech developers to identify areas where innovation can be introduced. This is especially important with the current trend towards mobile learning as well as the developments in learning designs. These findings thus enable developers to ensure new technologies are in line with the educational landscape of the day. Policymakers also learn from the study that will help them make informed decisions that are in line with educational technology trends. This paper gives an insight into how educational policies can inform strategies on matters of curriculum transformation or infrastructure upgrade to keep pace with international standards. Students benefit immensely from these plans as more advanced teaching methods give an education that is in line with digital age requirements—engaging students in an effective way while making them future-ready. Lastly, for investors interested in investing in edtech startups or research programs in academia; the study gives insight into how they can invest their resources to ensure promising returns on investment. The analysis provides insights on learning design technology journey from past to future that allow stakeholders to make decisions based on it.

REFERENCES

Aria, M., & Cuccurullo, C. (2017). bibliometrix: An R-tool for comprehensive science mapping analysis. *Journal of Informetrics*, *11*(4), 959–975. DOI: 10.1016/j.joi.2017.08.007

Bhandari, A. (2022). Design thinking: From bibliometric analysis to content analysis, current research trends, and future research directions. *Journal of the Knowledge Economy*, •••, 1–56. DOI: 10.1007/s13132-022-00907-1

Bornmann, L., & Mutz, R. (2015). Growth rates of modern science: A bibliometric analysis based on the number of publications and cited references. *Journal of the Association for Information Science and Technology*, *66*(11), 2215–2222. DOI: 10.1002/asi.23329

Branch, R. M., & Merrill, M. D. (2012). Characteristics of instructional design models. In Reiser, R. A., & Dempsey, J. V. (Eds.), *Trends and issues in instructional design and technology* (3rd ed., pp. 8–16). Pearson.

Callon, M., Courtial, J. P., & Laville, F. (1991). Co-word analysis as a tool for describing the network of interactions between basic and technological research: The case of polymer chemistry. *Scientometrics*, *22*(1), 155–205. DOI: 10.1007/BF02019280

Ertmer, P. A. (2005). Teacher pedagogical beliefs: The final frontier in our quest for technology integration? *Educational Technology Research and Development*, *53*(4), 25–39. DOI: 10.1007/BF02504683

Ertmer, P. A., & Newby, T. J. (2013). Behaviorism, cognitivism, constructivism: Comparing critical features from an instructional design perspective. *Performance Improvement Quarterly*, *26*(2), 43–71. DOI: 10.1002/piq.21143

Goldie, J. G. S. (2016). Connectivism: A knowledge learning theory for the digital age? *Medical Teacher*, *38*(10), 1064–1069. DOI: 10.3109/0142159X.2016.1173661 PMID: 27128290

Goodyear, P., & Retalis, S. (2010). *Technology-enhanced learning: Design patterns and pattern languages*. Brill. DOI: 10.1163/9789460910623

Haustein, S. (2016). Grand challenges in altmetrics: Heterogeneity, data quality and dependencies. *Scientometrics*, *108*(1), 413–423. DOI: 10.1007/s11192-016-1910-9

Holmes, W., Bialik, M., & Fadel, C. (2019). *Artificial intelligence in education: Promises and implications for teaching and learning*. Center for Curriculum Redesign.

Huang, H. M., Rauch, U., & Liaw, S. S. (2010). Investigating learners' attitudes toward virtual reality learning environments: Based on a constructivist approach. *Computers & Education*, *55*(3), 1171–1182. DOI: 10.1016/j.compedu.2010.05.014

Johann, D. A., Nunes, A. D. F. P., Santos, G. B. D., Silva, D. J. C. D., Bresciani, S. A. T., & Lopes, L. F. D. (2020). Mapping of scientific production on design thinking as a tool for entrepreneurship education: A bibliometric study of a decade. *World Journal of Entrepreneurship, Management and Sustainable Development*, *16*(4), 271–285. DOI: 10.1108/WJEMSD-05-2019-0028

Johnson, L., Becker, S. A., Cummins, M., Estrada, V., Freeman, A., & Hall, C. (2016). *NMC Horizon Report: 2016 Higher Education Edition*. The New Media Consortium.

Jonassen, D. H., & Rohrer-Murphy, L. (1999). Activity theory as a framework for designing constructivist learning environments. *Educational Technology Research and Development*, *47*(1), 61–79. DOI: 10.1007/BF02299477

Marshall, S. J. (2018). *Shaping the university of the future*. Springer., DOI: 10.1007/978-981-10-7620-6

Mayer, R. E. (2011). Multimedia learning and games. In Tobias, S., & Fletcher, J. D. (Eds.), *Computer games and instruction* (pp. 281–308). IAP.

Mayer, R. E., & Moreno, R. (2003). Nine ways to reduce cognitive load in multimedia learning. *Educational Psychologist*, *38*(1), 43–52. DOI: 10.1207/S15326985EP3801_6

Mishra, P., & Koehler, M. J. (2006). Technological pedagogical content knowledge: A framework for teacher knowledge. *Teachers College Record*, *108*(6), 1017–1054. DOI: 10.1111/j.1467-9620.2006.00684.x

Morrison, G. R., Ross, S. J., Morrison, J. R., & Kalman, H. K. (2019). *Designing effective instruction* (8th ed.). John Wiley & Sons.

Morrison, G. R., Ross, S. M., Kemp, J. E., & Kalman, H. (2011). *Designing effective instruction* (6th ed.). John Wiley & Sons.

. Park, E. J., & Lee, S. (2022). Creative thinking in the architecture design studio: Bibliometric analysis and literature

Radu, I. (2014). Augmented reality in education: A meta-review and cross-media analysis. *Personal and Ubiquitous Computing*, *18*(6), 1533–1543. DOI: 10.1007/s00779-013-0747-y

Reigeluth, C. M. (1999). The elaboration theory: Guidance for scope and sequence decisions. In Reigeluth, C. M. (Ed.), *Instructional-design theories and models* (Vol. 2, pp. 425–453). Lawrence Erlbaum Associates.

Reiser, R. A. (2001). A history of instructional design and technology: Part I: A history of instructional media. *Educational Technology Research and Development*, *49*(1), 53–64. DOI: 10.1007/BF02504506

Roblyer, M. D., & Doering, A. H. (2007). *Integrating educational technology into teaching* (5th ed.). Pearson.

Saçak, B., Bozkurt, A., & Wagner, E. (2022). Learning design versus instructional design: A bibliometric study through data visualization approaches. *Education Sciences*, *12*(11), 752. DOI: 10.3390/educsci12110752

Sharples, M., de Roock, R., Ferguson, R., Gaved, M., Herodotou, C., Koh, E., . . . Wong, L. H. (2016). Innovating pedagogy 2016: Open University innovation report 5. Institute of Educational Technology, The Open University. https://oro.open.ac.uk/48153/

Siemens, G. (2004). Connectivism: A learning theory for the digital age. Elearnspace. https://www.elearnspace.org/Articles/connectivism.htm

Siemens, G. (2013). Learning analytics: The emergence of a discipline. *The American Behavioral Scientist*, *57*(10), 1380–1400. DOI: 10.1177/0002764213498851

Sugimoto, C. R., & Larivière, V. (2018). *Measuring research: What everyone needs to know*. Oxford University Press. DOI: 10.1093/wentk/9780190640118.001.0001

Tlili, A., Huang, R., Shehata, B., Liu, D., Zhao, J., Metwally, A. H. S., Wang, H., Denden, M., Bozkurt, A., Lee, L.-H., Beyoglu, D., Altinay, F., Sharma, R. C., Altinay, Z., Li, Z., Liu, J., Ahmad, F., Hu, Y., Salha, S., & Burgos, D. (2022). Is Metaverse in education a blessing or a curse: A combined content and bibliometric analysis. *Smart Learning Environments*, *9*(1), 1–31. DOI: 10.1186/s40561-022-00205-x PMID: 40477962

Vygotsky, L. S., & Cole, M. (1978). *Mind in society: Development of higher psychological processes*. Harvard University Press.

Wu, W.-H., Wu, Y.-C. J., Chen, C.-Y., Kao, H.-Y., Lin, C.-H., & Huang, S.-H. (2012). Review of trends from mobile learning studies: A meta-analysis. *Computers & Education*, *59*(2), 817–827. DOI: 10.1016/j.compedu.2012.03.016

Zawacki-Richter, O., Marín, V. I., Bond, M., & Gouverneur, F. (2019). Systematic review of research on artificial intelligence applications in higher education – Where are the educators? *International Journal of Educational Technology in Higher Education*, *16*(1), 1–27. DOI: 10.1186/s41239-019-0171-0

Zupic, I., & Čater, T. (2015). Bibliometric methods in management and organization. *Organizational Research Methods*, *18*(3), 429–472. DOI: 10.1177/1094428114562629

Chapter 2

Blended Learning in the Age of Artificial Intelligence: Transforming Education Through Innovation

Narender Suhag
https://orcid.org/0000-0002-3836-2133
Lovely Professional University, India

Amrik Singh
https://orcid.org/0000-0003-3598-8787
Lovely Professional University, India

ABSTRACT

Artificial Intelligence (AI) is revolutionizing the educational landscape by enabling personalized learning experiences, automating administrative tasks, and enhancing student engagement. Through adaptive learning systems, AI can tailor instruction to meet the needs of individual learners, offering real-time feedback and dynamic learning pathways. Predictive analytics further supports student success by identifying at-risk learners and allowing for timely interventions. Virtual tutors and AI-generated content are enhancing accessibility and engagement, making learning more interactive and scalable. However, the integration of AI in education raises important challenges, including concerns about data privacy, algorithmic bias, and the ethical implications of AI-driven decision-making. This paper examines the opportunities and risks associated with AI in education and explores how future policies can guide the ethical and equitable implementation of AI tools.

DOI: 10.4018/979-8-3373-3815-6.ch002

right © 2026, IGI Global Scientific Publishing. Copying or distributing in print or electronic forms without written permission of IGI Global Scientific Publishing is prohibited. Use of this chapter to in generative artificial intelligence (AI) technologies is expressly prohibited. The publisher reserves all rights to license its use for generative AI training and machine learning model development.

INTRODUCTION

Education is one of the areas where the use of Artificial Intelligence (AI) has been rapidly developed in the past ten years due to the dramatic changes in machine learning, natural language processing, and big data analytics. With the development of AI technology, it is being implemented more and more in educational systems to improve learning outcomes, simplify administration, and create more interactive and personalized learning experiences. One of the long-term objectives of educators has been personalized learning, a pedagogical strategy that can adapt teaching methods to meet the needs, skills, and interests of each of the learners, potentially overcoming persistent challenges such as one-size-fits-all instructions, high dropout rates, inaccessibility to quality education, and variations in learning opportunities (Sharma & Singh, 2024). Such customized experiences, however, are frequently unable to be offered within traditional classroom environments due to resource and teacher-to-student ratio constraints. In particular, intelligent tutoring systems (ITS) can analyze whether a student has a proper comprehension of current information, what misconceptions he has formed, and provide feedback and exercises which will be personal and exercise-oriented. Other uses of AI beyond adaptive learning include its use to predict student performance, detect students who are at risk of failing academically, and prescribing interventions in time. Predictive analytics leverage past and current information to predict a course completion outcome, grades and student engagement. This initiative will enable teachers to adopt a proactive rather than a reactive stance and eventually enhance retention and achievement rates among the students. In addition, AI-based chatbots and virtual tutors support learners with on-demand guidance, providing answers to queries, explanations of concepts, and an overview of learning materials without requiring a human instructor to constantly monitor them. AI is also essential in the creation and evaluation of content.

Quizzes and summaries can be generated with natural language generation and automated content tools, and even lesson plans can be generated, alleviating educator workload and providing a uniform quality of teaching resources. The AI-based assessment tools can analyze objective and subjective responses, provide instant feedback, and assist students in seeing what they need to work on. In addition, AI promotes accessibility and inclusivity in learning. Speech recognition devices can support students with visual or reading disabilities and multilingual translators can help overcome language barriers so students of different origins can access the content in their native language. In the future, AI and other new technologies, including virtual reality (VR), augmented reality (AR), and the metaverse, are more likely to influence the future of education. Overall, AI-driven immersive environments have the potential to transform student engagement with content, peers, and instructors and make learning more experiential, engaging, and connected to the real-world environment. Though it opens up an entire new world of opportunities in terms of personalization and efficiency, it also demands an in-depth examination of ethical, legal, and social implications. This model combines the advantages of human teachers and AI technology to enhance the learning process, student interaction and efficiency in administration.

Figure 1. Key Components of the Blended Learning Model

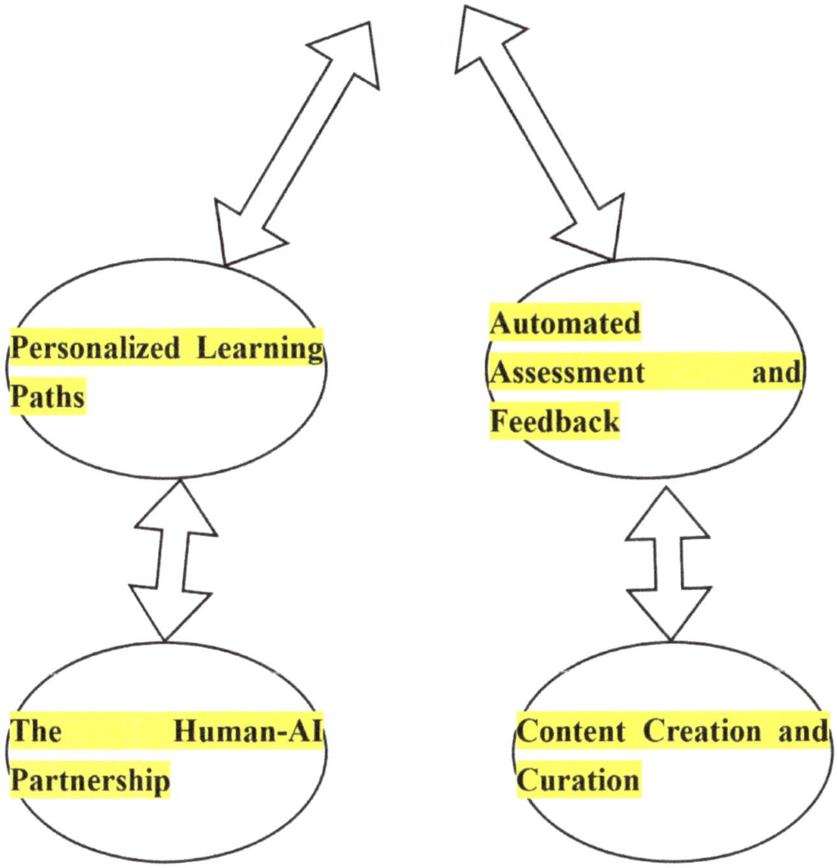

Sources: Author's own conceptual framework

Individual Learning Plans

Personalized Learning Paths have become an effective tool in changing the traditional approaches to teaching in the age of AI-driven education. This model goes beyond the one size fits all paradigm by applying artificial intelligence to the data of a student and designing a truly adaptive learning process. AI has the capacity to deliver specific assistance that can help the student to achieve his or her full potential by understanding the individual needs, strengths, and weaknesses of each student. Theshinse is an AI-based tutor that serves as a personal mentor, providing one-on-one guidance, and real-time feedback. Using the example of a student with a bad grasp of a specific concept in math, the system will automatically give the student more examples or practice problems to work on based on the error that the student has. The level of difficulty and content changes dynamically so that students can work as slowly as they need to, but as fast as they are able to learn, whether they are in need of skills to master the basics or they are able to learn more high level information. Not only is this level of personalized attention, previously only achievable with a human tutor, now open to all students, but AI also enables Curriculum Customization. Rather than all students being given the same materials, AI can create and suggest additional materials that match the preferred style of learning of a student. To a visual learner, the system may recommend a video or an interactive simulation, whereas a learner who learns through reading may be pulled to another article or text. This makes sure that each pupil receives the best type of teaching, which improves understanding and interest. AI can provide a highly effective and motivating learning environment by delivering the correct content, in the correct format and at the correct time.

Automated Assessment and Feedback

Automated assessment and feedback, powered by AI, are fundamentally changing how educators evaluate student performance and provide support. This technology streamlines a once time-consuming process, benefiting both instructors and learners. A primary advantage is Automatic Grading. AI can rapidly grade a vast array of assignments, from multiple-choice quizzes to more complex, open-ended responses. This capability frees up a significant amount of an educator's time, allowing them to focus on more impactful activities like one-on-one student interaction, lesson planning, and mentorship. The instant feedback also means students don't have to wait days or weeks for their results, enabling them to understand their standing almost immediately. Beyond just a score, AI provides Targeted Feedback. Instead of a simple grade, the system can analyze a student's work to identify specific errors or common misconceptions. For example, in an essay, AI can highlight sentences with grammatical mistakes or suggest ways to strengthen an argument. This detailed, constructive criticism helps students understand exactly where they went wrong and what they need to do to improve, fostering a more effective learning cycle. This is far more valuable than a simple letter grade and accelerates a student's mastery of the material.Finally, Predictive Analytics adds a powerful layer of proactive support. By analyzing patterns in a student's performance and engagement data, AI can flag students who are at risk of falling behind. This early warning system allows educators to intervene proactively, offering timely support before a small issue becomes a significant academic problem. This shift from reactive to proactive intervention ensures that no student is left behind, creating a more inclusive and supportive educational environment.

Production and Editing of Information

Content creation and curation AI tools are changing the education landscape in fundamental ways, as they provide educators with the means to produce and structure instructional content more effectively than ever. These tools allow educators to create lesson plans on the fly, create a wide variety of quiz questions, design interesting discussion prompts, and create slick presentations. This automation of routine workload is a huge relief on the administrative part of a school, as it eliminates teachers from the tedious chores they have to face and allows them to concentrate on the human side of the school business, which includes mentorship, developing critical thinking and helping students develop a positive relationship with one another. This capability to generate numerous types of materials at a rapid pace also means that there is increased experimentation and innovation in the classroom, which results in more active and engaging lessons. There is so much information out there on the internet that it can be overwhelming to locate relevant and reliable educational materials. Systems based on AI can scan through large databases of articles, videos, simulations and interactive exercises to identify and suggest quality, current resources. This will keep the teachers up to date in their area of interest and will allow them to offer a more diverse range of learning materials to their students. It replaces the educator as an informant in favor of a knowledgeable mentor who can guide the students to the most useful resources and can tailor the learning process to their interests and needs. What it produces is an educational environment that is more informed, flexible, and responsive.

The Human-AI Partnership

The Human-AI Partnership is the most disruptive part of AI in education. It is not to make artificial intelligence substitute teachers, but enhance their performance so that they can concentrate on the actual factors that are very important in instruction. This kind of symbiotic relationship creates a new role of an educator who no longer supplies most of the material, but instead serves as a facilitator and mentor. As administration tasks, such as grading and general instruction, are taken up by AI, teachers gain time and energy to do tasks that impact the process positively. This new model will enable teachers to spend more one-on-one time with students, facilitate energized group conversations, and create hands-on, project-based learning processes, which AI, as a formidable resource, cannot fully duplicate. Human-to-human interaction plays an important role in directing students to complex, open-ended problems, team projects and delicate conversations. These tasks require thinking at a higher level, creativity, and the capacity to cooperate with othersall qualities that are essential to succeed in the real world. Through AI efficiency, teachers now have the freedom to spend their face-to-face time developing these distinctly human capabilities, so that learners get a well-rounded education that extends well beyond memorization and recitation of information. The relationship results in a more efficient, customized, and, most importantly, a more humanized educational process.

LITERATURE REVIEW

AI-Improved Blended Learning Models

The usage of AI into blended learning and education makes it more personalized and interactive one. It improves on three popular models known as the Flipped Classroom, the Flex Model and the Enriched Virtual Model. This combination of physical education with AI-based internet solutions provides a more efficient and effective learning experience by both students and teachers.

The Flipped Classroom Model

The traditional Flipped Classroom involves students watching videos or reading assigned material at home and spending classroom time collaborating with their instructor and solving problems together. This model is even more powerful when supported with AI. AI is able to review the work done by a student on pre-class content and design individualized learning plans, providing them with additional learning resources or alternative instructional formats to help them ready them to do the in-class work. Student work can be accompanied by instant feedback via AI-powered tools during the classroom, allowing the teacher to assume a mentoring role and guide students through the intricate process of learning concepts and making decisions.

The Flex Model

The Flex Model focuses on internet learning where on-site support is provided on request. The central point of this is AI, which becomes an intelligent hub. A machine-intelligent platform offers intelligent curriculum which adjusts to the advancement of every student in real time. It is able to automatically modify the sophistication of a lesson or suggest fresh practice issues in accordance with student achievement. It is a data-based solution that enables teachers to track the progress of students on a central dashboard and easily detect struggling students. This allows the teacher to give specific proactive interventions so that no student can be left behind.

The Enriched Virtual Model

The Enriched Virtual Model refers to the situation where students complete the majority of the course work online but have a number of scheduled meetings in person. The virtual part is totally streamlined with AI. The online section of the course can be very efficient with AI tools automating the content delivery, assessment, and feedback. The face-to-face sessions, consequently, turn into a valuable time of intensive joint work that is hard to achieve through the Internet. Teachers can spend this in-person time on complex project-based learning, practical labs, or interactive Socratic seminars and exploit the collective intelligence of the group in a way that AI cannot perform.

Individualized/Adaptive Learning

Adaptive learning and personalized learning are two closely related pedagogical strategies that have become quite popular in today's education, especially with the advent of technology and artificial intelligence. Although both seek to make the learning process personal to the individual learner, they work under varying philosophies. Personalized learning represents a larger scale form of teacher-driven strategy aimed at tailoring a student-learning plan to his/her needs, interests, and objectives. It is a process done together by the student and the educator of establishing a learning goal, selecting the content to cover and the type of learning to follow. This can be in the form of a student choosing a project topic of their interest or as an educator creating a differentiated curriculum to a student with special learning needs. All it boils down to is providing students with greater agency and voice in their learning process. On the other hand, adaptive learning is a more automated and data-driven process. It uses algorithms and artificial intelligence to change the learning experience in real-time depending on the performance of a student (Nuong et al., 2024). To explain the point, when a student encounters an issue with a given concept in math, an adaptive learning platform will automatically provide the student with extra practice problems, a video explanation, or a new learning module to comprehend the concept. On the other hand, when the student mastered a subject within a very short time, the system will skip some basic stuff and introduce a little harder one to continue holding the student. This is a dynamic movement which does not leave any student behind. These two approaches are most powerful when they are combined together. One can relate personalized and adaptive learning model as the best of both worlds. The teacher as a facilitator develops a personal learning plan that has a goal and an overall orientation of the student (Singh and Hassan, 2024). Then the adaptive technology becomes a powerful tool to put this plan into action and provide the continuous, data-oriented transformations that would keep the student on track. There are many advantages of this integrated model. It helps in creating interest and enthusiasm among the students through offering content that is neither too hard nor too easy to handle. It facilitates further insight because students get immediate specific feedback that focuses on their particular bias. It also enables teachers by liberating them, relieving them of the burden of repetitive chores such as grading and content delivery so that they can do what they are best at; mentoring, helping them to work together and developing critical thinking skills. However, it will require an attitude change and investment in technologies and professional growth to be efficient. This does not seek to replace the human element, but instead to use technology as an excellent resource, providing a more efficient, equitable and student-centered learning experience to all. This might be the most radical element of AI in blended learning(Singh, 2024). Artificial intelligence (AI) applications are capable of processing large volumes of information about the performance, learning rate, and interests of a student in real-time. According to this analysis, the system is able to:

- **Modify content challenge:** When the student is making good progress, the system can automatically feed him with more challenging material. It can give simplified descriptions or correction materials when they are in distress.
- **Design bespoke learning journeys:** AI can suggest that a particular student take a particular module, video, or quiz that addresses their weaknesses so they can get the help they need to grasp a concept.
- Intelligent tutoring: AI-based tutors can be customized to provide real-time, one-on-one feedback and advice, which resembles a human tutor and enables learners to access learning 24/7. This leaves teachers free to do more advanced activities that are practical.

Famous Smattering Learning Models

- The best-known blended learning models include the Rotation Model, the Flex Model, the A La Carte Model and the Enriched Virtual Model.
- Rotation Model - This is possibly the most popular, mainly in the K-12 environment. In this model, students are assigned to alternate between the various

modalities of learning in a predefined rotation, and at least one of the modalities is online learning. Some sub-models within this category include the Station Rotation, in which students switch back and forth in the same classroom between various so-called stations (e.g., a teacher-led station, a collaborative project station, and a self-paced online station); the Lab Rotation, which is a kind of rotation between a physical classroom and a computer lab; the Individual Rotation, which is a rotation in which each student has an individualized schedule; and the Flipped Classroom, where students receive lecture material at home and use classroom-time to solve problems, discuss with peers and the teacher, and collaborate

- Flex Model is a student-centred concept where the curriculum is mostly presented online. The learners get to study modules and tasks at their speed, and the teacher can provide individual or small-group guidance as necessary. This is the most flexible model, and it is frequently applied in alternative education programs or to learners who need an extremely personalized course of study.
- The A La Carte Model enables the students to enroll in a combination of online and on-campus studies. This is mainly prevalent at high school or university level where college students can opt to pursue some courses online as they complete others in a standard classroom. It provides students with agency and the capacity to design their course load to achieve their personal and academic aspirations.
- The Enriched Virtual Model resembles a full-time internet school except that it has a few required face-to-face classes, usually to do lab work, collaborative work or exams. Most of the learning occurs over the internet, although the face-to-face aspect assists in creating a sense of community and offers great face-to-face interaction with the instructors and fellow students.

Blended learning models are associated with a plethora of benefits (Sharma and Singh, 2024). The online dimension opens access to a wealth of content including multimedia, interactive simulators and a variety of learning tools. This also contributes to the creation of the required 21 st century skills, including digital literacy, self-regulation, and critical thinking. Even with the advantages, blended learning has challenges when implementing the system. It involves a lot of investment in technology and teacher training. Teachers should be trained not just on how to use the technology, but how to create an effective learning experience that will bring together on-line and face-to-face elements in an organic manner. Moreover, equity and access factors must be taken into account with all students able to have good internet access and a qualified device in their residences. In the hands of the right people, blended learning may turn the classroom into an exciting, dynamic, and highly effective learning experience that will equip students to live in a future where technology and teamwork are paramount.

Blended Learning as a Reduction Measure

- Educational mitigation strategies are forward-looking initiatives that help reduce the adverse effects of disruptive occurrences, including pandemics, natural disasters, or other crises, on the continuity of learning. The aim is to sustain the provision of high-quality education to all students irrespective of the external challenges (Singh, 2024). Blended learning is one of the foundations of any viable mitigation plan, as it creates a flexible infrastructure that can be easily modified to meet new needs. When a disruption happens in schools, by incorporating online and in-person instruction as a regular operating procedure, schools are not beginning anew. Rather, they are able to smoothly transition between modalities.
- Flexibility and Adaptability: The online aspect of a blended model can be up-scaled to a fully remote model without much disturbance in the event of a school closure. The technology platforms, trainer training, and the student level interaction with online tools already exists. On the other hand, when only a few students need to be isolated they can still continue to study at home and their colleagues are able to attend the classroom. This eliminates a total shutdown and offers an opportunity to learn to all.
- Equity and Access: Blended learning may also be an effective equity tool. In the case of a crisis, content delivery is not the only issue, but also when all students are able to access the learning. The mitigation plans should involve the provision of devices and internet to students in low-income families. By its very nature, the blended model promotes the creation of digital resources and infrastructure that may be deployed during a crisis.
- Teacher Training and Support: An effective system should have an available labor force. An extremely important mitigation strategy is the constant professional growth of teachers in the area of online instruction design, digital tools, and distance communication. This training gives educators confidence and ability to offer top quality education in any form.

A Foundation of Policy and Governance

Although blended learning offers the effective policy and governance. Even the strongest technical infrastructure cannot work without having clear policies.

Clear and Flexible Policies: Policies can define a clear line of command and decision making between the various levels of disruption. It involves the identification of the criteria based on which the schools will be shut down or transition towards remote learning. One policy could be, by way of example, allowing a district superintendent to issue an immediate decision based on local health data, as opposed to waiting on a state-level directive.

Data and Accountability: The governance should have a data collection and data analysis system. This includes monitoring student engagement, academic achievement and welfare throughout remote learning seasons. This kind of information is critical in the diagnosis of students behind track and in the provision of certain interventions. Expectations regarding student attendance, academic integrity, and communication should also be laid down as part of holding them accountable.

Mitigation plans are properly funded and the allocation of resources is appropriate. This involves technology, professional development and support staff budget allocation. Efforts to proactively make policy choices to invest in a more robust educational infrastructure in advance of a crisis strike will save more resources and cause even less damage to the academic futures of students. Simply, a defined policy and governance framework can turn blended learning into a pedagogical option and make it a fundamental operational approach to resilience.

The Opportunities in AI-Powered Education

Adaptive Learning Algorithms

Adaptive learning algorithms are one of the greatest improvements in AI-driven education. These algorithms optimize the learning process by adapting the content, speed, and method of instruction according to the performance, behavior and preferences of a learner. The very nature of adaptive learning systems is that the learning data collection and analysis continuously follows the learners wherever they are and provides each of the students with a unique knowledge acquisition process with its own support and at its own pace (Singh, 2022). Such systems track the interactions of the students, evaluate learning of the concepts and determine the student behavioral patterns. With this information, they dynamically vary the content and paths of instruction they present to the student. Adaptive learning, like Knewton and DreamBox Learning, is a perfect example of a personalized approach that improves engagement and motivation, as well as improves learning outcomes by targeting the individual gaps in knowledge and skills. Knewton utilizes online analytics to customize online lessons that provide personalized recommendations based on the performance of a specific student (Pane et al., 2017). DreamBox, which has been demonstrated to be successful in K8 mathematics education, uses an intelligent adaptive engine that modulates the difficulty and presentation of materials based on over 40000 data points captured each hour of student interaction with the system (Sharma & Singh, 2024a). The effectiveness of adaptive learning has been proven in enhancing educational outcomes through such platforms, which would have been challenging or nearly impossible to achieve with human instructors in a traditional classroom setting. In one study by Walkington and Bernacki (2014), it was observed that students enrolled in adaptive mathematics software achieved significantly higher results compared to students enrolled in traditional instruction, particularly when the adaptive mathematics software was designed to include personalized contexts and scaffolds. Similarly, VanLehn (2011) reviewed various intelligent tutoring systems and found that many were as effective as human tutors in facilitating learning gains. Additionally, adaptive learning technologies enable a mastery-based pedagogical approach, according to which students can only move forward when they prove to have fully mastered the previous content. This minimizes the risk of foundational holes, which may build up with time and prevent learning in the future. Adaptive systems create a more collaborative and less punitive learning environment through the provision of feedback in real-time and just-in-time interventions. There is no matter how promising adaptive learning may be, there are challenges. Transparency of algorithmic choice is one of those issues. How adaptive systems can be used to make instructional decisions is often unknown to students and teachers, casting concerns of trust and accountability (Popenici & Kerr, 2017; Sharma & Singh, 2024a). The teachers should also be taught how to read and respond to the data produced by adaptive systems. Without a clear view of what is being given, it is likely that useful information could remain unused or misunderstood. So, the benefits of using adaptive learning technologies with the help of AI can be maximized with the help of professional development and collaborative practices. These technologies can empower students, assist teachers and help make learning experiences more equitable and inclusive when developed thoughtfully and implemented in an ethical way.

Predictive Analytics

Predictive analytics has quickly emerged as one of the most effective educational tools, and it provides institutions with an opportunity to make data-driven decisions that directly influence student success. Predictive analytics forecasts the risk of poor performance, engagement, and retention of students as it uses past and real-time data to infer the risk of poor performance, engagement, and retention through machine learning models and statistical techniques. Early identification of at-risk students can be listed among the most important uses of predictive analytics because it helps respond to academic and behavioral issues of students in a timely manner and prevent the recurrence of such problems. These algorithms are used with a set of data points such as grades, attendance, learning management system

(LMS) activity, social interaction, and demographic data to extract patterns that can be causal indicators of a struggling academic student or one who is disengaged (Arnold and Pistilli, 2012). Predictive analytics such as the Course Signals system at Purdue University can then help educators and academic advisors to implement specific interventions before students get too far behind, such as academic counseling, tutoring, or personal learning plans. The trick here is that predictive analytics is a self-improving system which did learn. The more data is gathered, the more accurate the models are when it comes to predicting the student outcomes. Such dynamic flexibility turns predictive analytics into a crucial part of AI-based education systems, in particular when combined with learning management systems that automatically modify instructional materials according to a student projected path. Besides its advantages, predictive analytics in education raise some fundamental ethical and practical concerns as well. All three issues (data privacy, informed consent, and algorithmic bias) must be addressed to make all students fairly and equally treated (Slade & Prinsloo, 2013). In addition, the risk of self-fulfilling prophecies also exists when educational institutions design predictive systems differently, which will, in turn, adversely affect the results of students deemed at-risk; to address it, it is necessary to ensure that the findings obtained with the help of analytics are used beneficially to support, rather than penalize students. Predictive analytics can be an innovation in personalized learning and student success when it is used responsibly.

DISCUSSION AND INTERPRETATION

Artificially Intelligent Response and Evaluation

AI-driven feedback and assessment systems are changing how learning is measured and academic development is supported by teachers. Conventionally, assessment, and especially summative assessment, has been time-consuming, labour-intensive and often restricted to the measurement of superficial knowledge. A more dynamic and scalable alternative is offered by AI technologies, which now can evaluate a variety of student inputs, including multiple-choice questions, as well as more complex and open-ended tasks like essays, problem-solving activities, and short-answer responses. Systems such as the e-rater by ETS and Pearson Intelligent Essay Assessor are based on natural language processing (NLP) algorithms that analyze the student writing on the basis of content relevance, grammar, organization and coherence. Studies conducted by Shermis and Burstein (2013) have demonstrated that even with human supervision, these AI systems have an equivalent ability to assess writing with a reasonable consistency as human graders. Instead of spending days or weeks to get the results of tests, the student gets the feedback instantly and can contemplate their mistakes, misconceptions and correct them instantaneously. This can support a culture of lifelong learning and growth, allowing the students to have greater control over the learning process, and it can also reduce teacher workload, particularly when it would be costly to mark and comment on assignments one-on-one in a large classroom (Nicol and Macfarlane-Dick, 2006). Even with these benefits, challenges do exist that could lead to data-driven instruction to give educators insight into student performance patterns, the most frequently misunderstood areas, and content that might need reteaching or reinforcement. Artificial intelligence systems can be weak at creative, subtle, or situation-specific answers, and they are more effective in some fields than in others. In conclusion, AI-based evaluation is not to be used instead of human evaluation, but rather as a complement that can help students learn more efficiently.

Virtual Tutors and Chatbots

Chatbots and virtual tutors based on AI become a staple of the educational industry, providing students with on-demand one-on-one assistance 24/7. Based on the principles of the latest natural language processing (NLP) and machine learning algorithms, these systems should be able to communicate with students in real-time and answer, explain, and guide them immediately. A key advantage of AI-based virtual tutors, such as IBM Watson Tutor, is that they can provide 24/7 assistance to students with a variety of tasks, including answering specific questions and helping them to comprehend complex material and theories in mathematics, science, and language arts (Luckin et al., 2016; Sharma and Singh, 2024a). These AI tools are available 24 hours a day, unlike human tutors, who are only available in limited quantities and thus the students can seek help at their own convenience and even during non school hours. Virtual tutors and chatbots can be used as supplements to the more human interaction of human instructors, but they cannot substitute the sympathetic, supportive process of sustained, unlimited learning.

AI Simulations and Generated Content

Simulations and artificially intelligent (AI) generated content is changing how educational content is produced and delivered, particularly within the field of science, technology, engineering, and mathematics (STEM). Through natural language generation (NLG) and the use of machine learning, AI can automatically generate quizzes, summaries, study maps, and even lesson plans on its own, saving time and effort that instructors would otherwise need to create learning content. Besides improving the efficiency of the content creation process, these tools can also make educational materials more adaptive (such as generating quizzes based on the level of performance of a particular student) by introducing more difficult questions as they advance in learning or reviewing questions based on the weaknesses identified (Holmes et al., 2019; Nuong et al., 2024). It is an active way to retain the interest rate and not to annoy the students because they are constantly tested. Intelligent software such as Socrative and Quizlet generate dedicated and individualized quizzes according to their past responses to give tailored feedback and encourage further study and memorization in STEM subjects with the use of algorithms. Laboratories and online simulations enable students to carry out experiments or perform complicated tasks in a secure controlled setting without the constraints of physical equipment or time. The use of AI involves platforms such as Labster which simulate real-life science labs, providing students with opportunities to test their hypotheses, manipulate variables, and view their results in a way that would pose a challenge or be impossible in a traditional classroom environment (Holmes et al., 2019; Singh, 2022). They are most useful in chemistry, physics and biology, where physical resources (both costly equipment and laboratory area) may be scarce. Scalability is also a benefit of AI-based simulations. Many students could be tutored at the same time in virtual labs and institutions could offer high-quality learning with hands-on activities without investing in the expensive physical facilities. In addition, AI systems do not only track the interactions among the simulating students, but also can provide immediate feedback and custom-made instructions to each student, which enhances the learning process. This information can also be utilized to pinpoint areas of frustration to provide instructors with specific assistance where necessary. Although the advantages of AI-generated content and simulations become obvious, there are still difficulties. AI systems should be well structured, so that the content generated is correct, applicable and in line with curricular objectives. Besides, the growing popularity of AI-based simulations also leads to the question of the digital divide: students in under-resourced communities might not have access to technology required to properly make use of them. Finally, to achieve successful experiences and outcomes of inclusive education, it is essential to ensure that AI-created content and simulations are available to everyone equally and offer scalability, interactivity, and personalization to students (Sharma & Singh, 2024a).

CHALLENGES IN AI INTEGRATION

Data Privacy and Security

The application of AI in the educational process requires recording and processing of large volumes of data on students. This data can be used to power AI-driven personalized learning systems based on personal details, academic performance, behavior patterns, and engagement with the educational platforms. Nonetheless, the sheer size of data gathering creates some major issues in terms of data privacy and data security, not mentioning the fact that the educational institution needs to be very vigilant to uphold the privacy of such data and the right of the student. Stealing students information or breaches of data have the potential to cause identity theft, cyberbullying, and other types of damage. Also, the application of AI systems will place education institutions in a dilemma between gathering sufficient information to customize learning and taking into account that data collection activities will not violate the privacy of students (Slade & Prinsloo, 2013). To use AI as an example, it can get not only academic information, but also behavioral and psychological information, and the latter can be easily abused, which is why the use of AI-based data collection makes ethics a blind street. Students and their families should be told what information is being gathered, how this information will be utilized and who will be allowed to access this information. Informed consent is an important element of responsible data use in education (Popenici & Kerr, 2017; Singh & Hassan, 2024). Implementing a policy that aligns with the international data protection regulations, such as the General Data Protection Regulation (GDPR) in Europe, can help to ensure that AI solutions in education are operating in a manner that is ethical and safe.

Both Algorithms and Fairness

One of the most important issues that need to be addressed in the context of the integration of Artificial Intelligence into education is the concept of algorithmic bias that leads to unequal and unfair learning outcomes. To fuel AI systems, such as those in the fields of personalized learning, predictive analytics, and automated assessments, machine learning algorithms are trained on large volumes of data. However, these datasets can include some underlying biases that represent past disparities, community stereotypes, or disproportionate representation of specific populations. Until these biases are identified and addressed, AI models can reproduce such disparities and, in the long run, lead to discrimination by educational institutions. AI bias can take on many different shapes. In particular, predictive models created to target at-risk students can tend to prioritize some population groups over others, including more privileged ones, and fail to consider students represented by marginalized populations. Likewise, AI-related grading software or computer-based assessment will favor specific linguistic or cultural standards, which will disfavour other students (Binns, 2018). However, when machine learning models are trained on data that is not diverse or even representative of the entire range of student experiences, they have been found to yield inaccurate results (Angwin et al., 2016). When applied in this way, bias algorithms may result in false identification of student abilities, incorrect predictions of student performance, and potentially risky interventions. The problem of algorithmic bias is also complicated by the fact many AI systems are opaque. The algorithms are often perceived as blackboxes, i.e. the mechanisms of making decisions that lead to making predictions and evaluations are not completely transparent to teachers or learners.

In order to overcome the problem of algorithmic bias, educators and developers of AI must emphasize the importance of fairness, transparency, and inclusivity in AI system design and implementation. The first is to make training data sets as heterogeneous as possible, and reflective of various student groups. Moreover, algorithms need to be actively monitored and audited to identify bias, and the decisions made by AI systems need to be interpretable and explainable to hold them accountable. Through proactive efforts to combat algorithmic bias, AI can deliver on its promise of fair and personalized learning experiences to serve the needs of all learners, irrespective of their background.

Metaverse and Immersive Learning

One concept that is likely to transform the education market is immersive learning, which is a synthesis of artificial intelligence (AI) and technology, including augmented reality (AR) and virtual reality (VR). The most encouraging application of these technologies is the metaversean interconnected virtual universe where students will be able to communicate with other students, read instructional content and engage in learning simulators. When AI is combined with AR and VR, the metaverse can provide dynamic, personalized immersive interactive learning spaces that are both exciting to use and can be expanded and accessible anywhere on the planet (Singh, 2022). One such example is that medical students can do complicated surgeries in a simulated operating room and engineering students can model and test structures in a simulated laboratory. Within these immersive environments, AI-based simulations can dynamically adjust to the actions of the learner, giving instant feedback and varying the difficulty level to suit the skills of the learner (Sharma and Singh, 2024). The concept of gamification has been demonstrated to enhance the performance of learners by making learning process more enjoyable and interactive through the use of game elements like points, levels and rewards. Gamification is also enhanced in the context of an AI-based metaverse, where learners can play in competitions, work in teams, and get rewards according to their results. Not only do these elements facilitate a sense of achievement, but they also facilitate teamwork, problem-solving, and critical thinking in a virtual environment. The metaverse may be used to create global classes, like having students in a language lesson learn a vocabulary by telling an interactive story or having students in a history lesson play an online scavenging mission to discover historical artifacts. Virtual environments also provide students across various regions of the globe with a chance to unite and study in one place, and overcome geographic and socio-economic boundaries that usually restrict the access to high-quality education. Among the most important functions that AI could perform in this is the translation of language in real-time and the dynamism of delivering the content based on the requirements of particular learners. To illustrate this point, multilingual students will be able to communicate and study in the same virtual classroom without any problems because AI-powered tools can translate between languages and provide full immersion in the virtual world to simulate a real-life situation. Students are able to experiment and see the results in a virtual science laboratory without having to deal with time, space, or the high cost of equipment.

The simulations provide a risk environment in which students are free to fail, experiment, and determine how theoretical knowledge can be put into practice. Despite the fact that AI continues to develop, the dystopia of the immersive learning in the metaverse can be achieved only, a range of issues require to be addressed. The second issue is to make sure that the required technology is available to everyone equally, because not all students in the world will have access to the latest VR devices or a high-speed internet connection needed to experience it best. Moreover, people are concerned about the ethical aspects of AI and VR, especially the issue of data privacy and security and the possibility of excessive dependence on technology. In conclusion, the combination of AI with immersive technologies like AR, VR, and the metaverse has a huge potential to reshape the field of education. By giving students a personalized, interactive, and engaging study process, the metaverse can allow them to acquire more knowledge on challenging subjects, engage in group work, and eliminate the barriers to the global process of education. But, to achieve the full potential of these technologies, we need to tackle the issues associated with equity, access, and ethics in AI-enhanced immersive learning environments in the future of education, governance structures that can guarantee equitable access, sufficient teacher education, and the creation of a robust technology infrastructure need to be a primary concern. The adoption of AI in education can generate vast inequalities in access when policies fail to consider the various socioeconomic circumstances within which learners exist. The other urgent field of AI governance is the area of teacher training, which, at all costs, should promote the use of AI-driven learning technologies even by students with disabilities (Zawacki-Richter et al., 2019). Teachers need to be provided with the skills and knowledge that will enable them to incorporate AI into their classrooms successfully. This involves the knowledge of AI system operation, interpretation of AI-generated findings, and how AI can be used to improve student learning (Holmes et al., 2019).

Motivation and Retention

AI-based tools can have a significant impact on the motivation and retention rates of students, which is two vital aspects that affect the results of an education. By transforming traditional learning processes into customized learning experiences and gamified content, AI can help students build a more interactive and accommodating learning environment that encourages them to not give up in the face of failure and remain committed to the learning process. Personalization of learning experiences is one of the main ways that AI improves motivation. In contrast to the traditional one-size-fits-all solutions, AI-based platforms have the capability to detect student behavior, preferences, and performance in real-time, adjusting content and resources to reflect the needs, strengths, and weaknesses of an individual (Nuong et al., 2024). AI also enhances the personalization aspect since it tracks the performance of students and provides feedback promptly. Students are in a better position to identify areas that need improvement once they are given instant feedback on their work and take realistic measures to improve their learning. It is a feedback loop that keeps students level-headed and motivated as learning experiences become more realistic and applicable. The gameification that brings the aspects of the game to the learning process can be listed among the strongest motivation tools that have been proven to be the most likely to be integrated into the learning process, along with the custom learning paths which include the DreamBox and Knewton platform (Pane et al., 2017). Gamified learning can be enhanced with AI, making it more difficult based on the students' progress, rewarding the progress with points, badges, and leaderboards, and challenging the students in a way that feels more like a game than a classroom task. Not only does this feeling of accomplishment and competition make the learning process more enjoyable but it also encourages students to keep reading through the material and to keep trying to master it. Gamification helps students to overcome challenges because the game elements provide a reward system that gives users a physical sense of achievement despite the complexity of the task, thereby affecting the student retention rates greatly. It has been proven that engaged and motivated students are less likely to drop out of school or college (Heffernan and Heffernan, 2014; Sharma and Singh, 2024a). The capability of AI to monitor the initial signs of disengagement, including declines in participation or performance, can allow educators to respond promptly with a customized intervention. The interventions can be through adjustment of learning materials, provision of additional materials, or the provision of incentives to ensure that learners follow the learning process.

In summary, AI can be effectively used to address the issue of retention in educational facilities by mitigating the problem proactively and offering students a more comprehensive learning experience, including elements of gamification. Through real-time feedback, personalized content, and dynamic engagement experiences, AI enables students to overcome challenges and stay motivated toward their learning objectives, which ultimately lead to higher academic achievements and reduced dropout rates.

Limitations of Blended Learning, Barriers To Practice

In spite of all the benefits, it is necessary to also mention that there are quite many disadvantages and practical traps to the blended learning: being flexible and personalized, in practice, this method can be complex and hard to implement. One of its major weaknesses is the digital divide. Not every student has access to the required technology and a stable connection to the internet at home. This could further increase the gaps that already exist with the better-off students doing well in the online section and the poorer students lagging far behind in their studies.Not just the supply of the equipment but the stable home conditions, where it can be practiced, and the technical assistance in fixing the issues.

Pedagogical, Social Problems

The other major weakness is the quality of online training. Making old classroom resources available to students online does not necessarily imply effective blended learning. It requires radical redefining of pedagogy which can be quite taxing to the teacher (Nuong et al., 2024). Not only should teachers be trained to use new technology, but they should also be trained to create an interactive online module that is engaging and more than a delivery of passive content. The physical nature of the interaction can also cause isolation and non-engagement by some students due to the absence of physical interaction in the online component. It is not always easy to achieve social and emotional advantages of face-to-face collaboration, such as spontaneous discussion and non-verbal communication, in a virtual environment.

Implementation Hurdles

Blended learning models also come with a plethora of challenges when it comes to practical implementation. Teacher training and professional development is one of the most important ones. Most teachers do not have the skills and confidence to use technology properly in their instructions. It also needs quite a significant amount of investment in the continuous training and not a workshop. The other major problem is the cost of technology. Educational institutions must spend a great deal of money on various hardware and software, including computers and tablets, as well as learning management systems and dedicated educational applications. This technology needs a committed IT support team, which may also be a separate financial cost.

In addition, there is a developing concern on data operations and confidentiality. Blended learning systems will be able to store a large amount of information about the performance and behavior of students(Singh & Hassan, 2024). This knowledge is applicable in individualizing learning, but may also raise questions regarding ownership of information, how information is utilized, and student privacy of data. Lastly, the change of culture needed to implement a successful implementation is not always taken seriously. Blended learning is only effective when there is a shared vision and all stakeholders administrators, teachers, parents, and students buy-in. The transition process is chaotic and ineffective due to the lack of effective policy framework and structure of governance. These are not insurmountable hurdles but they demand lots of planning, lots of investment and a resolve to tackle the underlying equity and pedagogical problems.

CONCLUSION

A convergence between blended learning and artificial intelligence is a recent field in education, but it is not limited to digitizing content to create a learning ecosystem that is intelligent and responsive. Through the application of AI-enabled solutions, including customized and tailor-made learning platforms, automatic evaluation and feedback mechanisms, and intelligent content selection systems, education will be more efficient and fair. Meanwhile, it gives the human educator a higher profile, taking them off the administrative treadmill and enabling them to do the most important job in education, which is to encourage critical thinking, promote collaborative learning, and offer the human touch and relationship-building that technology alone cannot accomplish. Probably, it will be the AI which will occupy the main position in defining the future of education as it will allow making the process of obtaining knowledge more personal, more inclusive and more efficient. By using adaptive learning algorithms, predictive analytics, intelligent tutoring systems, AI-based feedback mechanisms, and other tools, education can be made more responsive to the needs of individual learners. AI provides teachers with efficient tools to tailor the content delivery process, recognize at-risk students early, offer immediate feedback, and provide learners with virtual tutoring and multilingual accessibility tools and simulated immersion. These abilities not only have the capacity to improve learning outcomes, but also have the potential to close achievement gaps and improve retention rates in different learning environments. But the implementation of AI in education does not come without serious pitfalls. Data privacy, algorithmic bias, equity, and ethical use of student data need to be taken into account. AI systems rely heavily on data sets, which fail to reflect the population in general, or when the data sets are incorrectly processed, the systems themselves can perpetuate existing inequities and make faulty forecasts. Moreover, the lack of transparency, fairness and security of most of the AI algorithms, referred to as the black box problem, will force the governance and regulatory systems to maintain pace with technology. Overall, AI opens up transformative opportunities, as well as important responsibilities. Properly incorporated into robust ethical and policy frameworks, AI can be used to promote scalable, equitable, and effective learning environments that are customized to the individual learner and which equip learners with skills to function in a world that continues to change rapidly.

REFERENCES

Angwin, J., Larson, J., Mattu, S., & Kirchner, L. (2016). *Machine bias: There's software used across the country to predict future criminals. And it's biased against blacks*. ProPublica.

Arnold, K. E., & Pistilli, M. D. (2012). Course signals at Purdue: Using learning analytics to increase student success. *Proceedings of the 2nd International Conference on Learning Analytics and Knowledge*, 267–270. DOI: 10.1145/2330601.2330666

Binns, R. (2018). Fairness in machine learning: Lessons from political philosophy. *Proceedings of the 2018 CHI Conference on Human Factors in Computing Systems*, 1–14.

Heffernan, N. T., & Heffernan, C. L. (2014). The ASSISTments ecosystem: Building a platform that brings scientists and teachers together for minimally invasive research on human learning and teaching. *International Journal of Artificial Intelligence in Education, 24*(4), 470–497. DOI: 10.1007/s40593-014-0024-x

Holmes, W., Bialik, M., & Fadel, C. (2019). *Artificial Intelligence in Education: Promises and Implications for Teaching and Learning*. Center for Curriculum Redesign.

Luckin, R., Holmes, W., Griffiths, M., & Forcier, L. B. (2016). *Intelligence unleashed: An argument for AI in education*. Pearson Education.

Nicol, D. J., & Macfarlane-Dick, D. (2006). Formative assessment and self-regulated learning: A model and seven principles of good feedback practice. *Studies in Higher Education, 31*(2), 199–218. DOI: 10.1080/03075070600572090

Nuong Deri, M., Singh, A., Zaazie, P., & Anandene, D. (2024). Leveraging Artificial Intelligence in Higher Educational Institutions: A Comprehensive Overview. *Education and Law Review*, (30). Advance online publication. DOI: 10.1344/REYD2024.30.45777

Pane, J. F., Steiner, E. D., Baird, M. D., & Hamilton, L. S. (2017). *Informing progress: Insights on personalized learning implementation and effects*. RAND Corporation. DOI: 10.7249/RR2042

Popenici, S. A. D., & Kerr, S. (2017). Exploring the impact of artificial intelligence on teaching and learning in higher education. *Research and Practice in Technology Enhanced Learning, 12*(1), 1–13. DOI: 10.1186/s41039-017-0062-8 PMID: 30595727

Sharma, M., & Singh, A. (2024a). Embracing Technological Innovation: A Review of Hi-Tech Services in Hospitality Industry. *Evergreen, 11*(4), 2818–2830. DOI: 10.5109/7326926

Sharma, R., & Singh, A. (2024). Use of Digital Technology in Improving Quality Education: A Global Perspectives and Trends. In Nadda, V., Tyagi, P., Moniz Vieira, R., & Tyagi, P. (Eds.), *Implementing Sustainable Development Goals in the Service Sector* (pp. 14–26). IGI Global., DOI: 10.4018/979-8-3693-2065-5.ch002

Shermis, M. D., & Burstein, J. (Eds.). (2013). *Handbook of automated essay evaluation: Current applications and new directions*. Routledge. DOI: 10.4324/9780203122761

Singh, A. (2022). Conceptual framework on Smart Learning Environment- An Indian perspective. *Journal of Education and Law*, (25). Advance online publication. DOI: 10.1344/REYD2022.25.36706

Singh, A. (2024). Impact of E-learning on Student Motivation in Higher Education Institutions: An Indian Perspective. *Journal of Education and Law*, (29). Advance online publication. DOI: 10.1344/REYD2024.29.43214

Singh, A., & Hassan, S. C. (2024). Identifying the skill gap in the workplace and their challenges in hospitality and tourism organisations. In *Contemporary challenges in social science management: Skills gaps and shortages in the labour market* (pp. 101–114). Emerald Publishing Limited.

Slade, S., & Prinsloo, P. (2013). Learning analytics: Ethical issues and dilemmas. *The American Behavioral Scientist, 57*(10), 1510–1529. DOI: 10.1177/0002764213479366

VanLehn, K. (2011). The relative effectiveness of human tutoring, intelligent tutoring systems, and other tutoring systems. *Educational Psychologist, 46*(4), 197–221. DOI: 10.1080/00461520.2011.611369

Walkington, C., & Bernacki, M. (2014). Personalized learning in mathematics for adolescent learners. *Journal of Research on Technology in Education, 46*(4), 327–351.

Zawacki-Richter, O., Marín, V. I., Bond, M., & Gouverneur, F. (2019). Systematic review of research on artificial intelligence applications in higher education – Where are the educators? *International Journal of Educational Technology in Higher Education, 16*(1), 1–27. DOI: 10.1186/s41239-019-0171-0

Chapter 3
AI-Enhanced Network Learning Theory Transforming Education Through Personalized, Inclusive, and Ethical Artificial Intelligence

Benu Kesar
https://orcid.org/0000-0003-3207-5528
Symbiosis International University, Pune,India

Shaji Joseph
https://orcid.org/0000-0002-5268-1376
Symbiosis International University, Pune,India

Dev Kesar
https://orcid.org/0009-0004-0801-2257
Vellore Institute of Technology, Chennai, India

ABSTRACT

Artificial Intelligence (AI) is profoundly transforming education by enabling personalised learning and fostering inclusive access to knowledge. We have introduced AI-Enhanced Network Learning Theory (AI-NLT) that reconceptualises learning as the product of hybrid intelligence, emerging from the dynamic interaction between human cognition, artificial intelligence systems, and distributed digital networks. It emphasises six interrelated components: personalised and adaptive learning,

DOI: 10.4018/979-8-3373-3815-6.ch003

right © 2026, IGI Global Scientific Publishing. Copying or distributing in print or electronic forms without written permission of IGI Global Scientific Publishing is prohibited. Use of this chapter to in generative artificial intelligence (AI) technologies is expressly prohibited. The publisher reserves all rights to license its use for generative AI training and machine learning model development.

collaborative connectivity, inclusive intelligence, emotional-cognitive support, feedback and co-creation, and ethical AI. Together, these dimensions illustrate how AI can tailor learning pathways, facilitate global collaboration, dismantle barriers to participation, support learner well-being, enable co-creation of knowledge, and uphold transparency and accountability. A case study on Collaborative Learning with AI Speakers (CLAIS) exemplifies human-AI co-construction of knowledge, highlighting both potential and limitations.

1. INTRODUCTION

In the field of education, Artificial Intelligence (AI) is playing an increasingly significant role. AI not only helps personalize learning but also makes administrative tasks more efficient. It also helps provide access to quality education to a large number of people (Hwang et al., 2020; Rane, 2024). As these exchanges between humans and AI grow, human-centered machine learning (HCML) has evolved. AI is based on algorithms, a set of rules and instructions that computers follow to solve complex problems (Tammets et al., 2023).

Algorithms give AI and Machine Learning systems step-by-step instructions. Machine Learning (ML) uses statistical methods and data to solve complex problems. AI and ML analyze data to find patterns, build models, and then predict values based on those models (Akgun & Greenhow, 2022). AI is increasingly used to automate assessment and feedback processes (Kumar, 2024). AI assists educators in grading multiple-choice questions, math problems, and essays (Farhood et al., 2024). As a result, AI enables educators to focus on essential tasks, such as mentoring and student support. AI can also provide real-time feedback, helping students understand and learn from their mistakes (Kolluru et al., 2018).

These days, AI is used to analyze students' learning patterns, identify their strengths, areas for improvement, and learning preferences. This helps personalize learning instead of following a fixed curriculum (Karroum et al., 2024). Such flexibility is expected to lead to higher engagement and better academic results (Wu, 2023; Saputra et al., 2023). With AI, educational content and pacing are increasingly tailored to individual needs (Tulasi & Rao, 2023). Personalized learning allows students to take charge of their learning process and achieve educational goals aligned with their interests. Intelligent tutoring systems go further by providing one-on-one guidance, acting as personal tutors, and analyzing students' learning patterns, weaknesses, and strengths to customize content and pace for each learner (Ng et al., 2022; Sari et al., 2024).

Even outside classrooms, AI's influence is evident in automating administrative tasks. Schools and academic administrations become more efficient with AI-optimized class scheduling and timetables tailored to teacher preferences, room availability, and student needs (Thuy & Tien, 2024). Chatbots and virtual assistants are common, answering routine questions about coursework, deadlines, and administrative matters (Sajja et al., 2023). AI-powered translation tools also help reduce language barriers, making educational resources more accessible to students from less privileged backgrounds and those who do not speak English.

AI tools such as text-to-speech, speech-to-text, and visual aids foster a more inclusive learning environment for students with learning difficulties. The use of AI in language learning led to the creation of the Intelligent Computer-Assisted Language Learning (ICALL) system. Automated education governance assemblage evaluates how AI-driven decision-making supports institutional accreditation, policy development, and overall educational management. However, this also raises several ethical issues, including data privacy, algorithmic biases, and unequal access to AI tools (Saxena & Bajotra, 2024; Holmes et al., 2022).

AI-powered learning platforms collect a large amount of student data, including academic records and personal information. Therefore, it is important to prevent this data from being misused for personal gain (Córdova & Vicari, 2022). A well-designed data governance policy is crucial to ensure that sensitive student information remains protected from security breaches, unauthorized access, or even commercial exploitation by third-party vendors (Saxena & Bajotra, 2024).

Laws such as the Family Educational Rights and Privacy Act (FERPA) and the General Data Protection Regulation (GDPR) are crucial steps in preventing AI misuse. These laws clearly define rules for collecting, storing, and sharing student data and stress the need for user consent before gathering sensitive information. In practice, this involves using strong encryption, anonymizing data, and enforcing strict access controls to protect student privacy. Misusing this data can deepen existing educational inequalities. Algorithms trained on biased data can increase disparities related to gender, race, or socioeconomic status.

For example, an AI-driven admissions tool, mainly built on data from elite schools, might favor applicants from similar backgrounds while disadvantaging students from underrepresented groups (Holmes et al., 2022). This can be addressed by ensuring that training datasets are diverse and include all student groups (Rane, 2024).

Human-in-the-Loop (HITL) systems are an effective way to reduce bias. They require educators to review AI-generated feedback, grades, or recommendations before making any decisions. These systems help prevent AI from making unchecked choices and improve accountability (Córdova & Vicari, 2022). Schools should also establish AI ethics committees that regularly review AI applications in education to ensure adherence to high ethical standards and compliance with evolving regulations.

1.1 History of AI in Education

Artificial intelligence has transformed education over time, leading to a major shift in how we teach and learn. This change has happened in multiple stages, fueled by key technological breakthroughs, changing roles in teaching and learning, and more advanced AI tools. A pivotal moment was the development of intelligent tutoring systems, which brought AI into the classroom by providing personalized support to students (Sarnato et al., 2024).

At the start of the 21st century, online learning platforms saw a sharp increase, speeding up the integration of AI in education. The rise of Massive Open Online Courses (MOOCs) and other digital learning tools allowed AI to play a bigger role in delivering content, assessing students, and engaging learners. New digital tools began to supplement traditional assessments and classroom activities, leading to a shift toward more technology-driven teaching methods.

Another major breakthrough in AI development was the rise of machine learning, a subfield that creates algorithms enabling systems to learn from data without being explicitly programmed (Russell & Norvig, 2024). This breakthrough opened the door for various machine learning techniques, including supervised, unsupervised, and reinforcement learning. Later, deep learning emerged and revolutionized the field. Using multilayered artificial neural networks, deep learning allowed for analyzing complex, high-dimensional data, paving the way for today's most advanced AI applications. At the same time, Natural Language Processing (NLP) changed how machines interact with human language. This AI technology allows machines to understand, interpret, and generate language, leading to significant advancements in applications such as chatbots and translation services.

Early Beginnings (1950s-1970s): The history of AI in education started with early teaching machines and programmed instruction. B.F. Skinner's teaching machines in the 1950s laid the foundation for computer-aided instruction. One of the first notable AI-based educational systems was SCHOLAR, developed by Jaime Carbonell in 1970, which was capable of having conversations with students about geography (Carbonell & Collins, 1974).

Intelligent Tutoring Systems Era (1980s): In the 1980s, Intelligent Tutoring Systems (ITS) attracted more attention. John Anderson's ACT* theory fueled the development of cognitive tutors at Carnegie Mellon University. These systems could track student progress and provide personalized feedback based on cognitive models of learning.

Multimedia and Expert Systems (1990s): In the 1990s, multimedia and expert systems saw notable growth. The rise of multimedia computers opened the door for more sophisticated educational AI tools. Roger Schank's work on goal-based scenarios and practical learning significantly influenced the development of adaptive learning environments (Schank et al., 1994). Expert systems started to be used for curriculum planning and educational assessments. As multimedia computing became more integrated, AI applications in education advanced, including adaptive learning environments and intelligent decision-making systems. The expansion of the internet also fueled the development of web-based learning platforms that used AI to analyze student learning patterns and improve educational outcomes.

Web-Based Learning Revolution (2000s): The internet transformed AI in education through Learning Management Systems (LMS) and adaptive learning platforms. Carnegie Learning's cognitive tutors became widely used in mathematics education (Koedinger & Corbett, 2006). This period saw the integration of data mining techniques to analyze patterns of student learning. At the same time, the rise of Massive Open Online Courses (MOOCs) democratized access to education and sped up the adoption of AI-driven personalization, automated assessment, and learner engagement strategies.

Modern Era (2010s-Present): Recent advancements include machine learning algorithms for personalized learning paths, natural language processing for automated assessments, learning analytics for predicting student success, and virtual and augmented reality in education (Kumari, 2024). The rise of generative AI tools, like ChatGPT, has opened new possibilities for AI-assisted writing and customized learning experiences, while also creating challenges related to academic integrity and critical thinking skills (Perkins, 2023).

As shown in Table 1, the development of AI tools in education has caused significant shifts in roles, approaches, and technologies through various stages. These stages range from traditional, teacher-centered models that depend on simple digital tools to more advanced, future-oriented scenarios. In these scenarios, educators are increasingly supported by AI, students receive broader assistance, and technologies such as emotional AI, IoT, blockchain, and advanced machine learning become more common. Notably, students' roles have changed from passive recipients to self-directed learners and, ultimately, to co-creators. Teachers now often act as facilitators, learning guides, and educators enhanced by AI (Snehalatha, 2024).

Table 1. The Progression of AI in Education

Education stage	AI's role	Learning approach	Student's role	Teacher's role	Technology used
Traditional education	Limited or none	Teacher centric	Passive recipient	Knowledge provider	Basic digital tools
Early AI integration	Automatic assessment	Blended learning	Active participant	Facilitator	Adaptive learning platforms
Advanced AI in education	Personalized learning	Student-centric	Self-directed learner	Learning guide	AI tutors, VR/AR, ML algorithms
Future of AI in education	Holistic support	Continuous lifelong learning	Co-creator	AI augmented educator	Emotional AI, IoT, blockchain, advanced ML

Source: Author's own work

Table 1 illustrates the evolving role of AI in education, highlighting its transformative impact on teaching and learning processes across different stages:

1. Traditional Education: Represents the pre-AI baseline, characterized by teacher-centered instruction and limited technological support.
2. Early AI Integration: Marks the initial phase of AI adoption, primarily in automated assessment, administrative support, and basic forms of personalization.
3. Advanced AI in Education: Reflects the current stage, where AI-driven platforms enable personalization, adaptive learning, and data-informed pedagogy.
4. Future of AI in Education: Looking ahead, AI is expected to become deeply embedded in education, shaping lifelong, collaborative, and holistic learning ecosystems.

One key trend is the rise of AI guardrails in schools and universities. AI is evolving rapidly, making it difficult to create policies that cover every possible situation. Instead, many institutions now focus on broad guidelines that emphasize student safety, data privacy, and ethical use (Córdova & Vicari, 2022). Educational institutions have recognised that while AI has lots of potential, its adoption must be managed carefully. Enhancing learning should not compromise core values. To ensure this, institutions are increasingly introducing AI guardrails in schools and universities.

According to cognitivism, learning happens through mental processes such as receiving, organizing, storing, and retrieving information. This approach views learning as a mental activity that relies on memory, attention, and problem-solving. Conversely, behaviourism emphasizes external factors like stimuli and reinforcement to shape habits. We gain knowledge through rewards or punishments, according to this perspective. In contrast, constructivism uses a learner-centered approach, where individuals actively build their understanding by connecting new information to their existing knowledge, which is acquired through real-life experiences and social interactions (Lee et al., 2023).

Connectivism is the new age theory. This theory acknowledges that knowledge is spread across networks of people, tools, and information. Learning occurs through continuous connection-making and collaboration. As AI transforms education, numerous questions arise. How do students work with AI as if it were a peer or partner in learning? How do they assess whether AI's contributions are trustworthy and helpful for their goals? How do teachers orchestrate classroom dynamics when AI is integrated into group learning? These questions emphasize the need to look beyond just efficiency and outcomes and focus on the more profound ways AI might enhance knowledge creation.

To address these questions, we introduced the AI-Enhanced Network Learning Theory (AI-NLT). This framework combines advanced AI technologies with ethical considerations to create a model of hybrid intelligence where human cognition, AI systems, and digital networks work together continuously to shape learning. Unlike older views that see AI as a passive tool, AI-NLT considers AI an active partner: one that helps build knowledge, provides adaptive feedback, fosters collaboration, and promotes inclusivity.

1.2 Research Objectives

1. To explore the applications of Artificial Intelligence in transforming teaching, learning, and educational administration.
2. To evaluate the role of AI in enabling personalized, inclusive, and emotionally responsive learning experiences.
3. To examine the ethical implications of AI integration in education, including data privacy, algorithmic bias, and equitable access.
4. To assess the effectiveness of AI-powered tools in improving academic outcomes and overall educational outcomes.

5.To propose a comprehensive framework for the responsible and pedagogically sound integration of AI into educational ecosystems.

1.3 Research Questions

1. How is AI reshaping pedagogical practices, student engagement, and instructional personalization in education?
2. In what ways do AI technologies support inclusivity and accessibility for diverse learner populations, including those with disabilities and language barriers?
3. What are the ethical concerns surrounding AI use in education, and how can institutions mitigate risks related to data privacy and bias?

4. How does AI-Enhanced Network Learning Theory (AI-NLT) guide the effective and ethical deployment of AI in education?

2. LITERATURE REVIEW

AI has changed education from traditional methods to adaptive, data-driven, and personalized learning (Graesser et al., 2018; Ng et al., 2022). Now, machine learning algorithms are used to analyze student data and customize both content and pace to fit individual needs (Gligorea et al., 2023; Yadav, 2024). Researchers are also exploring emotional AI, also known as affective computing, which detects students' emotional states and adjusts instructional strategies in real-time. By addressing frustration, motivation, or disengagement as they occur, these systems enhance both well-being and learning outcomes (Aly et al., 2023; Singh et al., 2023).

AI-powered tools have enhanced accessibility through features like text-to-speech, speech-to-text, and real-time translation. Šumak et al. (2024) argue that these tools help reduce barriers for students with disabilities or language challenges. Tools such as Duolingo and Google Translate provide instant feedback to learners, aiding them in refining their pronunciation and grammar. AI, while identifying individual strengths and weaknesses and offering personalized exercises, supports a tailored learning environment.

AI's role is expanding with machine learning algorithms that predict student performance, identify at-risk students, and customize learning pathways (Graesser et al., 2018; Ng et al., 2022; Dash & Bhoi, 2024; Saifi, 2024). In higher education, these predictive analytics are valuable for early intervention, reducing dropout rates, and guiding students toward success. AI-powered academic advising systems can assist students in selecting the right courses based on their learning styles and career goals (Aly et al., 2023).

Advanced AI technologies can identify emotions through facial expressions, speech patterns, and physiological cues, allowing for real-time adjustments to learning materials (Singh et al., 2023). Emotional AI, also called affective computing, includes technologies that detect, interpret, and respond to learners' emotional states by analysing facial expressions, speech patterns, and physiological signals (Aly et al., 2023; Singh et al., 2023; Alm et al., 2005; Gremsl & Hödl, 2022; He et al., 2022; Kort et al., 2002).

Lately, AI-powered Virtual Teaching Assistants (VTAs) have gained popularity in higher education. These tools help automate grading, provide real-time feedback, and increase student engagement (Tack & Piech, 2022). Perkins (2023) states that these assistants not only ease students' cognitive workload but also improve self-directed learning and increase student satisfaction.

Transparency helps build trust by making it easier to identify and fix mistakes or unfair results. The human-in-the-loop approach is an effective way to improve transparency. Holmes et al. (2022) emphasize that human educators should review AI-generated grades and feedback before they are finalized. This process can help minimize harm caused by algorithmic biases and maintain the personal and contextual understanding that only human judgment provides (Karroum et al., 2024).

AI governance requires ongoing evaluation and adjustments. Policies cannot stay the same, they must evolve with advances in AI and changing societal priorities (Chan, 2023). To ensure AI in education aligns with fundamental academic and democratic values, continuous research, stakeholder input, and collaboration among institutions are essential (Córdova & Vicari, 2022).

Using AI in education in an ethical manner involves creating and using artificial intelligence systems that are transparent, fair, accountable, and respect data privacy (Córdova & Vicari, 2022). This requires careful attention to biases in algorithms, obtaining informed consent, and having humans oversee the process to ensure that AI contributes to just, fair, and inclusive learning for all students (Holmes et al., 2022).

Sustainable Development Goal 4 aims to ensure inclusive and equitable quality education and to promote lifelong learning opportunities for everyone. AI is a tool that can boost progress by making education more inclusive, accessible, and personalized.

As shown in Figure 1, AI's diverse role in education includes personalized learning, automated assessment and feedback, accessibility and inclusive intelligence, intelligent content creation, multimodal learning, and data-driven decision making.

Figure 1. Role of AI in Education

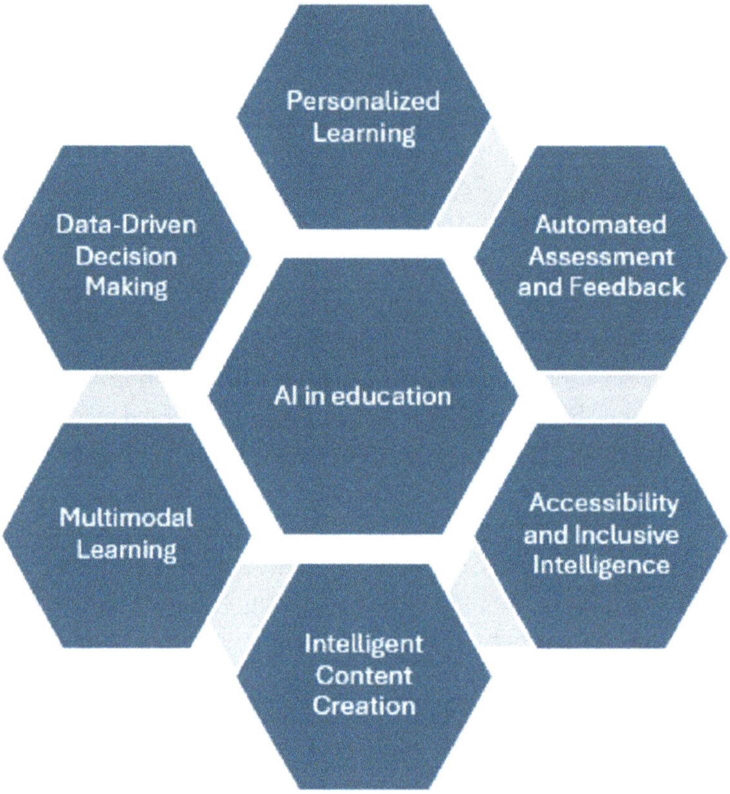

Source: Author's own work

2.1 Personalized Learning

AI enhances customized educational experiences by adapting to each student's unique needs, pace, and learning style. This is accomplished through machine learning algorithms that analyse performance, interaction data, and engagement signals to build dynamic learner models (Kolluru et al., 2018; Gligorea et al., 2023). These systems employ both collaborative and content-based filtering to create personalized learning paths that adjust presentation formats, content difficulty, and pacing in real-time. They accommodate different learning styles by offering visual and auditory content based on individual preferences (Karroum et al., 2024). Furthermore, AI improves cognitive load management through content chunking and scheduling (Saputra et al., 2023). AI algorithms detect behavioural patterns, such as optimal study times, and facilitate social learning through strategic peer matching. They also provide personalized assessment methods (Gligorea et al., 2023; Alenezi, 2024).

2. 2. Automated Assessment and Feedback

Automated assessment systems use item response theory and computerized adaptive testing to create tailored evaluation experiences (Dash & Bhoi, 2024). With natural language processing, complex and open-ended responses can be evaluated through semantic analysis, rather than just matching keywords. By integrating continuous assessment, evaluations become ongoing learning monitors, rather than just periodic events. AI systems analyze response patterns, solution strategies, and error types in real-time, providing immediate diagnostic feedback (Hwang et al., 2020).

2.3. Accessibility and Inclusive Intelligence

AI breaks down barriers for learners with disabilities and language challenges using speech-to-text tools, translation, and adaptive interfaces (Farhood et al., 2024). These systems automatically tailor interaction patterns, content presentation, and assessment formats to individual learner profiles (Šumak et al., 2024). The technology does more than convert text to speech - it transforms content in a sophisticated way that preserves educational value while making it more accessible.

AI systems can now recognize speech patterns associated with various disabilities, accents, and language variations, providing accurate transcription and response capabilities. AI systems can modify content presentation, break down information into manageable segments, provide additional processing time, and offer alternative explanation methods tailored to individual cognitive profiles (Kumar, 2024)

2.4. Data-Driven Decision Making

AI enables institutions to predict outcomes such as dropout risks, course success, or enrolment patterns. These insights drive proactive interventions and institutional planning. Data analytics transforms classroom information into actionable insights for administrators and teachers. Students' interaction clicks, response times, answer patterns, and engagement levels create data points that reveal learning patterns. Modern learning management systems continuously capture this information, building comprehensive profiles of student progress and behaviour (Gligorea et al., 2023; Yadav, 2024; Kolluru et al., 2018; Alawneh et al., 2024).

2.5. Multimodal Learning

AI supports "immersive learning experiences" across behavioural, emotional, and cognitive dimensions; here, we refer to multimodal learning (Samsonovich, 2020). This approach recognizes that effective learning engages multiple psychological processes and sensory channels at the same time (Kolluru et al., 2018). AI systems can analyse behavioural data (click patterns, time spent on tasks), emotional indicators (through sentiment analysis of text responses or facial recognition), and cognitive load markers (response accuracy, completion times) to create what we call "holistic learner profiles." These profiles inform adaptive content delivery that matches not just what students need to learn but also how they learn best (Suntharalingam, 2024; Samsonovich, 2020).

2.6. Intelligent Content Creation

AI systems now use advanced algorithms and machine learning to analyze large amounts of student data. This helps generate personalized educational materials that match each student's learning style and preferences (Kolluru et al., 2018). When students struggle with a concept, AI systems can provide extra explanations or alternative methods. If a student demonstrates mastery, they can accelerate their learning (Šumak et al., 2024; Ayeni et al., 2024). The ability to automatically generate content is rapidly expanding.

Machine learning algorithms first engage in robust pattern recognition to analyse extensive datasets on student performance, engagement, and learning behaviours. This initial stage involves training machine learning models to identify fundamental patterns and correlations within student data, such as common misconceptions, effective study habits, and typical progression curves for different subjects. This foundational understanding of learner characteristics and patterns provides the basis for developing dynamic, personalised learning experiences.

Transitioning from pattern recognition to adaptive learning is a sophisticated application of machine learning principles. These systems employ collaborative filtering and content-based filtering algorithms. Collaborative filtering identifies students with similar learning styles and suggests content that benefited similar learners. Content-based filtering examines the distinct features of educational materials that resonate with individual students. The growing use of chatbots like ChatGPT in education demonstrates how large language models (LLMs) are being utilized in teaching settings (Wu, 2023; Essel et al., 2022).

As shown in Table 2, the literature review highlights that AI platforms effectively tailor content and pacing to meet the individual needs of learners, supported by key research in the field.

Table 2. Overview of studies from literature review

Themes	Key Insights	Key studies
Personalized Learning	AI platforms tailor content and pace to individual learners, enhancing engagement and academic outcomes.	Kolluru et. al., (2018); Gligorea et al., (2023); Graesser et al., (2018); Sari et al., (2024); Yadav (2024); Karroum et al., (2024)
Accessibility and Inclusion	AI tools like speech-to-text, translation, and gesture recognition support learners with disabilities and language needs.	Šumak et al., (2024); Kolluru et. al., (2018)
Administrative efficiency	AI streamlines processes like enrollment forecasting, scheduling, and chatbot support for student queries.	Ayeni et al., (2024); Ajuwon et al., (2024); Kumar (2024)
Emotional AI	Affective computing adapts content based on students' emotional states, improving motivation and retention.	Singh et al., (2023); Aly et al., (2023); Kort et. al., (2002); Gremsl & Hödl, (2022); Villegas-Ch et al., (2023); González-Hernández et al., (2018)
Ethical AI	Data privacy, algorithmic bias, and transparency are key concerns; solutions include XAI, federated learning.	Saxena & Bajotra (2024); Holmes et al., (2022); Bazoukis et al., (2024); Kaur et al., (2024); Córdova & Vicari (2022); Akgun & Greenhow, (2022)

Source: Author's own work

3. THEORETICAL FRAMEWORK

AI-Enhanced Network Learning Theory (AI-NLT) offers a fundamental re-evaluation of learning processes in the era of artificial intelligence. Building on Siemens' (2004) Connectivism learning theory, it highlights the importance of networks and connections in the digital age, suggesting that knowledge exists within distributed networks of people and technology. AI tools support and expand these learning networks by connecting learners to relevant peers, resources, and communities. This promotes collaboration, knowledge sharing, and lifelong learning, thereby improving the overall educational experience.

AI-NLT proposes that learning is the product of hybrid intelligence, a dynamic interplay between human intelligence, AI systems, and digital networks. Unlike earlier approaches that positioned AI as a passive instructional tool, AI-NLT conceptualizes AI as an active, co-constructive agent within learning environments.

These networks facilitate bidirectional knowledge exchanges, allowing information, insights, and feedback to flow seamlessly between human learners and AI systems. Through this interaction, AI not only personalizes learning paths but also influences the development of knowledge.

The networks are constantly evolving, with connection strengths and pathways adapting based on learning patterns and outcomes. This dynamic adaptation enables the integration of human intuition with AI's analytical capabilities, creating a more resilient and effective learning environment than either could achieve alone (Karroum et al., 2024). The AI systems in this framework do not simply process information; they actively help build knowledge by identifying patterns, making connections, and suggesting new learning pathways that might not be immediately obvious to teachers.

The theory suggests that individual cognitive limitations do not restrict learning capacity but are significantly expanded through AI-enhanced information processing and distributed cognitive load management. Here, AI is not merely delivering personalized content but is engaging in adaptive knowledge synthesis, recognizing cross-domain patterns, constructing learning pathways, and shaping epistemic development in real-time.

The main idea of AI-NLT is network intelligence, where learning effectiveness comes from improving hybrid intelligence through AI mediation. AI-NLT emphasizes that learning no longer exists solely within an individual's mind or within a social network but instead occurs through the dynamic interaction of human intelligence, AI systems, and distributed digital networks.

The framework is based on six interconnected components, each emphasizing a key aspect of learning in AI-mediated environments. The first component is Personalized and Adaptive Learning, where AI systems utilize multimodal analytics, natural language processing, and reinforcement learning to deliver tailored content, pacing, and scaffolding. This enables context-aware instruction that reduces cognitive load, anticipates learner challenges, and fosters mastery learning.

The second component, Collaborative Connectivity, allows peer-to-peer and learner-expert interactions across distributed networks. With intelligent matching, multilingual support, and sentiment-aware grouping, AI enhances social presence and promotes global, interdisciplinary learning communities.

Equally important is the principle of Inclusive Intelligence. AI actively eliminates barriers to participation through real-time translation and adaptable user interfaces. These features make learning more equitable for diverse learners, including those with disabilities and from marginalized backgrounds. This is not just an optional aspect of the theory but a core ethic; AI-enhanced learning must be accessible to everyone and should be culturally responsive.

Another element of the framework is Emotional-Cognitive Support. By using affective computing, AI can identify emotional states like anxiety, frustration, or disengagement (Picard, 1999). By adjusting pedagogical strategies in real time, AI promotes motivation, resilience, and ongoing learner engagement (González-Hernández et al., 2018).

Feedback and co-creation involve Generative AI transforming learners from mere knowledge consumers into co-creators. This enables interactive content creation, adaptive feedback, and creative collaboration. As a result, AI becomes a partner in the learner's intellectual journey, and the lines between instruction, reflection, and creation become more fluid.

Finally, the theory places Ethical AI at its foundation. The framework underscores transparency, fairness, accountability, and human oversight as foundational safeguards. Principles such as Explainable AI (XAI), algorithmic auditing, federated learning, and human-in-the-loop (HITL) mechanisms ensure responsible deployment of AI in education. It is not just a theory for how we learn with AI; it is a theory for how we learn better, together.

Figure 2 illustrates the main components of AI-enhanced Network Learning Theory, including personalized and adaptive learning, collaborative connectivity, inclusive intelligence, emotional-cognitive support, feedback and cocreation, and ethical AI.

Figure 2. Components of AI-enhanced Network Learning Theory

Source: Author's own work

3.1 Personalized & Adaptive Learning

Definition: AI systems continuously customize content, pacing, and instructional strategies to match each learner's unique profiles. By utilizing machine learning and real-time analytics, educational experiences are tailored based on performance and engagement data (Yekollu et al., 2024).

AI Techniques Involved:

- Multimodal Large Language Models (MLLMs) for cross-modal content adaptation.
- Advanced knowledge tracing with Bayesian networks and deep learning.
- Item response theory with continuous calibration.
- Contextual Natural Language Processing for personalized language, examples, and cultural references.
- Reinforcement learning for optimizing learning path recommendations.
- Computer vision for gesture and facial expression analysis.
- Adaptive assessment algorithms with immediate difficulty adjustment.

Educational Impact:

- Enhanced multimodal engagement through personalized content delivery.
- Improved retention rates through optimized cognitive load management.
- Accelerated mastery-based progression with real-time competency assessment.
- Reduced learning time while maintaining or improving comprehension levels.
- Dynamic scaffolding that adapts to cognitive states.
- Predictive intervention before learning difficulties manifest.

3.2 Collaborative Connectivity

Definition: AI dynamically manages and improves interactions among learners, experts, communities, and digital content across distributed learning networks.

AI Techniques Involved:

- Social Network Analysis (SNA) with graph neural networks.
- Intelligent peer matching algorithms using compatibility scoring and learning goal alignment.
- Cross-cultural communication with cultural context awareness.
- Multilingual conversational agents for seamless collaboration.

- Collaborative filtering with deep learning for expert-learner connections.
- Sentiment-aware group formation algorithms.
- Real-time translation with context preservation.
- Virtual collaboration environment optimization.
- Collective intelligence harvesting through AI-mediated group insights.

Educational Impact:

- Global learning communities with seamless cross-cultural knowledge exchange.
- Enhanced social presence in digital environments through AI-mediated interactions.
- Distributed expertise access connecting learners with global subject matter experts.
- Collaborative problem-solving enhancement through optimized team formation.
- Peer mentoring networks with AI-facilitated matching and support.
- Cultural competency development through diverse collaboration experiences.
- Collective knowledge construction that exceeds individual learning capabilities.

3.3 Inclusive Intelligence

Definition: AI systems actively identify, forecast, and eliminate systemic and individual barriers to learning across various aspects, including language, neurodiversity, and cultural diversity.

AI Techniques Involved:

- Advanced speech-to-text and text-to-speech with accent and dialect recognition.
- Real-time multilingual translation with cultural context preservation.
- Computer vision for accessibility (screen readers, gesture recognition, eye tracking interfaces).
- Predictive analytics for at-risk identification using early warning systems.
- Bias detection and mitigation algorithms in content and assessment.
- Adaptive user interfaces that modify based on accessibility needs.
- Socioeconomic barrier prediction and resource recommendation.
- Neurodiversity-aware content adaptation.

Educational Impact:

- Significant reduction in dropout rates for marginalized learners.
- Enhanced participation from learners with disabilities and learning differences.
- Global educational access regardless of geographical or economic constraints.
- Cultural responsiveness that honours and incorporates diverse learning traditions.
- Inclusive excellence achievement where diversity strengthens learning outcomes.

3.4 Emotional-Cognitive Support

Definition: Affective computing enables AI to recognize and respond to learners' emotional states, such as motivation, frustration, or anxiety, in real time (Thompson & McGill, 2012).

AI Techniques Involved:

- Multimodal affective computing integrating facial recognition and voice analysis.
- Advanced sentiment analysis from text, and speech.
- Predictive mental health analytics for early intervention.
- Cognitive load assessment through pupillometry and interaction pattern analysis.
- Personalized motivational AI coaching.
- Stress pattern recognition and adaptive response systems.
- Emotional state prediction using data from facial expressions, speech, text, and gestures.
- Mindfulness and wellness integration with guided interventions.

Educational Impact:

- Enhanced intrinsic motivation via personalized encouragement and goal setting.
- Reduced academic anxiety and stress through proactive intervention.
- Better self-regulation skills developed through AI-guided reflection.
- Increased learning engagement by maintaining optimal emotional states.
- Mental health awareness and early problem identification.
- Supportive learning environments that prioritize learner wellbeing

3.5 Feedback & Co-Creation

Definition: AI-powered tutors offer one-on-one guidance by providing diagnostic insights and tailored explanations aligned with individual progress (Thompson & Mcgill, 2012). Automated feedback mechanisms deliver timely corrections and foster a more profound understanding.

AI Techniques Involved:

- Large Language Models (LLMs) fine-tuned for educational feedback and content generation.
- Automated formative assessment with detailed diagnostic capabilities.
- Conversational AI refers to AI-powered systems such as chatbots and virtual assistants that interact with users through natural, human-like dialogue in text or voice formats.
- Generative content creation tools for multimedia educational materials.
- Code generation and debugging assistance for programming education.
- Creative AI collaboration for art, music, and creative writing projects.
- Peer review facilitation through AI-mediated feedback exchange.
- Knowledge synthesis AI that helps learners connect concepts across domains.

Educational Impact:

- Immediate high-quality feedback that rivals human instructor guidance.
- Enhanced creativity and innovation through AI-human collaboration.
- Deeper conceptual understanding via interactive content creation.
- Accelerated skill development in creative and technical domains.
- Improved metacognitive awareness through reflective feedback processes.
- Active knowledge construction where learners become content creators.

3.6 Ethical AI

Ethical AI is based on principles such as fairness, data privacy, accountability, and transparency (Yadav, 2024). It also highlights the importance of explainable AI (XAI) and regulatory compliance frameworks to ensure systems are transparent, fair, accountable, and culturally responsive (Holmes et al., 2022). It also highlights the importance of ongoing monitoring, stakeholder involvement, and adaptive governance structures in sustaining trust and integrity in AI-driven learning environments (Córdova & Vicari, 2022).

Key Principles & Techniques:

- Fairness:

  a) Inclusive Design: AI user interfaces and systems should be mindful of cultural differences and stakeholder inclusiveness.
  b) Transparent Algorithms: AI should include fairness, helping students and teachers during decisions like grading, admissions, and providing feedback.

- Transparency

Transparency means that the processes, data sources, and reasoning behind AI-driven decisions are clear and accessible to all stakeholders, including students, educators, administrators, and families. In practice, this involves explaining how AI systems select, process, and interpret student data, as well as the types of outputs they produce, such as feedback, grades, or recommendations (Holmes et al., 2022). Transparent AI policies should specify data collection routines, algorithmic parameters, and institutional guidelines, enabling users to understand and question the rationale behind automated results (Córdova & Vicari, 2022).

Explainable AI (XAI) progresses further by ensuring that every decision made by an AI system is understandable and justifiable. This is especially important in educational settings, where automated assessments or interventions can significantly influence learners' outcomes. Explainable AI allows educators and students to trace decision paths, such as understanding why a specific learning resource was recommended or how a student's progress was assessed. Implementing transparency and explainability in educational AI systems includes a) providing clear documentation of AI decision-making, b) offering user-friendly explanations of the reasoning behind AI-based decisions, c) establishing a review and appeal process if the learner is dissatisfied, and d) conducting algorithmic audits to prevent bias.

- Accountability:

Accountability means that organizations and individuals are responsible for overseeing how AI systems are developed, deployed, and used, ensuring they operate transparently, ethically, and in line with societal values. It includes a) Clear Role Assignments: Designate specific individuals or teams (e.g., IT staff, educators, AI developers) with the responsibility for monitoring AI performance and decision-making. b) Audit Trails: Maintain detailed logs of all AI actions and decisions, enabling regular review and external audits to track performance, identify issues, and ensure compliance. c) Stakeholder feedback mechanisms: Provide channels for students, parents, and educators to give feedback or contest AI decisions, ensuring human rights and agency are respected. d) Ethics Committees or Oversight Boards: Establish formal bodies within institutions responsible for continuously evaluating the ethical use of AI and ensuring alignment with institutional values.

- Privacy:

Privacy involves safeguarding personal data collected and used by AI systems, particularly by adhering to legal frameworks such as the GDPR and FERPA. Privacy principles include reducing unnecessary data collection, ensuring strong data security through encryption and anonymization, obtaining informed user consent, and giving users control over their information (Holmes et al., 2022). It includes a) Federated learning for data privacy. b) Differential Privacy (DP) as a policy approach for protecting individual privacy in data analysis and AI systems. c) Implementing secure encryption protocols, access restrictions, and robust anonymization techniques that ensure only authorized stakeholders can handle student data.

- Human Oversight:

To ensure oversight of AI use, there is a need for a) a Human-in-the-Loop (HITL) model where human review or approval is required for AI-generated feedback, assessments, or recommendations before implementation; b) compliance with legal regulations such as GDPR and FERPA; and c) preventing bias and errors in AI algorithms through human intervention.

Educational Impact:

- Enhanced trust in AI-mediated educational systems.
- Critical digital literacy development among learners and educators.
- Protection against surveillance and inappropriate data profiling.
- Culturally responsive AI systems that respect diverse values and practices.
- Empowered stakeholder participation in AI governance and development.
- Sustainable AI deployment that evolves with ethical standards and regulations.
- Model ethical AI use that prepares learners for responsible technology citizenship.

Table 3 illustrates the components of AI Enhanced Network Learning Theory, their definitions, AI methods, outcomes, and implementation considerations.

Table 3. Components of AI-Enhanced Networked Learning Theory

Component	Definition	AI Methods	Outcomes	Implementation Considerations
Personalized & Adaptive Learning	Dynamically customizes learning experiences across multiple modalities (text, visual, audio) based on real-time assessment of cognitive and behavioural data. Predicts learning outcomes, identifies at-risk students, and recommends interventions before problems occur.	Multimodal Large Language Models (MLLMs), Cognitive neuropsychology-based AI, Real-time biometric monitoring, Adaptive assessment algorithms, Learning path optimization. Machine learning prediction models, Early warning systems, Pattern recognition algorithms, Risk assessment tools	Enhanced mastery learning, Increased engagement and retention, Improved accessibility for diverse learners, and reduced cognitive overload	Digital divide considerations Cultural sensitivity in AI training, Quality control of peer interactions Proactive learning support
Collaborative Connectivity	Facilitates AI-mediated peer interactions, expert connections, and community building through intelligent matching and social learning analytics. Virtual and augmented reality spaces are enhanced with AI for experiential learning and simulation-based education.	Social Network Analysis (SNA), Intelligent recommendation systems, Natural Language Processing for communication enhancement, Collaborative filtering algorithms, Virtual collaboration environments, VR/AR with AI integration, Spatial computing, Haptic feedback systems 3D learning environments	Enhanced social learning, Cross-cultural knowledge exchange, Peer mentoring networks, Collective intelligence development, Safe practice environments, Increased engagement and motivation	Digital divide considerations, Cultural sensitivity in AI-based matching, Quality control of peer interactions
Inclusive Intelligence	Eliminates learning barriers through AI-powered accessibility tools, real-time translation, and adaptive interfaces that accommodate diverse learning needs and disabilities	Computer vision for accessibility, Real-time language translation, Voice recognition and synthesis, Gesture-based interfaces, Predictive text, and communication aids	Universal accessibility, reduced educational inequality, enhanced learning for neurodiverse students, and Global participation in learning networks	Bias mitigation in AI algorithms, Cost of accessibility of technologies, Training requirements for educators

continued on following page

Table 3. Continued

Component	Definition	AI Methods	Outcomes	Implementation Considerations
Emotional-Cognitive Support	Monitors and responds to emotional states, stress levels, and cognitive load through multimodal assessment, providing personalized emotional support and motivational interventions.	Affective computing, Sentiment analysis, Physiological monitoring (e.g., heart rate, eye tracking), Facial emotion recognition, Predictive mental health analytics	Improved emotional resilience, Enhanced motivation and persistence, Early identification of learning difficulties, Better stress management	Ethical concerns about emotional monitoring, Privacy and consent issues, Need for human counsellor integration
Feedback & Co-Creation	Provides instant, personalized feedback and enables collaborative content creation through generative AI tools that adapt to individual learning styles	Large Language Models (LLMs), Generative AI for content creation, Interactive AI tutoring systems, Creative AI collaboration tools	Immediate formative feedback, Enhanced creativity and innovation, Deeper conceptual understanding, Active knowledge construction	Quality control of AI-generated content, Academic integrity concerns, Need for human oversight
Ethical AI	Implements transparent, fair, and explainable AI systems with human oversight, reducing algorithmic bias and ensuring equitable decision-making.	Explainable AI (XAI), Algorithmic auditing systems, Bias detection and mitigation tools, Federated learning for privacy, Human-in-the-loop monitoring	Safe and responsible learning environments, Trust in AI-enhanced education Ethical digital citizenship	Regulatory compliance Ongoing ethical evaluation, Stakeholder education on AI ethics

Source: Author's own work

4. CASE STUDY: COLLABORATIVE LEARNING WITH AI SPEAKERS (CLAIS)

AI speakers have become one of the most widely used AI services, integrated into daily life, with millions of users interacting with platforms like Apple's Siri, Microsoft Cortana, and Amazon Alexa every day. Using speech recognition, natural language processing (NLP), and cloud-based machine learning, these devices are increasingly capable of providing context-aware responses and personalized services. In education, this technological advancement has led to the creation of AI Speakers in Education (AISEd), which positions smart speakers as intelligent agents capable of answering students' questions, guiding learning activities, and supporting inquiry in natural spoken language.

Collaborative Learning with AI Speakers (CLAIS) is a design-based instructional system developed by Lee et al. (2023) using the Analysis, Design, Development, Implementation, and Evaluation (ADDIE) model, a standard instructional design framework. The CLAIS system was created to involve three to four human learners teaming up with an AI speaker to form a small group, where humans and AI are regarded as peers participating in the Jigsaw learning process. The development used the NUGU AI speaker platform.

The CLAIS system was successfully implemented in a Science Education course session with 15 pre-service elementary science teachers (Lee et al., 2023). The AI speaker processes learner input through several stages: speech recognition, natural language understanding, dialog management, natural language generation, and text-to-speech before delivering a spoken response. For example, when asked to explain Vygotsky's concept of the Zone of Proximal Development (ZPD), the AI responded that it is the distance between a learner's current level of independent performance and their potential level of development under the guidance of a more knowledgeable other. In this role, the AI provided explanations, addressed learner questions, and acted as a peer participant.

Participants evaluated the CLAIS system through mixed-method surveys involving teachers, learners, peers, and users. Qualitative findings indicated that participants anticipated future changes in the science classroom learning process, despite recognizing technical issues like speech recognition and response delays. Quantitative results showed significant improvement in participants' Intelligent-Technological, Pedagogical, and Content Knowledge after the CLAIS session. They also reported a positive experience with CLAIS, with varied peer assessments of AI speakers and human peers, and a mixed user experience.

This study emphasizes the power of human-AI collaboration in co-creating knowledge in classrooms. Essentially, AI-Enhanced Network Learning Theory suggests that learning happens through dynamic and adaptable interactions among human cognition, artificial intelligence, and digital networks. The CLAIS study applies this theory by utilizing "jigsaw" group activities, where human learners and an AI speaker on the NUGU platform collaborate to build knowledge. In this setup, the AI acts as both a content expert and a peer, sharing facts and promoting reflective discussion.

Findings from the CLAIS pilot support several proposals of AI-NLT. The data showed that participants achieved notable improvements in Intelligent Technological Knowledge (ITK), Pedagogical Knowledge (PK), and Content Knowledge (CK). Results confirm that hybrid intelligence networks can boost learning outcomes beyond what traditional, standalone methods offer.

Qualitative insights further validated the theory in practice; participants described changes in their epistemic expectations, envisioning a future science classroom where AI is regarded as a trustworthy partner, rather than just an information source. This supports the idea that knowledge is constructed through ongoing, two-way interactions between humans and AI, not only through one-way transmission. The system offered real-time feedback loops and opportunities for cross-domain pattern recognition, enhancing both individual and group understanding.

The CLAIS study also highlights challenges in unlocking the potential of networked hybrid intelligence. Technical issues, such as speech recognition errors and response delays, occasionally interrupted the collaborative flow, underscoring the need for AI systems to develop more advanced emotional and interpretive capabilities.

The CLAIS case study illustrates both the potential and current limitations of AI-enhanced network learning. It supports the core idea of the AI-NLT theory, which posits that hybrid and inclusive intelligence networks, collaborative connectivity and feedback, and co-creation combining AI's capabilities with human intelligence and digital networks are transforming education. As AI systems improve in recognizing emotions and engaging in multimodal discourse, the lines between teacher, tool, and peer will continue to shift, leading to a new era of collaborative knowledge building in education.

5. RESULTS AND DISCUSSION

The analysis of literature led to the development of the AI-NLT. The theory introduces six core components, each representing essential nodes in transforming learning processes through the use of artificial intelligence. The CLAIS case study, employing a mixed-methods survey approach, identified both promising results and notable challenges. Quantitative data revealed significant improvements in participants' Intelligent-Technological Knowledge (ITK), Pedagogical Knowledge (PK), and Content Knowledge (CK).. Although learners found value in the system, their user experience was somewhat mixed.

The qualitative data provided more depth, revealing that participants expected meaningful changes in how knowledge is developed in future science classrooms. They viewed AI not just as a passive information source but as an active partner in knowledge processes. However, they also pointed out technical issues, such as speech recognition errors and response delays, which occasionally disrupted the learning flow.

These findings highlight the potential of human–AI collaboration in co-creating knowledge within classroom environments. The CLAIS case uses AI-NLT through jigsaw group activities, where human learners and an AI speaker on the NUGU platform work together to build understanding. In this setup, AI acts both as a content expert and as a peer conversational partner, guiding discussions, sharing information, and encouraging reflection.

Evidence from this study strengthens AI-NLT's core ideas. Participants not only showed clear improvements in ITK, PK, and CK but also reported changes in how they view AI, seeing it as a trustworthy partner instead of just a digital tool. This supports AI-NLT's claim that knowledge arises from hybrid and inclusive intelligence networks, collaborative connections and feedback, and co-creation where human intelligence, AI's capabilities, and digital networks work together to develop knowledge.

6. CONCLUSION

This chapter presents the AI-NLT as a comprehensive framework for understanding how artificial intelligence is transforming the education sector. It explores six areas: Personalized & Adaptive Learning, Collaborative Connectivity, Inclusive Intelligence, Emotional-Cognitive Support, Feedback & Co-Creation, and Ethical AI. The framework provides scholars and practitioners with a clear way to envision AI's future in education. AI-NLT encourages us to see AI as more than just a simple teaching tool. Instead, it considers AI as a social and educational partner that can actively influence how knowledge is created, shared, and experienced.

Through the CLAIS case study, participants not only observed measurable improvements in PK and CK but also started to see AI as a collaborative partner in knowledge building. These findings strongly support AI-NLT's core idea that learning advances through hybrid and inclusive intelligence networks, collaborative connections and feedback, and co-creation where human intelligence works dynamically with AI's capabilities and digital networks. Ultimately, this work emphasizes a simple yet powerful idea: the future of learning is not about humans or machines alone, but about how we learn better together.

REFERENCES

Ajuwon, O. A., Animashaun, E. S., & Chiekezie, N. R. (2024). Integrating AI and technology in educational administration: Improving efficiency and educational quality. *Open Access Research Journal of Science and Technology*, *11*(2), 116–127. DOI: 10.53022/oarjst.2024.11.2.0102

Akgun, S., & Greenhow, C. (2022). Artificial intelligence in education: Addressing ethical challenges in K-12 settings. *AI and Ethics*, *2*(3), 431–440. DOI: 10.1007/s43681-021-00096-7 PMID: 34790956

Alawneh, Y. J. J., Sleema, H., Salman, F. N., Alshammat, M. F., & Oteer, R. S., & ALrashidi, N. K. N. (2024). Adaptive learning systems: Revolutionizing higher education through AI-driven curricula. *2024 International Conference on Knowledge Engineering and Communication Systems (ICKECS), 1*, 1–5. DOI: 10.1109/ICKECS61492.2024.10616675

Alenezi, A. (2024). Evaluating the Effectiveness of AI-Powered Adaptive Learning Systems in Secondary Schools. [IJonSE]. *International Journal on Studies in Education*, *6*(4), 686–700. DOI: 10.46328/ijonse.264

Alm, C. O., Roth, D., & Sproat, R. (2005). Emotions from text: machine learning for text-based emotion prediction. In *Proceedings of human language technology conference and conference on empirical methods in natural language processing* (pp. 579–586). DOI: 10.3115/1220575.1220648

Aly, M., Ghallab, A., & Fathi, I. S. (2023). Enhancing facial expression recognition system in online learning context using efficient deep learning model. *IEEE Access : Practical Innovations, Open Solutions*, *11*, 121419–121433. DOI: 10.1109/ACCESS.2023.3325407

Ayeni, O. O., Hamad, N. M., Chisom, O. N., Osawaru, B., & Adewusi, O. E. (2024). AI in education: A review of personalized learning and educational technology. *GSC Advanced Research and Reviews*, *18*(2), 261–271. DOI: 10.30574/gscarr.2024.18.2.0062

Bazoukis, G. A., Halkidis, S. T., Pepes, E., & Venardos, P. (2024). AI in education: Pedagogical and ethical analysis of the implementation of ASSISTments in the school environment. *European Journal of Science and Mathematics Education*, *12*(4), 428–451. DOI: 10.30935/scimath/14902

Carbonell, J. R., & Collins, A. M. (1974). Natural semantics in artificial intelligence. *American Journal of Computational Linguistics*.

Chan, C. K. Y. (2023). A comprehensive AI policy education framework for university teaching and learning. *International journal of educational technology in higher education*, *20*(1), 38.

Córdova, P. R., & Vicari, R. M. (2022). Practical ethical issues for artificial intelligence in education. In *Communications in Computer and Information Science* (pp. 437–445). Springer Nature Switzerland.

Dash, S., & Bhoi, C. (2024). Exploring the Intersection of Education and Artificial Intelligence: A Comprehensive Review. *International Journal of Multidisciplinary Approach Research and Science*, *2*(2), 601–610. DOI: 10.59653/ijmars.v2i02.637

Essel, H. B., Vlachopoulos, D., Tachie-Menson, A., Johnson, E. E., & Baah, P. K. (2022). The impact of a virtual teaching assistant (chatbot) on students' learning in Ghanaian higher education. *International Journal of Educational Technology in Higher Education*, *19*(1), 57.

Farhood, H., Joudah, I., Beheshti, A., & Muller, S. (2024). Evaluating and enhancing artificial intelligence models for predicting student learning outcomes. *Informatics (MDPI)*, *11*(3), 46. DOI: 10.3390/informatics11030046

Gligorea, I., Cioca, M., Oancea, R., Gorski, A. T., Gorski, H., & Tudorache, P. (2023). Adaptive learning using artificial intelligence in e-learning: A literature review. *Education Sciences*, *13*(12), 1216. DOI: 10.3390/educsci13121216

González-Hernández, F., Zatarain-Cabada, R., Barrón-Estrada, M. L., & Rodríguez-Rangel, H. (2018). Recognition of learning-centered emotions using a convolutional neural network. *Journal of Intelligent & Fuzzy Systems*, *34*(5), 3325–3336. DOI: 10.3233/JIFS-169514

Graesser, A. C., Hu, X., Nye, B. D., VanLehn, K., Kumar, R., Heffernan, C., Heffernan, N., Woolf, B., Olney, A. M., Rus, V., Andrasik, F., Pavlik, P., Cai, Z., Wetzel, J., Morgan, B., Hampton, A. J., Lippert, A. M., Wang, L., Cheng, Q., & Baer, W. (2018). ElectronixTutor: An intelligent tutoring system with multiple learning resources for electronics. *International Journal of STEM Education*, *5*(1), 15. DOI: 10.1186/s40594-018-0110-y PMID: 30631705

Gremsl, T., & Hödl, E. (2022). Emotional AI: Legal and ethical challenges1. *Information Polity*, *27*(2), 163–174. DOI: 10.3233/IP-211529

He, T., Li, C., Wang, J., Wang, M., Wang, Z., & Jiao, C. (2022). An emotion analysis in learning environment based on theme-specified drawing by convolutional neural network. *Frontiers in Public Health*, *10*, 958870. DOI: 10.3389/fpubh.2022.958870 PMID: 36408050

Holmes, W., Porayska-Pomsta, K., Holstein, K., Sutherland, E., Baker, T., Shum, S. B., Santos, O. C., Rodrigo, M. T., Cukurova, M., Bittencourt, I. I., & Koedinger, K. R. (2022). Ethics of AI in education: Towards a community-wide framework. *International Journal of Artificial Intelligence in Education*, *32*(3), 504–526. DOI: 10.1007/s40593-021-00239-1

Hwang, G.-J., Xie, H., Wah, B. W., & Gašević, D. (2020). Vision, challenges, roles and research issues of Artificial Intelligence in Education. *Computers and Education: Artificial Intelligence*, *1*(100001), 100001. DOI: 10.1016/j.caeai.2020.100001

Karroum, S. Y. A., Elshaiekh, N. E. M., & Al-Hijji, K. Z. (2024). Exploring the role of artificial Intelligence in education: Assessing advantages and disadvantages for learning outcomes and pedagogical practices. *International Journal of Innovative Research in Engineering & Multidisciplinary Physical Sciences*, *12*(4), 231000. Advance online publication. DOI: 10.37082/IJIRMPS.v12.i4.231000

Kaur, S., Budhraja, K., Pahuja, A., Nayyar, V., & Saluja, S. (2024). Leveraging artificial intelligence in education: Enhancing learning experience. In *Ethical AI and Data Management Strategies in Marketing* (pp. 140–155). IGI Global Scientific Publishing. DOI: 10.4018/979-8-3693-6660-8.ch010

Koedinger, K. R., & Corbett, A. (2006). *Cognitive tutors: Technology bringing learning sciences to the classroom*. 61–77.

Kolluru, V., Mungara, S., & Chintakunta, A. N. (2018). Adaptive learning systems: Harnessing AI for customized educational experiences. *International Journal of Computer Science and Information Technologies*, *6*(3), 13–26. DOI: 10.5121/ijcsity.2018.6302

Kort, B., Reilly, R., & Picard, R. W. (2002). An affective model of interplay between emotions and learning: reengineering educational pedagogy-building a learning companion. *Proceedings IEEE International Conference on Advanced Learning Technologies*.

Kumar, D. (2024). Ai-driven automation in administrative processes: Enhancing efficiency and accuracy. *International Journal of Engineering Science and Humanities, 14*(Special1), 256–265. DOI: 10.62904/qg004437

Lee, G. G., Mun, S., Shin, M. K., & Zhai, X. (2023). *Collaborative learning with artificial intelligence speakers (CLAIS): Pre-service elementary science teachers' responses to the prototype*. arXiv preprint arXiv:2401.05400.

Ng, D. T. K., Lee, M., Tan, R. J. Y., Hu, X., Downie, J. S., & Chu, S. K. W. (2022). A review of AI teaching and learning from 2000 to 2020. *Education and Information Technologies*. Advance online publication. DOI: 10.1007/s10639-022-11491-w

Perkins, M. (2023). Academic Integrity considerations of AI Large Language Models in the post-pandemic era: ChatGPT and beyond. *Journal of University Teaching & Learning Practice*, *20*(2). Advance online publication. DOI: 10.53761/1.20.02.07

Picard, R. W. (1999). Affective computing for hci. In *HCI (1)* (pp. 829–833).

Rane, N. L. (2024). Education 4.0 and 5.0: integrating Artificial Intelligence (AI) for personalized and adaptive learning. *Journal of Artificial Intelligence and Robotics*. DOI: 10.61577/jaiar.2024.100006

Russell, S., & Norvig, P. (2024). *Artificial intelligence: A modern approach, global edition 5Yr subscription* (4th ed.). Pearson Education.

Saifi, A. G. (2024). Pedagogy and AI in Education. In *Advances in Educational Technologies and Instructional Design* (pp. 136–156). IGI Global. DOI: 10.4018/979-8-3693-6397-3.ch006

Sajja, R., Sermet, Y., Cwiertny, D., & Demir, I. (2023). Platform-independent and curriculum-oriented intelligent assistant for higher education. *International Journal of Educational Technology in Higher Education*, *20*(1), 42. Advance online publication. DOI: 10.1186/s41239-023-00412-7

Samsonovich, A. V. (2020). Socially emotional brain-inspired cognitive architecture framework for artificial intelligence. *Cognitive Systems Research*, *60*, 57–76. DOI: 10.1016/j.cogsys.2019.12.002

Saputra, I., Astuti, M., Sayuti, M., & Kusumastuti, D. (2023). Integration of artificial intelligence in education: Opportunities, challenges, threats and obstacles. A literature review. *The Indonesian Journal of Computer Science*, *12*(4). Advance online publication. DOI: 10.33022/ijcs.v12i4.3266

Sari, H. E., Tumanggor, B., & Efron, D. (2024). Improving educational outcomes through adaptive learning systems using AI. *International Transactions on Artificial Intelligence*, *3*(1), 21–31. DOI: 10.33050/italic.v3i1.647

Sarnato, A. Z., Sari, W. D., Rahmawati, S. T., Hidayat, R., & Patry, H. (2024). The evolution of E-learning platforms: From U-learning to AI-driven adaptive learning systems. *Journal of Social Science Utilizing Technology*, *2*(2), 289–300. DOI: 10.70177/jssut.v2i2.1131

Saxena, M. K., & Bajotra, V. (2024). Potential of artificial intelligence in education and ethical issues. *Far Western Journal of Education*, *1*(1), 1–18. DOI: 10.3126/fwje.v1i1.68773

Schank, R. C., Fano, A., Bell, B., & Jona, M. (1994). The design of goal-based scenarios. *Journal of the Learning Sciences*, *3*(4), 305–345. DOI: 10.1207/s15327809jls0304_2

Singh, K., Goel, N., Gupta, B., & Bansal, D. (2023). Emotion prediction through facial recognition using machine learning: a survey. In *In2023 International Conference on Computer Communication and Informatics (ICCCI)* (pp. 1–5). IEEE. DOI: 10.1109/ICCCI56745.2023.10128348

Snehalatha, M. (2024). AI and OpenAI in education: Unveiling the future of learning and teaching. In *Enhancing Higher Education and Research With OpenAI Models* (pp. 176–205). IGI Global Scientific Publishing.

Šumak, B., López-De-Ipiña, D., Dziabenko, O., Correia, S. D., De Carvalho, L. M., Lopes, S., Şimşek, İ., Can, T., & Kline, D. I. (2024). *Pušnik M. AI-Based Education Tools for Enabling Inclusive Education: Challenges and Benefits. In2024 47th MIPRO ICT and Electronics Convention (MIPRO)*. IEEE.

Suntharalingam, H. (2024). Enhancing digital learning outcomes through the application of artificial intelligence: A comprehensive review. *International Journal of Innovative Science and Research Technology*, *9*(4), 718–727. DOI: 10.38124/ijisrt/IJISRT24APR530

Tack, A., & Piech, C. (2022). The AI teacher test: Measuring the pedagogical ability of Blender and GPT-3 in educational dialogues. In *arXiv [cs.CL]*. https://arxiv.org/abs/2205.07540

Tammets, K., & Ley, T. (2023). Integrating AI tools in teacher professional learning: a conceptual model and illustrative case. *Frontiers in artificial intelligence*, *6*, 1255089.

Thompson, N., & Mcgill, T. J. (2012). Affective tutoring systems: Enhancing e-learning with the emotional awareness of a human tutor. [IJICTE]. *International Journal of Information and Communication Technology Education*, *8*(4), 75–89. DOI: 10.4018/jictc.2012100107

Thuy, P. B., & Tien, P. D. (2024). AI-Powered administration: The role of intelligent tutoring systems in education. *International journal of religion*, *5*(10), 4560-4569.

Tulasi, L., & Rao, C. S. (2023). Integration of AI-technologies into ELT: A brief study. *Journal for Research Scholars and Professionals of English Language Teaching*, *7*(38). Advance online publication. DOI: 10.54850/jrspelt.7.38.003

Villegas-Ch, W. E., García-Ortiz, J., & Sánchez-Viteri, S. (2023). Identification of emotions from facial gestures in a teaching environment with the use of machine learning techniques. *IEEE Access*, *11*, 38010-38022.

Wu, Y. (2023). Integrating generative AI in education: How ChatGPT brings challenges for future learning and teaching. *Journal of Advanced Research in Education*, *2*(4), 6–10. DOI: 10.56397/JARE.2023.07.02

Yadav, S. (2024). Artificial Intelligence (AI) Integration in Higher Education: Navigating Opportunities and Ethical Frontiers in Education with Advanced Technologies. In *Impact of artificial intelligence on society* (pp. 43–59). Chapman and Hall/CRC.

Yekollu, R. K., Bhimraj Ghuge, T., Biradar, S., & Haldikar, S. (2024). *Farook Mohideen Abdul Kader O. AI-driven personalized learning paths: Enhancing education through adaptive systems. InInternational Conference on Smart data intelligence*. Springer Nature.

Chapter 4

AI-Powered Personalization: Redefining Learner Pathways in Blended Classrooms

Mustafa Kayyali
https://orcid.org/0000-0003-3300-262X
Maaref University of Applied Sciences, Syria

ABSTRACT

The fusion of artificial intelligence with blended learning is reshaping how we define educational journeys. This chapter explores how AI-driven personalization enables more fluid, learner-centered pathways that adapt in real time to individual needs, habits, and aspirations. Moving beyond static models, AI offers the potential for dynamic interventions that respond to learner data with nuance and precision. But this transformation brings profound questions: How do we preserve student agency amid algorithmic influence? Where does ethical responsibility lie when data defines direction? Through a critical yet hopeful lens, the chapter unpacks the evolving role of personalization, not merely as a technological function but as a philosophical shift in pedagogy. In reimagining blended classrooms, we find both promise and provocation—an invitation to redefine what meaningful learning could truly look like in a digital age.

INTRODUCTION

Education, at its heart, is a deeply personal journey—one shaped not only by curriculum and pedagogy but also by the intricate weave of a learner's background, pace, interests, and struggles. For centuries, education systems have wrestled with a

DOI: 10.4018/979-8-3373-3815-6.ch004

right © 2026, IGI Global Scientific Publishing. Copying or distributing in print or electronic forms without written permission of IGI Global Scientific Publishing is prohibited. Use of this chapter to in generative artificial intelligence (AI) technologies is expressly prohibited. The publisher reserves all rights to license its use for generative AI training and machine learning model development.

singular challenge: how to honor the individuality of learners within the constraints of a standardized framework (Fraile-Martinez et al, 2025). While blended learning—an integration of face-to-face instruction with digital technologies—promised to add flexibility and autonomy to this structure, it still often fell short of truly adapting to the unique rhythms of each student. Now, with the emergence of artificial intelligence (AI), we are on the brink of a paradigm shift: a move from generalized instruction toward finely-tuned, dynamically adaptive learner pathways.

Personalization in education is not a new aspiration. Educators have long tried to adjust content and pace to meet the needs of individual students, whether through differentiated instruction, project-based learning, or formative assessments. Yet the scale and complexity of personalization often rendered it an unattainable ideal in traditional settings. Enter AI—capable of processing vast datasets, identifying subtle learning patterns, predicting needs, and offering targeted interventions in ways no human teacher could manage alone (Ravichandran, 2024). With AI embedded in learning management systems, intelligent tutoring platforms, and real-time analytics dashboards, we are beginning to witness the contours of a new educational architecture: one where learner experience is continuously shaped and reshaped in response to their evolving interactions, challenges, and preferences.

Blended learning environments are particularly fertile ground for this transformation. These hybrid models already carry within them the digital scaffolding that allows AI to operate: a repository of learner data, flexible content delivery systems, and opportunities for both synchronous and asynchronous engagement (Almusaed et al, 2023). What AI adds is a kind of silent, responsive intelligence—a way of tailoring the journey in real time, gently nudging the learner toward deeper engagement, offering support at just the right moment, and adapting content to match their cognitive and emotional states. Instead of treating all learners as if they move at the same pace or respond to the same methods, AI-powered personalization creates a more humane and realistic map of learning progressions. But with this opportunity comes a profound responsibility. What does it mean when algorithms begin to shape the routes learners take? Can personalization become too prescriptive, narrowing learning rather than enriching it? Where do we draw the ethical boundaries when AI systems use predictive analytics to determine who needs remediation—or who gets enrichment? And what happens to the teacher's role in this landscape—do they become mere facilitators of pre-programmed pathways, or can they reclaim agency in directing how AI supports rather than replaces pedagogical intent?

This chapter delves into these critical questions, weaving together research, case studies, and theoretical perspectives to examine the promise and perils of AI-powered personalization in blended classrooms. We begin by revisiting the theoretical underpinnings of personalization and blended learning, then explore how AI reconfigures these frameworks in practice. Through this lens, we consider not only the technical affordances of AI but also its pedagogical implications, ethical dilemmas, and the future roles of educators and learners. In doing so, we aim to present a nuanced vision—neither utopian nor alarmist—of what it means to redefine learning pathways in an age of intelligent systems.

RETHINKING PERSONALIZATION IN THE AGE OF AI: BEYOND ONE-SIZE-FITS-ALL

Personalization. The word rolls off the tongue like a promise, doesn't it? For decades, it has lingered in educational discourse like a dream deferred—a vision of classrooms molded around the unique contours of each learner's journey. We've spoken of it in staff meetings, written about it in policy drafts, dangled it as the golden thread of reform. But how often have we truly achieved it? More often than not, the reality has been cosmetic: a few choices here, a re-sequenced lesson there. At best, personalization has meant grouping students by ability or offering alternative formats of the same content. At worst, it has been a rhetorical flourish—something everyone claims to value but few genuinely understand or operationalize. Then came artificial intelligence. Quiet at first. Slipping into dashboards, nudging through analytics, making recommendations about learning materials and pace. Before we even fully noticed, AI was not just a tool; it was shaping the very structure of learning pathways (Makarenko et al, 2024). Suddenly, personalization was no longer just aspirational. It was being engineered—coded, quantified, embedded into algorithms that could analyze thousands of data points in milliseconds. The question was no longer *can* we personalize learning, but *how* we do it—ethically, effectively, and without losing the human soul of education in the process.

The idea that one educational path could suit everyone was always a convenient fiction—efficient for system builders, comforting for policy makers, but ill-fitting for the learners themselves. Children do not learn in lockstep. Adults do not process complexity in uniform ways. To teach as though they do has always been a compromise with reality, a trade-off between idealism and manageability. But what if we didn't need to make that compromise anymore? What if the tools now at our disposal allowed us to finally let go of the industrial-era myth of standardization? And yet, we must tread carefully. Because AI doesn't just "see" learners; it interprets them. It constructs profiles, predicts behaviors, and—here's where it gets tricky—makes choices about what comes next. This is where the veneer of neutrality cracks. Algorithms don't exist in a vacuum. They are shaped by the data we feed them, the assumptions we hard-code, and the blind spots we fail to notice. If we're not cautious, we risk building a new kind of uniformity: one dressed up in the language of personalization, but driven by patterns, averages, and probabilities.

Take, for example, an AI system that notices a student tends to perform poorly on open-ended tasks and excels at multiple-choice quizzes. A well-meaning personalization engine might start curating content toward the latter, gradually nudging the student into a narrower learning corridor. But what if the reason for the underperformance isn't aptitude, but lack of confidence? Or unfamiliarity with the format? Or a deeper cognitive barrier that needs human guidance, not algorithmic avoidance? In trying to help, the system might unintentionally reinforce limitations. Personalization, then, becomes path dependency. The learner's past performance becomes a predictor of future trajectory—unless a human intervenes.

Here's the deeper truth: personalization is not about matching content to performance; it's about understanding the learner's evolving relationship to knowledge, challenge, and self-belief (Kayyali, 2024 a). And that understanding can't be fully captured by numbers alone.

When we rethink personalization in the age of AI, we must resist the allure of false precision. Yes, AI can track clicks, time-on-task, error rates, and content mastery with dazzling granularity. But it cannot yet grasp the intangible: the sigh of frustration, the thrill of insight, the quiet persistence of a learner who is struggling but refusing to give up. These are human signals—subtle, messy, sometimes contradictory. And they are essential to truly personalized learning.

This is not a rejection of AI. Far from it. AI is a gift—an extraordinary amplification of our ability to see patterns, provide timely feedback, and scale support in ways never before imaginable. But it is a tool, not a compass. It should illuminate choices, not eliminate them.

Personalization, properly conceived, is not about wrapping the world around the learner's preferences (Kayyali, 2025 a). It is about crafting experiences that stretch, provoke, and inspire—experiences that are responsive, yes, but also aspirational. The goal is not comfort; it's growth. And growth, by its nature, is often uncomfortable. If AI-powered systems only lead learners along paths of least resistance, we may risk cultivating shallow understanding and fragile competence. Let's remember that students are not consumers of content. They are constructors of meaning. A Netflix-style recommendation engine that serves up the "next best module" based on past choices may improve engagement metrics, but does it deepen learning? Does it invite curiosity, ambiguity, critical thinking? Or does it simply reinforce patterns—making the learner's world smaller, more predictable, more self-reinforcing?

To truly rethink personalization, we must reclaim its complexity. We must move beyond the idea that tailoring content is enough. Real personalization considers identity, motivation, context, history, aspirations, and struggles (Segal, 2022). It honors not only where the learner is now, but where they *might* go—if challenged, supported, believed in. This rethinking also means expanding our understanding of what counts as data. It's not just keystrokes and quiz scores. It's reflections, questions, drawings, silences. It's conversations with peers, glimmers of insight in a discussion forum, or a sudden shift in engagement that hints at a deeper issue. These are the kinds of signals that good teachers notice—and which AI, for all its sophistication, often misses. So where does this leave us? At a crossroads, perhaps. Or maybe a threshold.

Table 1. Core Features of AI-Powered Personalization in Blended Classrooms

Feature	Function	AI Example
Dynamic Content Delivery	Adjusts learning material based on progress and preferences.	Recommender engines for lesson sequencing.
Real-Time Feedback	Provides instant suggestions and corrections during learning.	Chatbots or AI tutors offering tips during tasks.
Performance Tracking	Continuously monitors engagement and learning outcomes.	Dashboards tracking quiz scores and participation.
Student Profiling	Analyzes learner behavior to customize experiences.	AI models building learner profiles from interactions.
Adaptive Testing	Modifies assessments to match student level and growth.	Algorithms adjusting test difficulty dynamically.

On one side lies a future in which personalization becomes efficient but empty—driven by dashboards, divorced from empathy (Rahaman et al, 2023). On the other lies a richer vision: one where AI augments human insight, offering scaffolding without prescribing destiny. In this vision, personalization is co-authored. The learner plays an active role in shaping their path, supported by educators who interpret data not as conclusions but as conversation starters. It also requires a shift in mindset—from personalization as a product to personalization as a process. It is not something delivered, but something co-created. Not a fixed pathway, but a living map that evolves as the learner grows. And this requires trust. Trust in students to make meaningful choices. Trust in teachers to guide with judgment and care. Trust in systems to remain transparent, accountable, and open to critique (Bukko et al, 2021). Without that trust, even the most sophisticated AI will falter. With it, we may just be able to build learning environments that are not only intelligent, but wise.

I find myself returning, again and again, to a simple but urgent question: *What kind of learners are we trying to shape?* If our answer is citizens who can adapt, question, collaborate, and innovate—then personalization must do more than deliver tailored worksheets. It must cultivate agency. It must support resilience. It must embrace the messy, nonlinear, often unpredictable path that real learning takes. And that means putting people—learners and teachers alike—at the center of the system. It means designing technology not to replace human judgment, but to enrich it. It means holding fast to the values that brought us to education in the first place: curiosity, connection, compassion. So, let us go forward—not blindly adopting AI-powered personalization, but thoughtfully reimagining it. Let us ask harder questions, listen more closely, and design with humility. Let us aim not for perfectly efficient learning, but for deeply human growth. Because in the end, personalization is not about perfection. It's about possibility.

THE ANATOMY OF BLENDED LEARNING: WHERE FLEXIBILITY MEETS STRUCTURE

To truly grasp the anatomy of blended learning, we must begin not with technology or timetables, but with tension. A productive tension, perhaps, but a tension nonetheless. On one end of the rope: structure—order, predictability, curriculum, and benchmarks. On the other: flexibility—fluid pacing, learner choice, responsiveness, and personalization. Blended learning, in its most elegant form, exists not by resolving this tension, but by holding it—delicately, intentionally, and with a kind of pedagogical poise.

Yet too often, the term "blended learning" gets flattened—reduced to a buzzword, or worse, a box-ticking exercise (Kayyali, 2024 b). A couple of online modules here, a weekly Zoom session there, and voilà! Blend achieved. But that's not it. That's not it at all. True blended learning is not about sprinkling technology into a traditional classroom like seasoning over a dish. It's about redesigning the meal from scratch—rethinking how time, space, and presence are configured in the service of deeper learning.

Figure 1. Components of Learner Profile

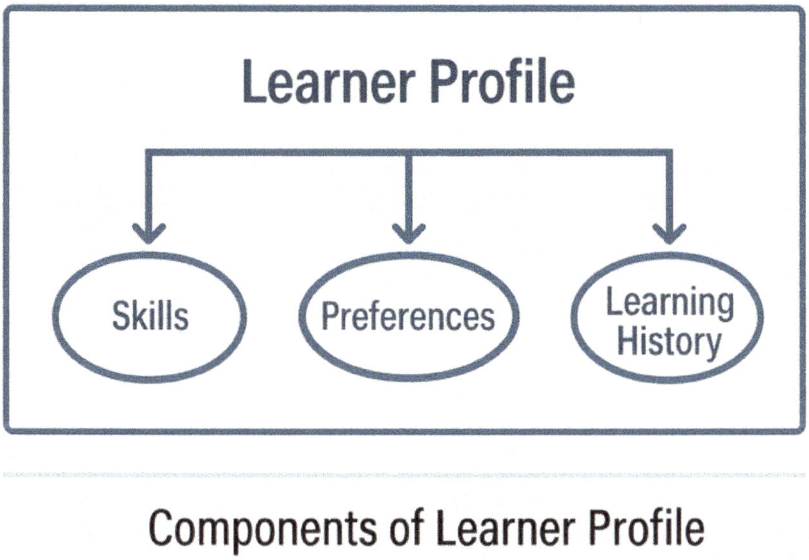

Let's break it down, not by modality, but by rhythm. In a well-designed blended environment, there's a cadence that you can almost feel. It breathes. There are moments of synchronous intensity—where learners gather in real time, physically or virtually, to wrestle with ideas, challenge one another, collaborate, ask messy questions. Then there are asynchronous stretches—quieter, more introspective, where learners move at their own pace, engage with content, reflect, revise, retry. It's a dance. Not always graceful, but alive.

At its core, blended learning is about rethinking presence. Not just physical presence—though that's part of it—but cognitive and emotional presence (Raes, 2022). When are students truly *there*, fully engaged? When does the medium amplify their thinking, and when does it dull it? These are not technological questions. They are deeply human ones. And so, the anatomy begins with intentionality. What do we want learners to experience? Not just what content we want to "cover," but what kinds of cognitive work we want them to do. Do we want them to explore, apply, critique, co-create? Depending on the goal, the blend must shift. Maybe foundational content lives online, in adaptive modules that let students revisit concepts as needed (Caulfield, 2023). Maybe higher-order discussions happen in person, where nuance and tone can flourish. Maybe group projects unfold in hybrid spaces, crossing the boundary between school and home, between now and later. But even the most flexible blended model needs scaffolding. Without a strong backbone of design, learners drift. The paradox is this: flexibility requires structure. Not rigid scheduling, but coherent framing. Learners need signposts—clear goals, meaningful tasks, timely feedback, and visible progress. They need to know not just *what* to do, but *why* it matters, and *how* it connects to the whole.

This is where many implementations falter. They confuse freedom with lack of guidance. They assume that giving students a menu of options is the same as fostering autonomy. It's not. Autonomy must be nurtured, supported, and slowly expanded. Otherwise, it becomes overwhelming—a kind of pedagogical abandonment dressed up as student-centeredness.

Technology can either help or hinder here. At its best, it provides a transparent learning journey—dashboards that show progress, recommendations based on performance, alerts when engagement dips. At its worst, it fragments the experience—too many platforms, too many passwords, too many clicks between thinking and doing. The tools we choose matter. But more than that, the *integration* of those tools matters. The learner should feel like they are on a single, coherent journey—not juggling puzzle pieces from three different courses (McMurtry, 2024). And let's not forget the social dimension. Blended learning is not solitary learning. The myth that online means alone has done real harm. In fact, some of the most vibrant blended classrooms are those where community is cultivated across modalities. A discussion thread can be just as rich—sometimes richer—than an in-person seminar, if it's well facilitated. A peer review done asynchronously can allow for deeper reflection than a rushed in-class critique. The key is not the format. It's the *framing*. How we design for connection, presence, reciprocity.

Which brings us to the role of the teacher. If you thought teaching was complex before, try teaching in a blended environment. You're now a designer, a facilitator, a coach, a technologist, a curator, and occasionally, a crisis counselor. You manage not just a room, but a whole ecosystem. You don't deliver content—you orchestrate experiences. And you do so while navigating digital fatigue, inequity in access, platform glitches, and wildly variable learner needs. It's a lot. And yet—there's something liberating about it. The chance to be more than a lecturer. To create spaces that adapt. To observe learners in multiple contexts. To use data not just for grading, but for guiding. To shift from coverage to depth. From pacing guides to learning arcs. Let's talk briefly about space and time—two elements that get reconfigured in blended learning, often in underappreciated ways.

Space, first. The traditional classroom is bounded—walls, desks, a front and a back (Ali Reza Beigi, 2021). The digital classroom is fluid—tabs, tools, hyperlinked rabbit holes. The blended classroom is both. It asks us to think spatially: Where does this learning best happen? Where do students feel safe to fail? Where can curiosity stretch its legs? Some things work better face-to-face: role plays, debates, spontaneous questions, the shared electricity of group insight. Some things thrive online: simulations, interactive tutorials, self-paced skill-building (Kayyali, 2026 a). The magic happens when we match the activity to the medium *with intention*—not because it's trendy or convenient, but because it amplifies the learning.

Now, time. Blended learning bends time. It allows us to escape the tyranny of the 45-minute period. Learners can pause, rewind, revisit. They can sprint through things they've mastered and linger where they struggle. Time becomes elastic—not infinitely so, but enough to respect the reality that learning is not linear. Some days are productive. Some aren't. Some concepts click instantly. Others marinate. This elasticity can be dangerous if unchecked—deadlines still matter—but it can also be profoundly humane. It respects that learners are people with lives, moods, energy cycles. It invites a slower kind of depth. And still, structure is essential. You need anchors: weekly check-ins, milestones, group syncs. Not to restrict, but to tether. So students don't float off into digital ether. So teachers don't lose the thread of who's where and why.

Equity looms large in all of this. Blended learning can widen gaps if we're not careful. Not all students have the same access to devices, stable internet, quiet spaces (Rose et al, 2023). Not all students have the same self-regulation skills. We must design with the margins in mind—create redundancies, offer offline options, teach metacognitive strategies, build in flexibility that doesn't assume privilege. So what, then, is the anatomy of blended learning? It is not a fixed formula. It is a choreography. A balancing act. A series of design decisions, constantly adjusted. It's pedagogical jazz—improvised within a structure, responsive to the moment, attuned to the players. And it's personal. Deeply so. Because the best blended classrooms don't just work (Kayyali, 2026 d). They feel right. They carry an energy—a rhythm that supports inquiry, a flow that respects the learner, a coherence that invites confidence. They are not seamless, but they are sincere. And they are never finished. The anatomy shifts as the context shifts. As tools evolve. As learners change. That's the challenge—and the beauty—of blended learning. It refuses to be static. It insists on being alive. So yes, blended learning is where flexibility meets structure. But more than that—it's where design meets empathy. Where innovation meets reflection. Where content meets context. And perhaps, most importantly, where learners meet themselves—again and again, across multiple spaces, moments, and modes.

AI AS AN ARCHITECT OF ADAPTIVE LEARNING JOURNEYS

Not long ago, a learning journey was mapped by hand. A teacher, perhaps with the help of a curriculum guide and some instinctual wisdom, charted the path: lesson after lesson, assessment after assessment, a mostly linear trek through content and concepts (Rose et al, 2023). The students walked that path, more or less together—

some sprinting, some lagging, most trying to keep pace with a rhythm that may or may not have been theirs. Adaptation, if it happened, was reactive (Butler, 2021). A late-night rework of lesson plans. An improvised mini-lesson at the whiteboard. A whispered conversation with a struggling student after class. The effort was human, heartfelt, and often heroic—but limited by time, capacity, and the sheer complexity of tracking multiple learners in real time.

Then artificial intelligence entered the scene—not with a bang, but with a whisper. First in the background: an algorithm recommending which videos to watch next, or a system flagging students at risk based on performance trends. Nothing flashy. Just quiet nudges. But the whisper is growing louder. AI is no longer a passive tool. It's becoming an active designer of learning experiences—a kind of invisible architect, shaping the contours of individual learning pathways, often before the learner even realizes it. And that raises a profoundly human question: What does it mean when an algorithm begins to co-author the learning journey? Let's sit with that for a moment. Because this isn't just a technical shift—it's a pedagogical and philosophical one. AI isn't just streamlining delivery. It's starting to make decisions that have traditionally been the domain of teachers: What content comes next? What level of difficulty is appropriate? When should we intervene? How much challenge is too much? What pace is just right?

The phrase "adaptive learning" is tossed around frequently, but what does it really mean? At its best, it's not about spoon-feeding or making things easier. It's about dynamic responsiveness. A learner encounters a concept—say, fractions. They struggle with the application, breeze through identification, and hover uncertainly over equivalence. The system notices. It recalibrates. It offers a scaffolded exercise here, a challenge there, a brief conceptual video just in time. Not three days later. Now. That immediacy is part of what makes AI feel so powerful—and so eerie. It anticipates. It reacts. It personalizes with uncanny accuracy. It's as if the system is listening. And in a way, it is. Listening to every click, every hesitation, every wrong answer, every revisit. Noticing what human eyes might miss: the subtle signals of confusion or disengagement. The fatigue hidden behind a string of correct but robotic answers. But here's the tension: responsiveness is not the same as understanding.

AI does not feel the student's frustration. It cannot interpret a sigh or read between the lines of a hesitant question (Jose & Jose, 2024). It doesn't know if the learner was distracted by noise at home, or if they're masking confusion with bravado. What it *does* know is data—lots of it. Patterns, correlations, probabilities. And based on that, it builds a version of the learner. A data-shadow. A profile that becomes the basis for adaptation. This shadow learner is useful—but incomplete.

That's where educators come in. The human role in adaptive learning is not diminished by AI. If anything, it becomes more complex. Teachers must now interpret not just student behavior, but system behavior. Why did the platform assign this task?

What does this progress dashboard actually reveal? Is the learner being challenged appropriately, or are they trapped in an algorithmic echo chamber—circling the same types of tasks because that's what they've done well in the past?

The promise of AI in learning design lies in its ability to handle complexity at scale (Carvalho et al, 2022). To track thousands of micro-interactions and surface meaningful insights. To support differentiated instruction in ways that were previously impossible. But this promise can only be realized if we treat AI not as a replacement for human judgment, but as a collaborator.

Consider this: AI can design a personalized math sequence tailored to a learner's performance patterns. But it can't yet understand that the student's lack of progress this week is because her grandmother passed away. Or that he's disengaged because he no longer sees the relevance of the topic to his life. That understanding—relational, contextual, emotional—still belongs to the teacher. And it always will. But let's not romanticize either. Humans miss things too. We carry biases, get tired, overlook quiet learners. AI, for all its limitations, can help level the playing field. It can draw attention to students who might otherwise slip through the cracks. It can identify trends across a classroom that a single teacher might not notice. It can provide a kind of second set of eyes—a data-informed intuition that complements the teacher's lived experience.

There's power in that partnership. When human insight meets machine precision, the learning journey becomes not just adaptive, but *attuned*. Responsive not only to performance, but to potential. To the quiet signals of readiness. To the gentle nudges toward challenge or rest. To the idea that learning is not a straight road, but a landscape of peaks and valleys, plateaus and sudden leaps (Kellogg, 2021). AI as an architect does not mean the blueprint is fixed. It means the design is alive. Responsive. Iterative. But that also demands transparency. Learners—and teachers—must understand how these systems work. What data is being used? How are decisions made? What can be overridden, and by whom? Without that, adaptive learning becomes a black box. A maze designed by someone else, with no map. And that's not empowerment. That's manipulation.

So, we must teach not only with AI, but *about* it. Digital literacy must include algorithmic literacy. Learners should be able to question why they're seeing certain content (Spurava & Kotilainen, 2023). They should be able to push back, to ask for alternative paths, to understand the logic behind their learning sequence. Only then can adaptive learning be truly learner-centered. And let's not forget the design layer. AI is not a neutral force (Kayyali, 2025 b). The decisions about what counts as "mastery," how difficulty is calculated, what learning models are embedded—these are human choices. Often made by developers and data scientists far removed from the classroom. We must bring educators into those conversations. Into the development of platforms, the calibration of feedback, the ethics of adaptation. Because adaptation is not just technical. It's pedagogical. It's cultural. It's deeply human.

A system that adapts by removing challenge is not adaptive—it's regressive. One that isolates learners in silos of tailored content is not personalized—it's atomized. The goal is not to shield learners from struggle, but to support them through it. To stretch them just enough. To scaffold, not smother. And sometimes, adaptation means slowing down. Or pausing. Or asking questions that don't have right answers. Not everything can be optimized. Some of the richest learning comes from detours. From ambiguity. From failing forward. Can AI design for that? Maybe. With the right prompts. The right data. The right design philosophy. But more often, it's the teacher who must build in those spaces. Who must recognize that the adaptive path is not always the straightest one. That the learner who appears "off-track" may, in fact, be doing the most meaningful work of all.

I've seen it firsthand. A student flagged by the system as "behind" because she spent twice the expected time on a module (Zakaria et al, 2022). But when you talk to her, she's not struggling—she's exploring. She's connecting the concept to a project she's working on. She's reading beyond the required material. She's learning deeply, not just quickly. The system doesn't know that. But the teacher does. And so, again, we come back to partnership. AI can be an extraordinary architect. But it needs a co-designer. Someone who brings empathy, intuition, context. Someone who sees beyond the metrics. Someone who believes that the learner is more than their data profile. Because in the end, adaptive learning is not just about matching content to capacity. It's about honoring the learner's humanity. Their curiosity, their fears, their quirks. It's about building a journey that is not only efficient, but meaningful. AI can help us do that. But only if we stay awake. Only if we ask questions. Only if we keep the learner—messy, beautiful, unpredictable—in the center of the frame. The algorithm may sketch the walls. But it's the learner who walks the halls. And it's the teacher who lights the way.

DATA, ETHICS, AND AGENCY: NAVIGATING THE RISKS OF HYPER-PERSONALIZATION

We live in an age that worships data. It's the new oil, the new currency, the new oracle. In education, it promises clarity—insight into what learners know, what they don't, how they move, where they stumble, what they might need next. It's seductive, this promise of personalization powered by cold, clean lines of code. Every click, every pause, every misstep—captured, processed, converted into feedback, recommendations, dashboards. The language is crisp: *optimize*, *streamline*, *adapt*. But somewhere behind those shiny graphs and predictive heatmaps is a human being—conflicted, emotional, non-linear—and here's the rub: human learning isn't always measurable, and it certainly isn't always clean. There's a point at which personalization tips from helpful to haunting. Where adaptation morphs into surveillance. Where support becomes steering. And the line between guidance and control? It's thinner than we like to admit.

The promise of AI-powered personalization is, on the surface, dazzling: bespoke learning experiences for every student, fine-tuned to their pace, their style, their gaps, their goals (Asfour, 2024). But behind that veneer lie complex questions—ethical landmines, really—that we can't afford to sidestep. Because at the center of this glittering algorithmic scaffolding is data. And where there's data, there's power. And where there's power, there's potential for harm.

Let's start with the data itself. What gets collected? Who decides? And more importantly—what doesn't? Most systems gather quantitative metrics: time on task, accuracy, frequency of login, completion rates. Fine. But that's a sliver of the story. What about the kid who reflects quietly, scribbles notes in the margins, connects dots in her head but says little on the discussion board? She might look disengaged to an AI system trained to reward activity. But she might be doing the deepest thinking of all.

Figure 2. Personalized Learning Model

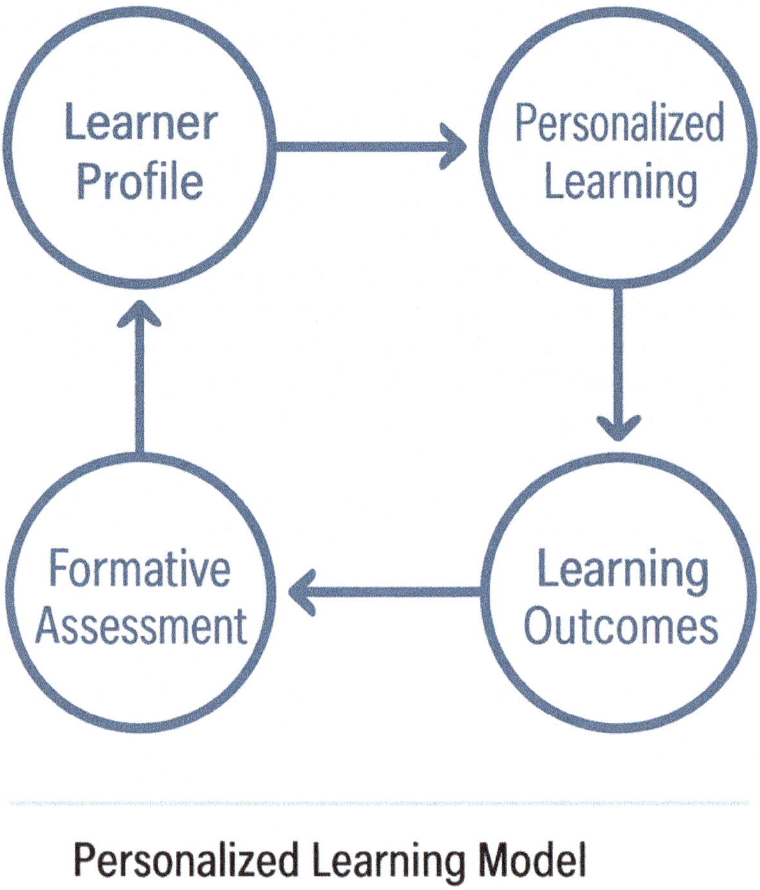

What's more, the data collected is only as good as the assumptions baked into its interpretation. Algorithms don't understand context; they recognize patterns. A drop in engagement? Must be disengagement (Poiroux, 2024). Or confusion. Or boredom. But maybe it's grief. Or hunger. Or burnout. The point is: the system can only guess, and those guesses can become scripts. Scripts that follow the learner. Scripts that decide which resources to offer, which level of difficulty to assign, even which learning outcomes to prioritize. This is where the ethical stakes rise.

When personalization becomes hyper-personalization—when the system starts curating not just content but *possibility*—we must pause. Whose values are shaping this path? Is the learner being nudged toward excellence, or corralled by probability? Is the AI reinforcing equity, or perpetuating quiet biases baked into its training data?

Because make no mistake—bias is not a glitch. It's a feature of systems trained on historical data. And education, historically, has not been an equal playing field.

Take a predictive model that identifies "at-risk" students based on past performance and demographic data (Fazlul et al, 2022). Sounds useful. But what happens when that label becomes a prophecy? When teachers start expecting less, when systems start limiting access to challenging material, when learners internalize a sense of limitation? What was meant to support becomes a cage. Agency erodes silently. And the most dangerous thing about this erosion is how invisible it is. When personalization works too well, it creates the illusion of choice while quietly scripting the options. It presents recommendations as neutral, when they are anything but. It nudges learners without their consent, without dialogue. And in doing so, it steals something vital: the learner's right to wander. To explore outside the predicted path. To struggle on purpose. To surprise themselves.

It's worth asking—when did struggle become a flaw to fix? Why have we become so obsessed with frictionless learning? Yes, no one wants students to flounder. But friction is often where the learning happens. The ambiguity, the detour, the question with no easy answer—these are not bugs. They are features of deep intellectual growth. And personalization systems, for all their strengths, are rarely designed to embrace that ambiguity. Which brings us back to agency.

True personalization should empower the learner, not just accommodate them. It should expand possibility, not narrow it (Kushwaha, 2024). It should be transparent—letting learners see *why* a path is being recommended, *how* it was determined, and *what* alternatives exist. Otherwise, it becomes a subtle form of programming: compliant learners on optimized tracks, all very efficient, all very polished—and all somewhat hollow. The solution is not to reject data, but to contextualize it. To complement quantitative analytics with qualitative understanding. To design systems that invite questioning, not just compliance. Systems that show learners the map, not just the route. Systems that ask, "What do you want to learn next?" instead of only predicting what you're likely to succeed at.

This is not easy work. It requires humility—from educators, developers, and institutions alike. Humility to admit that data does not tell the whole story. Humility to invite learners into the process. Humility to see AI not as the brain, but as the co-pilot. And it requires courage (Kayyali, 2026 c). Courage to ask hard questions about who owns the data. Who benefits. Who is accountable when the system fails. Because it *will* fail—inevitably, unpredictably, and in ways we can't fully foresee.

Already, we are seeing signs of tension. Parents concerned about surveillance. Students wondering why they were placed in certain tracks. Teachers overwhelmed by dashboards that don't match their own assessments. These are not fringe concerns. They are cracks in the system that demand honest reckoning. There is also the question of permanence. Educational data, once captured, doesn't just evaporate (Yu, &

Couldry, 2022). It lingers—on servers, in models, in institutional memory. What happens when a student's early struggles follow them across years, across systems? When they are tagged by algorithms long after the original context has faded? Do they get to reinvent themselves, or are they forever shadowed by their data double?

If we are not intentional, we risk building an educational infrastructure where every action is recorded, every path is predicted, and every deviation is quietly discouraged. That is not personalization. That is domestication. And so, we return to values. What do we believe about learners? Are they consumers of content, or creators of meaning? Are they to be optimized, or empowered? Are we building systems that trust them, challenge them, invite them into ownership—or systems that gently guide them into docility? Hyper-personalization, unchecked, tends toward the latter. It's comfortable. It reduces uncertainty (Al Balushi, 2024). But it also reduces serendipity, divergence, rebellion—the very things that make education transformative. So, what can we do?

We can design for transparency. Show learners the logic behind their pathways. Let them toggle settings, reject recommendations, see the bigger picture. We can prioritize dialogue. Make space for learners to reflect on their data. Invite teachers to interpret dashboards through the lens of lived experience (Kaliisa & Dolonen, 2023). Build systems that support conversations, not just conclusions. We can embrace friction. Let learners struggle, make odd choices, veer off track. Sometimes, the best insights come from the worst detours. And we can center ethics—not as an afterthought, but as a foundation (Kayyali, 2026 b). Every data point, every algorithmic decision, every personalized recommendation should be guided by questions like: *Is this fair? Is this empowering? Who is being left out?* Because the goal is not just smart systems. It's wise systems. Human systems.

In the end, the real measure of AI-powered personalization is not how efficient it is, or how well it predicts success. It's how deeply it honors the learner's agency. Their right to self-direct. Their capacity for surprise. Their humanity. Because data is not destiny. And education is not a script. It is, and always should be, a conversation.

CHARTING THE FUTURE: PERSONALIZED LEARNING AS A PEDAGOGICAL PARADIGM SHIFT

When we gaze forward into the horizon of education, there's an undeniable sense of unfolding—a gradual yet profound reimagining of what learning means, how it happens, and who holds the reins. Personalized learning, once a whispered hope or niche experiment, is asserting itself as more than a method or a tool; it is emerging as a tectonic shift in pedagogy. But to chart its future is to venture into both exhilarating possibility and complex uncertainty.

Personalized learning demands that we reconsider foundational assumptions (Strekalova-Hughes et al., 2021). No longer can education cling to the one-size-fits-all garment, hastily patched to cover diverse bodies and minds. Instead, it invites us to weave a fabric of infinite threads, each learner's unique story woven into the educational tapestry. This is not mere customization; it is a wholesale paradigm shift—a movement from standardization toward singularity, from prescriptive pacing toward fluid, learner-driven trajectories. But what does this shift look like, really? It is not just the presence of adaptive algorithms or the proliferation of digital platforms. Those are surface phenomena, symptoms of a deeper evolution. The real change lies in the relationship between learner, teacher, content, and context. It is a shift from transmission to transformation. From passive reception to active co-creation.

In this emerging paradigm, learners are no longer vessels to be filled but architects of their own knowledge. They navigate not a fixed curriculum but a constellation of experiences, guided by curiosity, reflection, and agency. Teachers become less gatekeepers and more facilitators, designers, mentors who scaffold not only knowledge acquisition but self-regulation, critical thinking, and resilience (Nunes et al, 2023). At the heart of this change is an embrace of complexity. Learning is messy, non-linear, and unpredictable. It resists neat categorization or simple metrics. Personalized learning acknowledges this messiness—it doesn't try to iron it flat but to hold it with respect and intention. It cultivates spaces where ambiguity is not a threat but a resource. Where failure is not a pitfall but a pivot. Where learning pathways are dynamic, flexible, and evolving.

Table 2. Benefits of Personalized Learning In Blended Environments

Benefit	Description	Example Scenario
Enhanced Engagement	Learners interact more when content reflects their pace and interest.	Students selecting project themes aligned with their goals.
Improved Retention	Personalized feedback helps learners retain and apply knowledge.	Quizzes revisited based on errors and explanations provided.
Equity and Access	AI helps support learners from diverse backgrounds with tailored content.	Translation and accessibility tools supporting varied needs.
Instructor Support	Teachers receive actionable data to better support individual students.	Teachers alerted when a student struggles repeatedly.
Scalable Customization	Systems personalize learning at scale without compromising quality.	Large classrooms receiving individualized learning paths.

This shift is catalyzed by technology, yes, but technology alone is not the agent of change. The real driver is a philosophical reorientation—toward learners as whole persons, toward learning as a lifelong, contextual, socially embedded process. Technology is the brush; pedagogy is the art. Yet, we must be vigilant not to fall into technocratic traps. It would be easy—and tempting—to think that if we build smarter algorithms, collect more data, or deploy more immersive platforms, personalized learning will naturally follow. But technology is neither neutral nor sufficient. Without intentional design, critical reflection, and ethical grounding, it risks becoming a seductive façade that obscures persistent inequities and flattens human complexity. So, what are the contours of this pedagogical revolution? What questions must we wrestle with as we chart this future?

- First: **How do we balance personalization with social learning?** Learning is not a solitary journey. It is woven through dialogue, collaboration, conflict, and community. Personalized pathways must not isolate learners in silos but connect them across difference and shared inquiry. Technology can support this, but only if designed to foster genuine interaction—not just algorithmic matching or shallow engagement.
- Second: **How do we preserve learner agency amid increasing automation?** Personalization powered by AI risks veering into predestination if not carefully managed. Learners must retain the power to question, resist, and shape their own trajectories. This calls for transparency, critical digital literacy, and systems designed for co-creation rather than top-down prescription.
- Third: **What does equity mean in a personalized paradigm?** Personalized learning holds promise for addressing diverse needs and dismantling barriers. But without deliberate focus, it may reproduce existing disparities—privileging those with access, support, and digital fluency. We must center equity not as an afterthought but as a foundational principle.
- Fourth: **What new competencies do educators need?** The pedagogical shift demands a new professional identity. Teachers must be data interpreters, ethical stewards, technologists, and compassionate guides. This calls for re-imagined training, support structures, and recognition of the intellectual and emotional labor embedded in personalized teaching.
- Fifth: **How do we measure success in personalized learning?** Traditional assessments fall short here. The paradigm shift invites more nuanced, formative, and multi-dimensional evaluations—capturing growth, creativity, collaboration, and metacognition. These measures are harder to quantify but vital to honoring the richness of learning.

From these challenges arise opportunities. Personalized learning can unleash creativity, foster deeper motivation, and cultivate lifelong habits of inquiry (Vaghela & Parsana, 2024). It can bridge formal and informal learning, connect school to life, and honor the fluid identities learners inhabit. It invites us to think holistically about learning ecosystems—not just classrooms but homes, communities, digital spaces. And as the pandemic reminded us painfully, adaptability is essential. Personalized learning, at its best, offers resilience—systems flexible enough to respond to disruptions, to meet learners where they are, to support well-being alongside cognition. Yet, the shift is neither smooth nor inevitable. It demands courage to question entrenched norms, to disrupt comfort zones, to embrace uncertainty. It requires humility to listen deeply—to learners, to communities, to critics. It calls for solidarity across disciplines—educators, technologists, policymakers, and learners themselves.

I often wonder what this future feels like on the ground. What does a day in a personalized classroom look like? Not a utopian fantasy, but a real, lived experience. I imagine a space buzzing with asynchronous and synchronous activity—students engaged in projects that reflect their interests, teachers circulating to facilitate, AI providing subtle nudges without overshadowing human connection. A space where failure is met with encouragement, curiosity is kindled, and every learner's voice matters. This future is neither dystopian nor utopian. It is deeply human—imperfect, evolving, full of promise and pitfalls.

The pedagogical paradigm shift toward personalized learning is not a destination but a journey—one that asks us to rethink what education is for and how it can honor the fullness of human potential (Zohuri & Mossavar-Rahmani, 2024). It invites us to embrace complexity without despair, to balance innovation with reflection, and to hold technology as servant rather than master. As we chart this future, we do so not with certainty, but with open questions and a shared commitment: to make learning more responsive, more just, more alive. And in that commitment lies the heart of the transformation.

CONCLUSION

As we look toward the future of blended education, one thing becomes increasingly clear: the integration of artificial intelligence into learning environments is not a fleeting trend but a profound shift in how we conceptualize, design, and experience education. AI-powered personalization, when thoughtfully implemented, holds the capacity to humanize education in ways we have long imagined but rarely achieved—meeting learners where they are, responding to their needs in real time, and creating flexible, nonlinear pathways that honor the complexity of individual growth. Yet this shift is not without tension. The promise of AI is often couched in language of efficiency, optimization, and scalability. These are important, certainly—but education is not a manufacturing line, and students are not datasets. As we turn to intelligent systems to guide learning, we must remain vigilant about the values we encode into these systems. If personalization becomes synonymous with control—if it limits rather than expands opportunities, or if it subtly steers learners along preordained paths—we risk exchanging the limitations of standardization for a new, algorithmic rigidity.

The key, then, lies in balance. AI should not dictate the journey, but rather illuminate possibilities. It should not replace teachers, but empower them—offering insight, scaffolding, and support while leaving room for human judgment, creativity, and care. Educators must be at the center of these transformations, not only as users of AI tools but as co-designers of the learning experiences they enable. Only then can we ensure that the power of personalization serves learning, rather than the other way around.

Moreover, we must ensure that students are not passive recipients of AI-driven recommendations. Instead, they must be equipped with the digital literacy, critical thinking, and self-awareness needed to navigate these personalized pathways with agency. A personalized learning journey is most powerful when the learner retains the ability to question, choose, and reflect—not simply to follow.

Ultimately, AI-powered personalization invites us to rethink what education can be. It challenges us to abandon the notion of linear progressions and fixed benchmarks in favor of more dynamic, learner-responsive models. It asks us to redefine success—not as conformity to a standard, but as the realization of individual potential within a supportive, flexible, and inclusive environment.

In this reimagined future, the classroom becomes less a place of delivery and more a space of co-creation—a collaborative ecosystem where data informs practice, technology supports growth, and learners are seen not just as recipients of knowledge, but as active, evolving participants in their own educational narratives. As we stand at the crossroads of pedagogical tradition and technological innovation, the question is not whether AI will change blended classrooms, but how we will shape that change—and whether we will do so with clarity, intention, and humanity at the core.

REFERENCES

Al Balushi, N. S. Z. (2024, November). Developing Innovative AI-Based Educational Guidance Systems to Meet the Needs of Each Student Individually: A Comprehensive Review. In 2024 2nd International Conference on Computing and Data Analytics (ICCDA) (pp. 1-6). IEEE.

Ali Reza Beigi, S. (2021). In between continuity and rupture: On taskified classroom practices.

Almusaed, A., Almssad, A., Yitmen, I., & Homod, R. Z. (2023). Enhancing student engagement: Harnessing "AIED"'s power in hybrid education—A review analysis. *Education Sciences*, *13*(7), 632. DOI: 10.3390/educsci13070632

Asfour, A. (2024). *AI-Powered Productivity*. Asma Asfour.

Bukko, D., Liu, K., & Johnson, A. H. (2021). Principal Practices That Build and Sustain Trust: Recommendations from Teachers in a High-Trust School. *Planning and Changing*, , 50.

Butler, S. F. (2021). *Moving Learning Forward in Christian Schools: A Practical Guide for a Mission-Focused Curriculum*. Wipf and Stock Publishers.

Carvalho, L., Martinez-Maldonado, R., Tsai, Y. S., Markauskaite, L., & De Laat, M. (2022). How can we design for learning in an AI world? *Computers and Education: Artificial Intelligence*, *3*, 100053. DOI: 10.1016/j.caeai.2022.100053

Caulfield, J. (2023). *How to design and teach a hybrid course: Achieving student-centered learning through blended classroom, online and experiential activities*. Taylor & Francis.

Fazlul, I., Koedel, C., & Parsons, E. (2022). Using Predicted Academic Performance to Identify At-Risk Students in Public Schools. *Educational Evaluation and Policy Analysis*, , 01623737231212163.

Fraile-Martinez, O., García-Montero, C., Fraile-Martinez, M., Pekarek, L., Barrena-Blázquez, S., López-González, L., Álvarez-Mon, M. A., Pekarek, T., Casanova, C., Álvarez-Mon, M., Saez, M. A., Diaz, R., & Ortega, M. A. (2025, March). From Greek paideia to modern educational systems: Evidence for the need to integrate physical activity into academic settings. [). Frontiers Media SA.]. *Frontiers in Education*, *10*, 1541876. DOI: 10.3389/feduc.2025.1541876

Jose, J., & Jose, B. J. (2024). Educators' academic insights on artificial intelligence: Challenges and opportunities. *Electronic Journal of e-Learning*, *22*(2), 59–77. DOI: 10.34190/ejel.21.5.3272

Kaliisa, R., & Dolonen, J. A. (2023). CADA: A teacher-facing learning analytics dashboard to foster teachers' awareness of students' participation and discourse patterns in online discussions. Technology. *Knowledge and Learning*, *28*(3), 937–958. DOI: 10.1007/s10758-022-09598-7

Kayyali, M. (2024 a). Global Perspectives on Personalized Learning: Case Studies and Best Practices. In Transforming Education for Personalized Learning (pp. 66-84). IGI Global.

Kayyali, M. (2024 b). Quality Assurance in Online and Blended Learning Environments. In *Quality Assurance and Accreditation in Higher Education: Issues, Models, and Best Practices* (pp. 227–292). Springer Nature Switzerland. DOI: 10.1007/978-3-031-66623-0_5

Kayyali, M. (2025 a). The Impact of Personalized Learning on Student Engagement and Achievement in STEAM. In *Integrating Personalized Learning Methods Into STEAM Education* (pp. 51–78). IGI Global Scientific Publishing. DOI: 10.4018/979-8-3693-7718-5.ch003

Kayyali, M. (2025 b). Digital Literacy for Sustainability: Preparing Students for the AI-Driven World. In Rethinking the Pedagogy of Sustainable Development in the AI Era (pp. 197-224). IGI Global Scientific Publishing.

Kayyali, M. (2026 a). Online and Blended Learning in Doctoral Studies: Opportunities and Challenges. Improving Doctoral Education and Research Development for Sustainability, 103-138.

Kayyali, M. (2026 b). Ethical AI and Automation in the Workplace. In Leading Inclusive Workplaces Through Digital Transformation and Organizational Change (pp. 103-138). IGI Global Scientific Publishing.

Kayyali, M. (2026 c). AI in Higher Education: The Risk of Excluding Vulnerable Learners. In AI and New Forms of Exclusion (pp. 57-82). IGI Global Scientific Publishing.

Kayyali, M. (2026 d). The Impact of AI on Classroom Dynamics in Higher Education: Shifting Roles for Professors and Students. In Responsible AI Integration in Education (pp. 151-180). IGI Global Scientific Publishing.

Kellogg, S. P. (2021). The Mountain in the Machine: Optimization and the Landscapes of Machine Learning. *Culture Machine*, , 20.

Kushwaha, U. (2024). 17 EMPOWERING EVERY ABILITY: PERSONALIZED LEARNING PATHS IN FUTURE-SPECIAL EDUCATION. Future of Special Education in India, 217.

Makarenko, O., Borysenko, O., Horokhivska, T., Kozub, V., & Yaremenko, D. (2024). Embracing artificial intelligence in education: Shaping the learning path for future professionals. Multidisciplinary Science Journal, 6.

McMurtry, A. (2024). Learning theory and interdisciplinarity: reframing learning in terms of evolving coherences rather than "true" representations or correspondences. In *Handbook of Interdisciplinary Teaching and Administration* (pp. 13–24). Edward Elgar Publishing. DOI: 10.4337/9781035309870.00009

Nunes, K., Gagné, A., Laliberté, N., & Rawle, F. (2023). Evidence-informed Practices for Fostering Self-regulated and Resilient Learners. In Pandemic Pedagogy: Preparedness in Uncertain Times (pp. 49-71). Emerald Publishing Limited. DOI: 10.1108/S2055-364120230000049004

Poiroux, J. (2024, October). Disengagement through Algorithms: How Traditional Organizations Aim for Experts' Satisfaction. In Proceedings of the AAAI/ACM Conference on AI, Ethics, and Society (Vol. 7, pp. 1145-1156).

Raes, A. (2022). Exploring student and teacher experiences in hybrid learning environments: Does presence matter? *Postdigital Science and Education*, *4*(1), 138–159. DOI: 10.1007/s42438-021-00274-0 PMID: 40477740

Rahaman, S. U., Abdul, M. J., & Patchipulusu, S. (2023). AI-DRIVEN EMPATHY IN UX DESIGN: ENHANCING PERSONALIZATION AND USER EXPERIENCE THROUGH PREDICTIVE ANALYTICS. [IJCET]. *Technology*, *14*(2), 255–268.

Ravichandran, K. (2024). Identifying Learning Difficulties at an Early Stage in Education with the Help of Artificial Intelligence Models and Predictive Analytics.

Rose, R. M., Smith, A., Johnson, K., & Glick, D. (2023). Ensuring equitable access in online and blended learning. In *Online, blended, and distance education in schools* (pp. 71–83). Routledge. DOI: 10.4324/9781003446194-9

Segal, A. (2022). When the student is the 'problem'and the teacher is not the solution: Teacher professional identity in an era of accountability and personalized instruction. *Learning, Culture and Social Interaction*, *32*, 100597. DOI: 10.1016/j.lcsi.2021.100597

Spurava, G., & Kotilainen, S. (2023). Digital literacy as a pathway to professional development in the algorithm-driven world. *Nordic Journal of Digital Literacy*, *18*(1), 48–59. DOI: 10.18261/njdl.18.1.5

Strekalova-Hughes, E., Nash, K. T., Schmer, B., & Caldwell, K. (2021). Meeting the needs of all cultureless learners: Culture discourse and quality assumptions in personalized learning research. *Review of Research in Education*, *45*(1), 372–407. DOI: 10.3102/0091732X20985081

Vaghela, V. S., & Parsana, D. F. (2024). *Teaching and Learning: Fostering Student Engagement*. Critical Thinking, and Lifelong Learning Skills.

Yu, J., & Couldry, N. (2022). Education as a domain of natural data extraction: Analysing corporate discourse about educational tracking. *Information Communication and Society*, *25*(1), 127–144. DOI: 10.1080/1369118X.2020.1764604

Zakaria, A. L. J., Anas, B. O. U. A. Y. A. D., & Oucamah, C. M. M. (2022). Intelligent system for personalised interventions and early drop-out prediction in MOOCs. *International Journal of Advanced Computer Science and Applications*, *13*(9). Advance online publication. DOI: 10.14569/IJACSA.2022.0130983

Zohuri, B., & Mossavar-Rahmani, F. (2024). Revolutionizing education: The dynamic synergy of personalized learning and artificial intelligence. *International Journal of Advanced Engineering and Management Research*, *9*(1), 143–153. DOI: 10.51505/ijaemr.2024.9111

KEY TERMS AND DEFINITIONS

Adaptive Learning Systems: Intelligent platforms that adjust the difficulty, sequence, or format of content in real-time based on learner behavior.

AI-Powered Personalization: The use of artificial intelligence to tailor learning content, pace, and assessments based on each student's unique needs.

Blended Classrooms: Educational environments that integrate face-to-face instruction with digital learning tools and platforms.

Formative Feedback: Ongoing, data-informed guidance that helps students reflect, revise, and grow throughout the learning process.

Learner Pathways: Customizable routes through educational content that adapt to learners' goals, interests, and performance data.

Learning Analytics: The collection and analysis of learner data to inform decisions about instructional strategies and student support.

Personalized Assessment: Evaluations that are modified in format, content, or timing to reflect the learner's profile and progress.

Chapter 5
From One-Size-Fits-All to Just-for-Me:
Adaptive Learning Algorithms Transforming Blended Education

Uddalak Mitra
https://orcid.org/0000-0002-5682-5218
JIS College of Engineering, India

Shafiq Ul Rehman
https://orcid.org/0000-0003-2266-218X
Kingdom University, Bahrain

Barnik Podder
https://orcid.org/0009-0009-5019-8186
JIS College of Engineering, India

Arpan Dutta
https://orcid.org/0009-0009-9284-1977
JIS College of Engineering, India

Bishtu Bhowmick
JIS College of Engineering, India

ABSTRACT

Blended learning has emerged as a transformative educational model, combining digital instruction with conventional classrooms. As academic institutions try to answer the growing demands of learners, AI-aided adaptive learning algorithms become a tool for personalized data-driven means of instruction. The chapter explores adaptive learning algorithms for maximizing effective use of a blended

DOI: 10.4018/979-8-3373-3815-6.ch005

right © 2026, IGI Global Scientific Publishing. Copying or distributing in print or electronic forms without written permission of IGI Global Scientific Publishing is prohibited. Use of this chapter to n generative artificial intelligence (AI) technologies is expressly prohibited. The publisher reserves all rights to license its use for generative AI training and machine learning model development.

learning environment by tailoring content, pace, and feedback to a student's needs in real-time. Focusing on the architecture and application of adaptive systems in various learning platforms, and discusses how AI models evolve continually on the basis of learner's behavior and performance. Real-world case studies provide the chapter with examples of adaptive algorithms in practice across disciplines. Issues of ethics like data privacy and biases in algorithmic decisions, are also critically analyzed. This chapter extends promising recommendations to instructors, instructional designers, and policymakers to develop an inclusive, efficient, and effective mode of AI-based education.

1. INTRODUCTION

The evolution of education in the digital age has prompted a fundamental rethinking of instructional strategies, with blended learning emerging as a preferred model for delivering flexible, accessible, and scalable education (Park, Y., & Doo, M. Y., 2024), Isaeva, R.et al. (2025). The quickly changing digital technologies have led to a complete rethinking of classical educational practices and a popular acceptance of blended learning as the new mode of instruction (Rohs & Ganz, 2015). Blended learning is accordingly considered an attractive concept appealing to a broad base of learners as it combines face-to-face instruction with digital tools and online content to create an environment that is flexible, accessible, and scalable (Park & Doo, 2024; Isaeva et al., 2025). This particular blended modality supports customization and learner independence, while engaging students through various avenues to absorb knowledge (Kumar et al., 2021; Müller & Mildenberger, 2021).

Still, several traditional limitations prevail in many of the existing blended learning environments: delivering static content, enforcing rigid linear instruction that does not cater to particular learning styles, speeds, or levels of grasping concepts (Sareen & Mandal, 2024; Bizami et al., 2023). Such a condition may cause mental stress on students (Mitra, U., & Rehman, S. U. (2025) a, Mitra, U., & Rehman, S. U. (2025) b). To better cover those gaps, creating an AI-assisted adaptive learning solution has been increasingly published by educators and technologists as a means to allow the personalized view of the learning path to be experienced really.

Adaptive learning is far beyond simple one-to-one personalization. Instead, via learning analytics, these systems dynamically evolve, learn, and modify their internal learner models to keep instruction aligned to the learner's specific knowledge gaps and cognitive needs (Kabudi et al., 2021; Gligorea et al., 2023). As of now, these systems find greater integration into digital and tech platforms, fostering learner engagement, retention, and delivering better results for K-12 institutions as well as higher education (Li & Wang, 2022; Halverson et al., 2023).

In the past several decades, the popularity of blended learning has stemmed from its flexibility, accessibility, and large-scale implementation, but many challenges still remain (Sareen & Mandal, 2024). The older systems (Rasheed et al., 2020) still rely on the use of static and rigid curriculum frameworks in content delivery, which are out of step with the current multifactorial instructional pathway requirements of learner heterogeneity with respect to styles, pace, and understanding levels. On the other hand, AI-assisted adaptive learning (Khine, 2024) attempts to address these challenges through blended learning's greater adaptive capacity with respect to dynamic individualization and progressive learner model adaptation. That said, still lacking is an in-depth scholarship of blended learning that tackles its architectural design and instructional frameworks alongside practical and pedagogical reflections. Beyond that, underexplored issues such as data privacy, algorithmic bias, and teacher agency from an equity and inclusion perspective stifle the creation of adaptive, blended learning models that are truly adaptive and responsive to learners from diverse and underserved backgrounds.

This chapter looks into adaptive algorithms in blended learning by way of architecture, in practice, and pedagogically. It also studies real-time platforms representing advantages of adaptive learning, while also considering ethical considerations of data privacy, algorithmic bias, and teacher empowerment, so that the technology might serve inclusive and equitable educational experiences.

2. ADAPTIVE LEARNING: CONCEPT AND ARCHITECTURE

Adaptive learning is a learning systems that dynamically adapt the content, sequence, pace, and format of opportunities to learn to the student's actual performance and requirements (Rachmad, 2022). Traditional instructional models move in a linear, predetermined fashion, but adaptive systems track learner behavior constantly to offer tailored paths to proficiency.

These systems work on a cycle of feedback that is data-driven, where the interactions of every individual learner are gathered, processed, and utilized to inform subsequent action in learning. This leads to an adaptive, personalised learning environment that aims to maximize outcomes for every learner. Driven by Artificial Intelligence (AI) and Machine Learning (ML) in most cases, these systems attempt to mimic the individualised attention a human tutor would offer but at scale. Three fundamental principles underpin adaptive learning algorithms (Tariq, 2024; Strielkowski et al., 2025) at their foundation.

Personalization: Personalization in adaptive learning is to tailor the learning path, content, and tests to the individual's skills, interests, and performance. The systems compute prior knowledge, learning capacity, and performance statistics to provide content that resonates with individual needs. Learners are provided with materials that are neither too difficult nor too simple, enhancing engagement and comprehension. In whatever form is diverse, such as videos, simulations, or text, personalization makes learning relevant, efficient, and best suited to the learner's current level.

Ongoing Feedback and Calibration: Adaptive learning systems employ ongoing data collection to continually monitor and react to learner behavior. A click, response, or pause is monitored to continually modify instruction. Where a learner is having difficulty, the system will offer hints or corrective content; where they are doing well, it will offer more advanced content. Ongoing feedback makes learning at the right rate and allows intervention in a timely manner. Ongoing feedback provides teachers with actionable data to better inform instruction and more accurately.

Mastery-based Progression: Mastery-based progression has students advance only after they have mastered prior learning. This principle minimizes knowledge gaps by not allowing students to advance too quickly. Adaptive systems track understanding and administer focused support until mastery is achieved. This strategy instills long-term retention, in-depth understanding, and confidence in learning. Mastery-based systems, as opposed to time-based systems, emphasize competence over velocity to establish a more personalized and effective learning experience measured in terms of the learner's readiness and cognitive development.

Current adaptive systems employ huge amounts of data and smart algorithms for pattern recognition, forecasting learning performance, and adapting pedagogy. The systems track learner performance and behavior to make content run in real time. Predictive analytics can identify when a learner is most likely to need assistance, adapting content accordingly. The system gets smarter as it learns from aggregated user data. The data-driven strategy makes scalable personalization possible, increases learning accuracy, and permits proactive intervention, leading to more responsive and more effective learning environments.

2.1 Adaptive Learning System Components

Every adaptive learning system is built around an advanced triadic architecture of three dependent models: Learner Model, Instructional Model, Domain Model (Ennouamani & Mahani, 2017; Barbosa et al., 2024). This three-dimensional structure guarantees that the system is able to respond cleverly and dynamically to the needs of the learner by grasping who the learner is, what content there is, and how that content must be provided. The role of each component is distinct yet complementary, and the synergy between them is what allows the adaptive system to work successfully.

Figure 1. Architecture of an Adaptive Learning System

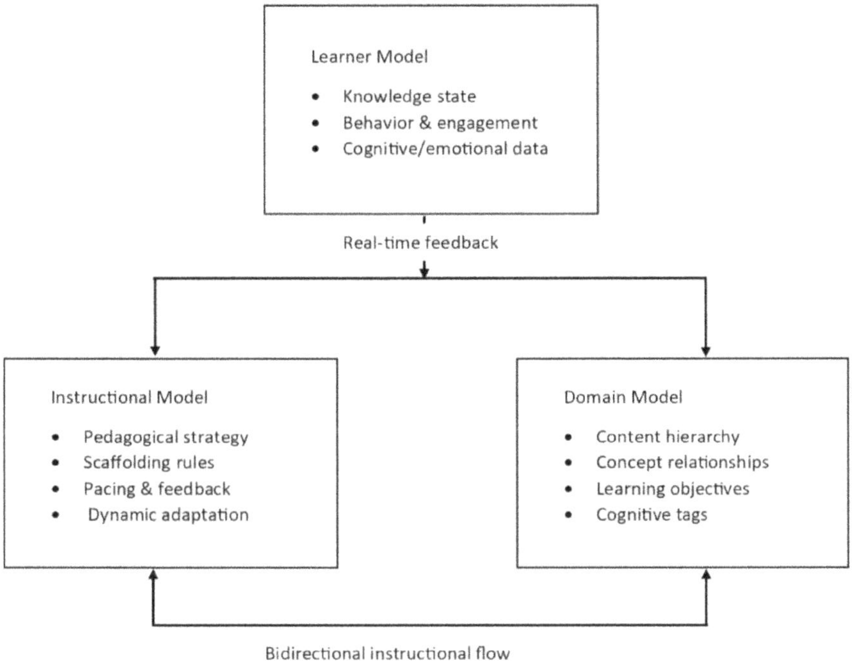

Figure 1 depicts the architecture of an adaptive learning system, highlighting how these three models are linked together by real-time data loops. The Learner Model updates continuously based on interactions with the user, informing the Instructional Model, which decides the best pedagogical approach. At the same time, the Instructional Model takes input from the Domain Model to retrieve suitable content sequences and learning objectives. The continuous circular flow of information between these elements enables the system to dynamically and at scale personalize instruction.

a) Learner Model

The learner model serves as the core intelligence center of the adaptive system. It continuously gathers and processes information from student interaction, creating a rich and dynamic profile that tells the system how it should best assist individual learners.

Tracks knowledge state: Adaptive systems continuously monitor the state of the learner's knowledge through monitoring what they know, partially know, or misinterpret. This is achieved through performance analysis on quizzes, answers to questions, and interaction patterns. The system determines what concepts are mastered and what needs more focus, creating an instantaneous map of the learner's capabilities and deficiencies. This changing knowledge allows the system to display content that is compatible with the learner's existing knowledge so as not to be redundant and correct misconceptions appropriately.

Monitors behavior and engagement: Aside from monitoring academic performance, adaptive systems pay close attention to learner behavior and interaction. They keep track of how much time a learner spends on certain activities, how many times they try questions, how long they take before they respond, and how often they engage with the system. These behavior metrics offer important background for learner commitment, fatigue, or distraction. By examining these indicators, the system can modify pacing, format, or level of interactivity to maintain attention and motivation.

Infers states of cognition and emotion: Sophisticated adaptive systems leverage analytics to make predictions about states of cognition and emotion like confidence, confusion, frustration, and motivation. These conclusions follow from trends in learner behavior—e.g., repeated failed attempts can indicate confusion, whereas rapid correct answers can mean high confidence. Some rely on sentiment analysis, eye-tracking, or face recognition to collect emotional information. Detection of these internal states enables the system to step in empathetically, providing encouragement, hints, or breaks to aid emotional well-being and cognitive preparedness.

Evolution over time: Adaptive learning platforms are not fixed; they change as the learner engages with the site. Every response, action, or behavioral prompt feeds into a constantly refreshed learner profile. This dynamic model allows for increasingly accurate personalization over time as the system becomes more sensitive to the learner's habits, likes, and progress. Consequently, instructional decisions become more focused, guaranteeing that learning experiences become more effective, relevant, and supportive with every new encounter, finally improving learning outcomes.

Through modeling of these factors, the system can make well-informed decisions regarding when to give extra assistance, shift the structure of the content, or provide advanced materials

b) Instructional Model

Instructional models within an adaptive learning system define the pedagogical approaches used when imparting, adapting, and sequencing instructional material to suit each learner's specific profile. Occurring at the core of content delivery, adaptive learning makes learning motivating, personalized, pedagogically sound, and in consonance with the principles of cognitive development. The system itself uses an instructional model when making transport decisions on how to teach content, what level of support to provide, when to give more assistance, or when to increase the challenge.

Content Delivery According to Learner Needs: A model good for instruction considers how best to deliver content for different kinds of learners. This means choosing from a number of modalities, including perhaps: text, video, or interactive simulations as well as real-time feedback; all of which may depend upon learner preference, past performance, or learning style. For example, graphical descriptions or animations may help visual learners; whereas verbal learners are served best through detailed written or audio descriptions. The model goes on to identify the right rate and structure suited for each concept so as to enrich the learning process, making it contextually interesting rather than generic and forbidding.

Scaffolding and Support: The Instructional model is one where scaffolding becomes relevant; temporary support systems assist learners toward growing independence. Accordingly, the adaptive systems are scaffolded by decomposing complex tasks into sequences of more straightforward steps and provide hints, cues, or guided practice when needed.

Scaffolding is phased out: As a demonstration of understanding is portrayed by the learner, scaffolding support is slowly withdrawn (called "fading"). For less able learners, this model might give easier versions of sub-concepts, graphics, or analogy explanations to build basic understanding and then move to more complex material.

Triggering Remediation or Acceleration: The primary purpose of the instructional model is to assess when a student needs remediation or can be accelerated. Using real-time performance data—such as multiple errors, long hesitation times, or disengagement—the system identifies trouble learning and then automatically offers content for remediation, including extra practice, alternative explanations, or review of prerequisite material. In contrast, if a student is completely successful in their work, the system may simply proceed ahead with challenging material or enrichment exercises to keep the student challenged and stimulated. These choices make learning more efficient, as well as avoiding frustration and boredom.

Adaptive Pacing and Differentiated Feedback: Adaptive pacing allows a student to proceed through material at a speed suited to his or her readiness. Unlike the traditional process-based training system, the adaptive system instantaneously adjusts to the learner's speed and allows for dynamic testing. Moreover, the system allows for differentiated feedback with respect to the nature and source of errors. For example, conceptual errors may trigger explanatory feedback, whereas careless errors would generate feedback requiring a review. Such concise feedback aids metacognition and allows learners to further comprehend their errors and ways to correct them.

Intelligent Reinforcement Learning and Dynamic Question Choice: Some highly adaptive systems have reinforcement learning algorithms that enable the instructional model to learn from previous experiences and improve decision-making over time. They can improve learning paths by understanding which methods yield the best results in the long run. Another dynamic question choice feature involves performance-based adaptation of question difficulty and question type by the system. Questions are not selected randomly but rather chosen to reinforce the learning objectives themselves, counteract misunderstandings, or leverage recent accomplishments.

This instructional model serves as the pedagogy of an adaptive learning system. Individualization of content presentation is maintained, whereas the quality factor of instruction is guaranteed through best teaching practices. With adaptive pacing, scaffolding, personalized feedback, and real-time decision-making, the instructional model has made the learning experience responsive and student-centered, motivating and promoting mastery.

c) Domain Model

The domain model is a system's core element that specifies the structure, organization, and pedagogical relationships of the subject material being taught. It serves as the system's internal map of the knowledge domain, which facilitates the accurate mapping between content, learner needs, and instructional strategies. By representing how concepts interconnect—sequentially, hierarchically, and logically—the domain model guarantees that content presentation is coherent, cumulative, and pedagogically valid. The domain model facilitates personalized learning by giving the structure for deciding what to teach, when, and how deeply, depending on a learner's existing knowledge state.

Content Hierarchies and Relationships: At the center of the domain model are representations of content hierarchies and relationships between concepts. These tend to be visualized through concept maps, knowledge graphs, or dependency networks, indicating how topics are built on top of previous ones. For example, in mathematics, understanding fractions could be a prerequisite for learning ratios and proportions. These hierarchical representations enable the system to order learning material in a logical way, so that basic ideas are explained prior to more complex ones. By defining prerequisite relationships, the domain model enables just-in-time remediation and helps avoid cognitive overload by refusing to introduce concepts learners are not yet ready to understand.

Learning Objectives: The domain model is also motivated by well-defined learning objectives, which specify the particular knowledge, skills, or competencies a learner will be able to learn. The objectives give the pedagogical rationale behind each content component and act as markers of learner advancement. In adaptive learning systems, every objective is frequently associated with several instructional resources and assessment tasks, enabling several paths to mastery. The model guarantees that instruction decisions—be it content suggestions or interventions—are matched with planned outcomes. This correspondence enables competency-based learning, whereby movement is based on mastery of goals instead of seat time.

Tags for Cognitive Complexity: In addition to enabling personalized instruction, the domain model contains metadata tags that classify content based on cognitive complexity levels, which are typically represented using taxonomies like Bloom's Taxonomy. Content can be tagged as needing lower-order thinking abilities, such as "remember" or "understand," or higher-order thinking such as "analyze," "evaluate," or "create." This tagging enables the adaptive system to align the content not just with the knowledge level of a learner but also with their stage of cognitive development. For instance, a learner having reached mastery of basic recall can be challenged with application or analysis-level activities, allowing for deeper learning and critical thinking.

Enabling Content Sequencing and Mapping: With the integration of hierarchies, objectives, and cognitive tagging, the domain model facilitates accurate content sequencing and mapping according to the learner's track. The model permits the adaptive system to determine exactly where a learner stands on the learning path, which concepts to introduce next, and how learning is organized pedagogically. This dynamic ordering is critical to mastery-based learning designs, in which students can take unique routes through the same domain depending on their previous knowledge, rate, and learning requirements. The domain model, therefore, serves as a master plan for curriculum development and a guiding system for customized learning paths.

The domain model supplies the disciplinary foundation of an adaptive learning system. It captures the organization of the subject matter in a form that supports intelligent sequencing, precise evaluation, and instruction alignment. Organizing content around relationships, objectives, and intellectual demands, the domain model allows adaptive systems to present learning experiences that are coherent, contextualized, and sensitive to individual learner progress.

2.2 Integration with Learning Management Systems (LMS) and Digital Learning Platforms

Adaptive learning platforms can exist as standalone software; they typically reveal their fullest potential, however, when integrated within a full-fledged Learning Management System (LMS) (Gunawan et al., 2024; Shafa, 2024), such as Moodle, Canvas, Blackboard, or Google Classroom. Such integration allows schools and colleges to centralize various areas of administration, instruction, and analytics within a single learning environment. The main enabler for this integration is the Learning Tools Interoperability (LTI) specification, which grants the adaptive platforms easy and secure communication with the LMS. Thus, through LTI, adaptive tools can be launched and accessed by end users from within the LMS while at the same time keeping session information, therefore lessening technical complexity. Single Sign-On (SSO) complements the ease of access since it allows the user to log in once and access multiple connected systems without having to recall passwords or other credentials.

As per Figure 2, an LMS is the management and entry layer for learners, providing access, course materials, and user data to the adaptive engine. From real-time synchronization and interoperability protocols (e.g., LTI and SSO), the LMS imputes the Learner Model, where, intermixed dynamically, it works with the Instructional Model and the Domain Model to customize learning pathways and provide feedback on analysis. This allows for operational administration and personalized instruction at scale.

Figure 2. Adaptive learning integration with Learning Management Systems (LMS)

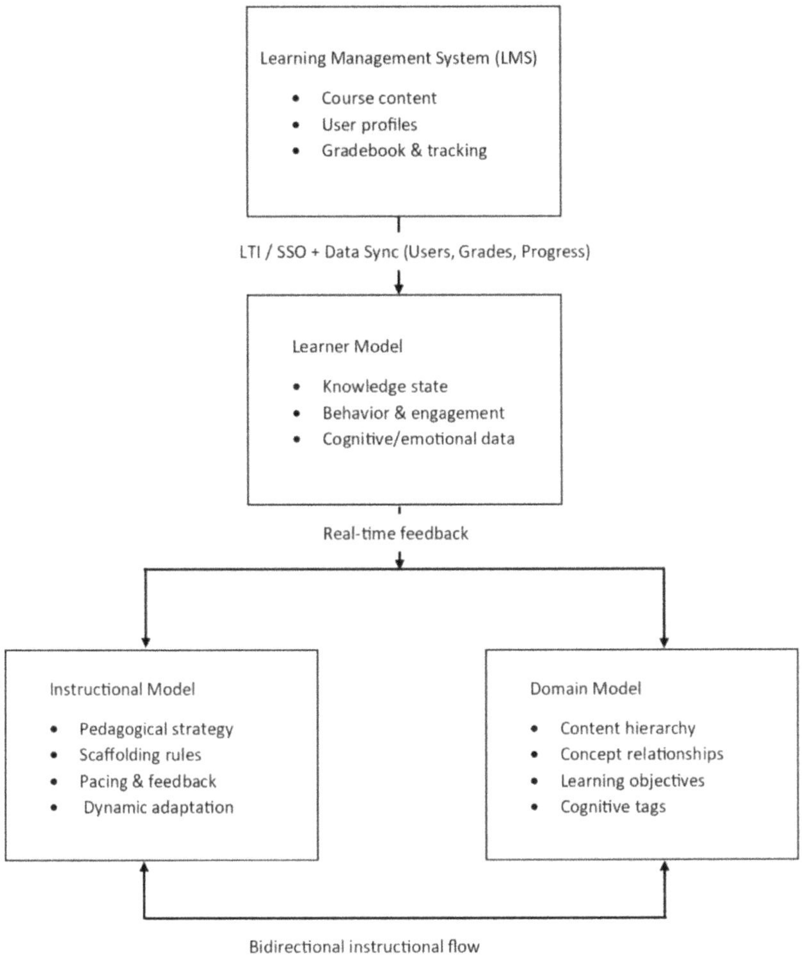

Adaptive modules can be integrated directly within current course designs, allowing instructors to place custom learning paths within mainstream curricula. This enables students to interact with personalized content such as adaptive quizzes, simulations, or tutorials without disrupting the fixed flow of thc course. Embedding also allows granular controls by which educators can specify the exact course timeline or unit structure to present adaptive elements. LMS integration, then, works to synchronize learning data in real-time concerning performance scores, engagement, time-on-task, mastery level, and progress toward objectives. This synchronized data allows adaptive systems to reflect up-to-date learner profiles and grades, as well as feedback, within the LMS gradebook, increasing transparency and reporting for educators and learners.

Also, the integration shall allow the adaptive system to use learner profiles, institutional settings, or accessibility options stored in the LMS for further instruction-at-a-glance customization.

For example, if a student has accommodations for extra time or audio assistance logged in the LMS, the adaptive system automatically changes the delivery mode or pacing, and hence, the system is made accessible to comply with accessibility guidelines such as WCAG and Section 508.

Moreover, integrated systems provide analytics dashboards offering instructors insight into student performance and student behavior on both the LMS and the adaptive platform. Such dashboards often contain comparative metrics, cohort analysis, and alerts for detecting students who are at-risk. This supports teaching with data and assures timely pedagogical intervention. Another emergent benefit of LMS integration is the scalability and interoperability of multiple platforms or campuses. Institutions having mixed digital environments possibly offer much consistency in the deployment of adaptive technologies, utilizing common standards to ensure interoperability regardless of vendor and LMS version. This, in turn, shall reduce costs for technical customizations and shall support sustainability in the long run for deployment.

Lastly, integration caters to blended and hybrid models of learning, where adaptive systems quietly accompany synchronous lectures, collaborative tools for peer interactions, and discussion forums within an LMS. It allows the adaptive learning system to co-exist with a robust digital adaptive learning environment instead of remaining in isolation. Certainly, by integrating with LMS, the adaptive learning system can extend both in depth and scope. This integration maximizes instructional flexibility; facilitates data management and storage; increases accessibility and personalization; and guarantees a unified learner experience. Such integration-equipped institutions would be able to undertake adaptive, data-rich, and student-centered education on a large scale.

2.3 How Adaptive Systems Change Over Time Through Real-Time Feedback and Learning Analytics

Admittedly, adaptive learning systems do adapt dynamically on the basis of real-time feedback from the learner. Contrasted with those systems that rely on predefined logic, adaptive platforms engage in real-time data collection and analysis as a dynamic and ever-increasing process to optimize instructional strategy. With such a high degree of interactivity, the response environment allows every move that a learner makes to affect a consequent choice of instructional action.

a. Real-time Feedback Loop

Four steps continue running from end to end as an active feedback loop for the adaptive process:

- Data Collection: Each unit interaction may fire many clicks, response cycles, events like hesitation time, repeated levels of submission, items missed, and is recorded and stored. This detailed behavioral information becomes an analytic base for the adaptive engine.
- Interpretation: This data is interpreted by machine learning algorithms, updating the Learner Model to detect learner patterns such as misconceptions, engagement levels, or cognitive fatigue under probabilistic modeling and pattern recognition processes.
- Adjustment: The Instructional Model gets adjusted based on the updated learner profile. Changes may be made to the question difficulty, scaffolding, review of previous concepts, or even to speed up the progress.
- Iteration: The process is ongoing and recursive, whereby every new input from the learner restarts the loop. With every session, the system learns more about how to cater to the learner's needs.

b. Learning Analytics Tools

To better support the adaptive process, systems utilize learning analytics, which can be subdivided into three categories.

- Descriptive Analytics: These tools provide real-time feedback on student behaviors and performance. Dashboards, heatmaps, and activity logs give teachers and administrators a gist of where students are thriving or struggling.
- Predictive Analytics: Predictive analytical tools forecast future performance based on current trends. For example, algorithms may predict which students are going to drop out, fall behind, or have difficulty grasping a certain concept.
- Prescriptive Analytics: This stage goes beyond predicting and providing insights, examining any possible set of specific next steps that can be followed. For instance, it might suggest the learner should focus again on the given topic, work somewhat slower or faster, or possibly complete more practice tests.

Collaborative filtering can be used by advanced systems, taking into consideration thousands of students' behaviors as data, to make greater instructional decisions on behalf of a student. Additionally, with the help of federated learning, adaptive systems learn from distributed data sets such as data from several platforms or schools without any compromise of data, thus detaching any suggestion offered by the system from the generalized ethical question. All in all, the coupling of real-time feedback loops with analytics has adaptive learning systems continuously improve instruction and support early intervention with learning outcomes at both an individual and institutional level.

2.4 Traditional vs. Adaptive Systems

Conventional e-learning systems mainly provide fixed one-size-fits-all environments where content is presented on a pre-defined path, irrespective of individual student needs. This results in all students having to work through the same material in the same order, usually receiving the feedback only at the end of either the assessment or the course module. Tests tend to be very generic, with fairly little variation in difficulty or format in response to student performance. Monitoring of the progress is also mostly manual-the instructor looks at student data and intervenes accordingly. In contrast, adaptive learning systems allow for dynamic and adaptive learning experiences. Content is adapted in real time based on the learner's performance, behavior, and interests. Feedback is immediate, thus allowing the learner to correct any misconceptions without delay. Assessments are adaptive, wherein based on the current knowledge of learners, they modify questions with respect to difficulty or type. Progress is monitored automatically along with present analytics, which supports immediate and targeted intervention decisions. A summary of these distinctions is depicted in Table 1 with an emphasis on the major differences between traditional e-learning and adaptive systems.

Table 1. Comparison of Traditional E-learning and Adaptive Learning Systems

Feature	Traditional E-learning	Adaptive Learning
Content Delivery	Static – same for all learners	Dynamic – adjusts based on learner data
Learner Path	Fixed – linear progression	Personalized – tailored learning paths
Feedback	Delayed – after quizzes or assignments	Real-time – immediate and contextual
Assessment	Uniform – same test for everyone	Adaptive – changes based on performance
Progress Tracking	Manual – by instructors	Automated – via analytics and AI

3. CASE STUDY: ADAPTIVE SYSTEMS IN PRACTICE

The case study ponders actual deployments of the top AI-powered adaptive learning platforms-Knewton, Smart Sparrow, DreamBox, and ALEKS-in a wide variety of educational settings. By examining the adoption of these platforms in K–12, higher education, and corporate training, we assess their impact on student performance and motivation. It then proceeds to discuss the burden of aligning adaptive systems with curricula and the shifting role of instructors within technology-aided classrooms.

3.1 Overview of Leading Adaptive Platforms

Knewton Alta is a courseware software that was first conceived as a test-preparation solution. Gradually, it developed into a rather potent adaptive learning engine for college-level education, most notably as part of Pearson MyLab for math, chemistry, and economics courses. It personalizes the learning through the gathering of student interaction information and continuously adapts the learning path in real-time to reinforce mastery.

Smart Sparrow, created at the University of New South Wales, is the most important design for adaptive tutorial customization. It applies in various fields such as health sciences, engineering, and science to design high-quality interactive learning environments based on learner responses and instructional requirements.

DreamBox Learning is a K–8 math program that uses real-time data to modify lessons depending on the learner's strategies, pacing, and types of errors. The program supports core math instruction with interactive visual models, games, and immediate feedback.

ALEKS is the system developed in collaboration with McGraw-Hill based on the knowledge space theory. It supports individualized instruction in math, chemistry, and business or accounts. It detects what gaps exist in the knowledge of the learners and directs them toward customized pathways toward mastery.

Each has a peculiar adaptive engine that merges learner modeling with instructional logic and domain expertise toward a personal, responsive learning experience.

3.2 Implementation Across Educational Contexts

K–12 Classrooms

The digital science education market speaks of DreamBox as one eminent player. School districts across the U.S. use the program, some of them as major and some as ancillary math tools. It is used by teachers in the classroom to differentiate instruction. In a number of studies, the implementation of DreamBox has led to mathematics achievement gains of above 1.5 grade levels in one year. It has an interactive, student-centered interface that encourages experimenting and persistence when working on problems.

Smart Sparrow has also been employed in high school STEM classes under university partnerships. For example, as part of a joint project with Arizona State University, students interacted with an adaptive course in astrobiology. Unlike students who used conventional digital learning materials, those who used Smart Sparrow reported stronger motivation, deeper curiosity, and a greater degree of retention.

Higher Education

Knewton Alta was established at Arizona State University for developmental math courses. More than 2,000 students were enrolled on the platform for four semesters. The results were a withdrawal rate drop of 56 percent and an increase in passing rates from 64 to 75 percent. Being that these students worked through early levels much ahead of time as a result of accelerated mastery-based progression, many were able to finish the class several weeks ahead of schedule. Smart Sparrow was used in biomedical engineering courses at the University of New South Wales. Adaptive tutorials take students through complex physiological systems. Students not only scored higher in exams but they also told us that they found it interesting and were confident to learn such abstract materials.

ALEKS has found widespread use in colleges in furtherance of developmental math and chemistry. ALEKS was installed by Cleveland State University, among others, to eliminate the traditional remedial math courses. By doing so, students moved into those gateway courses faster with a greater success rate in having achieved previously identified barriers.

Professional and Continuing Education

Adaptive learning found its way into workforce training and professional development. At Indian River State College, adaptive systems supported the flipped classroom and gateway course preparation. Pass rates increased by 20 percent, and withdrawal rates decreased substantially. Lorain County Community College has implemented adaptive math content in over 30 course sections. Adaptive students performed as well as or better than those in the previous traditional models, thereby confirming the implementation as an appropriate method of instruction in both credit-bearing and remedial courses.

3.3 Measurable Outcomes: Performance and Engagement

Concerning short two-day workshops with adaptive technology, reports consistently demonstrated a positive effect on student achievement, whereas static e-learning or lecture-style instruction generated results somewhere between nil and the negatively destructive. One large-scale analysis joint with Knewton reported that assignment completion percentages increased by 10 percent, accompanied by an increase in test scores. For each adaptive-engine-mastered learning objective, there was a 6.6-point boost associated with the related assessments, on average.

On DreamBox implementations, students using it for 60 minutes per week with fidelity saw significant gains on standardized math test scores, especially for younger and low-performing students. Because the platform responded to individual learning behavior, it enhanced persistence while lowering frustrations.

In the area of higher education, Smart Sparrow produced similar results. Faculty members cited enhanced student motivation, better use of class time, and more class interaction with the content outside the regular class hour. Students who did the activities on Smart Sparrow performed considerably better on post-tests than did the groups that did not have access to Smart Sparrow in several studies. At ALEKS, it was found that the speed at which students mastered core concepts was faster than how they underwent traditional remediation, and thus, they enrolled at higher-level courses more quickly. Faculty also stated that there were fewer drop-outs and that students were better prepared for upcoming coursework.

3.4 Alignment with Curriculum and Facilitation by the Teacher

These good adaptive systems also need to be highly aligned with curricula in institutions and teaching objectives. Systems like Knewton and ALEKS rely on in-depth domain models interrelating content hierarchies, prerequisites, and learning objectives. These models guarantee students are taught in a rational order and at the correct levels of cognition. For this to be facilitated, these adaptive systems integrate with LMSs, which allow grades, tests, and content to be synchronized and uploaded seamlessly to the LMS. Teachers integrate these adaptive activities with their course calendars and use LMS data strategically to make instructional decisions.

Teacher dashboards play an important role in adaptive learning. They present real-time student-performance analytics, mastery rates of concepts, and data on learner behavior. The teacher utilizes this data to identify students at risk, give them appropriately targeted interventions, and differentiate instruction in the classroom.

Those with adaptive systems increase teacher efficiency. Instead of sending the same material to all students, teachers can focus on encouraging deeper discussions, dispelling misconceptions, and mentoring select individuals in accordance with their level of progress. This transformation changes teaching from imparting content to supporting learning. Some organizations integrate adaptive rollouts with professional development initiatives. For example, when DreamBox is implemented in schools, teachers are trained to analyze learner analytics and adjust instructional methods based on this data to ensure adaptive technology is not viewed as a replacement for instruction but as a partner to student-centered data-based instruction.

3.5 Lessons Learned and Best Practices

While adaptive systems bring numerous advantages, their utilization must be carefully planned. The main challenge involves the initial investment in matching institutional standards to adaptive content. Teachers and administrators will need to invest time in actually mapping curriculum onto adaptive modules so that instructional coherence is maintained.

Adaptive learning might at first feel a bit alien or impersonal to students. Being upfront about the way the system operates and how it assists them in achieving their goals builds trust and motivation. Infrastructure is a big consideration too. The best examples have all of the students with stable access to their devices and internet connections. Institutions must also reflect upon the data privacy policies and ensure that adaptive systems provide inclusive education standards to accessibility. Finally, adaptive systems flourish in supportive, collaborative environments, so when instructional designers, administrators, and teachers collaborate and work cooperatively, the technology stands a better chance of being properly implemented and sustained over the longer term.

Knewton, Smart Sparrow, DreamBox, and ALEKS all provide evidence of how AI and data analytics could transform education. These systems, through real-time adaptation of instruction, allow students to learn more efficiently and with engagement. In K–12, higher education, and professional development contexts, adaptive systems demonstrated a measurable increase in learning results, a reduction in dropout rates, with teachers having access to actionable data. When aligned with curriculum and supported by trained teachers, adaptive systems become a powerful paradigm for scalable student-centered teaching.

The case studies demonstrate that adaptive learning is more than just a technology trend---it is a strategic tool that begs to change the future of teaching in various learning domains.

4. ENHANCING PERSONALIZATION THROUGH AI

Adaptive learning technologies have come a long way with the use of Artificial Intelligence (AI), which offers the computational smarts required to personalize education at scale. By harnessing methods like supervised and unsupervised machine learning, deep neural networks, reinforcement learning, and natural language processing (NLP), contemporary adaptive platforms provide real-time, data-driven learning experiences. These tools allow for smart systems to not just react to learner behaviors but also to forecast needs, identify cognitive difficulties, and suggest accurate instructional interventions.

4.1 Use of Machine Learning and Deep Learning in Predicting Learner Behavior

Machine learning (ML) and, in particular, algorithms like decision trees, random forests, support vector machines (SVMs), and gradient-boosted models, are key to adaptive learning systems. The models are learned from large datasets consisting of learner interactions—clickstreams, time-on-task, attempt sequences, and quiz scores—to classify, cluster, and predict student performance. For instance, classification models can forecast whether a student is likely to fail, whereas regression models predict time-to-mastery for a specific topic. A basic linear regression model employed in such scenarios can be shown as:

$$\hat{y} = \beta_0 + \beta_1 x_1 + \beta_2 x_2 + \cdots + \beta_n x_n$$

where $\hat{y}$ is the output (e.g., time to mastery), xi are attributes such as quiz scores or session length, and βi are the weights learned.

Deep learning models build upon these abilities by representing high-dimensional, unstructured data like handwriting, speech input, and emotion recognition. The characteristic neural network conversion within a feedforward deep model is:

$$a^{(l)} = f(W^{(l)} a^{(l-1)} + b^{(l)})$$

where a(l) is the activation of the current layer, W(l) are weights, b(l) is the bias, and f is an activation function (e.g., ReLU).

Natural language processing models like BERT or GPT can analyze open-text answers for misconceptions and provide individualized feedback. These models can be especially helpful in contextual understanding, sentiment analysis, and keyword matching, enabling adaptive systems to project student answers onto concept ontologies.

Through the application of these predictive technologies, adaptive platforms are able to execute activities like predicting the probability of dropout, finding "next best actions" (NBAs), and assigning instructional resources with accuracy according to ongoing learner profiling.

4.2 Reinforcement Learning for Real-Time Instructional Decision-Making

Reinforcement learning (RL) applies the principles of trial-and-error learning to instructional design by modeling the learning environment as a Markov Decision Process (MDP). In this context, the adaptive system acts as an agent that selects optimal instructional actions based on student state feedback.

The core mathematical representation involves the Q-learning update rule:

$$Q(s,a) \leftarrow Q(s,a) + \alpha\left[r + \gamma \max_{a'} Q(s',a') - Q(s,a)\right]$$

Here $Q(s,a)$ is the expected value of taking action α in state s, α is the learning rate, r is the immediate reward, and γ gammaγ is the discount factor for future rewards.

For instance, the system may learn that showing a worked example before a challenging question yields higher rewards (i.e., better performance and reduced error rates) for a particular student profile. This allows the adaptive engine to construct an optimal policy:

$$\pi^*(s) = arg \max_{a} Q(s,a)$$

which adjusts teaching approaches dynamically in real time.

This kind of real-time policy optimization enables fine-grained decision-making in instruction delivery, for instance, to choose the best modality (video, simulation, text), to decide when to trigger reflection, or to dynamically adjust the difficulty level.

4.3 Role of AI in Identifying Knowledge Gaps, Learning Styles, and Misconceptions

AI-driven learner modeling goes beyond mere score tracking to a rich learner state vector that captures cognitive, behavioral, and affective aspects. Knowledge tracing algorithms like Bayesian Knowledge Tracing (BKT) predict the probability that a learner has acquired a skill based on the history of performance:

$$P(L_t) = P(L_{t-1}) + (1 - P(L_{t-1})) . P(T)$$

Here, $P(L_{t-1})$ p is the prior, $P(L_t)$ p is the probability of mastery at time *t*, and *P*(*T*) p is the probability of learning from a single opportunity.

Deep Knowledge Tracing (DKT) is generally used to monitor a learner's evolving grip of concepts. Deep Knowledge Tracing (DKT), uses recurrent neural networks (RNNs) to capture sequential learning behaviors:

$$h_t = \sigma(Wx_t + Uh_{t-1} + b), \hat{y}_t = sigmoid(Vh_t + c)$$

where ht represents the hidden state at time t, xt is the input vector (e.g., question-response pair), and yt is the output predicted probability of a correct response.

These models revise probabilistic estimations of concept comprehension following every student action, enabling the system to recognize gaps in prerequisite knowledge or conceptual misinterpretations.

Clustering algorithms (e.g., k-means, hierarchical, DBSCAN) are used to find patterns in learning modes or behavioral prototypes. For instance, a cluster of students who keep looping back on video material might be well supported by visual scaffolding, and another group could do well with text-based drill.

In addition, AI systems utilize machine learning algorithms for semantic analysis and concept mapping to pin down misconceptions. For example, NLP-based classifiers can identify variations in student-written responses and re-route learners to clarifying examples or peer explanations. This real-time diagnosis and remediation system improves the accuracy and personalization of the learning process.

4.4 Adaptive Testing and Feedback Generation Based on Learner Profiles

Adaptive test engines apply item response theory (IRT), computer adaptive testing (CAT), and multi-dimensional scaling (MDS) to adapt the difficulty of questions and sequencing based on students' responses. The models choose test items that provide maximum information gain, enhancing the accuracy of the assessment while minimizing cognitive burden and test length.

Adaptive testing engines are powered by models like Item Response Theory (IRT), which connect the probability of a correct answer to learner ability θ and item difficulty *b*:

$$P(correct) = \frac{1}{1 + e^{-(\theta - b)}}$$

For a more discriminating model, the 2-parameter logistic (2PL) model involves the item discrimination parameter *a*:

$$P(correct) = \frac{1}{1 + e^{-\alpha(\theta - b)}}$$

These formulas control computer adaptive testing (CAT) so that the system can change item difficulty dynamically to fit a learner's current ability level, optimizing measurement accuracy and reducing test fatigue.

For instance, if a student correctly answers Level-2 Bloom's taxonomy questions (e.g., "comprehend") repeatedly, the engine can advance to Level-3 or Level-4 assignments (e.g., "apply" or "analyze"). The system has an adaptive item bank labeled by difficulty level, subject matter alignment, and cognitive complexity, dynamically creating assessment experiences as a function of learner ability and learning path.

At the same time, adaptive feedback engines tend to employ generative language models or template-based NLP to generate contextualized responses. For instance, a learner who tends to commit conceptual mistakes might be issued metacognitive prompts like:

"It seems you might be confusing force with mass. Would you like to review Newton's Second Law again?"

Certain platforms also integrate Explainable AI (XAI), which gives learners explanations for system choices. This may involve indicating how a mistake was diagnosed or the reason behind selecting a specific remediation route—establishing trust, transparency, and metacognitive knowledge.

Adaptive testing and feedback generation improve adaptive learning systems' personalization features through predictive analytics, independent decision-making, smart assessment, and intervention. The use of machine learning algorithms, deep learning networks, and reinforcement learning models allows these systems to simulate the dynamics of human learning at scale and in real time.

Adaptive testing and feedback generation-driven diagnostics reveal learner-specific misunderstandings, styles, and knowledge gaps, while adaptive testing and natural language feedback engines refine the learning and assessment cycle. With each advancement, the vision of personalized, mastery-based, data-informed education grows closer to reality—making learning more equitable, engaging, and effective for all learners.

5. ETHICAL, PRIVACY, AND PEDAGOGICAL CONSIDERATIONS IN AI-POWERED EDUCATION

Artificial intelligence applied to education can be used for very promising applications, such as individualized teaching, instant feedback, and administrative efficiency; however, this raises ethical issues about privacy, bias, transparency, and the role of the teacher. Educational centers must create a suitable environment for the development and implementation of these systems to ensure that the benefits of the students are put first while respecting their rights and well-being. The Section will entertain four pertinent concerns: data privacy, biases of algorithms, human-AI collaboration, and the matter of transparency.

5.1 Student Data Management - Privacy, Consent, and Regulation

Learning AI induces mass data collection containing personally identifiable information, academic data, behavioral data, and even biometric data. In the presence of students, who are, in particular, minors and an extremely vulnerable category, their data must respect their ethical standards.

a. Privacy and Consent

A good data privacy regime is at all times dependent on transparency. The school must teach the parents and students how any data is properly used, what data is collected and why, who has access to it, and how long the data will be retained. Informed consent must be:

- Voluntary-this means that access to education cannot be denied on such a basis.
- Specific-concerning only clearly defined purposes.
- Revocable-may be withdrawn voluntarily at any time.

Students must be able to access data about themselves, request unredacted information, or withhold consent for some of the ways their data can be used. Parental involvement is crucial in K-12. An informed guardian ought to be able to express concerns about how AI influences their child's learning experience.

b. Legal Protections: FERPA and GDPR

The two data protection laws most pertinent to using and applying AI in education are the following:

- FERPA (in the United States) protects students' education records and does so by requiring parental or student consent for the disclosure of personally identifiable information. AI companies must have the authorization of the school to operate and are bound by strict non-disclosure agreements concerning the sharing of data.

- GDPR (in the European Union) allows individuals the right to be forgotten, to allow data portability, and to refuse or accept explicit consent. Educational AI tools have to consider privacy from the design stage and conduct a data protection impact assessment whenever the system foresees processing sensitive data.

c. Best Practices for Governance

In order to work in an ethical and compliant manner, institutions develop explicit data policies and implement audits, enlist stakeholder participation in all decisions, and train their workforce in privacy issues pertaining to AI. The selection of a responsible vendor is also paramount. Protecting student data is beyond the rhetoric of legality; it pertains to building trust with students and respecting their dignity.

5.2 Minimizing Bias and Ensuring Fairness

An AI system cannot have more fairness than what the biases in its data and assumptions offer. Thus, if the training data portrays existing inequality, the AI might end up accentuating those prejudices.

a. The Origins of Bias

- Assessment tools traditionally based on historical data tend not to fairly portray students from existing different groups.
- Learning path recommendation systems disregard diversity among students and promote one-size-fits-all approaches.
- Predictive analytics might unjustly label certain students as being "at-risk," hence affecting the distribution of resources and the treatment of those students by educators.

b. Bias Mitigation

To stop the risks:

- Conduct audits on input data and output data.
- Make use of inclusive datasets with representation from various demographics and learning styles.
- Ensure that human intervention is still maintained as a window for educators to review AI decisions.

- Fairness-aware algorithms that can re-imbalance imbalanced data are to be applied during training and at prediction.
- There is a moral push for educational equity: it is never just a technical fix.

5.3 Automation and Teacher Roles

While software programs and algorithms may do grading, tracking, or content suggestion, putting too much emphasis on automation may destroy the human elements that are at the core of teaching.

a. Teachers as Primary Agents

Educators provide emotional sustenance, detect subtle struggles from the student, with an awareness of a larger social context that AI is incapable. Some of these suggestions may be made by AI, but they must be reviewed, interpreted, and integrated by teachers based on real-time constraints of the individual classroom.

b. Maintaining Pedagogical Control

It means that the AI system should enhance teacher autonomy rather than reduce it and thus:

- Provide teachers with the ability to create and edit lesson plans.
- Offer flexible tools that can be adapted to serve the needs of students.
- Allow the final judgment on evaluation and interventions to rest with the teacher.
- Give teachers the option to alter or override AI pathway recommendations.
- Educator authority helps to make education responsive, citizen-centric, and culturally relevant.

5.4 Transparency in AI Decision-Making

The"black-box" attribute in AI often presents difficulty in determining how particular decisions are arrived at. Such a secretive approach will engender mistrusting thoughts within students, parents, and staff.

a. The Need for Transparency

When students are not able to comprehend why they are labeled "at-risk" or assigned to a particular track, they feel dehumanized. When teachers do not have the means to interpret and justify the results produced by an AI, it engenders distrust. Conversely, parents may oppose AI involvement in high-stakes decisions if they are deprived of an explanation.

b. How to Make AI Transparent

An interpretability assurance looks something like this:

- The system should be Explainable AI capable of justifying the decision by human-understandable reasoning (for example, "the low reading speed contributed to this intervention suggestion").
- Provide an interactive dashboard for educators to understand how data results in outcomes.
- Demand from AI vendors the most detailed documentation on data sources, training methods, and known limitations.
- Try to explain things in plain English to the non-technical folks like parents, students, or teachers.

Thus, AI could just usher in a true revolution in access, personalization, and efficiency in education. But those very advantages can never get weighed against fairness, privacy, or human judgment. Ethical AI means protecting student data, challenging bias, empowering teachers, and making these systems transparent and accountable.

While laws like FERPA and the GDPR at least set a decent starting point, ethical AI asks for more than mere compliance: It asks for trust, inclusivity, and responsible design. As AI adoption grows, it becomes the collective responsibility of all stakeholders--educators, technologists, policymakers, and students--to stand together! Only then may AI truly help in learning while also safeguarding the integrity and humanity of education.

6. FUTURE DIRECTIONS AND CHALLENGES IN ADAPTIVE LEARNING TECHNOLOGIES

As AI disrupts and transforms education, adaptive learning is making shifts from regular classrooms to immersive settings and lifelong learning ecosystems. This very being of the evolution demands increasingly complex technical, ethical, and design challenges to be solved toward ensuring an effective, equitable, and sustainable realization.

6.1 Immersive Adaptive Learning: AR, VR, and the Metaverse

AR and VR allow learners to undergo situated interaction. While AR adds digital layers of information and interaction to the real world, VR takes students away to completely simulated environments. With content that can be adapted based on learner interaction, behaviors, or performance, developers can truly synergize double adaptive AR or VR experiences.

The metaverse takes this way further—creating shared learning spaces in which AI would mediate and tailor experiences across gamified, collaborative, and persistent platforms.

6.2 Developing Lifelong and Inclusive Learning

- Lifelong Learning and Corporate Training: Adaptive systems support adult learners by tailoring content to their prior knowledge, enabling flexible self-paced learning, and recommending certain career pathways by way of predictive analytics.
- Inclusive Education: Adaptive platforms can also be designed to suit learners with disabilities—interface changes can occur to accommodate voice and NLP support as well as gesture controls. However, the more important aspect is that this inclusivity is always embedded from scratch and never after the development process.

6.3 Technical Challenges

- Content Mapping: Personalization is affected by the structural robustness of knowledge maps, metadata tagging, and curriculum alignment. It is yet to be operationalized effectively.
- Scalability: Performance is bound to be affected on a larger scale due to the latency caused by cloud demands and limitations of hardware. Here, edge computing and lighter AI models look promising.
- Interoperability: Systems must allow open standards like SCORM and xAPI so that they don't get trapped within a particular ecosystem.

6.4 Research Junctions: Explainability and Design

- Explainable AI (XAI): To engender trust, AI systems must provide lucid explanations for the decisions they made, why a recommendation was made, what alternative courses of events exist, and what the confidence level of that decision is.

- Adaptive Learning Design: Issues under investigation pertain to how pedagogy informs adaptation, how learner autonomy may be balanced with guidance, and how AI may be used to foster collaborative or affective learning.

7. CONCLUSION

Personalized, responsive, and data-driven instruction is put forth by adaptive learning algorithms. Unlike one-size-fits-all traditional methods, adaptive systems keep content, pace, and feedback apt and in real-time feedback based on each learner's performance and preferences. This school's trio of a learner model, an instructional model, and a domain model furnishes the learning system with interactive pedagogy in real time. The technology behind adaptive learning systems is being proven and improving, and delivering results for educators in K–12, higher education, retraining, and professional development. DreamBox, ALEKS, and Knewton open the future for adaptive systems that will engage, train, and retain learners. Yet, they achieve success from far more than being mere algorithmic systems.

Trust and fairness cannot be ensured without ethical considerations such as data privacy, transparency, and algorithmic bias. Moreover, teachers still form the beating heart of the learning process. Because of this, these tools must support teachers so that their ability to serve diverse learner needs can be enhanced.

Simply put, adaptive learning has the power to democratize education by giving equal opportunities for quality, personalized instruction. Adaptively implemented ethical systems can foster inclusive environments in which learning is at the very core and, therefore, can bring forth the full power of blended education—that is, truly moving from "one-size-fits-all" to "just-for-me" learning.

REFERENCES

Barbosa, P. L. S., Carmo, R. A. F. D., Gomes, J. P., & Viana, W. (2024). Adaptive learning in computer science education: A scoping review. *Education and Information Technologies*, *29*(8), 9139–9188. DOI: 10.1007/s10639-023-12066-z

Bizami, N. A., Tasir, Z., & Kew, S. N. (2023). Innovative pedagogical principles and technological tools capabilities for immersive blended learning: A systematic literature review. *Education and Information Technologies*, *28*(2), 1373–1425. DOI: 10.1007/s10639-022-11243-w PMID: 35919874

Ennouamani, S., & Mahani, Z. (2017, December). An overview of adaptive e-learning systems. In *2017 eighth international conference on intelligent computing and information systems (ICICIS)* (pp. 342-347). IEEE. DOI: 10.1109/INTELCIS.2017.8260060

Gligorea, I., Cioca, M., Oancea, R., Gorski, A. T., Gorski, H., & Tudorache, P. (2023). Adaptive learning using artificial intelligence in e-learning: A literature review. *Education Sciences*, *13*(12), 1216. DOI: 10.3390/educsci13121216

Gunawan, R. D., Sutisna, A., & Ana, E. F. (2024). Literature review: The role of learning management system (LMS) in improving the digital literacy of educators. *Jurnal Inovasi Teknologi Pendidikan*, *11*(2), 116–123.

Halverson, L. R., Spring, K. J., Huyett, S., Henrie, C. R., & Graham, C. R. (2023). Blended learning research in higher education and K-12 settings. In Learning, design, and technology: An international compendium of theory, research, practice, and policy (pp. 3107-3135). Cham: Springer international publishing.

Isaeva, R., Karasartova, N., Dznunusnalieva, K., Mirzoeva, K., & Mokliuk, M. (2025). Enhancing learning effectiveness through adaptive learning platforms and emerging computer technologies in education. *Jurnal Ilmiah Ilmu Terapan Universitas Jambi*, *9*(1), 144–160. DOI: 10.22437/jiituj.v9i1.37967

Kabudi, T., Pappas, I., & Olsen, D. H. (2021). AI-enabled adaptive learning systems: A systematic mapping of the literature. Computers and education. *Artificial Intelligence*, *2*, 100017.

Khine, M. S. (2024). Using AI for adaptive learning and adaptive assessment. In *Artificial Intelligence in Education: A Machine-Generated Literature Overview* (pp. 341–466). Springer Nature Singapore. DOI: 10.1007/978-981-97-9350-1_3

Kumar, A., Krishnamurthi, R., Bhatia, S., Kaushik, K., Ahuja, N. J., Nayyar, A., & Masud, M. (2021). Blended learning tools and practices: A comprehensive analysis. *IEEE Access : Practical Innovations, Open Solutions*, *9*, 85151–85197. DOI: 10.1109/ACCESS.2021.3085844

Li, S., & Wang, W. (2022). Effect of blended learning on student performance in K-12 settings: A meta-analysis. *Journal of Computer Assisted Learning*, *38*(5), 1254–1272. DOI: 10.1111/jcal.12696

Mitra, U., & Rehman, S. U. (2025) a Integrating AI/ML With Wearable Devices for Monitoring Student Mental Health. In *Wearable Devices and Smart Technology for Educational Teaching Assistance* (pp. 257-284). IGI Global Scientific Publishing.

Mitra, U., & Rehman, S. U. (2025) b. Significance of AI/ML Wearable Technologies for Education and Teaching. In *Wearable Devices and Smart Technology for Educational Teaching Assistance* (pp. 1-26). IGI Global Scientific Publishing.

Müller, C., & Mildenberger, T. Facilitating flexible learning by replacing classroom time with an online learning environment: A systematic review of blended learning in higher education, Educational Research Review, Volume 34, 2021, 100394, ISSN 1747-938X, DOI: 10.1016/j.edurev.2021.100394

Park, Y., & Doo, M. Y. (2024). Role of AI in blended learning: A systematic literature review. *International Review of Research in Open and Distance Learning*, *25*(1), 164–196. DOI: 10.19173/irrodl.v25i1.7566

Rachmad, Y. E. (2022). Adaptive Learning Theory.

Rasheed, R. A., Kamsin, A., & Abdullah, N. A. (2020). Challenges in the online component of blended learning: A systematic review. *Computers & Education*, *144*, 103701. DOI: 10.1016/j.compedu.2019.103701

Sareen, S., & Mandal, S. (2024). Challenges of blended learning in higher education across global north-south: A systematic and integrative literature review. *Social Sciences & Humanities Open*, *10*, 101011. DOI: 10.1016/j.ssaho.2024.101011

Shafa, A. A. (2024). Implementasi Learning Management System dalam meningkatkan efektivitas pembelajaran. *Jurnal Teknologi Pendidikan*, *1*(4), 8–8. DOI: 10.47134/jtp.v1i4.658

Strielkowski, W., Grebennikova, V., Lisovskiy, A., Rakhimova, G., & Vasileva, T. (2025). AI-driven adaptive learning for sustainable educational transformation. *Sustainable Development (Bradford)*, *33*(2), 1921–1947. DOI: 10.1002/sd.3221

Tariq, M. U. (2024). Navigating the personalization pathway: Implementing adaptive learning technologies in higher education. In *Adaptive Learning Technologies for Higher Education* (pp. 265–291). IGI Global. DOI: 10.4018/979-8-3693-3641-0.ch012

Chapter 6
Artificial Intelligence-Supported Formative and Summative Assessment Approaches in Blended Learning Environments

Mehmet Yavuz
https://orcid.org/0000-0001-6218-232X
Bingöl University, Turkey

Bünyami Kayali
https://orcid.org/0000-0001-6419-9088
Bayburt University, Turkey

ABSTRACT

This chapter explores the role of artificial intelligence (AI) and summative assessment in blended learning environments, beginning with the historical evolution of assessment systems. It highlights the limitations of traditional methods in objectivity, validity, inclusiveness, and feedback. AI technologies address these issues through functions such as personalised learning, real-time feedback, automated scoring, and enhanced test security. AI not only reduces teachers' workload but also enriches students' learning through data-driven insights. While formative assessment guides learning based on immediate performance data, summative assessment evaluates outcomes effectively. These AI-supported approaches transform assessment into a continuous, integrated component of the learning process. The chapter also addresses ethical concerns, such as data privacy and algorithmic fairness, stressing

DOI: 10.4018/979-8-3373-3815-6.ch006

right © 2026, IGI Global Scientific Publishing. Copying or distributing in print or electronic forms without written permission of IGI Global Scientific Publishing is prohibited. Use of this chapter to in generative artificial intelligence (AI) technologies is expressly prohibited. The publisher reserves all rights to license its use for generative AI training and machine learning model development.

the importance of teacher competence and secure data handling. In conclusion, AI-enhanced assessment extends beyond traditional boundaries and becomes a dynamic tool to support learning.

INTRODUCTION

Blended learning (BL) refers to the deliberate combination of face-to-face and online teaching (Abu Bakar, 2021). In this model, traditional classroom activities are supported by digital learning resources to create flexible and multi-modelled learning experiences. BL aims to provide effective learning experiences by blending various approaches such as coaching, online courses, peer interactions, workshops and participation in online communities (Rossett et al., 2003). This design creates rich communication and interaction opportunities between students and teachers by integrating digital technologies and face-to-face interaction (Røe et al., 2022). In successful examples of blended learning, features such as flexibility, personalisation and active learning stand out; blended learning is considered not only as a technological integration but also as a pedagogical approach that encourages student engagement and individualised learning pathways (Margulieux et al., 2016).

This approach allows students to participate more flexibly in the learning process and provides instructors with the opportunity to enrich their teaching materials with various digital tools. Research shows that blended learning applications can increase student achievement levels and support individualised learning opportunities (Bernard et al., 2014; Graham, 2013).

However, there are also various difficulties in the implementation of blended learning. Especially for students with low levels of digital literacy, access and interaction with online components may be limited. In addition, the lack of pedagogical and technological competences of instructors may prevent the effective implementation of blended learning (Halverson et al., 2014). There are also challenges such as technological problems, the need for self-discipline, and possible feelings of isolation among students (Bandara & Jayaweera, 2024). All these situations can reduce educational effectiveness and deepen inequalities in the learning process.

In recent years, the use of blended learning has rapidly spread on a global scale due to the impact of the COVID-19 pandemic. After the pandemic, higher education institutions have turned more towards blended learning as a sustainable and accessible learning model, and many universities have made this model permanent (Hodges et al., 2020). In addition, the development of digital technologies and the widespread use of learning management systems have facilitated the diversification of blended learning applications and their integration into the education system.

With the widespread use of blended learning, not only teaching processes but also assessment and evaluation practices have undergone a significant transformation. The partial transfer of teaching activities to the online environment has necessitated the redefinition of teacher and student roles; this situation has also required rethinking assessment and evaluation activities (Koç et al., 2015). It is now important to design assessment strategies to be compatible with both online and face-to-face components. In this context, it has become a necessity for teachers to adopt flexible and multidimensional assessment tools suitable for blended learning models. Beyond traditional examinations, the potential of applications such as online tests, e-portfolios and digital monitoring tools are increasingly coming to the fore. Indeed, the use of online quizzes and similar digital tools in blended environments reinforces learning and increases participation by providing instant feedback to students. Thanks to such tools, assessment is moving from being a periodic measurement to a continuously integrated part of the learning process.

As a natural consequence of these developments, the impact of digital and technological tools, especially artificial intelligence-based applications, on assessment and evaluation processes attracts attention. With the digitalisation of education, advanced technologies such as AI have created significant transformations in the field of assessment and evaluation. While automated scoring systems provide instant feedback to students, intelligent teaching systems can offer question sequences tailored to students' individual progress (Hopfenbeck et al., 2023). In addition, data-driven approaches such as learning analytics allow for more in-depth analyses of student performance, making the teaching process more dynamic and adaptive. AI-based tools also contribute to the development of students' self-regulation skills by supporting peer assessment. In this way, teachers can quickly adjust their teaching strategies based on digital assessment data and instantly reflect the assessment findings into the educational process.

The use of AI technologies in assessment and evaluation processes significantly increases the efficiency of the evaluation process while increasing objectivity in education. Thanks to natural language processing and machine learning algorithms, it has become possible to automatically evaluate open-ended questions, which both reduces the evaluation time and increases the consistency of the evaluation (Bennett & Zhang, 2015). In addition, artificial intelligence-supported systems can identify learning deficiencies by analysing students' response patterns and support data-based decisions for instructional design (Ifenthaler & Yau, 2020). In this context, AI applications enable not only measurement but also the development of continuous and adaptive forms of assessment that support learning

However, the proliferation of AI-based assessment systems raises several ethical issues such as data privacy, algorithmic biases, reliability and impartiality. In particular, the secure storage and processing of large-scale data collected from students poses serious legal and ethical responsibilities (Williamson & Eynon, 2020). The lack of transparency in the decision-making mechanisms of algorithms may lead to systematic bias against certain student groups, which may undermine equal opportunities in education (Wieczorek et al., 2025). Therefore, it is necessary to clearly define ethical rules and establish control mechanisms in the development and use of artificial intelligence-based assessment and evaluation systems. Establishing ethical guidelines on the use of AI in education and supporting these guidelines with national policy documents will ensure that technological applications are used responsibly and in line with pedagogical goals

In addition, the widespread use of artificial intelligence-supported assessment and evaluation systems in education necessitates the development of teachers' not only technical but also ethical and pedagogical competences. It is critical for teachers to be able to use digital assessment tools effectively to enrich the learning process by utilising the analytical feedback provided by this technology (Christine, 2017). Therefore, a careful and pedagogically based approach is required to use the opportunities offered by AI in line with educational goals

Especially in the post-COVID-19 period, online exams became widespread, and the classification and ethical dimension of digital assessment activities came to the fore (Chowdhury et al., 2021). This process has shown that it is critical to align technology-supported assessment tools with pedagogical goals. Formative and summative assessment practices in blended learning environments also needed to be rethought. This transformation in practices requires not only a technical change but also a radical transformation in educational culture (Chan, 2021). To summarise, assessment and evaluation practices in blended learning environments are shaped by technological as well as pedagogical transformations. This new context makes it necessary for teachers to rethink their assessment tools and move towards student-centred, flexible practices. The sustainability of this transformation largely depends on the integration of innovative solutions based on AI into assessment processes.

FORMATIVE AND SUMMATIVE ASSESSMENT: FROM THEORY TO BLENDED LEARNING PRACTICE

Assessment and evaluation practices in education have undergone significant evolutions in the historical process. The first examples of systematic examinations date back to the imperial examinations in ancient China; these examinations were administered in written and proctored form and aimed at bureaucratic appointments based on merit (Farahsa & Tabrizi, 2015). In the 19th century, with the massification of education, centralised examination systems were developed and standardised multiple-choice tests came to the fore as the main measurement tools. In the early

20th century, reliability problems observed in the scoring of open-ended exams led to the development of multiple-choice question formats; thus, speed, objectivity and consistency were achieved in evaluation processes (Brown, 2022). The spread of quantitative scientific methods such as classical test theory and item analysis in the field of psychometrics has played a critical role in increasing the validity and reliability of measurement tools. In addition, assessment models have started to expand from focusing only on results to in-process and formative functions (Nicol & Macfarlane-Dick, 2006).

The foundations of modern formative assessment theory have been extensively shaped by the works of key scholars such as Sadler (1989), Nicol and Macfarlane-Dick (2006). Black and Wiliam (1998) emphasized that effective assessment should be embedded in everyday classroom practice, providing timely and constructive feedback to inform both teaching and learning. Sadler (1989) argued that formative assessment should clearly communicate to students their current performance, the desired standard, and the steps needed to close the gap. Nicol and Macfarlane-Dick (2006) proposed seven principles of good feedback practice, highlighting the importance of self-regulation, active learner engagement, and the co-construction of assessment criteria. These foundational perspectives underscore that formative assessment is not merely a measurement activity but a pedagogical process aimed at actively improving learning outcomes.

Formative assessment, which is one of the main pillars of assessment and evaluation methods used in education today, is a low-risk approach that is carried out throughout the learning process and provides continuous feedback to the teaching-learning process (Sadler, 1989). This method allows the identification of students' strengths and weaknesses and helps teachers to reorganise their teaching strategies instantaneously. Formative assessment contributes to the development of self-regulation skills by increasing students' awareness of their own learning process (Nicol & Macfarlane-Dick, 2006). In this context, tools such as classroom discussions, structured feedback, observation forms, self-assessment activities and teacher comments are widely used. Formative assessment is a pedagogical approach that aims not only to measure learning but also to support and deepen it.

Another main component of assessment and evaluation practices is summative assessment. This approach is usually carried out at the end of a unit, semester or learning process and aims to measure the level of knowledge, skills or performance of the student in line with certain criteria (Black & Wiliam, 1998). Summative assessment enables to document the final achievement of the student and to make classificatory decisions (e.g. pass/fail, grading) through structures such as high-stakes exams, projects, portfolios or performance tasks (Bennett, 2011). Such assessments are often standardised and positioned outside the teaching process (Brookhart, 2007). However, critics argue that such assessments do not contribute sufficiently to students' learning processes and may lead to the shaping of teaching according to the outcomes to be measured. For this reason, contemporary educational approaches emphasise efforts to make summative assessment more inclusive and process-oriented.

Integrating theoretical frameworks such as Bloom's taxonomy (Bloom et al., 1956; Anderson & Krathwohl, 2001) and the Assessment for Learning (AfL) model (Wiliam, 2011) provides a deeper pedagogical grounding for both formative and summative assessment. Bloom's taxonomy offers a structured approach for designing assessment tasks across cognitive levels—from basic recall to higher-order thinking skills such as analysis, synthesis, and evaluation. AfL emphasizes the formative use of assessment data to promote learning, where students understand learning objectives, engage with success criteria, and use feedback to regulate their own progress. In AI-enhanced environments, these frameworks can guide the design of digital assessment tools to target specific cognitive levels and ensure that feedback mechanisms align with pedagogical intentions.

Applying Bloom's taxonomy in AI-enhanced assessment could involve, for example, using adaptive testing algorithms to scaffold students from knowledge recall toward analysis and synthesis tasks. Within the AfL framework, AI-generated analytics could be presented in learner-friendly dashboards, enabling students to self-regulate their progress in real time.

Both types of assessment have been criticized by educational researchers due to various limitations. Traditional summative assessment practices based on standardized testing can lead teachers to focus only on the knowledge and skills measured by these tests, thereby narrowing the scope of the curriculum (Shepard, 2000). This situation promotes the phenomenon known as "teaching to the test," limiting students' opportunities to develop higher-order thinking skills such as deep learning, analysis, and synthesis (Popham, 2001). Such a constrained curriculum overlooks the multidimensional nature of the educational process and undermines the richness of learning experiences (Darling-Hammond & Adamson, 2014).

Excessive emphasis on high-stakes testing has adverse effects particularly on students from disadvantaged socioeconomic backgrounds. These tests reshape school resources and teaching strategies, reinforcing test-focused instruction in low-performing schools and consequently damaging the principle of equity in education (Au, 2007; Reardon, 2018). Research shows that schools in low-income areas often implement stricter disciplinary policies and less flexible teaching methods, which negatively affect students' motivation and academic achievement (Berliner, 2009).

Furthermore, the lack of timely feedback in summative assessments disrupts the learning process. Nicol and Macfarlane-Dick (2006) emphasize that timely and constructive feedback is one of the fundamental components of effective learning.

Delayed feedback prevents students from correcting conceptual misunderstandings and limits the development of self-regulation skills (Hattie & Timperley, 2007).

Standardized tests tend to assess lower-level cognitive processes such as recall and comprehension. However, the 21st-century skills targeted by modern education systems—such as critical thinking, problem-solving, collaboration, and creativity—are often overlooked by these assessments (Rotherham & Willingham, 2009; Pellegrino & Hilton, 2012). This raises questions about the alignment between what is taught and what is assessed, and fuels serious debates regarding the validity of assessment tools.

On the other hand, despite claims of objectivity, some assessment methods raise reliability issues in practice. In assessments based on open-ended questions, significant variation in scoring among teachers is frequently observed, suggesting that student achievement can be influenced by subjective judgments (Brookhart, 2013). Such inconsistencies not only undermine principles of fairness and reliability in education but also negatively affect students' academic self-efficacy (Stiggins, 2005).

In recent years, blended learning models, which have become widespread with the integration of digital technologies into educational settings, have introduced both new opportunities and challenges in assessment processes. In these models, issues such as ensuring academic integrity in online assessments, disparities in technological access, and monitoring student participation are commonly reported (Ocak, 2011; Limniou & Smith, 2010). Moreover, the validity and reliability of performance tasks conducted in online environments can be more complex compared to traditional in-class applications (Gikandi et al., 2011). Teachers' limited competence in effectively and pedagogically utilizing digital assessment tools is another factor negatively affecting the quality of assessment in blended learning environments (Delaney et al., 2010). Therefore, to enhance assessment practices in blended learning, both the strengthening of technological infrastructure and the improvement of teachers' digital pedagogical competencies are necessary.

All these criticisms indicate the need to pedagogically reconsider both traditional and contemporary assessment paradigms in terms of theoretical and practical dimensions. Assessment practices in education should be restructured with a multidimensional, process-oriented, and learning-centered approach that supports student development (Black & Wiliam, 1998). In this context, alternative approaches such as formative assessment and authentic assessment come to the forefront, as they promote active student engagement in the learning process, take individual differences into account, and aim for meaningful learning.

In line with these criticisms, the need for more inclusive, interactive and student-centred assessment approaches in education has increased and the opportunities offered by blended learning environments have come to the fore in meeting this need. Blended learning environments enable more flexible and multidimensional assessment approaches by combining face-to-face and online learning processes. In this context, formative and summative assessments can be used together to provide continuous feedback to students' learning processes (Kalkstein & Rheubert, 2024). Assessment processes can be designed in synchronous or asynchronous formats according to the structure of the learning environment. Synchronous assessment involves live classroom sessions or synchronous online activities in which students participate simultaneously. In these types of assessments, teachers can, for example, perform instant knowledge checks through mobile survey applications and immediately detect and correct misunderstandings (Hrastinski, 2008). Asynchronous assessment provides students with activities that they can access and complete at different times. Homework, reflective blog posts or online discussion forums are examples of this method (Hrastinski, 2008).

In addition to face-to-face assessments in blended practices, online quizzes conducted at regular intervals are effective tools in providing formative information by measuring students' immediate comprehension levels (Gikandi et al., 2011). E-portfolios provide rich evidence of the learning process by bringing together the student's work throughout the semester and provide depth in assessment (Barrett, 2007). While project-based assignments are usually included in summative assessment, constructive feedback given during the project process can also contribute to formative assessment (Darling-Hammond & Adamson, 2014). In addition, online forums support social learning and the development of critical thinking skills by allowing students to discuss content and learn from each other in an asynchronous environment (Garrison & Vaughan, 2008). Thanks to these diversified assessment methods, student achievement can be measured multidimensionally in blended learning environments and learning processes can be supported more effectively. However, ensuring the validity and reliability of formative assessments applied in online environments is an important challenge (Gikandi et al., 2011). Paying attention to these issues in the design of digital assessment applications is critical to ensure a fair and reliable learning experience for students.

In conclusion, formative and summative assessment types should be structured in a complementary manner in blended learning environments and supported by digital technologies. This balance both improves the quality of teaching and encourages students' active participation in the learning process. The integration of assessment approaches with digital tools is further enriched by artificial intelligence-based solutions. In the next section, the general role of artificial intelligence in education (AIEd) and its contributions in the context of blended learning will be discussed

ARTIFICIAL INTELLIGENCE IN EDUCATION: AN OVERVIEW

AI is an interdisciplinary field of research aimed at simulating human cognitive functions such as learning, reasoning, problem-solving, language processing, and decision-making through computer systems (Russell & Norvig, 2016). AI systems operate through algorithms that analyse data from the environment and develop optimal strategies to achieve specific goals. These systems encompass subfields such as machine learning, natural language processing, and deep learning, incorporating both symbolic logic-based models and statistical methods that learn from large datasets (Poole & Mackworth, 2010). AI technologies bring about not only a technical transformation but also a restructuring of cognitive processes at both individual and societal levels (Luckin & Holmes, 2016).

The use AIEd dates to the 1970s, when Intelligent Tutoring Systems (ITS) were developed to provide individualized instruction (Woolf, 2010). These systems aimed to model students' knowledge levels and deliver feedback tailored to their individual needs, thereby enabling a learning experience that surpassed traditional methods of instruction. During the 1980s and 1990s, with the advancement of cognitive sciences, AI-supported systems were redesigned to align more closely with human learning processes. In this period, systems such as Cognitive Tutor and ANDES emerged, offering personalized instructional strategies by analysing students' problem-solving processes (Koedinger et al., 1997).

Since the 2000s, with the widespread integration of digital technologies and the evolution of big data analytics, the role of AIEd has diversified significantly. Today, AI is utilized in learning analytics, adaptive learning systems, automated assessment tools, natural language processing-supported instruction, and learning management systems (LMS) (Holmes et al., 2019). Particularly after 2020, the COVID-19 pandemic necessitated the adoption of remote and digital education, accelerating the use of AI-based systems for student monitoring, performance analysis, and personalization in online learning environments (Zawacki-Richter et al., 2019). This transformative role of AIEd has prompted a redefinition of the teacher's role, increased the flexibility of learning environments, and enabled data-driven educational decision-making, thereby contributing to fundamental pedagogical shifts (Luckin & Holmes, 2016).

AI, as an increasingly important tool in the field of educational technologies, provides the opportunity to personalise, automate and analyse learning and teaching processes. Research reveals that AIEd has four main areas of use in education: student profiling and achievement prediction, assessment and evaluation processes, adaptive learning systems, and intelligent instructional systems (Zawacki-Richter et al., 2019). These titles reflect the main functions of AIEd and in each of them, AI targets different educational problems.

By analysing students' past performance and behaviour data, individual learning profiles can be created. Thus, predictions can be made about the student's future academic success and needs. For example, early warning signals can be generated by predicting which students are at risk of failing the exam through data mining methods (Zawacki-Richter et al., 2019). This proactive approach not only improves individual student achievement but also increases institutional effectiveness by identifying and supporting at-risk students in a timely manner (Gharkan et al., 2025). Indeed, a recent study has shown that machine learning-assisted models can provide high accuracy in predicting student performance (Gharkan et al., 2025). Thanks to such predictive models, schools and universities can increase success rates by intervening early with students who are likely to fail academically.

AI also contributes to measurement and evaluation processes through tools that automatically evaluate exams and assignments. These tools ease the workload of teachers by quickly evaluating student responses and providing detailed feedback (Ouyang et al., 2022). For example, automated grading systems can score many short answers or test responses in seconds without human error. In this way, speed and consistency in assessment processes are achieved, while students can receive immediate feedback without having to wait. AI also supports personalised learning experiences and real-time feedback mechanisms, thus contributing to formative assessment and automatic grading (Ogunsakin, 2024; González-Calatayud et al., 2021). In current research, it is emphasised that AI-based assessment tools increase accuracy and efficiency in assessment processes, provide customised feedback to students, and thus improve the learning experience. With such tools, teachers have the opportunity to adapt their teaching methods according to the needs by instantly monitoring the status of students.

Adaptive learning platforms use AI algorithms to deliver content according to each student's knowledge level and learning speed. These systems can dynamically adapt learning materials and the difficulty level of activities by monitoring the student's instant performance (Ouyang et al., 2022). By analysing students' behaviours, strengths and weaknesses, AI-based adaptive systems optimise learning by providing personalised recommendations and learning paths (Altaleb et al., 2023). For example, an adaptive platform that takes into account learning styles theories can create an experience that suits the student's preferences by presenting the same subject in different formats (videos, interactive simulations, text, etc.). Thus, engagement and academic results can be improved (Waladi et al., 2023).

ITS function as AI-supported virtual tutors or learning assistants. These systems provide instant feedback by interacting one-to-one with the student and adapt the course content according to the student's individual learning style (Crompton & Burke, 2023). ITSs aim to facilitate the whole teaching-learning process by supporting both students and teachers (Yacef, 2002). They usually include components such as personalised exercises, step-by-step hints, learning goal tracking and feedback mechanisms. For example, an AI-supported mathematics teaching software can provide hints in a problem step that the student cannot solve, enabling him/her to correct his/her mistake and understand the subject better. In this respect, ITSs can provide customised support to students even in crowded classes where a real teacher cannot provide individual guidance.

The advantages of AIEd are particularly noteworthy in terms of designing individualised learning experiences, automating teaching processes and supporting data-driven decision-making processes. These technologies increase the effectiveness of learning by providing content that is dynamically adapted to students' learning speed, prior knowledge and individual needs (Pellicelli, 2024). For example, AI-supported systems create individualised learning paths by developing recommendations based on students' previous achievements, errors and learning styles. This not only increases student motivation and interaction but also improves the quality of the learning process (Tapalova & Zhiyenbayeva, 2022).

Furthermore, AIEd has the potential to increase instructional efficiency by reducing teachers' workload. Automated grading systems save teachers considerable time, especially in the assessment of multiple-choice tests, short-answer questions and open-ended written responses, reducing human error and increasing consistency (Deckker & Sumanasekara, 2025). Likewise, through the automation of administrative processes (e.g. student progress tracking, absence analysis, feedback generation, etc.), teachers can spend more time on pedagogical planning and one-to-one student engagement. By analysing large-scale student data, AI-based decision support systems provide guidance to educational administrators and teachers in strategic decision-making processes, enabling the development of a data-driven culture that improves teaching quality and student achievement (Harry, 2023). In addition, the inclusive nature of AIEd contributes to equality of opportunity in education with its potential to produce adaptive solutions for students with learning difficulties, speaking different languages, or having access limitations. For example, voice response systems for visually impaired students or adaptive platforms that can provide explanations in different languages are concrete indicators of this inclusiveness. Over time, AIEd is becoming a powerful tool that supports not only individual learning experiences, but also the holistic fairness and accessibility goals of the education system

On the other hand, despite the opportunities offered by AIEd, there are also some significant disadvantages and risks. Pellicelli (2024) states that AI technologies may lead to excessive technology dependency in educational environments, which may lead to mechanisation of teaching processes and uniformity of learning experiences. In particular, the integration of all components of the learning process into automation systems may limit students' development of high-level skills such as critical thinking, creativity and social skills. The tendency for AI-supported systems to substitute the human interaction between teacher and student may harm the multifaceted nature of education, which includes not only cognitive but also affective and social dimensions (Holmes et al., 2019). Indeed, research shows that students deepen learning not only through digital feedback but also through meaningful pedagogical relationships and social interaction (Selwyn, 2019).

However, ethical issues are also seriously raised in AIEd applications. Biases in the datasets on which AI systems are trained can cause algorithmic injustices, which can lead to systematic errors to the detriment of certain socioeconomic, ethnic or gender groups (Binns, 2018). The lack of transparency, especially in automated decision-making processes, weakens accountability in education and can create situations that may violate students' rights. In addition, the large-scale processing of student data by AI systems poses significant risks to data privacy and security. Despite legal regulations such as GDPR, it is often not clear enough how personal data are collected, processed and shared (Williamson & Eynon, 2020). In this context, teachers need professional development support on digital ethics, data literacy and algorithmic awareness.

In conclusion, AIEd offers important opportunities for developing individualised learning experiences in education, increasing instructional efficiency and improving assessment and evaluation processes. However, these technologies need to be carefully evaluated in terms of pedagogical, ethical and social aspects and designed with a human-centred and value-oriented approach. Otherwise, the technological opportunities offered by AIEd may lead to risky results that may contradict basic principles such as justice, inclusion and integrity in education. Therefore, the integration of AI into educational environments should be carried out not only with technical competence, but also with ethical responsibility and pedagogical sensitivity

INTEGRATION OF ARTIFICIAL INTELLIGENCE INTO ASSESSMENT PROCESSES

With the digital transformation in the field of education in recent years, AI technologies have started to be integrated more and more into learning processes. This integration radically changes not only teaching methods but also assessment and evaluation approaches. While traditional assessment methods are mostly based on fixed-structure tests, manual scoring and delayed feedback processes, AI has the potential to make these processes more dynamic, individualised and data-driven (Saputra et al., 2024). Thanks to advanced algorithms, students' knowledge and skills can be measured more accurately, teachers are provided with instant analysis and feedback, and assessment processes become both instructive and guiding (Owan et al., 2023). It has been revealed that AI-supported assessment tools can take part in almost every stage of the measurement process - from determining the purpose and scope of the exam to item writing, from exam administration to scoring and reporting the results. In this section, various dimensions of the integration of AI into assessment processes will be discussed; the possibilities it offers and the transformation it can create will be analysed in a multidimensional way

Adaptive testing systems are dynamic testing environments that use machine learning algorithms to select the difficulty level of the next question after each student response based on the student's immediate proficiency. In such a computerised adaptive test, a high achieving student is presented with progressively more difficult questions, while a struggling student is presented with more basic questions on the subject. Thus, a measurement appropriate to the level of each student is ensured. In this way, instead of a fixed test, the knowledge and skill level of the student can be determined much more accurately through a personalised test. Some advanced systems can even consider additional parameters such as time spent in front of the screen, external resources used, and previous exam grades while evaluating the student's knowledge level (Lodhavia et al., 2020). Adaptive tests stand out as one of the most concrete examples of student-centred assessment and evaluation in the digital age. Especially in high-scale exams, it is possible to get more reliable results with fewer questions thanks to adaptive test applications.

AI can also automate the scoring of responses, which is one of the most laborious stages of the assessment process. Especially the assessment of open-ended questions, essays or project assignments is traditionally time-consuming for teachers and can be open to subjective judgements. This is where AI-based automatic grading systems come into play. Thanks to advanced natural language processing (NLP) techniques, an algorithm can make sense of a student's written response and score it consistently and in a short time according to predefined criteria (Yuvasri et al., 2025). For example, AI can evaluate an essay written in English in terms of grammar, coherence and vocabulary in seconds and produce an objective score. Similarly, AI models trained for short-answer questions can instantly determine accuracy by identifying key concepts and phrases in student responses. In recent studies, it has been emphasised that modern NLP-based scorers can evaluate written answers very quickly and consistently, thus providing significant convenience in cases where manual scoring is insufficient (Labadze et al., 2023). As a matter of fact, a review study on the automatic evaluation of text-based responses in higher education reveals that AI-supported systems can provide results with consistency and validity comparable to human raters in various courses (Gao et al., 2023). These developments offer significant advantages for both students and teachers by significantly reducing feedback time, especially in large-scale exams.

Another dimension of AI integration into assessment is the predictive analysis of learning data. Thanks to data mining and machine learning techniques, it has become possible to make predictions about students' future success by analysing their past exam performances and assessment results (Harsha et al., 2024). For example, when quizzes and assignments throughout the year are analysed in detail, it can be predicted which students may be at risk in the final exam with the help of AI. Such profiling and achievement prediction applications provide early warning signals to teachers and guidance units and enable timely preventive interventions. Much of the research in the field of AIEd focuses on modelling students' achievement patterns over large data sets and predicting critical outcomes (Zawacki-Richter et al., 2019). These predictive models support data-driven decision-making processes of educational institutions, enabling customised interventions

AI also plays important roles in the fields of exam security and academic integrity. Especially in online or remote exams, online proctoring systems have become increasingly widespread. These systems can detect unusual situations (e.g. cheating attempts) by monitoring the student's behaviour through the computer camera and microphone during the exam (Leong, 2025). For example, potential cheating attempts such as constantly avoiding eye contact with the screen, talking in a whisper, or using a non-exam application during the exam can be automatically detected and flagged thanks to behavioural patterns defined by machine learning algorithms. Similarly, advanced algorithms analyse whether the text answers given by students in exams contain plagiarism (Paul et al., 2024). These tools can detect possible plagiarism cases by comparing student answers with comprehensive databases. Although there is a risk that AI-based exam proctoring systems may give false alarms or misinterpret innocent behaviour, they have a high potential to increase reliability and fairness when used with appropriate calibration and human proctors (Labadze et al., 2023). These systems, which reduce the need for human proctors in large-scale online exams, are considered as an important innovation in ensuring exam security.

In the context of classroom assessment, AI offers powerful analytics tools that provide instant feedback to teachers. For example, learning analytics panels that are activated immediately after an exam can instantly identify students' common mistakes and common misconceptions in exam questions (Lin et al., 2023). In this way, teachers can determine which topics need to be revisited in the next lesson planning based on the data. Similarly, AI systems that gather and analyse the results of quizzes and activities throughout the semester can identify which students are falling behind the learning objectives. Thus, teachers can recognise students who need intervention at an early stage and provide them with additional support. Such learning analytics applications make it possible to make more informed and accurate educational decisions by revealing patterns that teachers may not recognise with traditional methods.

While the speed, scalability and personalisation opportunities provided by AI-supported assessment tools offer significant innovations in pedagogical processes, it should be noted that these advantages also bring some critical risks. The constructive alignment (Biggs & Tang, 2011) approach emphasises that assessment methods should be consistent with learning goals and instructional activities; however, technologies such as automated grading and instant feedback can create a tendency to focus on easily measurable outcomes rather than the higher-level cognitive skills targeted in instructional design. Similarly, within the framework of assessment for learning (Wiliam, 2011), formative feedback should support student self-regulation and interaction with the teacher, whereas excessive automation risks undermining the human interaction in the teacher-student relationship and mechanising the learning process. Moreover, ethical and institutional issues, such as data privacy violations, algorithmic biases and reduced teacher initiative, may overshadow the pedagogical value of these tools. Therefore, every technological achievement should be evaluated in the light of the pedagogical and ethical limitations that accompany it.

In conclusion, the integration of AI into assessment processes creates a major transformation by making assessment systems more personalised, faster and data driven. Algorithms can pose level-appropriate questions to students, score answers instantly and provide feedback, and process vast amounts of assessment data to provide meaningful insights. The goal of this integration is to improve assessment and evaluation practices in terms of effectiveness, efficiency and feedback. In an AI-supported assessment environment, teachers can monitor assessment data in real time and take action according to needs, while students can improve their learning by receiving continuous feedback. Thus, assessment becomes a proactive and continuously developing component of the learning process rather than just a measurement tool.

Table 1. Comparison of traditional and AI-supported assessment

Dimension	Traditional Assessment	AI-Supported Assessment
Pedagogical Approach	Teacher-centered, Summative focus	Learner-centered, Formative integration
Feedback	Periodic, Often delayed	Immediate, Adaptive
Scalability	Limited by teacher capacity	High scalability with automation
Ethical Considerations	Primarily fairness and transparency	Fairness, transparency, data privacy, algorithmic bias
Resource Requirements	Physical space, printed materials	Digital infrastructure, technical support
Teacher Role	Primary evaluator	Facilitator and human overseer

VALIDITY, RELIABILITY, AND CHALLENGES IN AI-SUPPORTED ASSESSMENT

While AI-supported assessment tools offer efficiency and scalability, their validity and reliability remain critical concerns. Construct validity must be ensured by aligning AI-generated tasks with intended learning outcomes, while reliability requires consistency in scoring across contexts and populations (Bennett & Zhang, 2015). Automated scoring systems may demonstrate high inter-rater reliability compared to human raters, yet they can still be vulnerable to biases embedded in training datasets (Gao et al., 2023). Additionally, challenges such as lack of transparency in algorithmic decision-making, difficulties in capturing higher-order thinking skills, and dependency on digital infrastructure may limit widespread adoption. Addressing these issues requires ongoing calibration, human oversight, and ethical governance frameworks.

Three main challenges stand out in the implementation of AI-based assessment systems. First, bias in algorithms can lead to systematic disadvantage of certain groups of students, especially if educational data underrepresent certain socioeconomic or cultural groups (Binns, 2018; Mehrabi et al., 2021). Second, over-reliance on AI can lead to a weakening of teachers' assessment literacy and pedagogical initiative (Selwyn, 2019) and mechanisation of the learning process. Third, interdisciplinary differences are ignored; while automated grading and structured tests can be applied more effectively in STEM fields, interpretive, context-sensitive assessments in the humanities may be supported by AI in a more limited way (Holmes et al., 2019). Therefore, AI-supported assessment strategies should be designed in accordance with both the nature of the discipline and pedagogical goals and should be supported by a human-centred moderation mechanism.

Pilot studies conducted in different educational contexts in recent years provide valuable data on how AI-supported assessment practices work in practice. For example, in a higher education project in Spain, an AI-based written assignment assessment system improved students' self-regulation skills, but teachers reported that automated feedback was limited due to a lack of contextual interpretation (González-Calatayud et al., 2021). In an adaptive learning platform trial in Australia, individual student progress data was analysed in real-time to provide teachers with targeted intervention opportunities, which increased student achievement; however, teachers' pedagogical initiative was partially reduced (Maity & Deroy, 2024). In another study conducted in STEM fields, automated grading systems provided high accuracy in evaluating short answers (Gobrecht et al., 2024), whereas they did not achieve similar success in tasks requiring interpretation and context in the humanities (Holmes et al., 2019). These findings suggest that the effects of AI-based assessment applications differ according to educational level, discipline type, and learning environment and should be carefully adapted in each context.

AI-supported assessment practices exhibit distinct challenges and opportunities across educational levels. In K–12 settings, issues such as equitable access to technology, the need for age-appropriate feedback, and safeguarding student data are paramount (Luckin, 2017). In higher education, academic integrity, disciplinary specificity, and the integration of AI into complex assessment rubrics take precedence (Zawacki-Richter et al., 2019). Addressing these differences requires context-sensitive policy design and professional development tailored to the unique needs of each educational stage.

For example, in a study conducted at a large state university in Kazakhstan, AI-powered peer assessment tools significantly reduced grading time while improving the quality of student feedback (Zheldibayeva, 2025). However, qualitative interviews revealed that some students perceived automated feedback as impersonal, highlighting the need for hybrid models in which AI plays a complementary role rather than replacing instructor interaction.

IDENTIFICATION OF ARTIFICIAL INTELLIGENCE APPLICATIONS IN FORMATIVE AND SUMMATIVE ASSESSMENTS

AI-supported assessment refers to the implementation of AI techniques within both formative and summative evaluation processes in educational contexts. This innovative approach holds the potential to offer a more dynamic, data-driven, and personalized assessment experience compared to traditional evaluation methods. AI systems can analyze student performance in real time, identifying learning difficulties as they arise, and providing individualized feedback tailored to the learner's specific needs. In this way, students' learning processes can be monitored and measured not only at the end of instruction but throughout the entire learning cycle.

Particularly in increasingly digital and blended learning environments, the speed, scope, consistency, and high analytical capacity afforded by AI contribute significantly to the enhancement of assessment practices. For instance, natural language processing (NLP) can be employed to evaluate students' written responses, while machine learning algorithms can generate predictive models based on past performance data. Furthermore, automated scoring systems, conceptual error analysis, and behavioral learning analytics help reduce the workload of educators while simultaneously offering deeper insights into learners' experiences. AI-supported assessment systems have the potential to increase the validity and reliability of measurement tools in education, thereby reshaping the quality and function of assessment from both pedagogical and technological perspectives.

AI-supported formative assessment includes technological applications that are carried out while the student's learning process is in progress and are intended to guide learning by providing instant feedback. These systems continuously collect data based on the student's knowledge level, learning speed and error patterns and shape the teaching process in real time by analysing these data. Intelligent Tutoring Systems (ITS) provide questions and directions that are appropriate to the individual learning needs of the student and reinforce learning with targeted feedback by instantly evaluating the responses (Lin et al., 2023). Such systems enable students to realise their mistakes in the learning process without delay and increase instructional effectiveness by filling learning gaps in a timely manner. In addition, these tools encourage active learning with interventions that re-explain certain concepts or offer alternative solutions based on the student's responses. These systems not only provide true-false feedback but also support metacognitive awareness by providing quality information about the student's thinking process.

In addition, the integration of generative AI technologies (e.g. GPT-based models) into formative assessment processes has added a new dimension to assessment practices. These models can provide personalised explanations and hints by detecting deficiencies or conceptual errors in students' open-ended responses with natural language processing techniques (Prompiengchai et al., 2025). In addition, systems that can generate automatic exercises and adapted questions according to the student's previous answers and progress level both facilitate the repetition process and increase the depth of learning. Open-ended questions, which traditionally require time and expertise to assess, can now be scored with high accuracy with AI, which improves teachers' time management and increases efficiency in education (Michael et al., 2014). Moreover, AI-supported analysis tools help teachers to restructure their teaching strategies by revealing common conceptual errors, learning tendencies and achievement patterns not only for individual students but also at the whole class level. Thus, assessment becomes an intrinsic and guiding component of the learning process, rather than just a measurement purpose. These technological solutions contribute holistically to the learning ecosystem by increasing the sustainability, inclusiveness and effectiveness of assessment processes while reducing the workload of teachers.

AI-supported summative assessment refers to the systematic use of AI technologies in exams, performance tasks and project-based assessment practices carried out at the end of the teaching process. In this type of assessment, AI aims to make the measurement of student performance faster, consistent and objective. In particular, automatic grading systems can perform high accuracy scoring without the need for human intervention by using machine learning (ML) and natural language processing

(NLP) techniques in assessment types such as short answer, open-ended text and written expression. Hybrid models developed in recent years can analyse not only keywords but also the holistic structure and content quality of the response, thus measuring the student's conceptual understanding more accurately (Gobrecht et al., 2024). In addition, the impartiality and high consistency of AI in the assessment processes contribute to the prevention of human-induced biases and inconsistent scoring, especially in large-scale exam applications. With these features, AI offers an important potential in terms of fairness, transparency and standardisation in assessment practices.

In addition, AI plays critical roles not only in grading but also in areas such as exam security and data analytics in summative assessment processes. AI proctoring systems used in online exam applications can detect academic integrity violations such as cheating or external interference during the exam with techniques such as face recognition, voice analysis, eye movement tracking, behavioural biometric analysis and anomaly detection. Such systems are important in terms of providing a reliable and valid assessment infrastructure, especially in distance education environments (Gao et al., 2023). On the other hand, AI-supported systems also contribute to test development processes, enabling dynamic updating of question banks, assigning questions at student-specific difficulty levels, and aligning test coverage with instructional objectives. In this way, teachers can perform processes such as question selection, item analyses, scoring and result reporting with less effort and higher accuracy. With comprehensive data analysis, achievement profiles can be created at the class level, common conceptual deficiencies can be identified and instructional interventions can be planned. As a result, AI-supported summative assessment offers a holistic and innovative assessment approach that aims to improve not only individual student achievement but also overall teaching quality.

As a result, AI-supported assessment applications offer the opportunity to monitor the learning process instantly and continuously in the formative context and to measure the final learning level of the student in a more objective, fast and reliable way in the summative context. These systems provide advantages such as speed, scope, consistency and scalability that cannot be achieved with traditional methods. Therefore, AI provides not only a technical support to assessment processes, but also a pedagogical contribution, both improving the quality of learning and reducing the workload of teachers. For education systems, this integration is the key to transition to a more effective and personalised assessment approach.

CONCLUSION

Organisations such as OECD (2021), UNESCO (2023) and ISTE (2022) emphasise that AI-supported assessment processes should be designed not only in terms of technical efficiency, but also in terms of pedagogical integrity, equity and ethical principles. OECD reports recommend that assessment tools measure students' cognitive, social and emotional skills in a holistic manner; UNESCO emphasises the principles of algorithmic transparency, data protection and inclusiveness. ISTE standards encourage the implementation of strategies to increase teachers' digital assessment literacy and students' data literacy. These frameworks reveal that AI-based assessment systems should be adaptable in terms of reliability, validity and ethics across different age groups and learning environments.

From a policy perspective, AI-supported assessment must align with national and international legal frameworks such as the EU General Data Protection Regulation (GDPR) and Ad Hoc Expert Group (AHEG)'s Recommendation on the Ethics of Artificial Intelligence (2020). Institutional policies should establish clear protocols for data governance, algorithmic transparency, and accountability mechanisms, ensuring that technological innovations uphold educational equity and integrity.

The 21st century digital transformation process has profoundly affected assessment approaches in education. Digital tools that go beyond traditional assessment methods now have the capacity to instantly monitor and guide not only the student's knowledge level but also the learning processes. This transformation makes it necessary to reinterpret the distinction between formative and summative assessment and integrate it with technological tools. AI, as one of the most powerful tools in this context, brings significant advantages such as speed, scalability and personalisation to assessment processes. Assessment is no longer a process that only measures past success; it has turned into a continuous and data-based component that guides learning.

AI-supported assessment systems are transforming not only in terms of automation and personalised feedback, but also the nature of instructional design and the nature of student learning outcomes. The OECD (2021) and UNESCO (2023) reports recommend more explicit definition of learning objectives, strengthening competency-based criteria and supporting student autonomy in formative and summative assessment applications of these technologies, while at the same time drawing attention to risks such as algorithmic bias, data privacy violations and "black box" decision processes. ISTE (2022) standards suggest that AI-based assessment tools should be designed in line with pedagogical goals, improving teachers' assessment literacy and increasing students' data literacy. Indeed, recent pilot studies (e.g. González-Calatayud et al., 2021; Maity & Deroy, 2024) show that the use of AI in adaptive learning ecosystems can increase students' self-regulation skills and motivation to learn. However, it is critical to develop human-centred and transparent hybrid models against the risk of weakening teachers' roles in the feedback process and skill loss.

The integration of AI with established educational assessment theories reinforces its pedagogical value. By aligning AI-driven feedback systems with the principles articulated by Black and Wiliam (1998) and the structure of Bloom's taxonomy, educators can ensure that technological innovations support—not replace—sound assessment practices. Furthermore, embedding AI tools within the AfL framework ensures that assessment data is used not only for measurement but also for advancing student learning through active engagement, self-regulation, and reflective practice.

Although AI-supported assessment tools theoretically offer significant advantages in terms of objectivity, speed and personalisation, various practical limitations are encountered in real-world applications. For example, infrastructure inadequacies, teachers' lack of digital assessment literacy, and technical standard incompatibilities between different institutions can limit the effective use of systems (Holmes et al., 2019). In a higher education pilot study conducted in Spain (González-Calatayud et al., 2021), although the AI-based written assignment assessment system improved students' self-regulation skills, teachers reported that the automated feedback did not adequately reflect contextual nuances. Similarly, in Maity and Deroy's (2024) study, adaptive learning platforms increased student achievement but partially limited teachers' pedagogical initiative. These findings suggest that over-reliance on automated systems can reduce the quality of teacher-student interaction and undermine the human aspect of the assessment process.

In digital learning environments, every student interaction turns into a data point. This abundance of data has made it possible to design assessment processes not only result-oriented but also process-oriented. Thanks to big data analytics, criteria such as the difficulty and discrimination level of exam questions, students' conceptual errors and the effectiveness of the teaching strategies applied can be continuously monitored. The instant feedback mechanisms offered by digital platforms support the student's learning process and enable teachers to monitor classroom dynamics in real time. Thus, assessment becomes an integral part of teaching rather than an independent activity.

AI-supported assessment systems offer significant advantages over traditional methods in terms of automation, personalisation, speed and scalability. The automatic generation of questions, instant scoring of answers and the provision of content that can be adapted according to student performance make assessment processes more effective and fairer. At the same time, AI systems can generate individualised feedback by analysing students' past performances and provide data-based insights to teachers, allowing them to restructure instruction. These multi-layered possibilities make assessment more meaningful and functional for both students and teachers.

Although AI-supported assessment systems have great potential, they also bring some ethical and security risks. Algorithmic biases can undermine the principle of fairness, and misclassifications can negatively affect students' academic development. In addition, it is of great importance to protect privacy in the processes of collecting, processing and storing student data. Basic measurement principles such as validity and reliability also apply to AI systems; therefore, the outputs obtained from these systems should be regularly monitored and verified by educators. At this point, it is suggested that institutions should establish ethical audit mechanisms to ensure transparency and accountability of AI applications (Elliott & Soifer, 2022). When using AI-based assessment tools, it is important to provide explanations about how the systems make decisions and to be open to human intervention when necessary in order to prevent possible erroneous decisions.

In the future, AI-supported formative assessment applications are expected to become more interactive, personalised and pedagogically integrated. In particular, more advanced versions of real-time learning analytics, adaptive content delivery and automated feedback systems will be able to instantly analyse students' individual learning paths and provide guidance accordingly (Maity & Deroy, 2024). Digital assessment models that overlap with learning objectives and include pedagogically valid measurement strategies should be supported not only by technological infrastructure but also by pedagogical understanding. At this point, an interdisciplinary approach should be adopted and more holistic assessment ecosystems should be created by bringing together learning sciences, AI engineering and instructional technologies (Viberg & Grönlund, 2024). In this way, student data can not only be monitored, but the system can also generate meaningful insights for intervention and guidance.

At the policy level, professional development of teachers should be considered as a priority area to effectively integrate AI-supported assessment tools into the teaching process. Teachers should be provided with access to continuing education programmes to improve not only their technical competencies but also their assessment literacy and digital pedagogical skills (Kimmons & Hall, 2020). Indeed, the successful execution of formative assessment processes in blended learning environments is directly related to teachers' self-efficacy in both pedagogical and technological fields (Chan, 2021). In addition, students' right to access their own learning data and their ability to analyse these data should be strengthened. Such data literacy practices increase learner autonomy and facilitate student ownership of their own learning process (Gašević et al., 2015). In other words, not only the teacher but also the student should take an active role in these new digital assessment paradigms; the main goal should be to raise individuals who can interpret learning data and shape their learning strategies according to these data.

In the context of summative assessment, it is predicted that artificial intelligence-supported automatic grading systems, digital proctoring tools used in online exams, and big data analytics-based validity-fidelity checks will become more sophisticated (Yang & Li, 2023). Thanks to the developing natural language processing (NLP) and machine learning techniques, the evaluation of open-ended questions can be carried out more holistically, covering not only content relevance but also conceptual depth, language use and reasoning ability (Persing et al., 2019). Likewise, in terms of exam security, AI-based surveillance systems with advanced features such as behavioural analysis, face recognition, voice command detection and environmental noise analysis offer important opportunities to ensure the integrity of the exam environment. With the widespread use of these systems, the workload of teachers and institutions is reduced, assessment processes are accelerated, and scoring inconsistencies caused by human error are minimised (Nguyen, et al. 2022). In addition, the ability to provide individually tailored test content based on learners' previous performance history supports fairer and more accurate results in measurement processes (Chen et al., 2021).

However, the widespread use of artificial intelligence-supported summative assessment practices also raises many ethical, legal and pedagogical issues. Issues such as algorithmic bias, data privacy, lack of transparency, and the exclusion of human control in decision-making processes pose serious risks (Mehrabi et al., 2021). Transparent monitoring of processes such as the criteria according to which automated decision-making systems assign grades and the reasons for which students are considered unsuccessful is essential for assessment reliability (Burrell, 2016). In this context, it becomes imperative for policymakers to create a comprehensive legislation including ethical principles, accountability mechanisms and legal regulations for AI-supported assessment systems (Jobin et al., 2019). In addition, all stakeholders in the education system, teachers, students, administrators, and technology developers should come together to develop common ethical standards and multi-stakeholder governance models for the fair and effective implementation of these systems (Floridi et al., 2018). Only in this way, the educational benefit can be maximised by managing the contribution of AI to summative assessment processes in balance with potential risks.

In conclusion, artificial intelligence-supported formative and summative assessment approaches reshape the understanding of assessment in education, especially in higher education. This transformation brings not only technological but also pedagogical and ethical change. Making assessment more effective, fair and data-based both supports students' learning process and strengthens teachers' decision-making processes. However, in order to use these opportunities in a sustainable way, educators need to approach AI technologies with a critical consciousness and structure these systems in line with pedagogical goals. Ultimately, AI forms the basis of a more equitable, flexible and student-centred educational ecosystem of the future by making assessment an integral and dynamic component of learning.

REFERENCES

Abu Bakar, R. (2021). Blended learning – An innovative process. *International Journal of Advanced Research in Education and Society*, *3*(4), 52–55. https://myjms.mohe.gov.my/index.php/ijares/article/view/16661

Ad Hoc Expert Group (AHEG). (2020). first draft of the Recommendation on the Ethics of Artificial Intelligence. https://unesdoc.unesco.org/ark:/48223/pf0000373434

Altaleb, H., Mouti, S., & Beegom, S. (2023, October). Enhancing college education: An AI-driven adaptive learning platform (ALP) for customized course experiences. In *2023 9th International Conference on Optimization and Applications (ICOA)* (pp. 1–5). IEEE.

Anderson, L. W., & Krathwohl, D. R. (2001). *A taxonomy for learning, teaching, and assessing: A revision of Bloom's taxonomy of educational objectives*. Longman.

Au, W. (2007). High-stakes testing and curricular control: A qualitative metasynthesis. *Educational Researcher*, *36*(5), 258–267. DOI: 10.3102/0013189X07306523

Bandara, K. M. N. T., & Jayaweera, B. P. A. (2024). Commentary on the applications of blended learning in the teaching and learning process–A review. *Journal of Research in Education and Pedagogy*, *1*(2), 83–97. DOI: 10.70232/jrep.v1i2.10

Barrett, H. (2007). Researching electronic portfolios and learner engagement. *The REFLECT Initiative. (ERIC Document Reproduction Service No. ED496586).*

Bennett, R. E. (2011). Formative assessment: A critical review. *Assessment in Education: Principles, Policy & Practice*, *18*(1), 5–25. DOI: 10.1080/0969594X.2010.513678

Bennett, R. E., & Zhang, M. (2015). Validity and automated scoring. In *Technology and testing* (pp. 142–173). Routledge. DOI: 10.4324/9781315871493-8

Berliner, D. C. (2009). Poverty and potential: Out-of-school factors and school success.

Bernard, R. M., Borokhovski, E., Schmid, R. F., Tamim, R. M., & Abrami, P. C. (2014). A meta-analysis of blended learning and technology use in higher education: From the general to the applied. *Journal of Computing in Higher Education*, *26*(1), 87–122. DOI: 10.1007/s12528-013-9077-3

Biggs, J., & Tang, C. (2011). *Teaching for quality learning at university* (4th ed.). McGraw-Hill Education.

Binns, R. (2018, January). Fairness in machine learning: Lessons from political philosophy. In *Conference on fairness, accountability and transparency* (pp. 149-159). PMLR.

Black, P., & Wiliam, D. (1998). Assessment and classroom learning. *Assessment in Education: Principles, Policy & Practice*, *5*(1), 7–74. DOI: 10.1080/0969595980050102

Bloom, B. S., Engelhart, M. D., Furst, E. J., Hill, W. H., & Krathwohl, D. R. (1956). *Taxonomy of educational objectives: The classification of educational goals. Handbook I: Cognitive domain*. Longmans, Green.

Brookhart, S. M. (2007). Expanding views about formative classroom assessment: A review of the literature. In McMillan, J. H. (Ed.), *Formative classroom assessment* (pp. 43–62). Teachers College Press.

Brookhart, S. M. (2013). *How to create and use rubrics for formative assessment and grading*. ASCD.

Burrell, J. (2016). How the machine 'thinks': Understanding opacity in machine learning algorithms. *Big Data & Society*, *3*(1), 1–12. DOI: 10.1177/2053951715622512

Chan, T. C. (2021). Formative assessment in blended learning environments. *Educational Technology Review*, *33*(2), 45–58.

Chen, L., Xie, H., & Heffernan, N. T. (2021). Personalized Adaptive Testing Based on Student Performance Using Machine Learning Techniques. *Computers & Education*, *164*, 104122. DOI: 10.1016/j.compedu.2020.104122

Chowdhury, R., Shrestha, A., & Nguyen, T. (2021). Assessment ethics in digital education: Lessons from COVID-19. *International Journal on E-Learning*, *20*(3), 123–140.

Christine, R. (2017). *European framework for the digital competence of educators*. Joint Research Centre.

Crompton, H., & Burke, D. (2023). Artificial intelligence in higher education: The state of the field. *International Journal of Educational Technology in Higher Education*, *20*(22), 22. Advance online publication. DOI: 10.1186/s41239-023-00392-8

Darling-Hammond, L., & Adamson, F. (2014). *Beyond the bubble test: How performance assessments support 21st century learning*. John Wiley & Sons.

Deckker, D., & Sumanasekara, S. (2025). The role of artificial intelligence in education: Transforming learning and teaching. *EPRA International Journal of Research and Development*, *10*(3), 5–18. DOI: 10.36713/epra20429

Delaney, D., McManus, L., & Ng, C. (2010). A blended learning approach to teaching first year accounting. In *ICERI2010 Proceedings* (pp. 4019-4026). IATED.

Elliott, D., & Soifer, E. (2022). AI technologies, privacy, and security. *Frontiers in Artificial Intelligence*, *5*, 826737. DOI: 10.3389/frai.2022.826737 PMID: 35493613

Farahsa, S., & Tabrizi, J. S. (2015). How evaluation and audit is implemented in educational organizations? A systematic review. *Research and Development in Medical Education*, *4*(1), 3–16. DOI: 10.15171/rdme.2015.002

Floridi, L., Cowls, J., Beltrametti, M., Chatila, R., Chazerand, P., Dignum, V., Luetge, C., Madelin, R., Pagallo, U., Rossi, F., Schafer, B., Valcke, P., & Vayena, E. (2018). AI4People—An ethical framework for a good AI society: Opportunities, risks, principles, and recommendations. *Minds and Machines*, *28*(4), 689–707. DOI: 10.1007/s11023-018-9482-5 PMID: 30930541

Gao, R., Merzdorf, H. E., Anwar, S., Hipwell, M. C., & Srinivasa, A. (2023). Automatic assessment of text-based responses in post-secondary education: A systematic review. *Computers and Education: Artificial Intelligence*, *6*, 100206. DOI: 10.1016/j.caeai.2024.100206

Garrison, D. R., & Vaughan, N. D. (2008). *Blended learning in higher education: Framework, principles, and guidelines*. John Wiley & Sons.

Gašević, D., Dawson, S., & Siemens, G. (2015). Let's not forget: Learning analytics are about learning. *TechTrends*, *59*(1), 64–71. DOI: 10.1007/s11528-014-0822-x

Gharkan, H. K., Radif, M. J., & Alsaeedi, A. H. (2025). Analysis of AI-empowered predictive models for predicting student performance in higher education. *Journal of Al-Qadisiyah for Computer Science and Mathematics*, *17*(1), 103–121. DOI: 10.29304/jqcsm.2025.17.11967

Gikandi, J. W., Morrow, D., & Davis, N. E. (2011). Online formative assessment in higher education: A review of the literature. *Computers & Education*, *57*(4), 2333–2351. DOI: 10.1016/j.compedu.2011.06.004

Gobrecht, A., Tuma, F., Möller, M., Zöller, T., Zakhvatkin, M., Wuttig, A., Sommerfeldt, H., & Schütt, S. (2024). Beyond human subjectivity and error: A novel AI grading system Preprint. *arXiv*. https://doi.org//arXiv.2405.04323DOI: 10.48550

González-Calatayud, V., Prendes-Espinosa, P., & Roig-Vila, R. (2021). Artificial intelligence for student assessment: A systematic review. *Applied Sciences (Basel, Switzerland)*, *11*(12), 5467. DOI: 10.3390/app11125467

Graham, C. R. (2013). Emerging practice and research in blended learning. In *Handbook of distance education* (pp. 333–350). Routledge. DOI: 10.4324/9780203803738.ch21

Halverson, L. R., Graham, C. R., Spring, K. J., Drysdale, J. S., & Henrie, C. R. (2014). A thematic analysis of the most highly cited scholarship in the first decade of blended learning research. *The Internet and Higher Education, 20*, 20–34. DOI: 10.1016/j.iheduc.2013.09.004

Harry, A. (2023). Role of AI in education. [INJURITY]. *Interdisciplinary Journal & Humanity, 2*(3), 1–10.

Harsha, S., Chandrappa, S. R., Priyanga, P., & Bhavanishankar, K. (2024, December). Strategic teaching enhancement through predictive analysis for individuals (STEP.AI). In *2024 IEEE International Conference on Teaching, Assessment and Learning for Engineering (TALE)* (pp. 1–6). IEEE.

Hattie, J., & Timperley, H. (2007). The power of feedback. *Review of Educational Research, 77*(1), 81–112. DOI: 10.3102/003465430298487

Hilton, M. L., & Pellegrino, J. W. (Eds.). (2012). *Education for life and work: Developing transferable knowledge and skills in the 21st century*. National Academies Press.

Hodges, C., Moore, S., Lockee, B., Trust, T., & Bond, A. (2020). The difference between emergency remote teaching and online learning. *EDUCAUSE Review, 27*(1), 1–9.

Holmes, W., Bialik, M., & Fadel, C. (2019). *Artificial intelligence in education promises and implications for teaching and learning*. Center for Curriculum Redesign.

Hopfenbeck, T. N., Decristan, J., & Stoeckigt, G. (2023). Artificial intelligence and feedback: New tools for old problems. *Assessment in Education: Principles, Policy & Practice, 30*(1), 10–28.

Hrastinski, S. (2008). Asynchronous and synchronous e-learning. *EDUCAUSE Quarterly, 31*(4), 51–55.

Ifenthaler, D., & Yau, J. Y. K. (2020). Utilising learning analytics to support study success in higher education: A systematic review. *Educational Technology Research and Development, 68*(4), 1961–1990. DOI: 10.1007/s11423-020-09788-z

ISTE. (2022). *ISTE Standards for educators*. International Society for Technology in Education. https://www.iste.org/standards/for-educators

Jobin, A., Ienca, M., & Vayena, E. (2019). The global landscape of AI ethics guidelines. *Nature Machine Intelligence, 1*(9), 389–399. DOI: 10.1038/s42256-019-0088-2

Kalkstein, D. A., & Rheubert, R. A. (2024). Implementing weekly mastery quizzes in a blended learning environment. *Journal of Educational Technology, 45*(2), 145–162.

Kimmons, R., & Hall, C. (2020). Professional learning and development for educational technology integration: The role of teacher learning communities. *Journal of Research on Technology in Education, 52*(3), 309–326. DOI: 10.1080/15391523.2020.1729387

Koç, M., Liu, X., & Wachira, P. (2015). Assessment strategies in online and blended learning. *Journal of Digital Learning, 29*(4), 201–216.

Koedinger, K. R., Anderson, J. R., Hadley, W. H., & Mark, M. A. (1997). Intelligent tutoring goes to school in the big city. *International Journal of Artificial Intelligence in Education, 8*, 30–43.

Leong, W. Y. (2025, March). Enhancing academic integrity in e-exams through AI-powered proctoring. In *2025 IEEE International Conference on Educational Technology (ICET)* (pp. 10–15). IEEE.

Limniou, M., & Smith, M. (2010). Teachers' and students' perspectives on teaching and learning through virtual learning environments. *European Journal of Engineering Education, 35*(6), 645–653. DOI: 10.1080/03043797.2010.505279

Lin, C.-C., Huang, A. Y. Q., & Lu, O. H. T. (2023). Artificial intelligence in intelligent tutoring systems toward sustainable education: A systematic review. *Smart Learning Environments, 10*(1), 41. DOI: 10.1186/s40561-023-00260-y

Lodhavia, J., Jain, V., Gupta, A., Prabhu, H., & Pandit, A. (2020, July). User-profiling based e-learning system using question adaptation. In *2020 Second International Conference on Inventive Research in Computing Applications (ICIRCA)* (pp. 723–728). IEEE. DOI: 10.1109/ICIRCA48905.2020.9183068

Luckin, R. (2017). Towards artificial intelligence-based assessment systems. *Nature Human Behaviour, 1*(3), 0028.

Luckin, R., & Holmes, W. (2016). Intelligence unleashed: An argument for AI in education.

Maity, S., & Deroy, A. (2024). Human-Centric eXplainable AI in Education. *arXiv preprint arXiv:2410.19822*. DOI: 10.35542/osf.io/k5u9b

Margulieux, L. E., McCracken, W. M., & Catrambone, R. (2016). A design for synthesis of asynchronous online and face-to-face learning environments. *Educational Technology Research and Development, 64*(4), 969–988.

Mehrabi, N., Morstatter, F., Saxena, N., Lerman, K., & Galstyan, A. (2021). A Survey on Bias and Fairness in Machine Learning. *ACM Computing Surveys*, *54*(6), 1–35. DOI: 10.1145/3457607

Michael, J., McMichael, J., & Vrugtman, J. (2014, March). Machine learning for continuous formative assessment. In *Proceedings of the 4th International Conference on Learning Analytics and Knowledge* (pp. 250–254). ACM.

Nguyen, Q. H., Nguyen, M. H., & Nguyen, T. T. (2022). AI-based Online Exam Proctoring: Techniques, Challenges, and Future Directions. *IEEE Access : Practical Innovations, Open Solutions*, *10*, 123456–123472. DOI: 10.1109/ACCESS.2022.3156789

Nicol, D. J., & Macfarlane-Dick, D. (2006). Formative assessment and self-regulated learning: A model and seven principles of good feedback practice. *Studies in Higher Education*, *31*(2), 199–218. DOI: 10.1080/03075070600572090

Ocak, M. A. (2011). Why are faculty members not teaching blended courses? Insights from faculty members. *Computers & Education*, *56*(3), 689–699. DOI: 10.1016/j.compedu.2010.10.011

Ogunsakin, R. E. (2024). The impact of artificial intelligence on personalized learning experiences. *Journal of Computer Assisted Learning*, *40*(1), 99–113.

Ouyang, F., Zheng, L., & Jiao, P. (2022). Artificial intelligence in online higher education: A systematic review of empirical research from 2011–2020. *Education and Information Technologies*, *27*(10), 7893–7925. DOI: 10.1007/s10639-022-10925-9

Owan, V. J., Abang, K. B., Idika, D. O., Etta, E. O., & Bassey, B. A. (2023). Exploring the potential of artificial intelligence tools in educational measurement and assessment. *Eurasia Journal of Mathematics, Science and Technology Education*, *19*(8), em2307. DOI: 10.29333/ejmste/13428

Paul, J. S., Farhath, O., & Selvan, M. P. (2024, April). AI-based proctoring system – A review. In *2024 International Conference on Inventive Computation Technologies (ICICT)* (pp. 1–5). IEEE.

Pellicelli, A. C. (2024). Challenges and risks of AI in education. In *Proceedings of EDULEARN24* (pp. 233–242). DOI: 10.21125/edulearn.2024.1767

Persing, I., Ng, V., & Adams, R. (2019). Modeling discourse moves for assessing argument quality in student essays. *Transactions of the Association for Computational Linguistics*, *7*, 507–521. DOI: 10.1162/tacl_a_00295

Poole, D. L., & Mackworth, A. K. (2010). *Artificial Intelligence: Foundations of computational agents*. Cambridge University Press. DOI: 10.1017/CBO9780511794797

Popham, W. J. (2001). *The truth about testing: An educator's call to action.* ASCD.

Prompiengchai, S., Narreddy, C., & Joordens, S. (2025). A practical guide for supporting formative assessment and feedback using generative AI Preprint. *arXiv*. https://doi.org//arXiv.2505.23405DOI: 10.48550

Reardon, S. F. (2018). The widening academic achievement gap between the rich and the poor. In *Social stratification* (pp. 536–550). Routledge.

Røe, Y., Rowe, M., Ødegaard, N. B., & Lie, A. (2022). Blended learning in higher education: A review of the literature. *Technology, Pedagogy and Education*, *31*(1), 1–18.

Rossett, A., Douglis, F., & Frazee, R. V. (2003). Strategies for building blended learning. *Learning Circuits*, *4*(7), 1–9.

Rotherham, A. J., & Willingham, D. (2009). 21st century. *Educational Leadership*, *67*(1), 16–21.

Russell, S. J., & Norvig, P. (2016). *Artificial intelligence: A modern approach.* Pearson.

Sadler, D. R. (1989). Formative assessment and the design of instructional systems. *Instructional Science*, *18*(2), 119–144. DOI: 10.1007/BF00117714

Saputra, I., Kurniawan, A., Yanita, M., Putri, E. Y., & Mahniza, M. (2024). The evolution of educational assessment: How artificial intelligence is shaping the trends and future of learning evaluation. *The Indonesian Journal of Computer Science*, *13*(6), 112–128. DOI: 10.33022/ijcs.v13i6.4465

Selwyn, N. (2019). *Should robots replace teachers?: AI and the future of education.* John Wiley & Sons.

Shepard, L. A. (2000). The role of assessment in a learning culture. *Educational Researcher*, *29*(7), 4–14. DOI: 10.3102/0013189X029007004

Stiggins, R. (2005). From formative assessment to assessment for learning: A path to success in standards-based schools. *Phi Delta Kappan*, *87*(4), 324–328. DOI: 10.1177/003172170508700414

Tapalova, O., & Zhiyenbayeva, N. (2022). Artificial intelligence in education: AIEd for personalised learning pathways. *Electronic Journal of e-Learning*, *20*(5), 639–653. DOI: 10.34190/ejel.20.5.2597

UNESCO. (2023). *Guidance for generative AI in education and research.* United Nations Educational, Scientific and Cultural Organization. https://www.unesco.org/en/articles/guidance-generative-ai-education-and-research

Viberg, O., & Grönlund, Å. (2024). Exploring teachers' (future) digital assessment practices in higher education: Instrument and model development. *British Journal of Educational Technology*, *55*(3), 1–19. DOI: 10.1111/bjet.13462

Waladi, C., Sefian, M. L., & Khaldi, M. (2023). Kolb's learning styles: Implementation and integration in an adaptive e-learning system. In *Handbook of Research on Scripting, Media Coverage, and Implementation of E-Learning Training in LMS Platforms* (pp. 398–413). IGI Global.

Wieczorek, M., Hosseini, M., & Gordijn, B. (2025). Unpacking the ethics of using AI in primary and secondary education: A systematic literature review. *AI and Ethics*, *5*(5), 1–19. DOI: 10.1007/s43681-025-00770-0 PMID: 40959538

Wiliam, D. (2011). What is assessment for learning? *Studies in Educational Evaluation*, *37*(1), 3–14. DOI: 10.1016/j.stueduc.2011.03.001

Williamson, B., & Eynon, R. (2020). Historical threads, missing links, and future directions in AI in education. *Learning, Media and Technology*, *45*(3), 223–235. DOI: 10.1080/17439884.2020.1798995

Woolf, B. P. (2010). *Building intelligent interactive tutors: Student-centered strategies for revolutionizing e-learning*. Morgan Kaufmann.

Yacef, K. (2002, December). Intelligent teaching assistant systems. In *International Conference on Computers in Education (ICCE)* (pp. 136–140). IEEE. DOI: 10.1109/CIE.2002.1185885

Yang, L., & Li, H. (2023). Advances in AI-Based Automated Scoring and Proctoring Systems: Enhancing Assessment Validity and Integrity in Online Education. *Computers & Education*, *189*, 104620. DOI: 10.1016/j.compedu.2022.104620

Yuvasri, J., Senbagavalli, M., Rahul, R., & Saravana Kumar, C. S. (2025, March). Automated subjective answer evaluation using GenAI and NLP by enhancing accuracy, fairness, and feedback in education. In *2025 International Conference on Intelligent Computing and Control Systems (ICICCS)* (pp. 648–654). IEEE.

Zawacki-Richter, O., Marín, V. I., Bond, M., & Gouverneur, F. (2019). Systematic review of research on artificial intelligence applications in higher education–where are the educators? *International Journal of Educational Technology in Higher Education*, *16*(1), 1–27. DOI: 10.1186/s41239-019-0171-0

Zheldibayeva, R. (2025). The impact of AI and peer feedback on research writing skills: a study using the CGScholar platform among Kazakhstani scholars. *arXiv preprint arXiv:2503.05820*.

Chapter 7

How AI Chatbots Enhance Student Support in Higher Education:

Exploring the Opportunities and Challenges

Amira Saif Abdullah
https://orcid.org/0009-0007-4637-0380
Universiti Sains Malaysia, Malaysia

Hanan Aldowah
https://orcid.org/0000-0003-1020-2389
Universiti Sains Malaysia, Malaysia

Samar Ghazal
USCI, Malaysia

ABSTRACT

In recent years, higher education institutions adopt speedy adoption of Artificial Intelligence (AI) where they have developed AI-powered chatbots to optimize their student support roles. This paper demonstrated the main opportunities that provided by AI chatbots, including 24 hours a day, enhance student engagement, personalize academic support, and improve administrative efficiency. This paper provides evidence on how capabilities of AI chatbot system can impact institutions as they attempt to implement student support solutions through practical technological advice. By analyzing these opportunities and challenges, this paper provides a balance perspective and vision for institutions that aiming to adopt AI chatbots solutions for student support. This discussion recommended future developments should focus

DOI: 10.4018/979-8-3373-3815-6.ch007

ight © 2026, IGI Global Scientific Publishing. Copying or distributing in print or electronic forms without written permission of IGI Global Scientific Publishing is prohibited. Use of this chapter to n generative artificial intelligence (AI) technologies is expressly prohibited. The publisher reserves all rights to license its use for generative AI training and machine learning model development.

more on adapting the chatbot, and it also suggested future directions for research and development to explored how the ethical use in AI chatbots can be effective in higher education environments.

1. INTRODUCTION

Artificial intelligence technology is increasingly being adopted by all areas of the society including higher education institutions in higher numbers. AI-driven tools in educational organizations are considered as an essential element for improving supportive learning structures and learning experience to develop their educational projects. Therefore, AI chatbots are important tools of education, as students can be able to interact with them to get academic consultancy, quickly access to educational information, and enhance their engagement with services of education.

University life creates special problems for students, who are starting their first year of study. Many academic, social, as well as administrative changes that first-year that students face create extensive effects on their academic success and total success. According to Van Rooij et al., (2018), academic adjustment consists of four influential elements which include learning motivation, academic work application together with academic task effort, and satisfaction about academic environments. Consequently, students will face some of these difficulties and challenges with their studies because these issues can affect how their performance in classes as they start their time at university. Similarly, a study conducted by Hassan et al. (2023) found that when students feel good about themselves and can handle stress or problems, it directly impacts their academic outcome. It can be seen from these results that students' struggles and problems during their academic journey are not only reflected on their performance, but also in design of the support systems that can be implemented. Additionally, the resources of traditional academic advising and help centers are still really helpful, but they are not flexible enough to consistently meet all students' needs. AI chatbots take care these issues by providing continuous automated support all the time to answer the students' questions and suggest solutions. The continued availability of student services is still necessary as it helps students inquire more about admission, registration, as well as important deadlines for courses, as a result improve their educational activities. The customizing feature of AI chatbots uses students' profiles, observations, and what they have done to help change the way they communicate with them. These chatbots look at a student's profile and their grades and likes to give them help that matches their requirements and needs. These AI tools suggest what study materials to use and remind students when their homework is due, even suggest some activities they can join after course.

Therefore, when the students find personal attention, they will actively participate and acquire knowledge more efficiently (Korda et al., 2024).

This research discusses how AI chatbots can support the students who enrolled in higher education institutions. It reviews the main operational aspects of these chatbots and their types in educational settings and highlights the main opportunities that provided by AI chatbots, including 24 hours a day, personalized academic support, enhance student engagement, and improve administrative efficiency. Furthermore, it revealed the challenges that associated with implementing chatbots system, such as data privacy concerns, lack of emotional, and limited functionality. This research discusses and reviews the benefits and challenges of using chatbots in order to provide a balance perspective and vision for institutions that aiming to adopt AI chatbots solutions for student support.

2. BACKGROUND OF STUDY

2.1 AI Chatbots in the Context Higher Education

Higher education institutions make use of AI chatbots as an intelligent digital system developed to simulate human conversations, through text and voice for students (McTear, 2022). Several studies explain the combination between machine learning algorithms with natural language processing (NLP) to read student conversation, produce appropriate replies, and enhance their capabilities through cumulative interaction learning in AI chatbots systems (Suta et al., 2020; Alazzam et al., 2023).

AI chatbots are widely used in higher education institutions for educational support and administrative practice. These information technologies have developed substantially in the last year following the advancement of conversational Artificial Intelligence during the 21st century. chatbots now serve as foundational components within standard e-learning systems that educational institutions use (Neto et al., 2019; Lien et al., 2022). The educational purpose-specific chatbots use natural language processing (NLP) to create conversations between students and instructors (Kumar et al., 2021). They provide personalized educational guidance, respond to questions from students, provide learning materials, and foster engaging, student-centered learning experiences (Lo, 2023). These chatbots are useful to students, enabling understanding of university systems, and reducing staff assistance. Furthermore, AI chatbots improve learning satisfaction, involvement and retention because their service is timely, reliable, and personal.

In general, two kinds of chatbots are employed in the educational settings:

- **Rule-based chatbots** use decision trees and prewritten programs to function. In addition to completing basic, repetitive activities like providing office hours or course deadlines, they are efficient at responding to often requested queries (Dogan & Gurcan, 2024).
- **AI-driven chatbots** understand context, learn from interactions, and provide more dynamic and customized answers by utilizing machine learning and natural language processing. These bots have the ability of handling more complicated queries, adjusting to the demands of various students, and even identifying emotional signs or learning gaps. (Dogan & Gurcan, 2024).

Higher education chatbot integration aims to improve student experience, reduce stress on staff, and provide scalable, reliable, and consistent support services (Labadze et al., 2023; Winkler & Söllner, 2018). In higher education, chatbots are increasingly used for:

- **Academic advising:** assisting students with course selection, program requirements, and academic progress monitoring.
- **Administrative tasks:** answering students' questions about financial aid, registration, and admissions.
- **Student support**: respond to inquiries about events, programs, and mental health resources available on campus.

AI chatbots represent a way to revolutionize different aspects of education by improving its effectiveness, personalization, and making interactive experience more engaging. These AI-driven tools allow personalized tutoring where each student needs real time customized assistance. By monitoring student learning progress smart chatbots deliver complex explanations with resource recommendations to support individual learning stages. The system enables personalized educational help for students instead of providing standardized educational methods.

Additionally, AI chatbots are useful for educational tasks, because they are able to provide quick feedback, answer student's questions, and summarizing important learning materials. Through reducing the need for teachers to make small clarifications, chatbots enable students to increase the academic confidence and also improve problem solving skills by teaching themselves. In addition to academic assistance, chatbots also see to administrative functions, including answering common questions like deadlines, course timetables or university policies. Automating the responsibilities of administration can save teachers and administrative personnel time to work directly with students. Additionally, AI chatbots can be used to review quizzes and assignments where they will yield immediate results without limiting the teachers' hands to assignments that require direct input from teachers. AI chatbots improve efficiency and engagement and open the door to new creative and innovative approaches for education. Using customizable chatbots, educators can create authentic environments, smart discussion tools, and playful learning methods that turn the traditional teaching models to a more dynamic and student-center setting.

2.2 Studies in the Field of Education

Since the last several years, a rapid growth of usage of artificial intelligence (AI) technology has been developed in education, transforming administrative, teaching and learning processes. Some of the AI-driven technologies that were found in studies to enhance the result of learning are very fast feedback, individualized learning paths, and wise use of resources- virtual teaching assistants, automated assessment platforms, and intelligent tutoring systems (Abrar et al., 2025; Kathleen Yekollu et al. 2024; Sumathy and Navamani, 2024). AI chatbots in this transitioning context became a flexible tool that can help to enhance student engagement and services as well as academic learning.

Educational technology has emerged as an area of increasing research regarding the application of AI for the improvement of student experiences inside and outside the classroom is concerned. Chatbots find their application in variety of ways, including answering of the frequently asked questions (FAQs), assisting in course registration, availability 24/7 for receiving institutional help, giving advice on mental health and wellness issues, among other uses. These applications give staff members in higher education institutions less administrative work while also giving students immediate access to help. A systematic literature review in education investigated 67 studies concerning AI chatbots, where emphasis on the benefits of these tools for both the educators and their learners. Chatbots assist students in doing their homework; they provide individual instruction and upgrade their skills, and they also save time for the teachers and make their pedagogical approach better, although problems with precision, reliability and morality still remain (Labadze, 2023). Another review that reviewed 37 studies, which show that AI chatbots make students more willing to learn and facilitate learning of language skills. They offer instructors reduced burden and cost-effectiveness. However, they somehow face a problem of the lack of interaction, giving a wrong response and plagiarism (Gökçearslan et al., 2024).

Furthermore, recent research has shown that how introducing chatbots into the online and blended learning environment can stimulate the self-regulated learning and motivation. A systematic review demonstrated that educational chatbots help students identify where to access learning materials, how to learn them using effective study techniques, and monitor their progress. However, a study discovered that chatbots provide a limited amount of help for defining the learning goals (Guan et al., 2025). Others have examined AI applications for self-regulated learning in online education and demonstrated that students considered AI technologies useful for behavioral, cognitive and metacognitive control, but not for motivation (Jin et al., 2023). The possibility of chatbots to deliver microlearning content, simulate conversational learning, and modify responses in response to learner input in line with existing educational approaches that place a high value on learner-centered design A study conducted by Kumar (2021) on educational chatbots in project-based learning revealed that chatbots stimulate human conversations to enhance learning outcome and team collaboration, and that chatbots improve team-based design courses' engagement and facilitate individual learning. Li et al., (2025) investigated the ways of how chatbots help the learner autonomy and engagement. The systematic review discovered that AI-driven conversational programs help to practice students in language skills through adaptive responses, especially regarding the need to adopt a learner-centered instructional design. Similarly, research on chatbot-based microlearning has studied the effects of AI-based conversational learning agents in learning motivation and performance. A quasi-experiment showed that learner in chatbot-supported microlearning environments had greater intrinsic motivation compared to traditional learning methods (Yin et al., 2021).

The use of AI chatbots in education is becoming more popular, as they provide students instant help, personalised learning support, and administrative convenience. Although, their short-term pros-readily availability, engagement, and better study habits, remain well documented, long-term effects seem a target to further research.

Educational Equity: The equal access to resources using the AI chatbots demonstrates hope for bridging the gap between different levels of education among students. Differential distribution of technology access, digital literacy level, and chatbot performance rate differences among groups may even reinforce the existing social inequalities, rather than modify them. Further research should be directed to investigate the degree to which AI systems provide equal educational opportunities for every student group, including those who are still rather unclear in terms of their demographic weaknesses.

Student Satisfaction: AI-powered student learning systems provide more responsiveness and engagement features, but students have mixed opinions about the effectiveness of chatbots as tools to support education. There are various opinions on students' preference of chatbots based on the fact that some appreciate quick help, but others believe that robots are not able to provide emotional connection. Evaluating student satisfaction over long term will result in creating chatbot designs that correlate automated actions with meaningful human interaction.

Academic Performance: Artificial intelligence chatbots facilitate education through instant solutions in feedback and personalized learning methods. The long-term academic gains of automated academic assistance in the future cannot be predicted, because relying on AI based teaching system may lead to the lack of critical thinking and problem-solving skills between individuals. Research for a long term is required to see the effect of AI-driven tutoring systems on students' learning outcomes after initial implementation.

These emerging trends provide the basis that AI chatbots are not just assistant roles but are playing an active role in shaping the future of education. Research should be aligned with AI integration within the institution to allow ethical and efficient use of learning environment chatbots for fostering equitable educational outcomes.

2.3 Future Trends and Innovations in AI Chatbots

With the further development of AI, chatbots no longer remain the bots for questions and answers only, but become the emotionally intelligent and flexible learning devices. A number of critical developments are defining the next era of AI-driven student support:

Emotion-Aware Chatbots

The technology of affective computing is expected to appear in future chatbots because it enables machines to pick emotions and react appropriately. Prior knowledge from the detection abilities of AI models, which aimed at students' frustration, confusion, and disengagement, allows flexible tweaks to their exchanges, offering encouragement, alternative explanations, and human presence when students feel uncomfortable. Early research on sentiment analysis and emotion detection reveals that the use of chatbots promotes students' mental health and motivation in virtual learning environments. Chukwuere and Handoko (2024) conducted a study and reported findings on how AI-enable emotion recognition systems can shape supportive learning environments that enable to tailor their solutions to students who need special academic support. Through examining sentiments and behavior patterns, AI allows it to modify its responses that offer encouragement, alternative explanations and urgent time-sensitive interventions.

AI-Driven Mentorship Programs

Student advising positions that use faculty availability restrict the access to students who need help. Personalized career guidance, academic preparation, and personalized educational planning will be provided to the students through AI driven mentoring applications. AI-powered chatbots will analyse students' progress, personal interests, and learning style to develop individualized recommendations on course selection, prospective internships and skill acquisition. A number of educational institutions are currently developing AI-based career guidance systems that design virtual sessions that resemble personal mentoring communication. Batista, Mesquita, & Carnaz (2024) report that how AI-based advising systems analyze students' data to create personalized study plans and career counselling, filling the gap between the traditional services of faculty advising and digital scaling. Their review examined the uses of generative AI in higher education trends that include stakeholder reception, educational strategies, and ethical issues. Their research reveals the academic value of institutionalization of AI chatbots as an aspect of educational improvement, as well as inherent issues arising from a result of academic ethics and evaluation methods from the use of such tools.

Seamless AI-Human Collaboration

The future AI-based chatbots will work collaboratively with support staff and academic faculty to provide quick and human guided student services. The hybrid framework combines automated systems and human advisors, meeting the needs of students who need fast self-service solutions as well as personalized human help in grave or emotionally complex matters. AI systems should be an integral part in the operations of higher learning institutions because with such systems, it is easy to transition between student interactions with automated chatbots to manual human advisors, and this design forms an interactive support system. McGrath et al. (2024) demonstrated the need for a system that combines machine learning and human supervision in a way that allows students to benefit from automatic help with basic questions, as well as the help from human assistance with complex academic requirements and emotional support. The incorporation of automatic systems with human guidance aspects contributes to improve operational performance and continuous human direction procedures. They are conducting a systematic review of AI chatbots to assess empirical studies that have been conducted after releasing ChatGPT. Results of investigations concerning AI chatbots offer idealistic and disturbing findings that highlight the need for further studies to determine how the systems impact student education and administrative processes.

Predictive Analytics for Early Intervention

AI chatbots will develop their predictive analytics capabilities to identify students in need of intervention through data interactions, and outcomes as well as behavioral indicators. Predictive analytics through AI chatbots in universities enables the institutions to offer academic counselling, mental health and specialized study support to prevent major academic problems among students. AI-powered early warning systems are being piloted at various institutions to assist universities to retain success and retention rates of students. Institutes of learning measure AI-driven intervention systems that identify early signs of student distress and offer preventative measures towards retention and academic achievement (Chukwuere, 2024).

Multimodal AI Learning Assistants

Future AI chatbots will become multimodal assistants that will combine the voice recognition, the visual elements and the augmented reality (AR) to improve their interaction abilities. By using video tutorials, gesture recognition, and AR learning environments, students are able to improve their interaction with AI chatbots in order to make the interactions more immersive and dynamic. Studies have examined the use of gesture-based interaction, use of virtual simulation and real time adaptive tutoring in AI transformed learning spaces to develop more dynamic educational settings (Batista et al, 2024; Jahadakbar & Yao, 2025; Kostadimas et al, 2025).

The advancements have shown that AI chatbots act as fundamental aspects of modernizing educational systems. AI-driven student support systems have ethical aspects, pedagogical implications, and technological constraints that need constant research for the higher education institutions that are embracing the digital transformation.

3. RESEARCH METHODOLOGY

This research paper uses a literature review methodology to explore the opportunities and challenges of AI chatbots in supporting students in higher education. In order to ensure full coverage of the target articles, relevant studies were identified through searches in major academic databases, including Scopus, Web of Science, IEEE Xplore, and Google Scholar. Keywords such as "AI chatbots," "student support," "opportunities," "Challenges," and "artificial intelligence in education" were used to locate relevant publications. To ensure relevance, the research paper was limited to peer-reviewed articles, conference papers, and authoritative reports published between 2015 and 2025 were included, given that this period was associated with the active development of intelligent chatbot applications in education. The selection process focused on works discussing (a) the pedagogical role of chatbots in higher education, (b) opportunities for enhancing learning and student engagement, and (c) challenges related to technology, ethics, and implementation. After the initial search, duplicates and irrelevant articles were excluded. The final set of studies was synthesized in a thematic manner

4. OPPORTUNITIES OF AI CHATBOTS FOR STUDENT SUPPORT

One of the most important advantages of AI-powered chatbots is their ability to provide support 24 hours a day. Although human employees are only accessible during business hours, chatbots are able to help students at any time, even on the weekends, holidays, and nights. This kind of advantage is especially useful for undergraduate students who might be anxious or feel overwhelmed and require immediate responses to their administrative or academic questions outside the working hours of the offices. Due to their friendly nature, chatbots enhance the students' perception of support and reduce the time needed to obtain information that contributes to improved academic performance and high level of student satisfaction (Kuh et al., 2011). This is especially helpful in the large organizations or companies in which there may be several students under one employee. Research evidences have shown that 24/7 support helps users to be satisfied and help in handling routine requests more efficiently (Kuhail et al., 2023; Labadze et al., 2023). Moreover, where the students are from different regions of the world or where the class is entirely an online class, then there must be a synchronous support. They make services available to as many people as possible since the service can be offered at any time of the day as well as at any place.

Furthermore, it is important to note that AI-powered chatbots are not just a means of instant interaction in higher education, but an effective means and tool for students' data collection and analysis (Okonkwo and Ade-Ibijula (a), 2021). Every conversation and interaction with a chatbot can be saved and analyzed to derive data about the student behaviours, preferences, questions, and emerging issues (Pelau et al., 2021). These insights help institutions:

- Determine which areas students are having difficulties (it could be some subject matter or administrative issues).
- Monitoring the rates of engagement in various periods and services.
- Carefully classify students into groups according to their habits of interaction with educational materials.
- Identify existing challenges or shortcomings in providing services in order to enhance the decision-making process in an institution.

Hence, through the analysis of the data acquired through chatbots, universities can take a more proactive approach to enhance students' learning satisfaction.

AI chatbots can help educational institutions save money in the long run as administrative tasks that would have to be performed manually otherwise (Kobets & Kozlovskyi, 2022; Hwang & Kim, 2021). These tasks include: offering information on commonly asked questions, guiding the students through the registration and enrolment processes, giving them updates on the academic calendar or their courses, and offering constantly available administrative assistance without having to hire staff that will work at night. By executing numerous interactions, chatbots save on human resource costs and staffing, and at the same time, enhance efficiency (Kedi et al., 2024). Employers can benefit from a continual level of assistance that helps to increase the customers' satisfaction and simultaneously minimize the costs concerning the salaries, training, and infrastructure. Ultimately, it makes resources more efficient to focus on valuable or rather specific activities, enhance services without increasing the budget (Kobets & Kozlovskyi, 2022).

Besides, AI chatbots can contribute to increasing the sales and revenue of educational institutions in several ways, directly influencing the achievement of the objectives that are set.

- Improved Student Registration and Recruitment: Chatbots provide immediate responses to questions about classes, tuition costs, the admissions process, and scholarships. According to Anagnoste et al. (2021), this consistent online presence leads to increases the conversion rate.
- Enhanced User Experience: When students and parents get the solutions to their problems within the shortest time possible, they realize they have placed their trust in the right institution. This has the potential to attract more people through word of mouth and more students to further their education which means more longevity and more potential to generate more revenue.
- Upselling Additional Services: Chatbots can help inform students about the availability of premium services, training workshops, certificates, or products that may exist within the institution. Such a real-time promotion may also increase the sales of any other complementary educational materials, products, or services (Savastano et al., 2024).
- Supporting International Student Markets: In terms of outreach, since chatbots work 24/7, the schools can use them to target international students, who are generally more expensive to recruit.

Chatbots make the work faster and more effective so that users can complete some operations and avoid the mistakes. One advantage associated with these models is that they are able to process information quickly, follow sequences, and produce consistent outputs because they are the ideal tools for implementing regular, unchanging procedures (Sota et al., 2020). AI chatbots are expected to solve tasks that are pre-structured in some way, meaning that some form of behavior is built into the bot through machine learning algorithms (Suta et al., 2020). It is frequently used at School, College, and Universities level by automating sections like timetable, form submission, frequently asked questions and many more; thereby saving sufficient time and reducing the repetition of errors. In the context of students and staff, this means that all routine tasks like registration to certain classes, timetable, reminder of examination, are done properly and fast and in so doing improves efficiency and satisfaction of users' nature.

Moreover, the main advantage of the chatbot is the personalized and human-like experience ensured by technology that routines communication and makes it more easily accessible (Haugeland et al., 2022). This simulated conversation not only improves user satisfaction but will also help expand support services effectively. These new models of AI-Chatbots employ natural languages processing (NLP) to tend to engage in a natural conversation as a human one (Nguyen et al., 2022). In education settings, this reduce the shyness that learners experience whenever they have questions to ask since the interaction with a chatbot is like talking to a human. Furthermore, since the chatbot interacts through a number of accessible public technology platforms (e.g., website, applications, messaging services), it becomes quite possible for an institution to support a large number of students via the technology without an equivalent human resource implication.

5. CHALLENGES AND CONCERNS

Students face a variety of challenges that arise from dealing with the new institution systems, learning environment changes, time management, and timely access to help. These challenges can affect their academic achievements and cause some level of psychological harm to them (Ahmadi, 2023).

It has been observed that designing and applying AI chatbots in education presents a complex and resource-costly process because it requires some of the firsts of them such as natural language processing (NLP), machine learning algorithms, and design of user experience, (Ayanouz et al. 2020). They are sometimes a little difficult to integrate into your content, especially if the bot is elaborate. In most cases, it takes about 2 weeks before your chatbot can start working effectively after you learn to use the functionalities. The first task is to overcome the problem of development of chatbots learning to comprehend academic queries from students that are not identical, contain linguistic and contextual irregularities, and depend on difficulties (Winkler& Söllner 2018). But there is still a big issue in AI development to design a chatbot able to communicate with clients, decipher the message of the clients and respond in an intuitive way.

Another serious problem that concerns some AI chatbots is their limited access to real-time or complete data. Most educational chatbots use static or preloaded sets of data that implies that they do not possess information on the latest updates within institutions, student registers, or modifications to the curriculum (Kooli, 2023). Consequently, they may provide students with outdate or inaccurate information especially when institutional data is updated regularly. Moreover, the process of introducing new information to the system of the chatbot can be time-consuming because it usually can involve manual updates or synchronization at regular times with institutional databases. This delay reduces the performance and the appropriateness of timely support by chatbots to students. This problem is especially pressing in higher education when students require accurate and current information regarding registration, schedule for classes, deadlines and policies. Chatbots can lose people's confidence due to insufficient access to real-time information, and they also fail to meet students' expectations for immediate, reliable support.

However, despite the increasing use of AI-driven chatbots in higher learning, most suffer from their limited functionality (Naik, 2023). Essentially, most chatbots have a narrow width and only able to answer pre-defined or commonly asked questions (Gunnam, 2024; Grudin & Jacques, 2019). This reduces the option to serve complex or open-ended queries that frustrate users who expect a smarter or more flexible assistant. Furthermore, most educational chatbots are rule based and have little development in natural language understanding and reasoning abilities, which are essential for dynamic dialogue or personalized academic support. These limitations are frequently attributable to limited training data, limited interoperability with institutional databases, and lack of superior AI models. Therefore, users may end up being redirected to human support, which somewhat negates the reason why the chatbot should be used to enhance scalability and accessibility.

Moreover, the lack of emotional intelligence and empathy on the part of AI-powered chatbots, which is one of the most frequently mentioned shortcomings of them, is in the first place among the mentioned disadvantages (Rahsepar, 2024; Seitz, 2024). Chatbots, unlike human educators or advisors, are deprived of the possibility of comprehending or responding to the emotional state of students (Gkinko & Elbanna, 2022). Although some chatbots may be designed to identify particular phrases or words related to distress or frustration naturally, their answers are frequently rife with the superficiality and a lack of empathy that characterizes such interactions. This limitation, however, is especially problematic in an educational context when students may require emotional reassurances, motivation or psychological support, in addition to facts-based answers, especially if they are first-year or weak learners. Lack of empathetic interaction modes among chatbots may undermine user satisfaction; eliminate trust in system operation and reducing the possibility of creating supportive learning environments.

AI chatbots provided in higher education often need access to personal, academic, behavioral data in order to provide more tailored response and support. However, the collection, storage and processing of this sensitive data cause great privacy and data protection concerns (Kooli 2023). Students are not always fully aware of what information the collection process requires and how it will be used, which reaching data privacy laws and ethical standards. In addition, institutions stand the risk of exposing the student's data to breaches, misuse or unauthorized access, without strict observance of policies such as the General Data Protection Regulation (GDPR) or Family Educational Rights and Privacy Act (FERPA) (Hasal et al., 2021). Even with the appropriate work of anonymization, data shared with the third party chatbot providers can be risky if they're not secured properly. Concerns for privacy may also reduce trust in the systems of chatbots, especially if we consider the case of the students who are careful with personal information being posted on the internet (Okonkwo & Ade-Ibijola (b), 2021). So when we deploy chatbots in the education setting, transparency, informed consent and strong data security measures are important matters.

Table 1 provides a clearer overview of the findings, and summarizes the opportunities and challenges of AI chatbots in higher education. This structured representation highlights how chatbots positively impact student support, learning engagement, and institutional efficiency, while also revealing risks and limitations that need to be addressed.

Table 1. Summarize the opportunities and challenges of AI chatbots in higher education

Opportunities	**Challenges**
Provide support 24 hours a day.	A complex and resource-costly process.
Save students' data collection and analysis.	Restricted data availability and delayed updates.
Save money in the long run.	Limited functionality.
Increase the sales and revenue of educational institutions	Lack of emotional intelligence and empathy.
Able to process tasks quickly and effectively.	Student data privacy concerns.
Accessible personalized experience	

6. RESULTS AND DISCUSSION

This study has investigated nuances of the role of AI-powered chatbots in enhancing student support at higher education level. Based on existing literature and actual examples, the discussion points out that chatbots have a lot of opportunities, such as 24-day opening (even at weekends), the possibility to provide customized academic assistance (homework), and increased administrative efficiency. One of the benefits of these features is increased level of engagement and satisfaction among students, especially for undergraduate who needs a regular reassurance as he/she settles into the mode of life as a student in university. Further, the use of chatbots allows institutions to increase the range of support services while, perhaps, reducing financial and human resource burdens. Figure 1 presents a summary of the main opportunities and challenges of AI chatbots in higher education.

Figure 1. Opportunities and Challenges of AI Chatbots

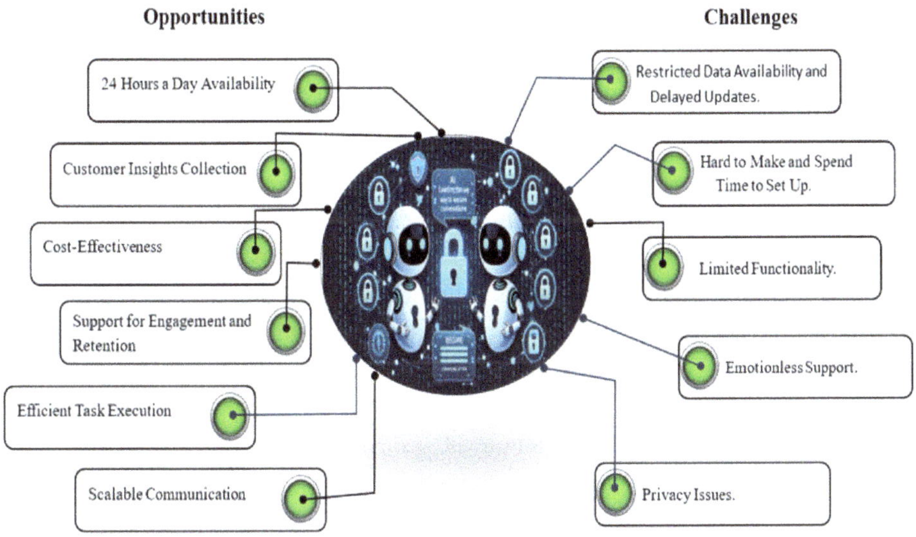

From the review of this study, many papers have shown that the AI chatbots can make a huge difference in the student support services. For instance, as report by Kuhail et al. (2023), students, who made use of chatbots indicated more levels of satisfaction and efficiency in answering common questions. Kedi et.al (2024) in another study revealed the effectiveness of chatbots in managing administrative work and leaving the staff with complex issues. Moreover, by processing thousands of the repetitive interactions, chatbots minimize the size of these support teams, decrease the operating costs and enhance efficiency. Organizations gain a scalable support solution that produces the same quality of service but at a smaller cost of salaries, training and infrastructure. Chatbots have also ability of handling a lot of interactions at the same time so while all the students receive timely assistance, there are realized no overburdening of the human staff.

However, several of these challenges need to be taken into account, even with these benefits. Generations of intelligent and reactive chatbots is a challenging task that requires high level of technical knowledge and resources. In addition, the possibility of availability of data, delays on providing the data updates and limited functionality can be considered obstacles in delivering quality or timely information to the chatbot. Chatbots also lack emotional intelligence and empathy and they can demote the quality of student interactions in sensitive situations. Moreover, uncertainty that surrounds data privacy and security questions still exist, in the form of questions of student trust and institutional accountability. Therefore, AI chatbots promote promising solutions, and it is advisable to conduct in a thoughtful design, constant improvement and clear standards of proper behaviour.

This reviewed addresses a common trend of the necessity in personalization and adaptive training in the system of the chatbot. In the area of effective implementation, there needs to be more than reliable algorithms and an important hybrid support model which combines automated services with the oversight by humans. Addition either accuracy, relevance and a trusting user calls for constant improvements to chatbot algorithms and ethical systems of data governance.

Finally, the integrating of AI chatbots into the student support services offers providers with a huge advantage. Although they are scalable, available, and efficient, they can change student experience in higher education, but the full realization of their potential requires continuous development, ethical oversight, and a student-centered approach. Based on the reviewed studies; therefore, personalization, transparency and supportive combination of technology with the human touch must be emphasized in successful implementation.

7. CONCLUSION AND RECOMMENDATIONS

AI chatbots have the capable of transforming the efforts in improving the student support in higher education. As this technology continues to develop, institutions must deal with a strategy and an ethical approach to implementation. Future developments should focus more on adapting the chatbot further, standardizing features that make it suitable for multilevel usage, and adding active integration with other academic and administrative systems so that using the chatbot becomes an integral part of the student experience.

Further study is needed in order to test chatbot effectiveness in different disciplines and levels of education. Furthermore, longitudinal studies may provide insight into the long-term effects of chatbot utilization on student performance, retention and overall satisfaction. The issue of further investigation of students' trust in the systems of the chatting bots especially concerning the issue of privacy and the question of security of data is also of pivotal importance.

A few recommendations may be made according to the current findings obtained. Institutions need to be investing in training and maintaining high-quality chatbot systems, updating the data that lies behind them and providing human backup support in the emotionally sensitive or complex cases. There is a need to define ethical guidelines clearly for the protection of student data and openness in AI interactions.

In conclusion, although AI chatbots cannot replace human interaction, they are a powerful complement to existing student support services. By offering immediate, expandable, and easy-to-use support, chatbots can dramatically raise levels of students' engagement and efficiency at the institutional level. Careful design, a consistent process for second-guessing decision-making based on experience, and ethics in the wake of the technological revolution can make AI chatbots a treasured resource in the future of higher learning.

REFERENCES

Abrar, M., Aboraya, W., Khaliq, R. A., Subramanian, K. P., Al Husaini, Y., & Al Hussaini, M. (2025). AI-Powered Learning Pathways: Personalized Learning and Dynamic Assessments. *International Journal of Advanced Computer Science and Applications*, *16*(1). Advance online publication. DOI: 10.14569/IJACSA.2025.0160145

Ahmadi, A. (2023). ChatGPT: Exploring the threats and opportunities of artificial intelligence in the age of chatbots. *Asian Journal of Computer Science and Technology*, *12*(1), 25–30. DOI: 10.51983/ajcst-2023.12.1.3567

Alazzam, B. A., Alkhatib, M., & Shaalan, K. (2023). Artificial intelligence chatbots: A survey of classical versus deep machine learning techniques. *Inf. Sci. Lett*, *12*(4), 1217–1233. DOI: 10.18576/isl/120437

Anagnoste, S., Biclesanu, I., D'Ascenzo, F., & Savastano, M. (2021). The role of chatbots in end-to-end intelligent automation and future employment dynamics. In *Business Revolution in a Digital Era: 14th International Conference on Business Excellence, ICBE 2020, Bucharest, Romania* (pp. 287-302). Springer International Publishing. DOI: 10.1007/978-3-030-59972-0_20

Ayanouz, S., Abdelhakim, B. A., & Benhmed, M. (2020, March). A smart chatbot architecture based NLP and machine learning for health care assistance. In *Proceedings of the 3rd international conference on networking, information systems & security* (pp. 1-6). DOI: 10.1145/3386723.3387897

Batista, J., Mesquita, A., & Carnaz, G. (2024). Generative AI and higher education: Trends, challenges, and future directions from a systematic literature review. *Information (Basel)*, *15*(11), 676. DOI: 10.3390/info15110676

Chukwuere, J. E., & Handoko, B. L. (2024). The future of generative AI chatbots in higher education. *Journal of Emerging Technologies*, *4*(1), 36–44.

Dogan, O., & Gurcan, O. F. (2024). Enhancing E-Business Communication with a Hybrid Rule-Based and Extractive-Based Chatbot. *Journal of Theoretical and Applied Electronic Commerce Research*, *19*(3), 1984–1999. DOI: 10.3390/jtaer19030097

Gkinko, L., & Elbanna, A. (2022). Hope, tolerance and empathy: Employees' emotions when using an AI-enabled chatbot in a digitalised workplace. *Information Technology & People*, *35*(6), 1714–1743. DOI: 10.1108/ITP-04-2021-0328

Gökçearslan, S., Tosun, C., & Erdemir, Z. G. (2024). Benefits, challenges, and methods of artificial intelligence (AI) chatbots in education: A systematic literature review. *International Journal of Technology in Education*, *7*(1), 19–39. DOI: 10.46328/ijte.600

Grudin, J., & Jacques, R. (2019, May). Chatbots, humbots, and the quest for artificial general intelligence. In *Proceedings of the 2019 CHI conference on human factors in computing systems* (pp. 1-11). DOI: 10.1145/3290605.3300439

Guan, R., Raković, M., Chen, G., & Gašević, D. (2025). How educational chatbots support self-regulated learning? A systematic review of the literature. *Education and Information Technologies*, *30*(4), 4493–4518. DOI: 10.1007/s10639-024-12881-y

Gunnam, G. R. (2024). *The Performance and AI Optimization Issues for Task-Oriented Chatbots* (Doctoral dissertation, The University of Texas at San Antonio).

Hasal, M., Nowaková, J., Ahmed Saghair, K., Abdulla, H., Snášel, V., & Ogiela, L. (2021). Chatbots: Security, privacy, data protection, and social aspects. *Concurrency and Computation*, *33*(19), e6426. DOI: 10.1002/cpe.6426

Hassan, M., Fang, S., Malik, A. A., Lak, T. A., & Rizwan, M. (2023). Impact of perceived social support and psychological capital on university students' academic success: Testing the role of academic adjustment as a moderator. *BMC Psychology*, *11*(1), 340. DOI: 10.1186/s40359-023-01385-y PMID: 37849001

Haugeland, I. K. F., Følstad, A., Taylor, C., & Bjørkli, C. A. (2022). Understanding the user experience of customer service chatbots: An experimental study of chatbot interaction design. *International Journal of Human-Computer Studies*, *161*, 102788. DOI: 10.1016/j.ijhcs.2022.102788

Hwang, S., & Kim, J. (2021). Toward a chatbot for financial sustainability. *Sustainability (Basel)*, *13*(6), 3173. DOI: 10.3390/su13063173

Jahadakbar, M., & Yao, M. Z. (2025, January). The Routine: Enhancing Special Needs Education Through AI-Personalized Embodied Learning in Virtual Environments. In *2025 IEEE International Conference on Artificial Intelligence and eXtended and Virtual Reality (AIxVR)* (pp. 176-182). IEEE. DOI: 10.1109/AIxVR63409.2025.00034

Jin, S. H., Im, K., Yoo, M., Roll, I., & Seo, K. (2023). Supporting students' self-regulated learning in online learning using artificial intelligence applications. *International Journal of Educational Technology in Higher Education*, *20*(1), 37. DOI: 10.1186/s41239-023-00406-5

Kedi, W. E., Ejimuda, C., Idemudia, C., & Ijomah, T. I. (2024). AI Chatbot integration in SME marketing platforms: Improving customer interaction and service efficiency. *International Journal of Management & Entrepreneurship Research*, *6*(7), 2332–2341. DOI: 10.51594/ijmer.v6i7.1327

Kobets, V., & Kozlovskyi, K. (2022). Application of chat bots for personalized financial advice. *Herald of Advanced Information Technology*, *5*(3), 229–242. DOI: 10.15276/hait.05.2022.18

Kooli, C. (2023). Chatbots in education and research: A critical examination of ethical implications and solutions. *Sustainability (Basel)*, *15*(7), 5614. DOI: 10.3390/su15075614

Korda, D. R., Dapaah, E. O., & Akolgo, E. A. (2024). The Role of AI Chatbots in Education: A Review. *Academy Journal of Science and Engineering*, *18*(1), 79–87.

Kostadimas, D., Kasapakis, V., & Kotis, K. (2025). A Systematic Review on the Combination of VR, IoT and AI Technologies, and Their Integration in Applications. *Future Internet*, *17*(4), 163. DOI: 10.3390/fi17040163

Kuh, G. D., Kinzie, J., Schuh, J. H., & Whitt, E. J. (2011). *Student success in college: Creating conditions that matter*. John Wiley & Sons.

Kuhail, M. A., Alturki, N., Alramlawi, S., & Alhejori, K. (2023). Interacting with educational chatbots: A systematic review. *Education and Information Technologies*, *28*(1), 973–1018. DOI: 10.1007/s10639-022-11177-3

Kumar, J. A. (2021). Educational chatbots for project-based learning: Investigating learning outcomes for a team-based design course. *International Journal of Educational Technology in Higher Education*, *18*(1), 65. DOI: 10.1186/s41239-021-00302-w PMID: 34926790

Labadze, L., Grigolia, M., & Machaidze, L. (2023). Role of AI chatbots in education: Systematic literature review. *International Journal of Educational Technology in Higher Education*, *20*(1), 56. DOI: 10.1186/s41239-023-00426-1

Li, Y., Zhou, X., Yin, H. B., & Chiu, T. K. (2025). Design language learning with artificial intelligence (AI) chatbots based on activity theory from a systematic review. *Smart Learning Environments*, *12*(1), 24. DOI: 10.1186/s40561-025-00379-0

Lien, A. K., Randem, L. M., Taralrud, H. P. F., & Edalati, M. (2022). Implementing a Chatbot So-lution for Learning Management System. *arXiv*, arXiv:2206.13187. [**Google Scholar**]

Lo, C. K. (2023). What is the impact of ChatGPT on education? A rapid review of the literature. [Google Scholar] [CrossRef]. *Education Sciences*, *13*(4), 410. DOI: 10.3390/educsci13040410

McGrath, C., Farazouli, A., & Cerratto-Pargman, T. (2024). Generative AI chatbots in higher education: A review of an emerging research area. *Higher Education*, •••, 1–17.

McTear, M. (2022). *Conversational ai: Dialogue systems, conversational agents, and chatbots*. Springer Nature.

Naik, I., Naik, D., & Naik, N. (2023, September). Demystifying the working, types, benefits and limitations of chatbots. In *UK Workshop on Computational Intelligence* (pp. 558-566). Cham: Springer Nature Switzerland.

Neto, A. J. M., & Fernandes, M. A. (2019, July). Chatbot and conversational analysis to promote collaborative learning in distance education. In 2019 IEEE 19th International Conference on Advanced Learning Technologies (ICALT) (Vol. 2161, pp. 324-326). IEEE.

Nguyen, Q. N., Sidorova, A., & Torres, R. (2022). User interactions with chatbot interfaces vs. Menu-based interfaces: An empirical study. *Computers in Human Behavior*, *128*, 107093. DOI: 10.1016/j.chb.2021.107093

Okonkwo, C. W., & Ade-Ibijola, A. (2021a). Chatbots applications in education: A systematic review. *Computers and Education: Artificial Intelligence*, *2*, 100033.

Okonkwo, C. W., & Ade-Ibijola, A. (2021b). Evaluating the ethical implications of using chatbot systems in higher education. *digiTAL*, *2021*, 68.

Pelau, C., Dabija, D. C., & Ene, I. (2021). What makes an AI device human-like? The role of interaction quality, empathy and perceived psychological anthropomorphic characteristics in the acceptance of artificial intelligence in the service industry. *Computers in Human Behavior*, *122*, 106855. DOI: 10.1016/j.chb.2021.106855

Rahsepar Meadi, M., Bernstein, J. S., Batelaan, N., van Balkom, A. J., & Metselaar, S. (2024). Does a lack of emotions make chatbots unfit to be psychotherapists? *Bioethics*, *38*(6), 503–510. DOI: 10.1111/bioe.13299 PMID: 38735049

Savastano, M., Biclesanu, I., Anagnostc, S., Laviola, F., & Cucari, N. (2024). Enterprise chatbots in managers' perception: A strategic framework to implement successful chatbot applications for business decisions. *Management Decision*. Advance online publication. DOI: 10.1108/MD-10-2023-1967

Seitz, L. (2024). Artificial empathy in healthcare chatbots: Does it feel authentic? *Computers in Human Behavior: Artificial Humans*, *2*(1), 100067. DOI: 10.1016/j.chbah.2024.100067

Sumathy, V., & Navamani, G. (2024). AI-Driven Personalized Learning: Enhancing Student Success through Adaptive Technologies. *Library of Progress-Library Science, Information Technology & Computer, 44*(3).

Suta, P., Lan, X., Wu, B., Mongkolnam, P., & Chan, J. H. (2020). An overview of machine learning in chatbots. *International Journal of Mechanical Engineering and Robotics Research*, *9*(4), 502–510. DOI: 10.18178/ijmerr.9.4.502-510

Van Rooij, E. C., Jansen, E. P., & van de Grift, W. J. (2018). First-year university students' academic success: The importance of academic adjustment. *European Journal of Psychology of Education*, *33*(4), 749–767. DOI: 10.1007/s10212-017-0347-8

Winkler, R., & Söllner, M. (2018, July). Unleashing the potential of chatbots in education: A state-of-the-art analysis. In *Academy of management proceedings* (Vol. 2018, No. 1, p. 15903). Briarcliff Manor, NY 10510: Academy of Management. DOI: 10.5465/AMBPP.2018.15903abstract

Yekollu, R. K., Bhimraj Ghuge, T., Sunil Biradar, S., Haldikar, S. V., & Farook Mohideen Abdul Kader, O. (2024, February). AI-driven personalized learning paths: Enhancing education through adaptive systems. In *International Conference on Smart data intelligence* (pp. 507-517). Singapore: Springer Nature Singapore. DOI: 10.1007/978-981-97-3191-6_38

Yin, J., Goh, T. T., Yang, B., & Xiaobin, Y. (2021). Conversation technology with micro-learning: The impact of chatbot-based learning on students' learning motivation and performance. *Journal of Educational Computing Research*, *59*(1), 154–177. DOI: 10.1177/0735633120952067

Chapter 8
Integration of Artificial Intelligence in Blended Business Education:
Fostering Critical Thinking and Student Engagement

Sarra Berraies
https://orcid.org/0000-0001-8406-9678
Higher Institute of Management of Tunis, Tunisia

Wajdi Ben Rejeb
https://orcid.org/0000-0002-9454-0280
University of Lincoln, Tunisia

ABSTRACT

Blended learning is a dominant instructional model in business education, offering flexibility and accessibility while posing challenges around student self-regulation, engagement, and critical thinking. Artificial Intelligence (AI) integration within virtual learning environments offers opportunities to address these issues by personalizing support, scaffolding learning, and enhancing interaction. However, without thoughtful design, AI risks promoting automation bias, surface learning, and reduced critical thinking. This chapter proposes a framework for integrating AI into blended learning, grounded on three pillars: purposeful AI tools' alignment with cognitive outcomes, integrated design across modalities, and scaffolding for self-regulation and collaboration. A case study from a Strategic Management course in a UK Business School illustrates how AI functionalities can support deeper learning and engagement without eroding rigor. The chapter offers a pathway for leveraging AI while preserving analytical and ethical reasoning in business education.

DOI: 10.4018/979-8-3373-3815-6.ch008

right © 2026, IGI Global Scientific Publishing. Copying or distributing in print or electronic forms without written permission of IGI Global Scientific Publishing is prohibited. Use of this chapter to in generative artificial intelligence (AI) technologies is expressly prohibited. The publisher reserves all rights to license its use for generative AI training and machine learning model development.

1. INTRODUCTION

Blended learning has become a cornerstone of business education, merging online flexibility with the relational strengths of face-to-face interaction (Arbaugh et al., 2009; Garrison & Vaughan, 2008; Rasheed et al., 2020). To improve the entire learning experience, blended learning combines cutting-edge technological tools with conventional teaching methods (Benson et al., 2011). Due to the COVID-19 epidemic, universities around the world have experimented with different types of blended learning. This form of learning has proven to be beneficial for students as it provides them with personalized learning paths, accessibility, and flexibility (Belur & Bentall, 2024; Kumar et al., 2021; Joshi et al., 2023; Fathahillah et al., 2023). However, it has been also subject to criticisms as it imposes significant demands on students' self-regulation, digital competencies, and critical engagement (Rasheed et al., 2020; van der Stap et al., 2024). While some studies claim that interactive, reflective, and discussion-based activities in blended learning can boost learning outcomes (Belur & Bentall, 2024; Fathahillah et al., 2023), other studies find no discernible benefit or even difficulties because of ineffective instructional design or challenges in maintaining student motivation and engagement (Sareen & Mandal, 2024; Pavlidou et al., 2021).

In this line, recent developments in artificial intelligence (AI) are being investigated as possible remedies to these problems in order to improve the efficacy of blended learning settings (Fathahillah et al., 2023; Lee et al., 2024; Alshahrani, 2023). The expanding incorporation of AI is transforming blended learning systems. In this context, AI is increasingly perceived as a crucial facilitator, and educational institutions are under pressure to provide more flexible, effective, and captivating blended learning experiences (Lee et al., 2024). Rethinking instructional design is urgently needed by these universities, as seen by the growing use of generative AI tools in education such as ChatGPT and automated feedback systems. AI-enhanced blended learning is of paramount importance for business higher education institutions looking for scalable, customized, and data-driven solutions. But given how quickly these tools are being adopted, it is necessary to critically assess their educational consequences. Fathahillah et al. (2023) stressed that AI integration into the blended learning approach could further enhance the benefits of this type of learning and address its challenges. AI is transforming education by offering personalized support, adaptive feedback, and new forms of learner engagement (Holmes & Tuomi, 2022; Luckin et al., 2022; Al Nabhani et al., 2025).

Nevertheless, one of the most critical challenges of AI in higher education is the establishment of cognitive barriers that impede the development of critical thinking abilities of both students and instructors (Jose et al., 2025). Instead of encouraging deeper cognitive engagement, AI tools may unintentionally promote passive learning behaviours and create cognitive roadblocks if intentional instructional tactics are not used, since students may passively accept the AI-generated content without evaluating it or engaging in critical reflection (Ododo et al., 2024). Careful consideration should be given to this important issue as critical thinking emerges as one of the key skills needed by the workforce of the 21st-century (OECD, 2021; World Economic Forum, 2023).

While recent studies recognize AI's potential to address some of blended learning's challenges (Alshahrani, 2023; Park & Doo, 2024), there remains a lack of guidance on how to use AI tools in ways that preserve and enhance students' critical thinking essential for business graduates navigating complex, real-world problems (Popenici & Kerr, 2017). This chapter responds to this gap by proposing a framework for integrating AI into blended learning that addresses student engagement and self-regulation challenges while deliberately fostering critical thinking. Through theoretical grounding and a practical example, it offers business educators actionable strategies to balance the benefits of AI with the imperative of developing independent and reflective learners.

This chapter seeks to contribute to the emerging debate on AI-enhanced learning in business schools, particularly within the context of blended learning. By connecting the dots between AI innovation and blended learning pedagogy, this chapter advances our knowledge of how educational technology can present both opportunities and challenges. It provides useful advice for educators, instructional designers, and programme leaders looking to improve student experience in a blended learning setting without sacrificing critical thinking and student cognitive outcomes. It is crucial that educators go beyond superficial adoption and implement deliberate, critical, and careful integration strategies in light of AI's growing integration into educational tools and curriculum design. By doing this, we can make sure that AI is used as a catalyst for deeper learning, ethical reflection, and transformative education rather than just as a technological advancement.

To illustrate the practical relevance of the proposed framework, this chapter draws on an instructional intervention applied in November 2024 within a postgraduate Strategic Management course at a UK business school. Delivered in a blended learning format, the course integrated an AI-enhanced simulation activity planned to address persistent cognitive and engagement challenges. Traditional case studies in strategic management often rely on lengthy, static narratives that promote passive reading rather than critical inquiry or dynamic decision-making. These limitations are often exacerbated in blended learning environments, where reduced interaction can lead to student isolation and disengagement. To mitigate these challenges, the intervention utilized Blackboard Ultra's AI chatbot functionality to transform a conventional case study into an interactive, inquiry-driven simulation. This approach aimed to foster deeper engagement, encourage problem-solving, and support the development of critical thinking which are key outcomes that standard blended approaches may struggle to deliver without intentional design.

This chapter is organized as follows: Section 2 introduces blended learning and outlines the key challenges related. Section 3 examines the role of AI in tackling these issues and provides an overview of the main features and uses pertinent to blended education environments. Section 4 discusses the possible drawbacks of using AI in educational settings, with an emphasis on the threat of over-automation and the erosion of critical thinking. Section 5 presents the suggested strategic framework for integrating AI into blended learning, specifically based on the alignment, integration, and scaffolding principles. It also highlights critical recommendations for academic leaders, instructors, and instructional designers, in leveraging AI for blended learning. Section 6 offers an illustrative application of this framework via a real-world case study of the Strategic Management module. Finally, Section 7 concludes with reflections on the future of AI in higher business education, outlining directions for future research and institutional practice.

2. CHALLENGES OF BLENDED LEARNING

In the education setting, learning can take place in a variety of ways and is commonly divided into synchronous vs asynchronous learning and virtual vs face-to-face learning (Müller & Mildenberger, 2021; Chaeruman et al., 2018). Students and educators engage in real-time communication during synchronous learning, which can take place in a live online session or in a physical classroom. In turn, asynchronous learning enables students to access resources and finish assignments at their own speed without having to communicate with others at the same time. While asynchronous learning such as recorded lectures or discussion boards provides flexibility, synchronous learning such as online live sessions allows for real-time participation. In blended learning settings, striking the correct balance is essential because each has unique benefits.

In a similar vein, face-to-face learning happens in a conventional classroom, but virtual learning happens exclusively online. Combining these approaches results in blended learning, which maximizes the learning experience by integrating online and in-person learning. Blended learning is a hybrid deliberate approach integrating both traditional face-to-face classroom instruction and e-learning practices (Kumar et al., 2021; Su et al., 2023). However, it frequently involves an uneven rather than seamless integration of online and in-person instruction. It can range from completely online classes with sporadic in-person encounters to simply sharing lecture materials via virtual platforms (Fleck, 2012).

Blended learning, combining synchronous and asynchronous delivery across virtual and face-to-face modes, has gained widespread recognition in higher education (Müller & Mildenberger, 2021; Kumar et al., 2021), especially in several globally renewed universities, in recent years and its use increased dramatically during and after the COVID-19 lockout (Su et al., 2023; Bizami et al., 2023; Li & Hou, 2024). Institutions were compelled by the epidemic to quickly implement online learning programs, which hastened the incorporation of digital resources into conventional teaching techniques. Blended learning has then transformed from an alternative method to a mainstream educational model (Bizami et al., 2023).

The difference between content and instructional design is also important. While content design refers to what is taught i.e. the subject matter or knowledge, instructional design focuses on how the course material is taught including how it is arranged, presented, and made interesting for students. Effective blended learning carefully considers how students will interact with the material rather than merely posting it online (Fleck, 2012). With the growing popularity of OpenCourseWare and other easily accessible online resources, the focus in education is shifting from simply teaching content to helping students navigate and engage with it (Fleck, 2012).

Considering the increasing popularity of blended learning, it is crucial to assess both its benefits and implementation obstacles. Prior studies highlighted that students benefit greatly from a hybrid strategy (Belur and Bentall, 2024; Kumar et al., 2021; Webster et al., 2020). Students can study whenever and wherever they choose, which provides both educators and students greater accessibility, flexibility and opportunities for self-paced learning and removes geographical constraints (Belur & Bentall, 2024; Kumar et al., 2021; Goedhart et al., 2019).

Joshi et al. (2023) stressed that a dynamic learning environment that accommodates various learning preferences and styles is produced by combining in-person encounters with virtual activities. Students are more satisfied when they have the freedom to access course materials and take part in discussions whenever and wherever they choose, fostering a sense of control and ownership (Joshi et al., 2023).

Notwithstanding the advantages of blended learning, properly implementing it is not without its obstacles. Several persistent challenges accompany this model. Through a systematic literature review, Sareen & Mandal (2024) identified 16 key barriers to the effective implementation of blended learning. These include compromised self-regulation skills, where learners struggle with time management and organization; inactive learning, driven by lack of motivation and internal resistance; and individual paradoxes, such as low confidence, distrust in online assessments, and dissatisfaction (Sareen & Mandal, 2024). Mental-wellness constraints including isolation and stress also inhibit engagement. ICT infrastructure and digital connectivity challenges limit access to reliable devices and internet, especially in remote settings (Sareen & Mandal, 2024). Content-related and resource-management restrictions emerge from poor-quality materials and scattered information (Sareen & Mandal, 2024). Institutions also face a lack of institutionalisation, showing limited commitment to blended learning frameworks. Learners and instructors experience limited human connection and socialisation constraints, impacting collaboration and community building (Sareen & Mandal, 2024). Support deficiencies, including lack of technical help and unreliable platforms, further disrupt learning (Sareen & Mandal, 2024). Additionally, designing constraints, lack of purpose in tasks, reinforcement constraints like delayed feedback, and training deficiencies among educators and students all contribute to the complex challenges of blended learning (Sareen & Mandal, 2024).

A frequently mentioned difficulty in blended learning settings is keeping students engaged and motivated, especially when it comes to asynchronous or self-paced components. Students often experience isolation and a reduction in meaningful peer-to-peer and student-instructor interactions, which can negatively affect engagement and learning outcomes (van der Stap et al., 2024; Park & Doo, 2024). According to Pavlidou et al. (2021), students frequently view online discussions as less dynamic and interesting than in-person classroom discussions when it comes to peer interaction and student participation. Peer collaboration and trust-building are more challenging when there is a lack of physical presence since it weakens social bonds (Pavlidou et al., 2021). Additionally, because the actual presence of instructors and peers reduces the temptation of digital distractions like online browsing or multitasking on devices, students reported feeling more engaged and less distracted in face-to-face situations (Pavlidou et al., 2021). The disengagement in online settings may be exacerbated by the lack of direct instructor supervision in asynchronous or inadequately controlled online environments. Besides, Pavlidou et al. (2021) observe that students frequently express discontent with cursory talks and that there are insufficient quality exchanges on collaborative platforms. These authors concluded that because of these issues, the emotional and relational aspects of learning including such as presence, trust, and accountability, can be jeopardized in blended settings.

Students may feel isolated, less motivated, participate less, and feel less like they're contributing, if they don't have the immediate, intimate, and accountable interactions that come with in-person interactions (Li, 2022; Moallem, 2015; van der Stap et al., 2024; Park & Doo, 2024). Moallem (2015) demonstrated that the impact of quality and richness of the online interaction, whether synchronous or asynchronous, on learning and motivation depends on social presence, interaction, collaboration, intimacy, immediacy and self-regulation.

While online learning offers the flexibility to learn at one's own pace, it frequently lacks the social presence, emotional connection, and immediacy that face-to-face setting offers (Pavlidou et al., 2021; Chaeruman et al., 2018; van der Stap et al.,

2024). This could lead to passive learning attitudes and behaviours and a lack of interaction with classmates, instructors, or the course material. Students who require accountability and immediate feedback or lack internal motivation may find it especially difficult to be engaged in asynchronous blended learning, which could ultimately affect their learning outcomes and learning satisfaction (Sareen & Mandal, 2024). In this sense, limited interaction between students and their instructors is another enduring issue in blended learning settings (Li, 2022; Whiteside & Dikkers, 2016). Particularly in virtual settings, a lack of significant social presence might impede collaboration and diminish opportunities for feedback and discussion (Moallem, 2015; Pavlidou et al., 2021; Li, 2022; van der Stap et al., 2024). Asynchronous learning frequently leads to fragmented communication, in contrast to face-to-face environments where impromptu queries and informal interactions can boost the learning process (Moallem, 2015). Group projects, case studies, and project-based learning may become less dynamic and interesting as a result of this lack of immediacy. Furthermore, students may feel alienated from the course and the learning community if instructors are not available or take too long to respond.

Additionally, systematic reviews highlight issues such as poor self-regulation skills including procrastination, weak time management, and shallow learning approaches as well as difficulties managing the flexibility that blended learning affords (Sareen & Mandal, 2024; Moallem, 2015; Boelens et al., 2017; Rasheed et al., 2020). Students who lack time management capabilities or the capacity to organize and track their own work are more likely to lag behind because they are frequently expected to complete a portion of the course on their own (Sareen & Mandal, 2024). Some students struggle to maintain constant study habits, skip deadlines, or procrastinate in the absence of formal instruction (Pokryszko-Dragan et al., 2021; Sareen & Mandal, 2024). Online learning's flexibility can be a double-edged sword for students who lack the necessary skills to manage independence. This challenge is exacerbated in case of students' inexperience with goal-setting, structured routine and reflection (Sareen & Mandal, 2024).

Blended learning may also overlook each student's unique needs, skill level, and preferred learning method (Sareen & Mandal, 2024), which can hinder instructional personalization and differentiation. Instructors may struggle to manage both in-person and online components simultaneously, leading to overburdened students and lost interest. This may limit the efficacy of blended learning as an inclusive pedagogical strategy, as it may not provide personalized feedback or adapt instructional tactics and content to each student's needs.

Vaughan (2007) emphasizes also the serious challenges and dangers connected to the use of technology in education. Developing blended learning course modules presents several challenges, such as technology unavailability, inadequate assistance, a lack of resources and time for course material development, and the requirement to master new teaching and technological skills (Benson et al., 2011; Sareen & Mandal, 2024). Finally, the digital divide and related technological obstacles continue to be major problems when implementing blended learning, especially in university settings with limited resources. According to Joshi et al. (2023), important issues of blended learning are the digital divide, which is the unequal distribution of students' access to internet connectivity and technology, challenges with digital platform navigation, a lack of digital literacy and technical problems that can hamper students' engagement. On the one hand, blended learning poses challenges for students who have limited access to reliable internet or digital devices are (Bayyat et al., 2021; Joshi et al., 2023; Rasheed et al., 2020). On the other hand, inadequate digital literacy and perceived complexity with using learning tools can prevent students with access from participating. Notably, the skills needed to use the online platforms are constantly evolving, which is overwhelming for both instructors and students (Rasheed et al., 2020). The whole online learning experience can be also undermined by instructors and students being discouraged by the quality of the online platforms including bad user interface design, platform overload, and frequent technological issues.

Table 1 summarizes the blended learning challenges in higher education.

Table 1. Challenges of blended learning in higher education

Category	Challenges	References
Pedagogical design and delivery	- Balancing online and in-person modes and synchronous and asynchronous processes. -Ineffective educational design - Poor interface design (fragmented conversations, passive learning) - Insufficient individualization and distinction	Fleck (2012); Sareen & Mandal (2024); Moallem (2015)
Student engagement and motivation	- Low self-control and motivation (bad time management, procrastination) - Isolation and decreased involvement - Online conversations less engaging than in-person ones - Lack of accountability, presence, and immediacy.	Sareen & Mandal (2024); van der Stap et al. (2024); Li (2022); Pavlidou et al. (2021);
Social and emotional aspects	- Decreased trust-building and peer interaction - Weakened social ties - Reduced feeling of connection and community; - Stress and anxiety	Pavlidou et al. (2021); Moallem (2015)

continued on following page

Table 1. Continued

Category	Challenges	References
Instructional skills and support	- Instructors' insufficient instruction in blended learning -Limitations on time and resources for creating high-quality modules - Inadequate institutionalization and low institutional support - Managing in-person and virtual components.	Sareen & Mandal (2024); Benson et al. (2011); Vaughan (2007)
Assessment and feedback	-A lack of confidence in online tests - Lack of follow-up and reinforcement - Delayed or superficial feedback - Students' discontent with assessments' transparency	Sareen & Mandal (2024); Li (2022); Moallem (2015)
Content management and navigation	- Inadequate material and dispersed resources -Students' challenges utilizing digital platforms - Shallow involvement as a result of complexity or overload	Sareen & Mandal (2024); Fleck (2012); Rasheed et al. (2020)
Equity and inclusion	- A one-size-fits-all strategy overlooking various learning requirements. -Limited ability to adjust to the preferences, styles, or degrees of learners -Less tech-savvy students are marginalized.	Sareen & Mandal (2024); Joshi et al. (2023); Boelens et al. (2017)

3. THE ROLE OF ARTIFICIAL INTELLIGENCE IN ADDRESSING BLENDED LEARNING CHALLENGES

Artificial Intelligence (AI) materializes computer systems and algorithms equipped to realize tasks inherent to human intellect, such as solving problems, thinking, and making complex decisions. All sectors, including education, must adapt to the new reality shaped by AI, which stands at the core of current research debates (Fathahillah et al., 2023). AI has started to revolutionize higher education (Ruano-Borbalan, 2025; Kumar et al., 2024).

A literature review highlights important growth in the integration of AI within higher education (Park and Doo, 2024). In this context, AI is increasingly incorporated to automate administrative tasks, personalize learning experiences, support assessment, and enhance student engagement (Luckin et al., 2022; Al Nabhani et al., 2025). This higher education's quick adoption of AI has been fueled by blended learning, particularly in the aftermath of post-pandemic changes and digital transformation. In order to help educators meet the many demands of contemporary students, AI solutions such as adaptive learning platforms and intelligent tutoring systems are being incorporated to automate tasks and provide individualized, flexible training. AI-driven personalization, through adaptive content and tailored feedback, has emerged as a key mechanism for enhancing student engagement and learning efficiency (Bhutoria, 2022). Besides, recent studies have shown that AI tools can improve the assessment of students' performance (Mallik & Gangopadhyay, 2023; González-Calatayud et al., 2021) and predict learning outcomes with greater precision (Arizmendi et al., 2023). However, current AI applications in blended learning tend to focus primarily on asynchronous individual online activities, with limited integration linking online and face-to-face components (Park & Doo, 2024). This gap underscores the need for more comprehensive strategies that bridge virtual and in-person learning environments cohesively.

As blended learning gains traction, AI has the potential to significantly improve engagement, efficacy, and equity in hybrid or full online course delivery. For business education, AI offers specific solutions to blended learning difficulties. With careful integration into instructional design, AI can be a potent enabler in overcoming the constraints of when and how students learn, from virtual assistants and intelligent tutoring systems to predictive analytics dashboards and automated grading tools. It can improve pedagogical strategies by offering personalized and adaptive learning practices. In this perspective, adaptive learning platforms are e-learning platforms that tailor content according to the students' specific profiles and progress and in this sense customize the learning process through suggesting particular materials in the format that the students prefer, defining the degree of difficulty of assignments according to the students' skills and providing tailored feedback (Tan et al., 2025). AI offers support by scaffolding learning activities like recommending extra readings or videos to students based on their performance, thereby adjusting the learning content delivery (Huang et al., 2023). AI-powered or intelligent tutoring systems such as Chatbots can evaluate students' needs and preferences, respond to the students' questions immediately, guide them for complex assignments and provide feedback instantly, ensuring clear learning structure and tailored and engaging content and more effective blended learning environments (Lin & Mubarok, 2021). These systems can provide feedback to the instructors who can then intervene in synchronous or asynchronous settings. AI can assist instructors by creating flashcards and quizzes from course materials, select relevant videos or case studies, thereby ensuring high-quality resources and thus better instructional design and pedagogy (Lechuga & Doroudi, 2023).

Within the context of blended learning, by personalizing educational resources and assessments to each student's requirements and preferences, it can be utilized to personalize learning (Fathahillah et al., 2023). AI streamlines course structure, improves accessibility, and arranges learning materials according to student choices in content management and navigation. AI provides individualized learning, supports students with a range of requirements, and enhances accessibility for students with disabilities to advance equity and inclusion. Besides, by tailoring educational content to individual learners and ensuring assessments are delivered promptly and precisely, AI can enhance interactions between students and educators, fostering a more supportive, inclusive, and effective learning atmosphere (Al Nabhani et al., 2025). For instance, an AI-powered adaptive learning system can evaluate student performance information and offer tailored study suggestions, allowing each learner to comprehend and remember the course material better with this personalized approach (Fathahillah et al., 2023). Besides, AI can help educators develop and provide successful instruction through Natural Language Processing (NLP) approaches that can assess student comments, generate automatic feedback, help instructors detect challenging students and offer tailored actions to improve their learning (González-Calatayud et al., 2021; Fathahillah et al., 2023). Moreover, integrating AI with virtual and augmented reality technologies creates novel possibilities for delivering immersive learning experiences that enhance students' learning effectiveness (Al Nabhani et al., 2025). Ge et al. (2025), for example, show how gamified large language models (LLMs) can support goal-setting and metacognitive reflection, enabling students to successfully traverse hybrid learning paths. These resources aid in bridging the gap between the organized assistance frequently found in in-person learning environments and the flexibility offered by online learning (Ge et al., 2025). Also, AI offers automated grading and tailored feedback, giving students thorough, individualized and quick feedback (Huang et al., 2023). This feature improves the evaluation process overall in blended learning contexts by guaranteeing consistent and objective assessment. AI-driven platforms can enhance self-Regulation and autonomy by providing personalized scaffolding, real-time feedback, and adaptive task scheduling to help students manage time and engagement across online and face-to-face elements (Liao & Wu, 2022; Jovanović et al., 2017). For example, AI assistants could offer weekly prompts, alerts, and nudges to encourage on-time participation and task completion.

Moreover, to address the problems of isolation and motivation, emotion-aware AI bots can identify affective cues and react sympathetically, resulting in more human-like interactions even in digital environments (Huang et al., 2023). AI-based learning systems can even identify students' emotions and moods and adjust the learning content depending on their emotional state, aiding them to avoid anxiety and improving their self-confidence (Huang et al., 2023). In hybrid environments, this feature helps foster a stronger sense of community and support, which is essential for sustaining motivation and lowering dropout rates (Lin & Mubarok, 2021).

In this sense, Lin & Mubarok (2021) stressed that these systems are perceived as Smart learning partners and that chatbots are very popular interactive tools that can improve student achievement and provide more effective one-on-one learning experiences than typical classroom settings. AI can support affective engagement and motivation through fostering emotional engagement, clustering students based on learning behaviors and offering motivational nudges (Jovanović et al., 2017), or by using gamification features like badge systems to reward timely participation (Troussas et al., 2020). In business communication courses, for instance, gamified AI systems could encourage active participation in online discussions about cross-cultural negotiation.

Also, due to fragmented collaboration and low social presence, learner engagement and involvement frequently decrease in blended learning, AI helps address this by acting as a pedagogical agent (ChatGPT or AI tutors), as a direct mediator (AI-based learning platforms), and as a supplementary assistant (learning analytics tools) (Xu & Ouyang, 2022; Park & Doo, 2024). These roles offer diverse opportunities to address student challenges if strategically deployed. In particular, Chatbots can provide peer-like engagement, affective assistance, and intellectual support (Lin & Mubarok, 2021). Additionally, by grouping student contributions to promote richer in-class conversations and creating collaborative groups based on complimentary abilities or learning profiles (Lechuga & Doroudi, 2022), AI can maximize peer learning. It facilitates peer and instructor interaction by assisting in forming collaborative groups based on complementary skills (Lechuga & Doroudi, 2022), automating initial peer feedback on case analyses or project drafts (Pardo et al., 2019), and clustering discussion contributions to identify themes for further in-class debates (Liao & Wu, 2022). In a business strategy course, AI could match students for case study discussions based on their analytical strengths, ensuring deeper interaction both online and during seminars.

In addition to automating a variety of repetitive duties for educators such as quizzes generation, learning content updates and even grading students, AI also frees up time and mental energy for more complex, creative, and human-centered endeavors creating augmented instructors (Mariyono & Nur Alif Hd, 2025). It supports instructors by improving their teaching capabilities, suggesting improvement for their course material and instruction, and freeing them to focus on higher-order instructional design and student engagement (Fathahillah et al., 2023). AI-driven analytics can personalize learning content and monitoring progress by helping instructors customize course pathways, adjusting case study complexity or recommending additional resources based on students' demonstrated competencies (Phillips et al., 2020). For instance, in an operations management module, students struggling with supply chain simulations could be directed to supplementary AI-generated tutorials.

Table 2 summarizes the AI solutions to blended learning challenges in higher education.

Table 2. Mapping AI solutions to blended learning barriers in higher education

Challenge category	How AI Can Mitigate These Challenges	References
Pedagogical design and delivery	AI enhances instructional quality via intelligent tutoring systems, flashcard/quiz generation, NLP tools for auto-feedback, and differentiated learning paths.	Tan et al. (2025); Lin & Mubarok (2021); Lechuga & Doroudi (2023); Fathahillah et al. (2023); Al Nabhani et al. (2025); Ruano-Borbalan (2025); Kumar et al. (2024)
Student engagement and motivation	AI supports self-regulation with prompts and nudges; VR/AR and gamified AI boost critical thinking and motivation; emotion-aware bots enhance emotional connection and reduce disengagement.	Liao & Wu (2022); Jovanović et al. (2017); Ge et al. (2025); Huang et al. (2023); Troussas et al. (2020); Lin & Mubarok (2021); Bhutoria (2022)
Social and emotional aspects	AI fosters emotional support through affective computing and NLP; intelligent agents simulate human-like interaction; chatbots serve as peer-like companions; AI facilitates collaborative group formation and thematic clustering for rich social learning.	Huang et al. (2023); Xu & Ouyang (2022); Park & Doo (2024); Lechuga & Doroudi (2022); Lin & Mubarok (2021); Pardo et al. (2019)
Instructional skills and support	AI automates administrative tasks (quizzes, grading, content updates), provides teaching enhancement feedback, and supports instructors through content curation and analytics-based instructional suggestions.	Mariyono & Nur Alif Hd (2025); Phillips et al. (2020); Fathahillah et al. (2023); Lechuga & Doroudi (2023); Park & Doo (2024)
Assessment and feedback	AI enables instant grading, automated and tailored feedback, learning outcome prediction, and continuous student performance tracking with precision.	Mallik & Gangopadhyay (2023); Arizmendi et al. (2023); González-Calatayud et al. (2021); Al Nabhani et al. (2025); Fathahillah et al. (2023)
Content management & navigation	AI streamlines navigation and delivery of personalized content; platforms adapt material sequencing, suggest additional resources, and reduce overload through structured recommendations.	Tan et al. (2025); Fathahillah et al. (2023); Park & Doo (2024); Al Nabhani et al. (2025)
Equity and inclusion	AI promotes inclusion by adapting learning to individual needs, supporting accessibility for diverse learners (e.g., disabilities, low tech literacy), and offering personalized learning pathways to reduce inequality.	Fathahillah et al. (2023); Al Nabhani et al. (2025); Luckin et al. (2022); Huang et al. (2023)

4. THE RISKS OF AI FOR CRITICAL THINKING IN BLENDED LEARNING

Despite that the integration of AI into blended learning environments offers opportunities for personalization, feedback, and learner support, it may pose risks for students' critical thinking capabilities, which is a key learning objective (Kos'myna et al., 2025; Jose et al., 2025). Excessive dependence on AI tools can impede students' development of autonomous, analytical, and reflective thinking, which are essential elements of critical thinking. These risks fall under two primary categories: cognitive concerns and operational, equity and academic integrity risks.

4.1. Cognitive concerns

A new study performed by Kos'myna et al. (2025) at MIT's Media Lab highlights the cognitive cost of AI use, reporting alarming findings about how the use of ChatGPT alone can impede students' aptitude for critical thinking. Researchers asked three groups of participants including those who utilized Google search engine, those who utilized ChatGPT and those who used only their brain and did not use any AI tool (brain-only), to write essays. Results show that while the search engine group displayed moderate levels of engagement, the Brain-only group displayed the most robust and extensive brain network activity. The ChatGPT group displayed the least amount of total brain connection and signs of cognitive offloading and poor critical thinking, such as decreased neural engagement, memory recall, and creativity (Kos'myna et al., 2025). Similarly, Ju (2023) found that students relying exclusively on AI scored 25% lower on writing tasks related to comprehension and 12% lower on AI-assisted reading tests. These findings indicate that overreliance on AI can reduce cognitive effort and hinder deep processing, underscoring the need for careful instructional guidance.

Within blended learning, where independent online work complements in-person interactions, the risks to cognition are amplified. Without thoughtful instructional design, AI can undermine the competencies that blended learning aims to cultivate, including critical thinking, problem-solving, and independent analysis. While AI can free students from unnecessary cognitive load, allowing them to focus on higher-order thinking (Jose et al., 2025; Mariyono & Nur Alif Hd, 2025), it can also diminish the essential cognitive effort required for deep learning (Jose et al., 2025). Students may passively embrace AI outputs without critical evaluation, reducing engagement and reflective thinking (Ododo et al., 2024). Jose et al. (2025) emphasize that AI should augment, not replace, instructors' pedagogical roles, ensuring alignment with learning objectives.

Several mechanisms illustrate these cognitive risks. Blended learning inherently requires students to self-regulate, synthesize diverse sources of information, and engage actively during both asynchronous and synchronous phases (Rasheed et al., 2020; Boelens et al., 2017). However, the growing availability of AI-powered tools risks short-circuiting these processes. Automation bias occurs when learners uncritically accept AI outputs as authoritative, bypassing evaluation and reflection, and fostering cognitive complacency (Abuzar et al., 2025; Niloy et al., 2024). Reduced cognitive struggle arises because AI often provides immediate solutions, diminishing the productive cognitive friction needed to wrestle with complex problems and reducing opportunities for analytical skill development (Burns, 2025; Deng et al., 2024). Surface learning can occur when AI summarizes content or generates responses, causing students to engage less deeply and inhibiting critical synthesis, evaluation, and innovation (Kasneci et al., 2023; Farrokhnia et al., 2024; Burns, 2025). Without deliberate reflection and synthesis, learners may gain fragmented knowledge rather than deep mastery, mirroring past critiques of education that emphasize memorization over meaningful cognitive integration (Burns, 2025). These cognitive concerns may be exacerbated by design and delivery decisions involving AI. While instructors' over-reliance on AI may cause them to misalign their instruction with the desired learning outcomes, students may only interact superficially with AI-generated content (Jose et al., 2025; Park & Doo, 2024). AI tools may limit the amount of effort put into difficult activities and promote automation bias by lowering student motivation and impeding self-regulation (Ge et al., 2025; Lin & Mubarok, 2021). Poorly managed tailored content paths may fragment learning or cognitively overwhelm students, and excessive use of AI-generated assessments or feedback can promote surface-level reflection rather than in-depth analytical thinking (Mallik & Gangopadhyay, 2023; Tan et al., 2025; Rasheed et al., 2020).

Recent studies underscore these concerns. Niloy et al. (2024) highlight that AI chatbots can foster academic laziness and diminish critical inquiry during self-paced learning. Deng et al. (2024) and Lee et al. (2024) caution that AI used for direct answers rather than structured scaffolding may inhibit higher-order skills necessary for business leadership and strategic decision-making. In blended learning, these risks are compounded because asynchronous activities are designed to develop autonomy and independent learning. In business education, where the ability to critically evaluate complex problems, integrate diverse information, and make sound strategic judgments is essential, the blind adoption of AI tools into blended courses is particularly hazardous. Careful instructional strategies are needed to ensure AI acts not as a shortcut to answers but as a catalyst for deeper thinking, critical discussion, and collaborative knowledge building across both online and in-person components of blended learning (Jose et al., 2025). Adaptive AI-based blended learning strategies must be created to balance automation with cognitive competency development.

4.2 Operational, equity, and academic integrity risks

In integrated learning, issues pertaining to AI operations, equity, privacy, and integrity are intricately linked, even though cognitive challenges play a major role. It is impossible to study instructional design, inclusivity, data utilization, and fair evaluation separately because of their overlap. To give a more comprehensive picture of the difficulties AI presents for teaching and learning, the ensuing section combines these aspects.

Beyond cognitive risks, the use of AI in blended learning presents operational, ethical and equity concerns that impact instructors' skills, their instruction methods, social relationships, and inclusivity. These challenges may affect the efficacy, equity, and quality of learning outcomes. An important operational risk stems from pedagogical delivery and design. AI-generated content and automated recommendations can promote standardized instructional pathways that neglect different students' needs and lead instructors to misalign learning objectives with course activities (Jose et al., 2025; Park & Doo, 2024). Over-reliance on AI also limits adaptive strategies like experiential or problem-based learning by reducing instructors' capacity to use contextual judgment and creative teaching techniques (Phillips et al., 2020; Kassekhan et al., 2025). As AI becomes more prevalent, instructors' ability to critically assess and modify AI outputs may be compromised, leading to less adaptable and dynamic learning environments.

Social and emotional aspects of learning are also impacted. AI systems are unable to offer genuine mentoring, emotional support, or subtle social cues, all of which are essential for encouraging resilience, teamwork, and motivation (Xu & Ouyang, 2022; Huang et al., 2023). Asynchronous learning activities can cause students to feel isolated, and an excessive dependence on AI may limit opportunities for peer contact, teamwork and development of communication skills (Fang et al., 2021; Lechuga & Doroudi, 2022). These limits can be somewhat filled by intelligent agents and AI-enabled teamwork, but these agents cannot completely replace the advantages of social interaction and human direction.

AI adoption is further challenged by concerns about equity and inclusion. Learners from different social, linguistic, or cultural backgrounds may be at a disadvantage due to algorithmic bias in AI systems, which might exacerbate already-existing disparities (Luckin et al., 2022; Boelens et al., 2017). When AI platforms fail to accommodate students with disabilities, low digital literacy, or restricted access to technology, accessibility issues may occur. Ineffective customization might cause students to become cognitively overloaded or fragment their learning experiences, which lowers engagement and self-control (Kassekhan et al., 2025; Tan et al., 2025).

Additionally, when AI systems gather and store sensitive personal data, such as behavioral logs and performance metrics, student privacy may be jeopardized, leaving students vulnerable to breaches or unauthorized usage (Al Nabhani et al., 2025; Phillips et al., 2020). Additionally, students may abuse AI for plagiarism, automated essay writing, or cheating, which could compromise academic integrity and result in shallow engagement and difficulties with authentic evaluation (Mallik & Gangopadhyay, 2023; Arizmendi et al., 2023). These risks are increased in blended learning environments where students work autonomously since instructors are less present during asynchronous activities.

Risks related to operations, equity, and integrity are frequently intertwined. While algorithmic biases may disproportionately impact underrepresented learners, decreasing interest and motivation, an over-reliance on AI by instructors might make it more difficult to uncover misuse or privacy violations. Similarly, a lack of human interaction can exacerbate social and ethical issues, emphasizing the necessity of careful planning and supervision. Operations, equity, and ethical concerns must be carefully controlled to ensure that blended learning remains inclusive, fair, and effective, even while AI could expedite operations, deliver timely support, and customize learning (Jose et al., 2025; Xu & Ouyang, 2022; Huang et al., 2023).

5. A STRATEGIC FRAMEWORK FOR INTEGRATING AI INTO BLENDED LEARNING IN BUSINESS EDUCATION

According to Jose et al. (2025), a successful AI integration strategy in education requires careful planning to support, rather than replace, core cognitive processes. Educators should begin with needs' evaluation to align AI use with learning goals (Bloom, 1956), select tools that promote engagement, ensure a balanced mix of AI support and educator guidance, and implement monitoring and feedback systems to evaluate and adjust the impact on student learning. This needs' assessment should take into account the course learning objectives, the students' characteristics, and problems with the existing instructional method. Instructors may integrate simulations using AI to improve students' decision-making abilities for a real-case study scenarios in a business strategy course without taking the place of instructor for guiding students via moral discussions. In the line of Sweller's (1988) cognitive load theory, AI tools can reduce extraneous cognitive load and automate complex and routine activities, allowing students to focus on problem-solving and critical thinking rather than struggling with overly complex information presentation.

Kassekhan et al. (2025) advise integrating AI literacy within educational curricula in order to guarantee that students use AI tools for analytical analysis rather of depending on them in a mechanistic manner. Via specialized courses or reflection exercises, students can learn how to assess AI-generated outputs, challenge data sources, and comprehend AI tools' limitations. Jose et al. (2025) advocate that the application of AI in the higher education should be aligned with the core psychological needs as highlighted by Ryan & Deci (2000), namely competence, autonomy and relatedness, giving their effect on students' motivation. AI should offer timely, tailored feedback that promotes learning progress in order to develop competency (Zimmerman, 2002). Giving students options about how to use AI tools is also necessary to promote autonomy. Meaningful peer and instructor engagement should be included to AI interactions in order to foster relatedness. In this sense, by avoiding over-reliance on automated systems, AI should be integrated in a way that safeguards students' autonomy while enhancing their competence (Jose et al., 2025). It must be paired with meaningful human interaction to sustain students' social and emotional engagement and reinforce their sense of relatedness (Jose et al., 2025). Rather than replacing human instruction, AI should support students' development of autonomous thinking and interpersonal connection in the learning process (Jose et al., 2025). According to Lin & Mubarok (2021), combining AI chatbot assistance with mind map coaching in a flipped classroom can improve learning results and student engagement with the chatbot. The mix of mind maps and AI chatbots helps students arrange their ideas graphically before responding, which results in more structured and insightful answers. AI chatbots provide flexible, self-paced chances to reinforce their abilities, while the flipped model permits students to absorb material on their own and use class time for active practice (Lin & Mubarok, 2021).

Instructors should also prevent students from the dangers of an excessive reliance on AI, such as diminished cognitive effort, surface learning, and automation bias, that may hinder critical thinking. In this line, instructors could encourage debriefs, critical discourse, and reflection when using AI. Besides, when combined with AI, gamification like serious games can enrich blended learning environments and turns passive learning into engaging and rewarding learning (Troussas et al., 2020). For instance, instructors can use storytelling or narrative-based learning based on AI that can develop critical thinking for real-world scenarios and experiential learning (Gupta et al., 2024).

Abuzar et al. (2025) suggests improving AI literacy via workshops, encouraging efficient prompt drafting and output assessment techniques, and putting institutional regulations in place to direct ethical AI use. Institutions can promote critical engagement with AI and make sure it improves rather than detracts from educational outcomes by incorporating reminder prompts and AI literacy modules into their curricula (Abuzar et al., 2025).

To harness AI's potential while safeguarding the critical competencies essential in business education, we propose a strategic framework for its integration into blended learning environments. This framework is grounded in three core principles:

- **Purposeful alignment with learning outcomes:** AI applications must be explicitly aligned with the cognitive and metacognitive goals of the course, particularly critical thinking, problem-solving, and reflective judgment. This entails defining AI tools for business education that can perfect decision-making in the face of uncertainty, simulate strategic problems, and inspire ethical thought in addition to delivering material. Rather than simply accelerating content delivery, AI tools should be designed to scaffold students' analytical processes. For example, instead of providing direct answers during asynchronous online tasks, AI tools such as conversational agents (e.g., ChatGPT with customized prompts) can guide students through inquiry-based processes, posing follow-up questions that require analysis, synthesis, and evaluation (Lee et al., 2024). In business education, this could involve using AI to simulate complex decision-making scenarios where students must weigh conflicting stakeholder interests, rather than simply generating strategic recommendations. Adaptive AI must be used to encourage active involvement rather than passive information consumption, even while it has the potential to tailor learning experiences and simplify complex ideas (Jose et al., 2025)

- **Integrated design across online and offline learning phases:** To prevent the fragmentation often seen in blended courses, AI-enhanced activities must deliberately bridge the online and face-to-face components. To help instructors maintain cognitive momentum between learning stages, an online forum based on AI could serve as a starting point for in-class discussions. AI can be used to generate case studies or debate prompts from online discussions that feed directly into in-person seminars, thus maintaining continuity of critical engagement across modalities (Park & Doo, 2024). For instance, AI analytics can help instructors identify patterns in online discussion boards such as common misconceptions or emerging themes and use these insights to structure face-to-face workshops focused on critical evaluation of diverse viewpoints. In order to build critical viewpoints and reinforce important concepts across contexts, this cross-modal relationship is crucial.

- **Scaffolding for self-regulation and peer collaboration:** Given that self-regulation and peer interaction are recurring challenges in blended learning (Boelens et al., 2017; Rasheed et al., 2020), AI tools should be used to support but not replace these processes. Learners can take charge of their education by using AI-powered dashboards to get real-time feedback on their engagement, pace, and time-on-task. This can include AI-generated personalized feedback on time management, participation, and critical depth of contributions can help with self-regulation support.

Furthermore, students can be assembled based on their complimentary skills or ways of thinking using AI, which facilitates more complex peer-to-peer interaction and problem-solving exercises. AI-based clustering tools can form peer groups based on diverse thinking styles or past performance, ensuring rich peer-to-peer learning opportunities (Fang et al., 2021; Lechuga & Doroudi, 2022). For instance, in business education contexts, using AI to help students iteratively co-construct business plans or marketing strategies, encouraging negotiation, critique, and collaborative problem-solving.

The framework advocates for AI to be embedded not as a passive content provider but as an active, inquiry-driven, and socially connective agent within blended learning ecosystems helping to overcome blended learning's traditional challenges such as learner isolation and poor self-regulation without sacrificing the cultivation of the critical, reflective, and integrative thinking skills that business education demands.

Table 3 outlines strategic recommendations for mitigating the risks of AI when integrated to blended learning:

continued on following page

Table 3. Continued

Table 3. Strategic recommendations for mitigating AI-Related Risks in blended learning: An integrated framework

Challenge area	AI-related risks	Strategic recommendations	Key references
Pedagogical design and delivery	-Over-reliance of instructors on AI and misalignment with teaching objectives. -For students, learning at the surface level from content produced by AI and consuming content passively.	- Perform needs' assessment to match AI resources with learning objectives. -Integrate AI applications supporting research, problem-solving and critical thinking across online and offline learning sessions. - Employ flipped classroom under the direction of chatbots.	Jose et al. (2025); Park & Doo (2024); Tan et al. (2025); Lin & Mubarok (2021); Lee et al. (2024)
Student engagement and motivation	- AI tools can lessen motivation, promote automation bias, and hinder self-regulation. - Condensed effort in resolving challenging tests.	-Include challenging gamified AI-powered nudges. -Use of narrative-based learning. -Integrate emotion-aware bots. -Encourage the active usage of AI by using inquiry prompts. -Integrate adaptive chatbots.	Ge et al. (2025); Lin & Mubarok (2021); Huang et al. (2023); Jovanović et al., 2017 ; Troussas et al., 2020 ; Gupta et al. (2024) ; Jose et al. (2025)
Social and emotional aspects	Lack of human interaction in AI systems.	-To mimic human interaction, use intelligent agents that are sympathetically designed. -Encourage peer cooperation with AI-assisted group creation. - Maintain both AI and human connection.	Xu & Ouyang (2022); Huang et al. (2023); Fang et al., 2021; Lechuga & Doroudi, 2022
Instructional skills and support	Instructors' capacity to employ contextual judgment and innovative teaching methods may be restricted if they become overly dependent on AI technology.	-Use AI to lessen administrative burdens while maintaining instructor authority over course customization. -Educate educators on AI literacy.	Phillips et al. (2020); Kassekhan et al. (2025) Jose et al. (2025); Park & Doo (2024); Luckin et al. (2022)

Challenge area	AI-related risks	Strategic recommendations	Key references
Assessment and feedback	Overuse of automated tests might reduce reflective learning and result in superficial feedback.	- Steer clear of full automated assessments. -Utilize feedback produced by AI to scaffold reflection. -Achieve balance between instructor-led debriefs and immediate feedback. -For more thorough diagnostic insights and formative assessment, use AI analytics.	Mallik & Gangopadhyay (2023); Al Nabhani et al. (2025); Arizmendi et al. (2023)
Content management and navigation	AI-driven personalization may lead to fragmented learning pathways or cognitive overload if it is not properly guided.	-Use AI filters and smart dashboards to lessen overload. -Provide content paths that are tailored to cognitive load and scaffolded.	Tan et al. (2025); Rasheed et al. (2020); Fathahillah et al. (2023)
Equity and inclusion	The algorithmic bias and lack of accessible features of AI systems may marginalize learners with different needs or backgrounds.	-Adopt AI that can accommodate a variety of tech skill levels and is inclusive. -To remove obstacles to access, promote moral application and AI expertise .	Luckin et al. (2022); Boelens et al. (2017); Kassekhan et al. (2025)

An important facilitator of this framework is equipping instructors with the skills and knowledge needed to design AI-supported blended courses. To assist faculty in efficiently integrating AI tools, addressing ethical problems, and modifying pedagogical techniques to developing technologies, systematic professional development initiatives are required. These initiatives should include focused training programs, ongoing workshops, and peer-learning networks. Without such structured support, AI can be misused or undervalued in ways that impair learning quality. Guidelines at the national and institutional levels are also necessary for effective integration. Clear AI rules that cover ethical use, data governance, equity, and sustainability in higher education should be added to the framework. Including policy recommendations in the strategy framework guarantees long-term sustainability and ensures that AI adoption is not left to ad hoc initiatives but rather fits with larger educational objectives.

Although the principles highlighted above provide a framework for incorporating AI into blended learning, their usefulness becomes more apparent when used in a real-world teaching setting. The following section illustrates how some of these strategic guidelines can be applied via the design and execution of an AI-enhanced blended learning exercise in a Strategic Management module.

6. ILLUSTRATIVE APPLICATION: AI-ENHANCED BLENDED LEARNING IN A STRATEGIC MANAGEMENT MODULE

The preceding section described a broad strategic framework for AI integration, encompassing purposeful alignment with learning outcomes, integrated design throughout learning phases, scaffolding for self-regulation and peer collaboration. To guarantee both pedagogical coherence and successful AI integration, this section focuses on how these elements might be operationalized in practice. Building on this, it provides a real-world example from the deployment of an AI-enhanced blended learning case in a Strategic Management module. The case serves as an exploratory illustration of how the framework can be applied, rather than a fully validated empirical study.

In November 2024, we integrated an AI-enhanced case study simulation into a postgraduate Strategic Management curriculum offered via a blended learning format at a UK business school to illustrate the usefulness of the suggested framework. The over-reliance on long, static case studies that frequently encourage passive reading rather than critical inquiry and dynamic problem-solving is one of the cognitive and engagement issues that traditional strategic management education has. This issue is amplified in a blended learning settings as students may feel isolated and frustrated. This instructional intervention was created expressly to address these issues.

6.1. Activity design: From case study to AI-driven strategic simulation

The main goal of this project was to use Blackboard Ultra's AI chatbot functionality to turn a traditional case study into an interactive, inquiry-driven learning environment. Students were given a quick, one-page executive brief that summarized the background of a real-world organization and its main strategic dilemma, rather than a lengthy case study narrative. This intentional design choice served two educational purposes: (1) it lessened the cognitive overload (Sweller, 1988) that dense case texts often cause, and (2) it made students actively build their comprehension of the case through iterative questioning, a procedure that more closely resembles actual consulting engagements.

The position of strategy consultant was given to the students. They had to mimic a conversation with the AI chatbot, which was taught to pretend to be the client, in order to identify and address the company's strategic issues. The chatbot replicated the ambiguity and asymmetry of actual consulting situations by answering students' questions with pre-programmed prompts and natural language responses that mirrored a client's insider knowledge. To synthesize fragmented knowledge across time, students had to formulate meaningful questions and delve for contextual insights.

6.2. Pedagogical value and alignment with the AI integration framework

This design directly operationalized the AI integration framework in three ways:

Purposeful alignment with critical learning outcomes

The task was specifically linked to the learning objectives of the module, particularly LO3 ("produce workable strategic solutions") and LO4 ("assess short and long-term strategic recommendations"). Students were required to critically examine the client's context, independently apply strategic frameworks like PESTEL, Porter's Five Forces, and SWOT, and support their recommendations with dialogic evidence because they were interacting with the chatbot rather than being provided a completely completed case. The chatbot's answers required students to use higher-order thinking skills, negotiate trade-offs, and think about long-term effects in their ideas. It also offered layered information about internal conflicts, market dynamics, and operational limits.

Integration Across Online and Face-to-Face Components

Within the virtual learning environment, the chatbot-based simulation was run asynchronously. Following the documentation of student interactions and initial findings, peer groups discussed strategic interpretations and worked together to improve their recommendations in synchronous seminars. Socratic questioning and in-the-moment scenario modifications were used by instructors to allow systematic criticisms of emergent techniques. This demonstrated an integrated blended learning experience by guaranteeing the continuity of crucial engagement throughout the online and in-person stages.

Scaffolding for Inquiry, Self-Regulation, and Collaboration

By requiring students to formulate their questioning technique, test hypotheses repeatedly, and update their understanding in light of new evidence, the activity scaffolded inquiry. The AI chatbot encouraged students to think critically and reflectively by acting as a knowledge gatekeeper rather than an answer supplier. Tutors were able to identify students who needed more support by using Blackboard's analytics tools to track engagement patterns, such as the number of interactions and the complexity of questions asked. Collaborative debriefs also promoted perspective-sharing and peer teaching, which strengthened the analytical and social skills necessary for strategic consulting positions.

6.3. Impact on learning and student feedback

Evidence of the AI-enhanced case simulation's ability to support important learning outcomes for adult, part-time learners participating in the work-based distance program was obtained from feedback obtained through the end-of-module survey. When compared to conventional case study formats, students consistently expressed that the activity felt more engaging, authentic, and cognitively demanding.

It was especially well-received when an AI chatbot was used to mimic a real-time customer engagement. A number of students emphasized the experience's authenticity, saying, "*This felt more like a real consultancy scenario than a textbook exercise.*"

Others observed that the inquiry-based framework promoted more in-depth participation and autonomous thought: "*The exercise helped me assume greater responsibility for the case, I had to think more critically and actively seek out the information I needed*".

Because the chatbot's responses were dynamic, students were able to practice strategic inquiry and ambiguity management, two critical skills in both academic and professional settings:

> *"I couldn't just look up the answer. I had to pose questions and utilize the responses to construct a scenario. That seems a lot more like how real-world strategic decisions are made."*

Students also reported that the AI chatbot enhanced their learning in both the online and in-person portions of the module, adding coherence and interest to the blended format: "The chatbot kept me interested during the online portion of the course.". Another student stated: "*I felt more prepared when we had to debate it in class since it provided structure and gave the case a sense of activity.*"

"*It connected the online and classroom parts really well and helped deepen the learning and see other perspectives,*" said the students, who appreciated the way the synchronous, in-person talks and asynchronous chatbot interactions were integrated.

Lastly, the overall layout was regarded as both inspiring and pertinent: "*This was one of the most interesting aspects of the module, in my opinion. It was genuinely fun to execute and gave the theory a sense of application and practicality*".

The comments show that the exercise successfully tackled typical blended learning issues, especially those related to student engagement. In addition to increasing the convergence of online and in-person learning experiences, redefining the traditional case study as an AI-driven simulation assisted students in developing strategic thinking and inquiry abilities in a format that was viewed as both relevant and realistic. Even though the illustrative application is set in a business education setting and centers on a Strategic Management module, the pedagogical strategies and fundamental ideas of the AI integration framework, namely, inquiry scaffolding, blended delivery integration, and purposeful learning outcome alignment, are not necessarily discipline-specific. Law, healthcare, engineering, and social sciences are just a few of the fields to which the framework might be used with proper contextualization to material and analytical tools, such as substituting strategic frameworks for discipline-specific analytical tools. Its current validation and design, however, are particularly based on management and business education.

7. CONCLUSION

This chapter's objective was to investigate how AI can be strategically incorporated into blended learning settings to tackle engagement and cognitive challenges within higher business education. A conceptual framework was suggested highlighting how educators can integrate AI into blended learning processes aiming to address pedagogical challenges inherent to this type of learning. Specifically, through a thorough literature review, it outlines six important areas where blended learning frequently falls short namely instructional skills and training, social and emotional support, students' motivation and engagement, pedagogical design and delivery, assessment and feedback, and content management and accessibility. For each of the six major areas, this chapter outlined specific challenges that collectively weaken blended learning's pedagogical effectiveness such as design and delivery issues, student disengagement, and social and emotional disconnect to inadequate instructional support. In order to clarify how AI technology might facilitate more efficient, interesting, and inclusive learning environments, this research mapped matching AI-driven solutions to each of the major blended learning challenges. By enhancing knowledge delivery through intelligent support systems, encouraging students' autonomy and engagement through adaptive prompts and immersive environments, humanizing digital interactions through emotion-aware agents, providing educators with real-time analytics and simplified content management, improving assessment through and personalization, streamlining the flow and relevance of learning materials, and encouraging equitable participation through tailored, inclusive learning experiences, AI offers key improvements to blended learning while raises concerns including the erosion of critical thinking. Consequently, this chapter highlights main risks associated with AI overreliance within higher education such as automation bias in independent learning, cognitive struggle in problem-solving and surface learning during content synthesis.

In response to these cognitive threats, the chapter provides recommendations for using AI in blended learning settings to promote critical thinking including the purposeful alignment of AI tools with learning outcomes, the integration of AI across online and offline phases, the use of scaffolding to support self-regulation and collaboration. Additional suggestions incorporate the development of emotionally and cognitively stimulating learning experiences as well as the support of inclusive, moral, and instructor-led AI applications.

By focusing on the intersection of AI and blended learning, the framework presented in this chapter shows the importance of the intentional instructional design for the effective use of AI systems in blended learning settings providing opportunities for critical thinking, reflection, and students' autonomy to flourish. In the light of this research, educators, students and instructional designers must be aware of the challenges and risks posed by AI and blended learning and that the AI should not replace but augment their skills. They can use the proposed framework to implement AI within blended learning settings. Properly implementing AI entails purposefully aligning pedagogical strategies with learning objectives and particularly critical thinking. Universities should also invest in digital resources and organize training and workshops for students and instructors about the effective use of AI, to improve their AI literacy skills and to prevent.an overreliance on AI that can inhibit cognitive engagement. Educators should also ensure a balanced blended learning design that mixes online and in class learning and continuously evaluate the effect of AI and blended learning use on students' outcomes. They should offer continuous guidance to students on how they should reflect, solve problems and not passively use AI-generated content. Integrating gamification like serious play could also enhance students' engagement and motivation.

Nevertheless, this chapter is not without limitations. Its insights are drawn primarily from a single case study conducted within a specific institutional context, which may constrain the generalizability of the proposed framework. This study presents a single illustrative application of the AI integration framework within a UK business education context and therefore does not provide full empirical validation. Besides, although student feedback on the AI-enhanced simulation shows improved engagement and critical thinking, this evaluation remains self-reported. To offer more objective evidence, future research should support these perceptions with quantifiable learning outcomes, like engagement analytics or assessment results and larger, multi-institutional samples to strengthen methodological robustness. Additionally, the implementation of AI-enhanced blended learning requires careful consideration of institutional resources, including staff training, technical infrastructure, and time investment.

Furthermore, the evaluation of the framework's effectiveness relied heavily on students' feedback gathered through end of module surveys. As participation in such surveys is often voluntary and tends to underrepresent certain student groups, this introduces potential response and selection biases, particularly in qualitative feedback. Future research should aim to validate and expand the framework across diverse educational settings and student populations. To gain a more holistic understanding of AI's pedagogical impact, subsequent studies could adopt a mixed-

REFERENCES

Abuzar, M., Mahmudulhassan, , & Muthoifin, . (2025). University Students' Trust in AI: Examining Reliance and Strategies for Critical Engagement. *International Journal of Interactive Mobile Technologies*, *19*(07), 70–82. DOI: 10.3991/ijim.v19i07.52875

Al Nabhani, F., Hamzah, M. B., & Abuhassna, H. (2025). The Role of Artificial Intelligence in Personalizing Educational Content: Enhancing the Learning Experience and Developing the Teacher's Role in an Integrated Educational Environment. *Contemporary Educational Technology*, *17*(2), ep573. DOI: 10.30935/cedtech/16089

Alshahrani, A. (2023). Revolutionizing Blended Learning: Exploring Current Trends and Future Research Directions in the Era of ChatGPT. In *2023 7th International Conference on Business and Information Management (ICBIM)* (41–47). IEEE.

Arbaugh, J. B., Godfrey, M. R., Johnson, M., Pollack, B. L., Niendorf, B., & Wresch, W. (2009). Research in online and blended learning in the business disciplines: Key findings and possible future directions. *The Internet and Higher Education*, *12*(2), 71–87. DOI: 10.1016/j.iheduc.2009.06.006

Arizmendi, C. J., Bernacki, M. L., Raković, M., Plumley, R. D., Urban, C. J., Panter, A. T., Greene, J. A., & Gates, K. M. (2023). Predicting student outcomes using digital logs of learning behaviors: Review, current standards, and suggestions for future work. *Behavior Research Methods*, *55*(6), 3026–3054. DOI: 10.3758/s13428-022-01939-9 PMID: 36018483

Bayyat, M., Muaılı, Z. H. A., & Aldabbas, L. (2021). Online component challenges of a blended learning experience: A comprehensive approach. *Turkish Online Journal of Distance Education*, *22*(4), 277–294. DOI: 10.17718/tojde.1002881

Belur, J., & Bentall, C. (2024). Reviewing the 3C's of blended learning for police education: Assessing capacity, building capability, and conquering challenges. *Police Practice and Research*, *25*(2), 168–188. DOI: 10.1080/15614263.2023.2210249

Benson, V., Anderson, D., & Ooms, A. (2011). Educator's perceptions, attitudes and practices: Blended learning in business and management education. *Research in Learning Technology*, *19*(2), 143–154. DOI: 10.3402/rlt.v19i2.10353

Bhutoria, A. (2022). Dealing with online and blended education in modern challenging times. *Decision (Washington, D.C.)*, *49*(2), 179–180.

Bizami, N. A., Tasir, Z., & Kew, S. N. (2023). Innovative pedagogical principles and technological tools capabilities for immersive blended learning: A systematic literature review. *Education and Information Technologies*, *28*(2), 1373–1425. DOI: 10.1007/s10639-022-11243-w PMID: 35919874

Bloom, B. S. (1956). *Taxonomy of educational objectives: The classification of educational goals*. Handbook I: Cognitive domain. Longmans.

Boelens, R., De Wever, B., & Voet, M. (2017). Four key challenges to the design of blended learning: A systematic literature review. *Educational Research Review*, *22*, 1–18. DOI: 10.1016/j.edurev.2017.06.001

Burns, L. R. (2025). Beyond Problem-Solving: The Future of Learning in an AI-Driven World. *Creative Education*, *16*(4), 520–534. DOI: 10.4236/ce.2025.164031

Chaeruman, U. A., Wibawa, B., & Syahrial, Z. (2018). Determining the appropriate blend of blended learning: A formative research in the context of Spada-Indonesia. *American Journal of Educational Research*, *6*(3), 188–195. DOI: 10.12691/education-6-3-5

Deng, , Jiang, M., Yu, X., Lu, Y., & Liu, S. (2024). Deng, R., Jiang, M., Yu, X., Lu, Y., & Liu, S. (2024). Does ChatGPT enhance student learning? A systematic review and meta-analysis of experimental studies. *Computers & Education*, *227*, 105224. DOI: 10.1016/j.compedu.2024.105224

Fang, J. W., Chang, S. C., Hwang, G. J., & Yang, G. (2021). An online collaborative peer-assessment approach to strengthening pre-service teachers' digital content development competence and higher-order thinking tendency. *Educational Technology Research and Development*, *69*(2), 1155–1181. DOI: 10.1007/s11423-021-09990-7

Farrokhnia, M., Banihashem, S. K., Noroozi, O., & Wals, A. (2024). A SWOT analysis of ChatGPT: Implications for educational practice and research. *Innovations in Education and Teaching International*, *61*(3), 460–474. DOI: 10.1080/14703297.2023.2195846

Fathahillah, F., Fakhri, M. M., & Ahmar, A. S. (2023). Analysis of artificial intelligence literacy in the blended learning model in higher education. *EduLine: Journal of Education and Learning Innovation*, *3*(4), 566–575. DOI: 10.35877/454RI.eduline2049

Fleck, J. (2012). Blended learning and learning communities: Opportunities and challenges. *Journal of Management Development*, *31*(4), 398–411. DOI: 10.1108/02621711211219059

Garrison, D. R., & Vaughan, N. D. (2008). *Blended learning in higher education: Framework, principles, and guidelines*. Jossey-Bass.

Ge, W., Sun, Y., Wang, Z., Zheng, H., He, W., Wang, P., . . . Wang, B. (2025). SRLAgent: Enhancing Self-Regulated Learning Skills through Gamification and LLM Assistance. arXiv preprint arXiv:2506.09968.

Goedhart, N. S., Blignaut-van Westrhenen, N., Moser, C., & Zweekhorst, M. B. (2019). The flipped classroom: Supporting a diverse group of students in their learning. *Learning Environments Research*, *22*(2), 297–310. DOI: 10.1007/s10984-019-09281-2

González-Calatayud, V., Prendes-Espinosa, P., & Roig-Vila, R. (2021). Artificial intelligence for student assessment: A systematic review. *Applied Sciences (Basel, Switzerland)*, *11*(12), 5467. DOI: 10.3390/app11125467

Gupta, A., Lee, S., Mott, B., Chakraburty, S., Glazewski, K., Ottenbreit-Leftwich, A., Scribner, A., Hmelo-Silver, C. E., & Lester, J. (2024). Supporting upper elementary students in learning AI concepts with story-driven game-based learning. *Proceedings of the AAAI Conference on Artificial Intelligence*, *38*(21), 23092–23100. DOI: 10.1609/aaai.v38i21.30354

Holmes, W., & Tuomi, I. (2022). State of the art and practice in AI in education. *European Journal of Education*, *57*(4), 542–570. DOI: 10.1111/ejed.12533

Huang, X., Zou, D., Cheng, G., Chen, X., & Xie, H. (2023). Trends, research issues and applications of artificial intelligence in language education. *Journal of Educational Technology & Society*, *26*(1), 112–131.

Jose, B., Cherian, J., Verghis, A. M., Varghise, S. M., S, M., & Joseph, S. (2025). The cognitive paradox of AI in education: Between enhancement and erosion. *Frontiers in Psychology*, *16*, 1550621. DOI: 10.3389/fpsyg.2025.1550621 PMID: 40297599

Joshi, D., Zalte, S. M., Johny, K. R., & Mahajan, D. A. (2023). The impact of blended learning on student engagement in the digital era. *European Chemical Bulletin*, *12*(1), 727–735.

Jovanović, J., Gašević, D., Dawson, S., Pardo, A., & Mirriahi, N. (2017). Learning analytics to unveil learning strategies in a flipped classroom. *The Internet and Higher Education*, *33*, 74–85. DOI: 10.1016/j.iheduc.2017.02.001

Ju, Q. (2023). Experimental evidence on negative impact of generative AI on scientific learning outcomes (A Pilot Research). arXiv. https://doi.org//arXiv.2311.05629DOI: 10.48550

Kasneci, E., Seßler, K., Küchemann, S., Bannert, M., Dementieva, D., Fischer, F., Gasser, U., Groh, G., Günnemann, S., Hüllermeier, E., Krusche, S., Kutyniok, G., Michaeli, T., Nerdel, C., Pfeffer, J., Poquet, O., Sailer, M., Schmidt, A., Seidel, T., & Kasneci, G. (2023). ChatGPT for good? On opportunities and challenges of large language models for education. *Learning and Individual Differences*, *103*, 102274. DOI: 10.1016/j.lindif.2023.102274

Kos'myna, N., Hauptmann, E., Yuan, Y., Situ, J., Liao, X.-H., Beresnitzky, A. V., Braunstein, I., & Maes, P. (2025). Your Brain on ChatGPT: Accumulation of Cognitive Debt when Using an AI Assistant for Essay Writing Task, MIT Media Lab. arXiv, https://doi.org//arXiv.2506.08872DOI: 10.48550

Kumar, A., Krishnamurthi, R., Bhatia, S., Kaushik, K., Ahuja, N. J., Nayyar, A., & Masud, M. (2021). Blended learning tools and practices: A comprehensive analysis. *IEEE Access : Practical Innovations, Open Solutions*, *9*, 85151–85197. DOI: 10.1109/ACCESS.2021.3085844

Kumar, S., Rao, P., Singhania, S., Verma, S., & Kheterpal, M. (2024). Will artificial intelligence drive the advancements in higher education? A tri-phased exploration. *Technological Forecasting and Social Change*, *201*, 123258. DOI: 10.1016/j.techfore.2024.123258

Lechuga, C. G., & Doroudi, S. (2023). Three algorithms for grouping students: A bridge between personalized tutoring system data and classroom pedagogy. *International Journal of Artificial Intelligence in Education*, *33*(4), 843–884. DOI: 10.1007/s40593-022-00309-y

Lee, H. Y., Chen, P. H., Wang, W. S., Huang, Y. M., & Wu, T. T. (2024). Empowering ChatGPT with guidance mechanism in blended learning: Effect of self-regulated learning, higher-order thinking skills, and knowledge construction. *International Journal of Educational Technology in Higher Education*, *21*(1), 16. DOI: 10.1186/s41239-024-00447-4

Li, C. T., & Hou, H. T. (2024). Remote Blended Game-Based Learning: Integrating Synchronous Game-Based Learning with Asynchronous Inquiry-Based Learning. *Journal of Science Education and Technology*, *33*(5), 746–758. DOI: 10.1007/s10956-024-10118-8

Li, L. (2022). Students' isolation challenges in blended EFL learning during covid-19: How can social presence and interaction help develop sense of community? *Psychology Research and Behavior Management*, *2022*, 3117–3131. DOI: 10.2147/PRBM.S388317 PMID: 36317089

Liao, C. H., & Wu, J. Y. (2022). Deploying multimodal learning analytics models to explore the impact of digital distraction and peer learning on student performance. *Computers & Education*, *190*, 104599. DOI: 10.1016/j.compedu.2022.104599

Lin, C. J., & Mubarok, H. (2021). Learning analytics for investigating the mind map-guided AI chatbot approach in an EFL flipped speaking classroom. *Journal of Educational Technology & Society*, *24*(4), 16–35.

Luckin, R., Cukurova, M., Kent, C., & Du Boulay, B. (2022). Empowering educators to be AI-ready. *Computers and Education: Artificial Intelligence*, *3*, 100076.

Mallik, S., & Gangopadhyay, A. (2023). Proactive and reactive engagement of artificial intelligence methods for education: A review. *Frontiers in Artificial Intelligence*, *6*, 1151391. DOI: 10.3389/frai.2023.1151391 PMID: 37215064

Mariyono, D., & Nur Alif Hd, A. (2025). AI's role in transforming learning environments: A review of collaborative approaches and innovations. *Quality Education for All*, *2*(1), 265–288. DOI: 10.1108/QEA-08-2024-0071

Moallem, M. (2015). The impact of synchronous and asynchronous communication tools on learner self-regulation, social presence, immediacy, intimacy and satisfaction in collaborative online learning. *The Online Journal of Distance Education and e-Learning : TOJDEL*, *3*(3), 55–77.

Müller, C., & Mildenberger, T. (2021). Facilitating flexible learning by replacing classroom time with an online learning environment: A systematic review of blended learning in higher education. *Educational Research Review*, *34*, 100394. DOI: 10.1016/j.edurev.2021.100394

Niloy, A. C., Hafiz, R., Hossain, B. M. T., Gulmeher, F., Sultana, N., Islam, K. F., Bushra, F., Islam, S., Hoque, S. I., Rahman, M. A., & Kabir, S. (2024). AI chatbots: A disguised enemy for academic integrity? *International Journal of Educational Research Open*, *7*, 100396. DOI: 10.1016/j.ijedro.2024.100396

Ododo, E. P., Iniobong, U. B., Udoessien, A. I., Ukpe, I. U., & James, O. D. (2024). Artificial intelligence in the classroom: Perceived challenges to vocational education student retention and critical thinking in tertiary institutions. *American Journal of Interdisciplinary Innovative Research*, *6*(9), 30–39. DOI: 10.37547/tajiir/Volume06Issue09-05

OECD. (2021). OECD skills outlook 2021: Learning for life. OECD Publishing. https://www.oecd.org/content/dam/oecd/en/publications/reports/2021/06/oecd-skills-outlook-2021_6f4da936/0ae365b4-en.pdf

Pardo, A., Jovanovic, J., Dawson, S., Gašević, D., & Mirriahi, N. (2019). Using learning analytics to scale the provision of personalised feedback. *British Journal of Educational Technology*, *50*(1), 128–138. DOI: 10.1111/bjet.12592

Park, Y., & Doo, M. Y. (2024). Role of AI in blended learning: A systematic literature review. *International Review of Research in Open and Distance Learning*, *25*(1), 164–196. DOI: 10.19173/irrodl.v25i1.7566

Pavlidou, I., Dragicevic, N., & Tsui, E. (2021). A multi-dimensional hybrid learning environment for business education: A knowledge dynamics perspective. *Sustainability (Basel)*, *13*(7), 3889. DOI: 10.3390/su13073889

Phillips, A., Pane, J. F., Reumann-Moore, R., & Shenbanjo, O. (2020). Implementing an adaptive intelligent tutoring system as an instructional supplement. *Educational Technology Research and Development*, *68*(3), 1409–1437. DOI: 10.1007/s11423-020-09745-w

Pokryszko-Dragan, A., Marschollek, K., Nowakowska-Kotas, M., & Aitken, G. (2021). What can we learn from the online learning experiences of medical students in Poland during the SARS-CoV-2 pandemic? *BMC Medical Education*, *21*(1), 450. DOI: 10.1186/s12909-021-02884-5 PMID: 34445982

Popenici, S. A., & Kerr, S. (2017). Exploring the impact of artificial intelligence on teaching and learning in higher education. *Research and Practice in Technology Enhanced Learning*, *12*(1), 22. DOI: 10.1186/s41039-017-0062-8 PMID: 30595727

Rasheed, R. A., Kamsin, A., & Abdullah, N. A. (2020). Challenges in the online component of blended learning: A systematic review. *Computers & Education*, *144*, 103701. DOI: 10.1016/j.compedu.2019.103701

Ruano-Borbalan, J. C. (2025). The transformative impact of artificial intelligence on higher education: A critical reflection on current trends and futures directions. International Journal of Chinese Education, 14(1), 2212585X251319364.

Ryan, R. M., & Deci, E. L. (2000). Intrinsic and extrinsic motivations: Classic definitions and new directions. *Contemporary Educational Psychology*, *25*(1), 54–67. DOI: 10.1006/ceps.1999.1020 PMID: 10620381

Sareen, S., & Mandal, S. (2024). Challenges of blended learning in higher education across global north-south: A systematic and integrative literature review. *Social Sciences & Humanities Open*, *10*, 101011. DOI: 10.1016/j.ssaho.2024.101011

Su, Y., Lin, Y., & Lai, C. (2023). Collaborating with ChatGPT in argumentative writing classrooms. *Assessing Writing*, *57*, 100752. DOI: 10.1016/j.asw.2023.100752

Sweller, J. (1988). Cognitive load during problem solving: Effects on learning. *Cognitive Science*, *12*(2), 257–285. DOI: 10.1207/s15516709cog1202_4

Tan, L. Y., Hu, S., Yeo, D. J., & Cheong, K. H. (2025). Artificial Intelligence-Enabled Adaptive Learning Platforms: A Review. *Computers and Education: Artificial Intelligence*, 100429.

Troussas, C., Krouska, A., & Sgouropoulou, C. (2020). Collaboration and fuzzy-modeled personalization for mobile game-based learning in higher education. *Computers & Education*, *144*, 103698. DOI: 10.1016/j.compedu.2019.103698

van der Stap, N., van den Bogaart, T., Rahimi, E., & Versendaal, J. (2024). Fostering online interaction in blended learning through social presence and convergence: A systematic literature review. *Journal of Computer Assisted Learning*, *40*(4), 1712–1726. DOI: 10.1111/jcal.12981

van Der Stap, N., van den Bogaart, T., Rahimi, E., & Versendaal, J. (2024). Fostering online interaction in blended learning through social presence and convergence: A systematic literature review. *Journal of Computer Assisted Learning*, *40*(4), 1712–1726. DOI: 10.1111/jcal.12981

Vaughan, N. (2007). Perspectives on blended learning in higher education. [Association for the Advancement of Computing in Education] [AACE]. *International Journal on E-Learning*, *6*(1), 81–94.

Whiteside, A. L., & Dikkers, A. G. (2016). Leveraging the social presence model: A decade of research on emotion in online and blended learning. In Tettegah, S. Y., & McCreery, M. P. (Eds.), *Emotions, technology, and learning* (pp. 225–241). DOI: 10.1016/B978-0-12-800649-8.00013-4

World Economic Forum. (2023). The future of jobs report 2023. https://www3.weforum.org/docs/WEF_Future_of_Jobs_2023.pdf

Xu, W., & Ouyang, F. (2022). The application of AI technologies in STEM education: A systematic review from 2011 to 2021. *International Journal of STEM Education*, *9*(1), 59. DOI: 10.1186/s40594-022-00377-5

Zimmerman, B. J. (2002). Becoming a self-regulated learner. *Theory into Practice*, *41*(2), 64–70. DOI: 10.1207/s15430421tip4102_2

Chapter 9

From Passive Learning to Experiential Engagement: The Role of AI and Immersive Technologies in Tourism Education

Mishra Shreeansh
https://orcid.org/0009-0004-8847-6587
Central University of Tamil Nadu, India

Bhabani S. Mohanty
https://orcid.org/0000-0001-9130-6221
Central University of Tamil Nadu, India

Zakir Hossen Shaikh
https://orcid.org/0000-0003-4733-4166
Kingdom University, Bahraian

Saad Znad Darwish
Kingdom University, Bahrain

ABSTRACT

The landscape of higher education is undergoing a profound transformation, driven by the increasing integration of digital technologies. In tourism education, where experiential and contextual learning is paramount, traditional pedagogical methods—often characterized by passive content delivery—fall short in preparing students for the dynamic and multidimensional nature of the industry. Blended learning environments, which combine face-to-face and online instruction, offer flexibility and reach. However, these environments often struggle to replicate the

DOI: 10.4018/979-8-3373-3815-6.ch009

right © 2026, IGI Global Scientific Publishing. Copying or distributing in print or electronic forms without written permission of IGI Global Scientific Publishing is prohibited. Use of this chapter to n generative artificial intelligence (AI) technologies is expressly prohibited. The publisher reserves all rights to license its use for generative AI training and machine learning model development.

real-world experiences essential to tourism training. Artificial Intelligence (AI) and immersive technologies such as virtual reality (VR) and augmented reality (AR) are now emerging as powerful tools to bridge this gap. This study concludes that these technologies influence the motivation, participation, and perceived value of students and have transformative potential for tourism pedagogy, such as enhancing learning outcomes, student retention, and engagement in blended learning settings.

1. INTRODUCTION

The integration of Artificial Intelligence (AI) with immersive technologies, such as virtual reality (VR) and augmented reality (AR), is transforming the practice of tourism education, offering opportunities to move away from conventional passive learning approaches towards more experiential, student-oriented practices. This study investigates how these technologies influence the motivation, participation, and perceived value of students within blended tourism classrooms. A qualitative research approach was used, and semi-structured interviews were carried out with tourism educators and students from various higher education institutions. The respondents underwent thematic analysis to identify dominant themes from the respondents' experiences and perceptions. The study concludes that AI and immersive tools have important roles to play in enhancing experiential learning by simulating real-world tourism settings, enhancing the emotional intensity of learning, and enabling a greater sense of connection and meaning. The participants noted the enablement of greater interactivity, personalization, and context-rich discovery as major contributions, especially in education modules on cultural tourism, destination management, and sustainability. The study concludes that AI and immersive technologies have transformative potential for tourism pedagogy, not only enhancing learning outcomes but also reducing concerns with student retention and engagement in blended learning settings.

Tourism education has been prioritizing experiential learning for the past few years (Arcodia et al., 2020). Due to the customer-centric nature of the tourism business and hospitality industry, intercultural communication, destination management, and experiential knowledge exchange at a rapid pace, and traditional pedagogies are likely to be incapable of delivering experiential learning to build actual workplace competencies (Liang, 2021; Maumbe, 2014). Tourism education has been historically grounded in lectures, textbooks, and theoretical instruction, which may be incapable of offering students the hands-on skills and analytical expertise needed in the workplace. In an age where student engagement, motivation, and retention are key measures of learning success, there is a strong need to shift from passive learning pedagogies to more experiential and student-centered approaches to instruction (Hsu, 2017; Huang et al., 2022; Sheldon et al., 2011).

This study is born out of the mounting concern that blended learning environments, as convenient and flexible as they are, do not consider the contextual richness and sensory immersion that abound in conventional field-based tourism education. Whereas online learning has made access to learning materials more convenient, it can also lead to disengagement, alienation, and a sense of irrelevance for students (Raj et al., 2024) in practice and experience-oriented fields like tourism. With students increasingly expecting more interactive and participatory learning processes, the learning institutions now find themselves compelled to adopt innovative technologies in making teaching more effective and students more contented (Huang et al., 2022).

Within this provided framework, Artificial Intelligence (AI) and immersive technologies i.e., Virtual Reality (VR), Augmented Reality (AR), and Mixed Reality (MR) are increasingly regarded as potent drivers of educational change (Bec et al., 2020; Holt, 2022). These technologies allow for the creation of virtual worlds and tailored learning pathways that mirror real-world experiences and, as such, make far-off or intangible concepts more tangible (Papakostas et al., 2024). AI helps facilitate the personalization of content delivery, real-time measurement of student performance, and emotional or behavioral support through the use of chatbots and learning analytics (H. Liang et al., 2024). VR and AR, by their nature, allow students to "visit" various places, manipulate simulations, or participate in virtual cultural festivals without leaving the classroom (Beck et al., 2019). Through the integration of these tools, there is a possibility to transform the design and delivery of tourism education.

Despite the technological advancements and growing adoption of AI and immersive technologies in various educational fields, their integration into tourism education remains limited and underexplored (Hsu, 2017), especially in the context of developing countries (Anctil & Blanc, 2015; Mayaka & Akama, 2006). Most higher education institutions still rely on didactic teaching methods or rely on limited use of technology for administrative or assessment purposes rather than pedagogical innovation. Consequently, tourism students often find themselves disengaged, struggling to co-relate abstract academic content and practical industry scenarios.

Moreover, student motivation and retention have become important issues in blended learning environments. While digital teaching aids provide access and flexibility, most of the time it lacks social interaction, place-based context, and emotional engagement, which are important actors known to contribute significantly to learner satisfaction and persistence. As institutions seek to expand and diversify their digital and hybrid classroom setups, there is a crucial need to understand how AI and immersive technologies can be utilized not just to deliver content but to foster meaningful, connected, and motivational learning experiences. As tourism education continues to progress in response to global digitalization and industry requirements, understanding how to harness the power of AI and immersive tools has become a pedagogical necessity.

This research tried to fill a significant gap in theory and practice. Although there has been research on AI and immersive learning before, it primarily covers applied areas such as medicine, engineering, or computer science. Not much work has been conducted to examine their application in tourism education, one of the growing industries, inherently on sensory immersion, cultural experience, and locational knowledge. By exploring the pedagogical integration of these technologies, this research contributes to the broader discourse on technology-enhanced learning (TEL) and education 4.0, specifically in the context of tourism studies. It situates itself at the intersection of learning sciences, educational technology, and vocational education, providing actionable insights for curriculum designers, educators, and institutional policymakers.

The study is particularly relevant in the post-COVID-19 educational landscape, where digital and hybrid models are becoming mainstream. The pandemic has accelerated the shift toward online learning, but it has also revealed critical shortcomings in student motivation and emotional connection. The ability of AI and immersive technologies to simulate real-world experiences and offer emotional as well as cognitive support makes them especially promising tools for recovery and innovation in tourism education. The implications for curriculum design, faculty development, and policymaking are outlined, along with recommendations for future research studies.

2. LITERATURE REVIEW

Tourism education has long emphasized the value of experiential learning (Arcodia et al., 2020), given the inherently practical, place-based, and service-oriented nature of the tourism and hospitality industry (Chiou, Tien, & Tang, 2020; Mak et al., 2017). Scholars like Jennings et al. (2015) and Ruhanen et al. (2020) have emphasized the necessity for tourism students to learn in real-world settings, cultural environments, and industry-related problem-solving situations. Traditional pedagogies like lectures and learning from books frequently lack preparation of students in applied competencies and critical thinking skills expected of the industry (Mínguez et al., 2021). Field trips, simulations, internships, and role-playing exercises have long been used to fill this gap (Boon et al., 2024). However, with the proliferation of online and blended learning modes, induced by the COVID-19 pandemic, considerable challenges have come into play to sustain this experiential component in tourism education. Although blended learning provides ease of access and flexibility, it tends to be missing the active, sensorial-based activities upon which student engagement in vocational fields depends (Derntl & Motschnig-Pitrik, 2005).

New technological advancements present effective solutions to revitalize tourism pedagogy (Mínguez et al., 2021). Artificial Intelligence (AI) and immersive technologies like Virtual Reality (VR), Augmented Reality (AR), and Mixed Reality (MR) have shown promise to revolutionize the learning process across subjects (Crogman et al., 2025; Koumpouros, 2024). AI is gaining traction in education for personalization (Bate, 2025), intelligent tutoring, predictive analytics, and learner support through applications like chatbots and adaptive platforms (Zawacki-Richter et al., 2019; Holmes et al., 2019). Concurrently, immersive technologies have been extensively applied to mimic real-world scenarios (Rubio-Tamayo et al., 2017), particularly in fields such as medicine (Iqbal et al., 2024), architecture (Suryawinata, 2021), and engineering (Prabhakaran et al., 2025), with dividends in skill acquisition, knowledge retention, and learner motivation. These technologies provide learners with the ability to interact with complicated environments, carry out situational analysis, and rehearse decision-making—all within a safe, controlled digital environment (Suh & Prophet, 2018; Rubio-Tamayo et al., 2017).

While there has been progress in other areas of research on AI and immersive technology incorporation into tourism education is still in its infancy. As a field of study, tourism has only started to investigate virtual field trips (Guttentag, 2009; Hodgson et al., 2019) and immersive simulations for destination management training (Aldawsari et al., 2025). These research studies, although valuable, are generally technology-focused and neglect the pedagogical and affective learning aspects of student experience. In particular, there has been little research on how these technologies affect learner motivation, value perceptions, emotional engagement, or sense of belonging—factors all paramount to student retention and satisfaction in blended learning environments.

Student motivation has long been recognized as a primary driver of engagement and retention at the higher education level (Berry, 2020; Ferrer et al., 2020). Students logically deprioritize the tasks due to a sense of overburden and a gap between the online learning component and the expected outcome (Lomer & Palmer, 2021). Evidence indicates that AI has the ability to maximize motivation through personalized learning routes and assessments, timely feedback, and performance tracking (Chen et al., 2020). Similarly, immersive technologies have been discovered to enhance cognitive flow and emotional attachment to content, hence increasing learner engagement (Makransky & Lilleholt, 2018). In tourism education, however, scholars like Hsu (2017), Huang et al. (2022), and Kallou and Kikilia (2021) have explored these technologies through a pedagogical perspective that involves affective outcomes such as motivation, belonging, or value alignment. Most studies, instead, address cognitive outcomes like test results or memory retention, failing to capture the overall experience of learning.

AI is a useful tool in this age of digital acceleration since it has special applications that are accessible to all sectors of the economy, including supply chain management, robotics, healthcare, public safety, retail, human resources, financial services, and financial inclusion and governance, artificial intelligence (AI) is upending established paradigms. (Shaikh, et al, 2024, 2025, Soni et al, 2025, Mahapatra et al, 2025). The development of artificial intelligence (AI) and digital technology has drastically changed education. (Soni et al, 2025, Mohanty, B. S et al, 2025, Ratnakaram, S et al, 2025)

2.1. Conceptual framework

To fill this void, the current study suggests a conceptual framework that places AI and immersive technologies in the role of pedagogical facilitators that optimize experiential engagement to improve student motivation, emotional engagement, and eventually, academic persistence. The proposed framework is rooted in constructivist learning theory (Vygotsky, 1980) and self-determination theory (Deci & Ryan, 1985), which highlight autonomy of the learner, context-based learning, and the significance of relatedness as drivers of intrinsic motivation. The conceptual map illustrated in Figure 1 is centered on "AI and Immersive Technologies" as the key driver that is transforming tourism education. The map stretches into four interconnected spaces: Experiential Learning, Student Motivation, Student Engagement, and Tourism Education. Each of these spaces highlights a key aspect of impact—immersive experiences stimulate contextual and sensory learning; self-determination theory underpins understanding of how AI tools, such as feedback mechanisms and adaptive learning paths, drive motivation; social presence and belonging encapsulate how collaborative VR/AR environments constrain feelings of loneliness and optimize peer-to-peer interactions; and gaps in pedagogic practice and dropout figures in tourism education encapsulate the urgent need for digitally rich, inclusive learning models. Together, the map illustrates how the strategic use of AI and immersive technologies can make blended learning a more engaging, inclusive, and productive environment for tourism and hospitality students.

Figure 1. Conceptual Framework for AI and Immersive Technologies in Tourism Education

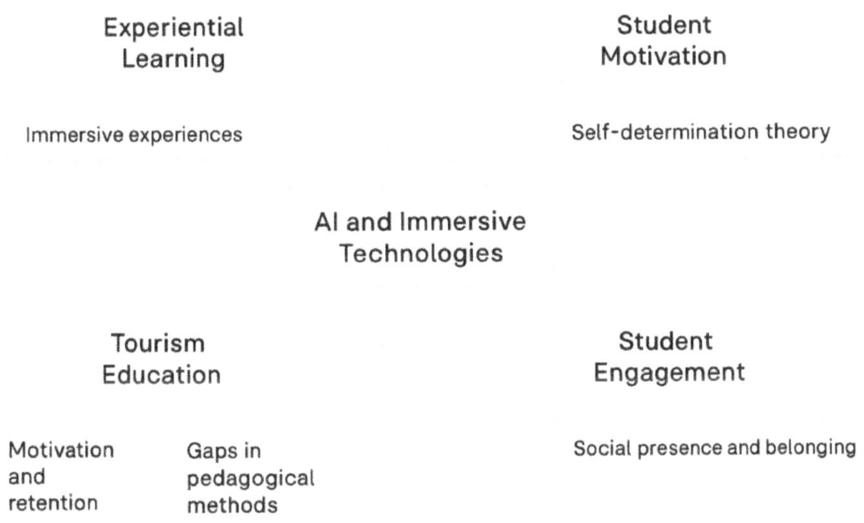

Source: *Author's compilation based on constructivist learning theory (Vygotsky, 1980) and self-determination theory (Deci & Ryan, 1985).*

In this model, the combination of AI and immersive tools is anticipated to create more interactive, personalized, and relevant learning, thereby engaging curiosity, enhancing self-efficacy, and decreasing dropout intentions for blended learning environments.

This research corroborates educational technology literature, confirming that AI and immersive tools can build more interactive and personalized learning experiences. Simultaneously, it puts to the test the hypothesis that mere technological integration is enough to improve the quality of education. The study enlarges the field in that it moves the focus away from tool orientation and places it on learner orientation, highlighting emotional as well as motivational elements that are usually given a backseat in tourism education studies. Furthermore, although existing research has centered on STEM fields, this study shines light on much-needed attention in tourism studies as well, where experiential, contextual, and humanistic dimensions of learning are especially pertinent.

2.2. Research Gap

The gap in research can be observed in three broad areas. First, there is limited insight into how AI and immersive technologies are to be methodologically incorporated within tourism education to make experiential learning more effective. Second, past research hardly touches on the emotional and motivational aspects of technology-enhanced learning in tourism. Third, there is no quantitative, in-depth research that records the lived experiences of learners and teachers when using these tools in blended learning contexts. Most studies are still quantitative, experimental, or theoretical, and few take direct engagement with the voices of teachers and learners.

Filling this gap is of core importance for a number of reasons. As tourism education evolves further into hybrid and digital mediums, instructors need to rethink not only what is being taught, but how it is being taught and how it connects with students. Neglecting the affective and experiential aspects of learning may isolate students, particularly in practice-oriented fields such as tourism. Furthermore, when schools are facing challenges of student dropout, digital fatigue, and decreasing classroom engagement, there is an immediate need to create pedagogical approaches that are technologically innovative yet emotionally supportive. By exploring how AI and immersive technology can enhance motivation, experiential value, and feelings of belonging, this study informs a learner-centered model of tourism education for the digital era.

3. RESEARCH METHODOLOGY

To explore the potential of AI and immersive technologies in reshaping tourism education, this study adopts a qualitative research design using semi-structured interviews and thematic analysis. The rationale for choosing a qualitative approach lies in its strength to capture complex, subjective, and context-specific insights from learners and educators, which is particularly important when dealing with emerging, understudied pedagogical technologies. Participants included faculty and students from tourism and hospitality programs across Indian universities that have adopted or experimented with immersive or AI-powered tools in their blended classrooms. The interviews probed areas such as: Students' emotional and cognitive responses to AI/immersive tools; Educators' perspectives on teaching transformation; Perceived advantages and limitations of these technologies; Influence on motivation, belonging, and intention to persist in learning. Thematic analysis based on Braun and Clarke's guidelines was used to seek patterns and make sense from the data. The NVivo software was used to facilitate thorough coding and development of themes.

3.1. Research Design

Qualitative research design was used within this research to seek to find out how AI and virtual reality technologies shape student motivation, engagement, and experiential learning in tourism education. As the research was exploratory in nature and aimed at grasping participants lived experiences and perceptions, a qualitative approach was found to be most suitable (Creswell & Poth, 2016). The research intended to bring forth deeper, detailed understandings of how these new technologies are included in blended learning environments and how they influence the affective and cognitive elements of student learning.

3.2. Participants and Sampling

Participants consisted of 25 people from both educators and students involved in undergraduate and postgraduate tourism and hospitality courses in Indian higher education institutions, as shown in Table 1. Purposive sampling was used to sample participants with immediate experience with AI tools (e.g., chatbots, learning analytics, adaptive systems) and immersive technologies (e.g., virtual field trips, VR simulations) in an integrated learning curriculum. The sampling method was used to ensure that the data gathered were relevant, information-rich, and representative of the particular teaching-learning contexts being researched (Patton, 2014).

Table 1. Details of respondents

Participant Category	Count (n)	Gender (M/F/ Others)	Academic Level / Role	Experience with AI/ Immersive Tech
Students	18	M: 9 / F: 9	UG: 10 / PG: 8	Basic to Intermediate
Educators	7	M: 4 / F: 3	Assistant Professors (5), HOD (1), Visiting Faculty (1)	Intermediate to Advanced
Total	**25**	M: 13 / F: 12		

Participants were recruited through institutional connections, referrals, and email invitations. Ethical standards were respected, such as informed consent, the voluntary nature of participation, confidentiality, and freedom to withdraw from participation at any stage. The research was submitted and cleared up by the host institution's academic ethics committee.

3.3. Data Collection

Data were gathered with the use of semi-structured interviews (Bryman, 2016), enabling guided question asking together with conversational adaptability. The interview protocol included the following questions: Types and extent of AI/immersive technology utilization; Perceived influence on student engagement, motivation, and learning quality; Feeling of belonging and connection in blended classrooms; Observed challenges and opportunities experienced in their use. Every interview took 45 to 60 minutes and was performed either face-to-face or through video conferencing facilities, based on participants' availability and choice. All interviews were recorded with permission and transcribed verbatim for analysis. The semi-structured style allowed the researcher to delve deeper into subjects as they arose and to adjust the question flow according to participants' answers (Kvale & Brinkmann, 2009). Flexibility was essential in revealing subtle aspects of learning involvement and emotional reaction that might not have been revealed in a more structured style.

3.4. Data Analysis

The data collected were analyzed with thematic analysis, a technique appropriate for identification, analysis, and reporting of patterns in qualitative data (Braun & Clarke, 2006). Braun and Clarke's six-step procedure was adhered to: (1) getting familiar with the data, (2) creating initial codes, (3) searching for the themes, (4) reviewing the themes, (5) refining and naming the themes, and (6) making the final report. Coding was done manually and with the assistance of NVivo 12 qualitative analysis software, which helped manage, categorize, and retrieve data segments efficiently. The themes were developed inductively, allowing them to emerge organically from the data rather than imposing a priori. Particular attention was paid to how participants described changes in learning behavior, perceived value, emotional engagement, and the relational aspects of using technology in blended environments.

To ensure the credibility of the findings, various methods were utilized. Credibility was dealt with using data triangulation (student and teacher viewpoints), member checking was done by presenting early interpretations to chosen participants for confirmation, and dependability was gained by maintaining a rich audit trail of coding and analysis procedures.

4. FINDINGS AND DISCUSSION

The viewpoint of respondents provided rich feedback regarding how AI and immersive technologies are affecting learning habits, motivation, and experience-based engagement in blended tourism education. Thematic analysis of the interview transcripts showed five dominant themes, as shown in Table 2.

Table 2. Thematic analysis of the interview transcripts

Main Theme	Sub-Themes	Description	Sample Participant Quotes	Frequency (No. of Respondents)
1. Experiential Enrichment	- Immersive field simulations- Contextual visualization	VR/AR tools enabled real-world tourism scenarios and contextual learning	*"The VR tour helped me understand biodiversity better than classroom lectures."* (Student 4)	21 (15 students, 6 faculty)
2. Enhanced Motivation	- AI feedback- Gamified learning	AI-supported quizzes and instant feedback improved motivation and engagement	*"After the AI quiz, I knew where to improve—it made learning feel like a game."* (Student 10)	18 (14 students, 4 faculty)
3. Real-World Relevance	- Industry-aligned simulations- Career preparation	Tools reflected practical challenges in tourism/ hospitality	*"The destination crisis simulation felt like a real-world management task."* (Faculty 2)	16 (10 students, 6 faculty)
4. Peer Connection & Belonging	- Collaborative VR- Shared digital experience	Students experienced greater belonging and teamwork in blended settings	*"Even online, we worked as a real team in the VR project."* (Student 12)	14 (11 students, 3 faculty)
5. Implementation Challenges	- Infrastructure gaps- Faculty preparedness- Tech access issues	Inequity in access and lack of training limited effectiveness	*"We don't have enough VR devices, so we took turns, which reduced learning time."* (Faculty 6)	20 (13 students, 7 faculty)

4.1. Experiential Richness and Contextual Learning

AI enhances tourism education by integrating experiential richness and contextual learning through gamified simulations, using points, badges, leaderboards, real-time quizzes, and interactive challenges to deepen engagement and sustainability understanding (Gao, 2024; Neophytou et al., 2025). The respondents reiterated consistently that immersive technologies delivered experiential and sensory learning opportunities that made theoretical knowledge come alive. VR-based destination simulations and virtual field trips allowed learners to virtually visit iconic tourism destinations, cultural landscapes, and eco-sensitive areas, and thus gain contextual knowledge that books or classroom lectures could not provide.

"The VR field trip to the Sundarbans made the biodiversity and challenges of ecotourism more real to me than reading about it," said a postgraduate student.

Teachers also reported that such technologies enabled students to exercise decision-making and critical thinking in a safe, simulated environment, which is very useful in dealing with complicated issues such as over-tourism management or crisis response planning. This is consistent with Guttentag (2009) and Dieck & Jung (2015), whose argument is that experiential technologies for tourism education promote greater understanding by placing learning in authentic settings. The results validate the hypothesis that experiential learning in virtual form can replace, to some degree, direct physical fieldwork, particularly in resource-poor environments.

4.2. Increased Student Motivation and Curiosity

AI-powered learning holds great promise to ignite student interest and curiosity through personalization, immediate feedback, and engagement-based learning (Aires & Schatten, 2025). Educational institutions need to work together on efficient implementation, so AI becomes a curiosity driver, motivating students to attend class, learn, and dive deeply into lessons. Students reported that AI-powered feedback systems and gamified VR environments raised their incentive to work through course materials. The interactive learning experiences, immediate feedback, and visual engagement triggered interest, especially among those who had been disconnected in conventional lecture courses.

"I learned through discovery, not from being instructed. The AI quiz following the VR tour informed me precisely where I needed to pay more attention," explained one undergraduate student.

Teachers reported students being more engaged and self-directed with assignments based on AI-recommended materials or AR-related tourism design challenges.

These results highlight the motivational theories of Deci and Ryan (2009), in which autonomy, competence, and relatedness are central to intrinsic motivation. AI and immersive technology, through their personalized pathways and salient challenges, meet these psychological needs, leading to greater student effort and interest in subjects. AI technologies used in tourism education, such as adaptive learning systems, chatbots, and game-based testing, tailor the learning process more engaging and tailored to every learner's interests. These technologies trigger curiosity by allowing students to experience real-time tourism destinations, investigate real tourism scenarios in an interactive environment, making them engage more.

4.3. Value Addition and Real-World Relevance

Another common theme identified was the experience of value-added learning. Students perceived AI and immersion tools as offering skills and exposure related to actual practice in real-world tourism, specifically in digital tourism marketing, sustainable planning, and cultural interpretation. Students are provided with hands-on experience through simulations, virtual site management activities, and decision-making based on data that is reflective of real-life problems. This alignment with what the industry requires makes students more confident and ensures that classroom learning is applicable to on-the-job success.

"The VR experience gave me a taste of what working with destinations could be like—it felt more like industry training than just class," said a final-year student.

Teachers recognized that such technologies were career preparation instruments, filling the gap between academic learning and workplace-based application. This view of real-world application was highly related to learning engagement and satisfaction because it made learning more concrete and job-focused.

4.4. Peer Connection and Sense of Belonging

Artificial intelligence and virtual reality/augmented reality-based collaboration tools enable learners to interact and collaborate with each other, even when studying remotely or in hybrid learning environments. Cooperative virtual tasks and team tasks make learners feel more connected to their learning community and peers, and this reduces loneliness and enhances feelings of belonging. This affective bond is essential in facilitating students' motivation and engagement in tourism education. Notably, some of the students explained how collaborative platforms enabled by AI and collective immersive experiences created a deeper sense of belonging and community, particularly when learning blended or remotely.

"We collaborated on the virtual simulation of designing a tourism product. Although we were online, we felt like we belonged to an actual team," said one student.

These tools seemed to minimize the loneliness that comes with distance learning, generating mutual experiences that mimicked group assignments or in-person collaboration. AI mentors and chatbots also offered effective and academic guidance, making students feel less "lost" in cyberspaces. This theme supports evidence by Makransky & Lilleholt (2018), who posit that emotional immersion—specifically the feeling of presence and social connection—can have strong effects on learning persistence and retention in virtual learning environments.

4.5. Institutional Readiness and Implementation Challenges

Even though AI and immersive technologies hold great promise to improve tourism education, their successful integration is always interrupted by institutional factors like weak digital infrastructure, the absence of faculty training, and unequal students' access to sophisticated tools. Most institutions lack the capacity to scale up these innovations owing to budget constraints, policy vacuums, and pedagogical resistance. Overcoming these barriers needs strategic thinking, capacity investment, and inclusive frameworks that promote equitable and sustainable use in a variety of educational environments. Despite the positive overall response, students and faculty pointed to some challenges in implementing these technologies optimally. These comprised:

Limitations in digital infrastructure, e.g., substandard VR equipment, slow internet speeds, or inadequate access to devices. Not all institutions can have equal access to the necessary technology to move from a traditional classroom to experiential learning. Limited funds, costly products, and installation are major challenges in institutes and universities, especially in developing countries. Moreover, maintenance and extra care required to keep the technology in use pose added challenges for authorities to adopt AI and related technology for advanced blended learning classrooms.

Training gaps in faculty, where teachers were not always equipped or confident in leading AI/VR-supported sessions. Teachers, being beginners and not so tech-savvy, face difficulty in using advanced technology efficiently and most of the time end up wasting a lot of time in transitioning from traditional teaching to AI applications. Teachers also feel unprepared or lack the training to effectively use AI tools, sometimes leading to hesitation or inconsistent adoption. One of the teachers suggested,

> *".. having a technical team or helpers who might help them when they get stuck in some process of technology application or assist them in arranging the setup while they continue the teaching module in lecture mode could ensure minimal disruption to the flow of class, allowing them to focus on efficient content delivery..."*

Issues of equity, with some students not having access to good-quality devices or home contexts suitable for immersive learning. Some students, owing to different family background and varyi g socio-economic circumstances may face difficulties in meeting the technological requirements necessary for participation in AI supported classrooms. Teachers highlighted calls for institutional investment, training initiatives, and budgeting support for both institution and students to grow these technologies inclusively and sustainably. This echo's the concerns of Holmes et al. (2022) regarding the inconsistent rate of AI uptake in education and to close technological access and capacity development in higher education.

The research indicates that AI and virtual technologies are not just ancillary resources, but pedagogical actors with the potential to greatly enhance experiential learning, increase student motivation, feeling of belonging, and maximize retention for tourism education. Image 2 shows the conceptual model, the TOURNET (Tourism Immersive Learning Network) Model, to complement the research findings. The technology, carefully embedded, serves both cognitive and affective purposes, facilitating knowledge acquisition, emotional engagement, and social connectedness. Concurrently, the research warns against unproblematic adoption, emphasizing the need for equal access, adaptive implementation at the local level, and pedagogic readiness.

Figure 2. The TOURNET (Tourism Immersive Learning Network) Model

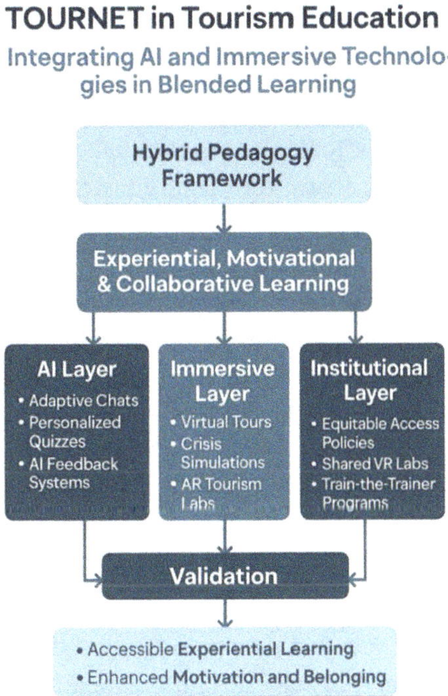

Source: TOURNET in Tourism education

5. IMPLICATIONS OF THE STUDY

The conclusions drawn from this research have significant pedagogical implications for tourism education, integration of educational technology, and the wider development of blended learning. As digital technologies increasingly become the key to the future development of higher education, especially in vocational areas such as tourism, this research makes a subtle contribution to an enhanced comprehension of how AI and immersive technologies can be used as drivers of experiential, emotionally charged, and socially interactive learning spaces.

5.1. Theoretical Implications: Affective and Experiential Dimensions of Technology-Enhanced Learning

The study advances the current literature in technology-enhanced learning (TEL) by concentrating not only on cognitive achievement but also on affective measures like student motivation, emotional investment, and feelings of belonging. While prior studies in TEL (Zawacki-Richter et al., 2019; Makransky & Lilleholt, 2018) have emphasized the efficacy of AI and VR in delivering content or developing hard skills, fewer have deeply investigated their role in shaping the emotional and relational dynamics of learning. This research reorients the conversation by positioning these technologies as tools for fostering experiential engagement, reinforcing self-determination theory (Deci & Ryan, 2009) and constructivist principles (Vygotsky, 1980) that highlight autonomy, competence, and social connection as foundations of meaningful learning.

Furthermore, the study provides a conceptual bridge between experiential learning theory and blended pedagogy, showing how digital simulations and AI-driven feedback can recreate the context-rich, situated learning typically achieved through physical site visits and internships in tourism education.

5.2. Practical Implications: Designing Blended Tourism Classrooms for Motivation and Retention

From a practical standpoint, the results suggest that educational institutions, particularly those offering vocational or practice-based programs, must move beyond content digitization and instead design blended learning environments that are emotionally engaging, interactive, and contextually meaningful. The integration of AI and immersive technologies should not be an add-on or novelty but a core instructional strategy to stimulate learner agency, motivation, and belonging. For educators in tourism and hospitality, this means curating AI-supported adaptive learning paths, integrating VR simulations for destination management, and facilitating AR-based collaborative projects that mirror real-world industry practices.

These tools can play a critical role in addressing common challenges of online and hybrid education, such as learner isolation, demotivation, and low persistence.

Institutional leaders and curriculum designers should also invest in faculty development programs to build digital pedagogical competence. As some participants noted, the full potential of these technologies is not realized unless instructors are trained in both the technological and pedagogical aspects of their application. This includes not just tool usage, but also designing assessments, supporting digital inclusion, and fostering emotionally safe learning spaces.

5.3. Comparison with Prior Studies

The study's findings echo existing literature that affirms the cognitive benefits of immersive and AI tools in higher education (Dieck & Jung, 2018). Like previous studies, this research confirms that such technologies enhance knowledge retention, visualization, and situational understanding. However, this study diverges from prior work by focusing explicitly on affective and relational benefits, which have been underexplored in tourism and hospitality education. While earlier works have discussed technology adoption from an infrastructure or usability standpoint, this research investigates how students feel, connect, and persist when learning through AI and immersive modalities.

Moreover, the emphasis on belongingness, a construct more common in psychology or sociology of education, is rarely explored in the context of blended tourism classrooms. This study introduces it as a central factor linking digital engagement to retention, thereby expanding the theoretical lens through which we understand learning in blended environments.

5.4. Contextualization within Tourism Education

Tourism education in India, and globally, is at a crossroads. The demand for digitally competent graduates, the need for accessible and scalable learning models, and the disruption of traditional field-based pedagogy have created a space where innovation is both necessary and overdue. Within this context, AI and immersive technologies are not just modern tools; they represent pedagogical pathways to bridge the gap between academic theory and industry reality.

The study contextualizes these technologies within curriculum innovation, suggesting that their implementation should align with core tourism competencies such as cultural sensitivity, sustainable practice, and customer experience design. For example, applying experiential simulations to learning conflict resolution in heritage sites or sustainability issues in ecotourism would make intangible principles more concrete, engaging learners through relevance and empathy.

5.5. The Big Picture: Rethinking Blended Learning as an Experiential Ecosystem

At the macro level, this research encourages a core rethink about what we mean by blended learning. Instead of considering it a middle path between offline and online modes, the research rethinks it as an experiential ecosystem, an unfolding learning space where AI and immersive tools facilitate multi-sensory, emotionally resonant, and socially interactive learning experiences.

It also disputes binary "online vs. offline" reasoning and offers a more sophisticated vision of "extended reality learning", in which physical boundaries no longer restrict student access to places, cultures, and operating scenarios. The findings emphasize the notion that learning presence the feeling of being cognitively, emotionally, and socially engaged in the learning environment, is as vital as physical presence. Essentially, this research offers a template for the development of blended learning from its current status as passive, transactional content consumption to being more comprehensive, affective, and applied learning experiences. This rethink speaks not merely to tourism education but to all fields that aim to promote student agency, belonging, and persistence in the digital age.

6. CONCLUSION

The study investigated the potential of AI and immersive technology in transforming tourism education from passive to experiential learning within blended learning environments. From thematic analysis of qualitative interviews between students and educators, this research identified that AI and immersive tools highly increase student motivation, promote contextual and practical learning, and develop a sense of belongingness, all of which are essential for retention and satisfaction of blended tourism learning classrooms.

Findings of key interest note that virtual and augmented reality technologies allow students to engage with actual tourism situations, thus making learning more relevant and industry-focused. At the same time, AI-based tools such as smart feedback systems and chatbots individualize learning and provide cognitive assistance, hence enhancing learner independence and motivation. Notably, the research points out that these technologies are also facilitating the affective aspect of learning, a vital but commonly neglected element of digital learning. In practical terms, this research underscores the need for tourism educators and institutions to rethink blended learning as an experiential ecosystem, not merely a mix of digital and face-to-face elements but a transformative, learner-centered model. The integration of AI and immersive technologies can significantly bridge the gap between theoretical instruction and practical application, making tourism education more adaptive, inclusive, and future-ready.

6.1 Limitations and Future Directions

The research was conducted with a relatively small sample size of 25 respondents, which may restrict the generalizability of the findings to a broader population. The reliance on self-reported data introduces the possibility of response bias, as participants' perceptions may be influenced by personal experiences, attitudes, or social desirability. Additionally, the study focuses on a specific context within tourism education, which may limit the applicability of the results to other disciplines or educational environments. While thematic analysis provided valuable insights, the subjective nature of qualitative interpretation means that alternative perspectives may exist.

Future research could address these limitations by incorporating larger, more diverse samples, employing mixed methods, and exploring longitudinal impacts of AI integration in educational settings. Quantitative studies, experimental designs, and comparative cross-national research can further validate and scale the findings. Additionally, research should examine ethical concerns, accessibility barriers, and faculty readiness in diverse institutional settings. A call to action is made for researchers, curriculum designers, and policymakers to collaborate in building evidence-based, technology-enhanced pedagogies. Future research could be conducted on the problems and prospects of educational institutions adopting AI-enabled technologies. The next steps involve developing inclusive frameworks that balance innovation with equity, ensuring that the shift toward experiential, AI-driven learning leaves no learner behind.

REFERENCES

Aires, T., & Schatten, J. (2025). Cultivating Curiosity through AI. In *Chapman and Hall/CRC eBooks* (pp. 63–75). DOI: 10.1201/9781003422433-3

Aldawsari, R., Buhalis, D., & Roushan, G. (2025). Immersive metaverse technologies for education and training in tourism and hospitality. *International Journal of Contemporary Hospitality Management, 37*(8), 2716–2736. Advance online publication. DOI: 10.1108/IJCHM-01-2025-0126

Anctil, A., & Blanc, D. L. (2015). An educational simulation tool for integrated coastal tourism development in developing countries. *Journal of Sustainable Tourism, 24*(5), 783–798. DOI: 10.1080/09669582.2015.1091463

Arcodia, C., Novais, M. A., Cavlek, N., & Humpe, A. (2020). Educational tourism and experiential learning: Students' perceptions of field trips. *Tourism Review, 76*(1), 241–254. DOI: 10.1108/TR-05-2019-0155

Bate, G. W. (2025). Gaining Traction with Gen AI in 2025. *Research Technology Management, 68*(2), 69–71. DOI: 10.1080/08956308.2025.2446136

Bec, A., Moyle, B., Schaffer, V., & Timms, K. (2020). Virtual reality and mixed reality for second chance tourism. *Tourism Management, 83*, 104256. DOI: 10.1016/j.tourman.2020.104256

Beck, J., Rainoldi, M., & Egger, R. (2019). Virtual reality in tourism: A state-of-the-art review. *Tourism Review, 74*(3), 586–612. DOI: 10.1108/TR-03-2017-0049

Berry, A. (2020). Disrupting to Driving: Exploring upper primary teachers' perspectives on student engagement. *Teachers and Teaching, 26*(2), 145–165. DOI: 10.1080/13540602.2020.1757421

Boon, Q. W., Sulaiman, T., & Razali, F. (2024). Innovative Integration of Experiential Learning in Hospitality and Tourism Management Education: A Systematic review. *Studies in Big Data*, 39–49. DOI: 10.1007/978-3-031-71213-5_4

Bryman, A. (2016). *Social research methods*. Oxford university press.

Chen, L., Chen, P., & Lin, Z. (2020). Artificial Intelligence in Education: A review. *IEEE Access : Practical Innovations, Open Solutions, 8*, 75264–75278. DOI: 10.1109/ACCESS.2020.2988510

Chiou, C., Tien, L., & Tang, Y. (2020). Applying structured computer-assisted collaborative concept mapping to flipped classroom for hospitality accounting. *Journal of Hospitality, Leisure, Sport and Tourism Education*, *26*, 100243. DOI: 10.1016/j.jhlste.2020.100243

Creswell, J. W., & Poth, C. N. (2016). *Qualitative inquiry and research design: Choosing among five approaches*. Sage publications.

Crogman, H. T., Cano, V. D., Pacheco, E., Sonawane, R. B., & Boroon, R. (2025). Virtual reality, augmented reality, and mixed reality in experiential Learning: Transforming Educational Paradigms. *Education Sciences*, *15*(3), 303. DOI: 10.3390/educsci15030303

Deci, E. L., & Ryan, R. M. (1985). Intrinsic Motivation and Self-Determination in human behavior. In *Springer eBooks*. DOI: 10.1007/978-1-4899-2271-7

Deci, E. L., & Ryan, R. M. (2009). 25 Self-determination theory: a consideration of human motivational universals. *The Cambridge handbook of personality psychology*, 441.

Derntl, M., & Motschnig-Pitrik, R. (2005). The role of structure, patterns, and people in blended learning. *The Internet and Higher Education*, *8*(2), 111–130. DOI: 10.1016/j.iheduc.2005.03.002

Dieck, M. C. T., & Jung, T. (2015). A theoretical model of mobile augmented reality acceptance in urban heritage tourism. *Current Issues in Tourism*, *21*(2), 154–174. DOI: 10.1080/13683500.2015.1070801

Ferrer, J., Ringer, A., Saville, K., Parris, M. A., & Kashi, K. (2020). Students' motivation and engagement in higher education: The importance of attitude to online learning. *Higher Education*, *83*(2), 317–338. DOI: 10.1007/s10734-020-00657-5

Gao, T. (2024). Research on the design of online gamified tourism education activities based on Moodle platform. *Entertainment Computing*, *52*, 100823. DOI: 10.1016/j.entcom.2024.100823

Guttentag, D. A. (2009). Virtual reality: Applications and implications for tourism. *Tourism Management*, *31*(5), 637–651. DOI: 10.1016/j.tourman.2009.07.003

Hodgson, P., Lcc, V. W. Y., Chan, J. C. S., Fong, A., Tang, C. S. Y., Chan, L., & Wong, C. (2019). Immersive Virtual Reality (IVR) in Higher Education: development and implementation. In *Progress in IS* (pp. 161–173). DOI: 10.1007/978-3-030-06246-0_12

Holmes, W., Bialik, M., & Fadel, C. (2019). Artificial Intelligence in Education: Promises and Implications for Teaching and learning. Center for Curriculum Redesign. https://circls.org/primers/artificial-intelligence-in-education-promises-and-implications-for-teaching-and-learning

Holmes, W., Persson, J., Chounta, I. A., Wasson, B., & Dimitrova, V. (2022). *Artificial intelligence and education: A critical view through the lens of human rights, democracy and the rule of law*. Council of Europe.

Holt, S. (2022). Virtual reality, augmented reality and mixed reality: For astronaut mental health; and space tourism, education and outreach. *Acta Astronautica*, *203*, 436–446. DOI: 10.1016/j.actaastro.2022.12.016

Hsu, C. H. (2017). Tourism education on and beyond the horizon. *Tourism Management Perspectives*, *25*, 181–183. DOI: 10.1016/j.tmp.2017.11.022

Huang, A., De La Mora Velasco, E., & Haney, A. (2022). Examining Instructional Technologies in Hospitality and Tourism Education: A Systematic Review of literature. *Journal of Hospitality & Tourism Education*, *36*(2), 113–131. DOI: 10.1080/10963758.2022.2109480

Iqbal, A. I., Aamir, A., Hammad, A., Hafsa, H., Basit, A., Oduoye, M. O., Anis, M. W., Ahmed, S., Younus, M. I., & Jabeen, S. (2024). Immersive Technologies in Healthcare: An In-Depth exploration of virtual reality and augmented reality in enhancing patient care, medical education, and training paradigms. *Journal of Primary Care & Community Health*, *15*, 21501319241293311. Advance online publication. DOI: 10.1177/21501319241293311 PMID: 39439304

Jennings, G., Cater, C. I., Hales, R., Kensbock, S., & Hornby, G. (2015). Partnering for real world learning, sustainability, tourism education. *Quality Assurance in Education*, *23*(4), 378–394. DOI: 10.1108/QAE-03-2015-0010

Kallou, S., & Kikilia, A. (2021). A transformative educational framework in tourism higher education through digital technologies during the COVID-19 pandemic. *Advances in Mobile Learning Educational Research*, *1*(2), 37–47. DOI: 10.25082/AMLER.2021.01.005

Koumpouros, Y. (2024). Revealing the true potential and prospects of augmented reality in education. *Smart Learning Environments*, *11*(1), 2. Advance online publication. DOI: 10.1186/s40561-023-00288-0

Kvale, S., & Brinkmann, S. (2009). *Interviews: Learning the craft of qualitative research interviewing*. sage.

Liang, A. R. (2021). Examining the factors of experiential learning and teaching style: A case study of a hospitality and tourism program. *Journal of Hospitality, Leisure, Sport and Tourism Education*, *29*, 100332. DOI: 10.1016/j.jhlste.2021.100332

Liang, H., Hwang, G., Hsu, T., & Yeh, J. (2024). Effect of an AI-based chatbot on students' learning performance in alternate reality game-based museum learning. *British Journal of Educational Technology*, *55*(5), 2315–2338. DOI: 10.1111/bjet.13448

Lomer, S., & Palmer, E. (2021). 'I didn't know this was actually stuff that could help us, with actually learning': Student perceptions of Active Blended Learning. *Teaching in Higher Education*, *28*(4), 679–698. DOI: 10.1080/13562517.2020.1852202

Mak, B., Lau, C., & Wong, A. (2017). Effects of experiential learning on students: An ecotourism service-learning course. *Journal of Teaching in Travel & Tourism*, •••, 1–16. DOI: 10.1080/15313220.2017.1285265

Makransky, G., & Lilleholt, L. (2018). A structural equation modeling investigation of the emotional value of immersive virtual reality in education. *Educational Technology Research and Development*, *66*(5), 1141–1164. DOI: 10.1007/s11423-018-9581-2

Maumbe, K. (2014). Teaching and Learning in Recreation and Tourism: A comparison of three instructional methods. *Journal of Teaching in Travel & Tourism*, *14*(4), 365–385. DOI: 10.1080/15313220.2014.955305

Mayaka, M., & Akama, J. S. (2006). Systems approach to tourism training and education: The Kenyan case study. *Tourism Management*, *28*(1), 298–306. DOI: 10.1016/j.tourman.2005.12.023

Mínguez, C., Martínez-Hernández, C., & Yubero, C. (2021). Higher education and the sustainable tourism pedagogy: Are tourism students ready to lead change in the post pandemic era? *Journal of Hospitality, Leisure, Sport and Tourism Education*, *29*, 100329. DOI: 10.1016/j.jhlste.2021.100329

Mohanty, B. S., Shaikh, Z. H., Mahapatra, D. M., Ratnakaranm, S., & Manikeswari, D. (2025). Wearable technologies in education: Advantages, limitations, and technical difficulties. In *Wearable devices and smart technology for educational teaching assistance* (pp. 309–330). IGI Global Scientific Publishing.

Neophytou, R., Liasidou, S., Pipyros, K., & Christofi, A. (2025). Artificial intelligence driven adaptive learning methods in sustainable tourism education. *Worldwide Hospitality and Tourism Themes*, *17*(1), 120–131. Advance online publication. DOI: 10.1108/WHATT-12-2024-0308

Papakostas, C., Troussas, C., & Sgouropoulou, C. (2024). Review of the Literature on AI-Enhanced Augmented Reality in Education. In *Cognitive technologies* (pp. 13–50). DOI: 10.1007/978-3-031-52005-1_2

Patton, M. Q. (2014). *Qualitative research & evaluation methods: Integrating theory and practice*. Sage publications.

Prabhakaran, A., Mahamadu, A., Booth, C. A., & Manu, P. (2025). Applications of immersive technology in architecture, engineering and construction. In *Routledge eBooks*. DOI: 10.1201/9781032662909

Raj, S., Sharma, S., & Dutt, D. (2024). Digital Disruption: 'Transforming Tourism Education for the 21st Century.' In *Emerald Publishing Limited eBooks* (pp. 137–145). DOI: 10.1108/978-1-83608-704-520241010

Ratnakaram, S. P. K., Manikeswari, D., Shaikh, Z. H., Mahapatra, D. M., Mohanty, B. S., & Soni, A. (2025). Wearables and AI-smart technologies: Transforming the education sphere. In *Wearable devices and smart technology for educational teaching assistance* (pp. 27–52). IGI Global Scientific Publishing.

Rubio-Tamayo, J., Barrio, M. G., & García, F. G. (2017). Immersive Environments and Virtual Reality: Systematic review and advances in communication, interaction and simulation. *Multimodal Technologies and Interaction*, *1*(4), 21. DOI: 10.3390/mti1040021

Ruhanen, L., Axelsen, M., & Bowles, L. (2020). Engaging students through authentic learning: Connecting with international tourism partners. *Journal of Hospitality, Leisure, Sport and Tourism Education*, *29*, 100291. DOI: 10.1016/j.jhlste.2020.100291

Shaikh, Z. H., Irfan, M., Nomran, N. M., Ratnakaram, S. P., Abey, J., & Anto, M. L. (2025). Measuring Vital Sign: A Case Study of India's Emerging Wearable Technology (EzeCheck) for Mass Screening and Health Monitoring. In Ul Rehman, S. (Ed.), *Wearable Devices and Smart Technology for Educational Teaching Assistance* (pp. 285–308). IGI Global Scientific Publishing., DOI: 10.4018/979-8-3693-7817-5.ch011

Shaikh, Z. H., Irfan, M., Vemavarapu, K. R., Sadayan, S., Hawaldar, I. T., & Rehman, S. U. (2024). Assessing the Effectiveness of Learning Outcomes: In Achieving Quality Education at Higher Learning Institutions in Bahrain. In Naim, A., Saklani, A., Khan, S., & Malik, P. (Eds.), *Evaluating Global Accreditation Standards for Higher Education* (pp. 50–65). IGI Global Scientific Publishing., DOI: 10.4018/979-8-3693-1698-6.ch004

Sheldon, P. J., Fesenmaier, D. R., & Tribe, J. (2011). The Tourism Education Futures Initiative (TEFI): Activating Change in Tourism Education. *Journal of Teaching in Travel & Tourism, 11*(1), 2–23. DOI: 10.1080/15313220.2011.548728

Soni, A., Shaikh, Z. H., Taqi, M., Bijja, V., & Ratnakaram, S. P. (2025). Enhancing Education in Bahrain With AI and ML: Through Wearable Technology. In Ul Rehman, S. (Ed.), *Wearable Devices and Smart Technology for Educational Teaching Assistance* (pp. 115–144). IGI Global Scientific Publishing., DOI: 10.4018/979-8-3693-7817-5.ch005

Suh, A., & Prophet, J. (2018). The state of immersive technology research: A literature analysis. *Computers in Human Behavior, 86*, 77–90. DOI: 10.1016/j.chb.2018.04.019

Suryawinata, B. A. (2021). Immersive technology as a tool for sustainable architecture. *IOP Conference Series. Earth and Environmental Science, 794*(1), 012185. DOI: 10.1088/1755-1315/794/1/012185

Vygotsky, L. S. (1980). Mind in Society. *Mind & Society*. Advance online publication. DOI: 10.2307/j.ctvjf9vz4

Zawacki-Richter, O., Marín, V. I., Bond, M., & Gouverneur, F. (2019). Systematic review of research on artificial intelligence applications in higher education – where are the educators? *International Journal of Educational Technology in Higher Education, 16*(1), 39. Advance online publication. DOI: 10.1186/s41239-019-0171-0

Chapter 10
Exploring the Integration of AI and Metaverse in Education:
Opportunities, Challenges, and Future Directions

Hanan Aldowah
https://orcid.org/0000-0003-1020-2389
Universiti Sains Malaysia, Malaysia

Amira Saif
https://orcid.org/0009-0007-4637-0380
Universiti Sains Malaysia, Malaysia

Shafiq Ul Rehman
Kingdom University, Bahrain

Samar Ghazal
UCSI University, Malaysia

Ahmed Alsswey
Al-Zaytoonah University of Jordan, Jordan

ABSTRACT

The convergence of Artificial Intelligence (AI) and the metaverse is reshaping the future of education by enabling personalized, immersive, and learner-centred experiences. This conceptual paper examines how the integration of AI-driven tools within metaverse environments can transform teaching, learning, and institutional practices. It explores the educational opportunities enabled by this convergence,

DOI: 10.4018/979-8-3373-3815-6.ch010

…yright © 2026, IGI Global Scientific Publishing. Copying or distributing in print or electronic forms without written permission of IGI Global Scientific Publishing is prohibited. Use of this chapter to …ain generative artificial intelligence (AI) technologies is expressly prohibited. The publisher reserves all rights to license its use for generative AI training and machine learning model development.

including intelligent tutoring, real-time analytics, immersive learning, and enhanced accessibility. A conceptual framework is proposed, built on three foundational pillars: Pedagogical Integration, Technological Infrastructure and Access, and Ethical and Data Governance all centered around supporting meaningful and equitable learner engagement. The paper also critically discusses the challenges and limitations associated with ethical concerns, the digital divide, data privacy, and institutional readiness. Implications for key stakeholders- educators, institutions, and learners- are considered, along with strategic recommendations for sustainable adoption.

1. INTRODUCTION

The educational world, notably higher education, is undergoing a fundamental change, driven mainly by the rapid advancements in digital technologies. The most critical changes dictating the future of education include AI and the metaverse, which have the potential to transform teaching and learning practices at a base level. AI technologies, such as machine learning (ML) and natural language processing (NLP), are increasingly being integrated into the educational systems to provide personalized learning opportunities, automate administrative work, and engage students more (Holmes, Bialik, & Fadel, 2019). Such tools allow educators to individualize content to students according to their learning styles, monitor student progress in real-time, and provide immediate feedback, thus improving learning outcomes. Concurrently, attention in the area of education is being increasingly drawn to the metaverse, which refers to a collective virtual shared space formed through the integration of physical and digital worlds. It provides immersive and interactive learning in which students can engage in 3D simulations, access virtual laboratories, and engage in real-time collaborations with peers and instructors all over the world (Maas & Hughes, 2020). The integration of AI into the metaverse further enhances the educational value of this technology as it develops adaptive and intelligent learning experiences. As these technologies expand further, they are bound to be the centre of revolutionizing the future of education through making learning more alive, accessible, and productive (Zawacki-Richter, Marín, Bond, & Gouverneur, 2019).

Although there is an increasing interest in the unique possibilities of AI and the metaverse in educational settings, their combined use is still not thoroughly examined, especially regarding practical and ethical aspects. Existing challenges include the absence of instructional frameworks for practical immersive AI applications, unequal infrastructure that hinders fair access, and a lack of focus on ethical governance and the protection of data. These obstacles highlight an urgent need to explore how AI and the metaverse can be merged responsibly to benefit a variety of learners. This paper offers a comprehensive conceptual framework that highlights ethical, technological, and pedagogical aspects, unlike earlier research that investigates AI or the metaverse separately. Although the perspective is positive, this work also acknowledges potential dangers such as data misuse, algorithmic bias, digital exclusion, and the need for educator readiness. The primary emphasis of this paper is on higher education, where the incorporation of AI and metaverse technologies is swiftly advancing.

1.1 Artificial Intelligence in Education

Artificial intelligence has been integrating into education for quite some time, with its early involvement tracing back to the 1960s when the first computer-assisted instructional systems were created (Woolf, 2010). At the beginning of AI applications, the concept focused on Intelligent Tutoring Systems (ITS), which aimed to mimic the adaptive guidance of a human tutor with rule-based reasoning and decision trees (Luckin & Holmes, 2016). These systems provided targeted feedback and learning materials to students based on their inputs, marking the beginning of personalized learning.

Subsequently, developments in machine learning and big data analysis, along with progress in natural language processing, have greatly improved the effectiveness of AI in educational environments (Holmes et al., 2019). Modern AI systems in education surpass traditional programming in their ability to analyze a significant volume of learner data, predict learning paths, and implement corresponding interventions. Now, AI is increasingly being applied to personalise learning pathways, add in-time flexibility to instructional materials, and provide personalised study for heterogeneous learners through differentiated instruction (Huawei & Aryadoust, 2023). AI tools also help instructors with administrative and instructional functions, such as automated grading and lesson planning for students' individualised feedback. For example, generative AI tools such as ChatGPT are currently being investigated in higher education for purposes including content summarization, development of the question lists, assistance in languages, and interactions with the students (Kasneci et al., 2023). These tools minimise cognitive load for educators and improve student access to timely support (Shan Wang et al., 2024).

Recent research indicates a substantial increase in the adoption of AI technologies within educational institutions worldwide. Educators are implementing AI to enhance administrative efficiency, facilitate personalized instruction, support differentiated learning, and promote inclusive educational practices (Huawei & Aryadoust, 2023; Kasneci et al., 2023). Implementation of generative AI tools like ChatGPT and other large language models is growing exponentially to assist in the creation of content, automatic feedback, and intelligent tutoring systems (Dwivedi et al., 2021; Joksimovic, Ifenthaler, Marrone, De Laat, & Siemens, 2023). Furthermore, there is an increasing focus on ensuring the ethical and responsible use of AI in education, which has resulted in the development of governance guidelines, AI literacy programmes, and policies regarding the privacy of data, as well as the transparency of algorithms (Shan Wang et al., 2024; Zawacki-Richter et al., 2019). The integration of AI into teaching and learning, therefore, is likely to expand at a deeper level with future applications targeting intelligent learning analytics, adaptive feedback mechanisms, and real-time intuition into emotional and behavioural aspects, to reinforce learning engagement.

1.2 The Metaverse in Education

Metaverse, a multidimensional digital environment that combines physical and virtual realities, has become a new transformative element for the world of education. It has been successfully described as an immersive, persistent, 3D interactive environment, where the metaverse allows learners to move, interact, and play in their personalized digital avatars and forms (Al-Sharafi, Al-Emran, Al-Qaysi, Iranmanesh, & Ibrahim, 2024). While the concept predates the pandemic, during the global shift to remote learning, its importance and momentum have gained increased traction due to the limitations of traditional online platforms and the need to create more immersive and social learning areas (Diao & Su, 2025).

In an educational setting, the metaverse provides experiential and constructivist learning opportunities, where the students can interact with digital simulations, carry out laboratory work in the virtual environments, and collaborate with peers in other geographies in real time (Onu, Pradhan, & Mbohwa, 2024). These capabilities are consistent with the concepts of active learning and multimodal engagement, thus enabling deeper conceptual understanding of and long-term retention of knowledge. Studies conducted recently have stressed that the metaverse supports the learners with various needs, and provides adaptive settings, individualizable interfaces, as well as real-time feedback (Al-Sharafi et al., 2024; Maghaydah, Al-Emran, Maheshwari, & Al-Sharafi, 2024; Mitani et al., 2025).

Higher education institutes are starting to experiment with pilot applications of coursework based on the metaverse, metaverse campuses, and a learning ecosystem with AI enhancement, which have the potential to improve students' motivation, cooperation, and inclusion better (Maghaydah et al., 2024; Singh, 2024). For instance, in the metaverse classrooms, students can manipulate virtual objects in STEM fields, engage in historical reenactments in humanities, or participate in global discussions in virtual environments. These contribute to greater involvement and critical thinking skills (Illi & Elhassouny, 2025; Yeganeh, Fenty, Chen, Simpson, & Hatami, 2025). In addition, the educators have also reported greater emotional presence, social connectedness, and learner satisfaction in metaverse-supported contexts than in traditional virtual learning systems (Diao & Su, 2025; Rodway & Schepman, 2023).

Despite the excitement, there are still several challenges, such as technological barriers, accessibility, privacy issues, and a lack of teacher training and institutional support (Illi & Elhassouny, 2025; Maghaydah et al., 2024). However, the technology of virtual reality (VR), augmented reality (AR), and AI integration will continue to develop, and the metaverse is expected to become a key element of future educational systems, which will provide an inclusive, engaging, and personalised learning experience (Villegas-Ch, García-Ortiz, & Sánchez-Viteri, 2024; Yeganeh et al., 2025).

1.3 Emerging Adoption Trends of AI and the Metaverse in Education

The application of AI and the metaverse in education is rapidly growing, driven by institutions' pursuit of innovative methods to boost learning engagement, improve operational efficiency, and enhance teaching effectiveness. The use of AI in education has notably increased compared to traditional intelligent tutoring systems. Contemporary tools such as ChatGPT, GPT-4, and other large language models are now being utilized by both educators and students for various purposes, including content creation and personalized tutoring, as well as for formative assessments and streamlining administrative tasks (Al-Emran, 2024; Jin, Yan, Echeverria, Gašević, & Martinez-Maldonado, 2025). A trending global survey indicated that an increasing number of higher education institutions are using generative AI to integrate into learning management systems for improving interactivity and offering real-time academic support (Bahroun, Anane, Ahmed, & Zacca, 2023; Ilieva et al., 2023; Jin et al., 2025).

Some of AI's existing applications are adaptive learning environments, automated grading systems, feedback generation, predictions, and multilingual support. These tools are already enabling educators to understand learner needs and determine at-risk students before adjusting instruction to meet the needs (Ouyang, Zheng, & Jiao, 2022). Additionally, as the availability of AI tools is enhanced, more inclusive and equitable educational experiences are constituted, especially for those learners with diverse linguistic, cognitive, and physical demands (Li, Guan, Wang, Chen, & Hwang, 2024).

Meanwhile, the metaverse is evolving as a platform for learning that promotes experiential and collaborative learning. Colleges and universities are piloting metaverse-based courses and virtual campuses to enhance student engagement, motivation, and social interaction (Diao & Su, 2025; Yeganeh et al., 2025). Platforms that support extended reality (XR) environments, avatars, and interactive digital spaces allow learners to participate in virtual labs, role-playing activities, and worldwide discussions in real time. These environments are particularly beneficial in fields that require spatial visualization or hands-on knowledge, such as medicine, engineering, and history (Shaofeng Wang & Zhang, 2024). Not only its readiness, but also the ability to solve old educational problems with accessibility, personalization, and learner isolation in web-based learner settings make this rise possible (Onu et al., 2024). These virtual spaces will allow educators to create rich context and learner-centred learning opportunities, which ensure deeper engagement and an active knowledge construction process (Illi & Elhassouny, 2025). Together, AI and the metaverse are essentially a paradigm shift in the delivery and experience of education. Their merging is set further to boost learning personalization, interactivity, and inclusiveness, and pressure educators to rethink pedagogies and digital literacy methodologies.

2. EDUCATIONAL OPPORTUNITIES ENABLED BY THE INTEGRATION OF AI AND THE METAVERSE

The involvement of AI and the metaverse in education opens up countless opportunities to revolutionise teaching and learning in the field. Together, these technologies contribute to building immersive, personalised, and accessible learning environments. The following key opportunities illustrate how such an integration supports diverse aspects of education:

2.1 Immersive Learning

Immersive learning environments allow students to engage in three-dimensional (3D) virtual spaces rooted in contexts that are a reflection of the real world or an abstract scenario. Learners immerse themselves in educational simulations that vary from virtual science laboratories and historical reconstruction to engineering prototypes and medical procedures employing modern technologies like virtual reality (VR), augmented reality (AR), and extended reality (XR). These experiences offer an opportunity for practical training in safe, controllable, and reproducible environments, something that cannot be achieved in a regular classroom or by e-learning.

The metaverse significantly improved immersive learning through establishing persistent, multi-user settings that students can use to collaboratively investigate, manipulate, and reflect on digital artefacts (Gilbert & Gilbert, 2024; Shaofeng Wang & Zhang, 2024). These environments can be accessed asynchronously or synchronously; the feature promotes flexible and continuous learning. The spatial organisation of information and the presentations with multisensory stimuli enable the learners to grasp meaning more effectively and retain knowledge for a longer period. Research emphasised that immersive learning increases cognitive involvement and motivation, better conceptual learning, especially in the STEM domains, architecture, and health sciences (Diao & Su, 2025; Oh, Kim, Chang, Park, & Lee, 2023; Villegas-Ch et al., 2024; Yenduri et al., 2023). Learners benefit from real-life testimonies that illustrate abstract theories, such as simulations of physics laws or virtual surgeries, which aid in understanding and building confidence. In addition, immersive technologies can minimise the cognitive overload through chunking information into spatial formats, attention management, and inquiry-based exploration (Al-kfairy, Sendaba, & Alfandi, 2025). In short, immersive learning environments facilitated by AI and AR not only improve content delivery but also change the role of the learner from a passive recipient of knowledge to an active creator of knowledge.

While immersive learning environments provide valuable opportunities to simulate real-world experiences, their integration with intelligent systems has not been extensively explored. Most studies consider immersive design and AI-driven guidance as separate entities, creating a gap in understanding how these can collaboratively enhance personalized virtual education.

2.2 Intelligent Tutoring Systems (ITS)

AI-driven Intelligent Tutoring Systems (ITS) use data analytics and machine learning (ML) algorithms for data collection and analysis, track learner behaviour, assess academic performance, and adapt the instructional content to meet individual-specific needs (Yeganeh et al., 2025). These systems use virtual tutors to provide real-time suggestions, scaffoldings, explanations, and individualised feedback that mimic an instructor in one-on-one interactions (Illi & Elhassouny, 2025). Unlike traditional e-learning systems that usually require a specific sequence to be followed, ITS can vary the level of difficulty, pace, and content flow to match any participant's activity during the learning process and their emerging understanding (Jin et al., 2025). One of the distinguishing competencies of the modern ITS is that they are capable of supporting adaptive learning. Through an analysis of patterns in the input, response time, and error rate of a student, ITS can understand knowledge gaps and adjust the instructional strategies appropriately. This leads to a personalised learning experience that is efficient and facilitates mastery learning, discouraging students from frustration and disengagement.

Recent advancements in generative AI and natural language processing (NLP) have significantly enhanced Intelligent Tutoring Systems (ITS). Models like ChatGPT now enable these systems to engage learners in open-ended discussions, answer complex questions, and explain concepts in various ways, promoting critical thinking (Kasneci et al., 2023; Zhang, Jiang, Xiong, & Zhao, 2024). For instance, a struggling learner might receive not just a solution but also contextual explanations or visual aids (Bansal, Chamola, Hussain, Guizani, & Niyato, 2024). These systems promote learner autonomy by allowing students to navigate content at their own pace, revisit ideas, and access immediate support, which helps reduce anxiety associated with traditional assessments. However, from the instructor's perspective, ITS markedly simplifies the instructional burden by automating all the routine actions, including paper marking, generating questions, and delivering materials; thus, time for more advanced instructional activities, as well as individual assistance, is available (Bansal et al., 2024; Jin et al., 2025). Also, the ITS platform can provide learning analytics dashboards to instructors that will help them know the trends in class performance, the level of concepts, and those areas that need refinement in the instruction (Onu et al., 2024).

Intelligent Tutoring Systems (ITS) are a prominent example of AI in education, offering scalable, customizable, and data-driven support tailored to each student's needs. Although research on ITS has made significant progress in adapting content for learners, the integration of these systems into immersive metaverse environments has not been fully explored. There is still limited conceptual work linking AI adaptability with spatial and social immersion, highlighting a clear opportunity for future development.

2.3 Enhanced Accessibility and Inclusion

The integration of AI and the metaverse in the learning process is driving significant advancements in accessibility and inclusivity.is contributing to significant changes in the sphere of accessibility and inclusivity in learning (Al-Zahrani & Alasmari, 2025). AI technologies assist students with various customised tools and assistive technology options. Such features as automatic language translation, real-time speech-to-text transcription, or text-to-speech synthesis allow students with hearing, visual, cognitive, or linguistic issues to consume and interact with educational content on par with their peers (Gadekallu et al., 2025; Orynbay, Razakhova, Peer, Meden, & Emeršič, 2024).

The inclusivity of the metaverse is enhanced by its capacity to create immersive and customizable learning environments. Students can personalize their avatars to reflect their identities, navigate the online space using voice commands or alternative inputs, and participate in virtual activities, even if they have physical limitations (Memon & Memon, 2025). Such affordances are particularly important for learners who have difficulties in a traditional classroom context, such as learners with physical disabilities, neurodiverse learners, or learners in remote or underprivileged regions (Diao & Su, 2025).

In addition to accessibility tools, AI plays a crucial role in promoting emotional and cognitive inclusion. AI algorithms can analyze behavioral indicators such as engagement rates, response times, and even facial expressions (when ethically collected) to identify signs of disengagement or learning difficulties. By utilizing this data, the system can offer timely and personalized interventions, which may include presenting more straightforward content, providing motivational prompts, or connecting users with a human tutor or counselor (Rekha et al., 2024). These capabilities not only enhance the learning experience but also promote educational equity. By overcoming physical and cognitive barriers, AI and the metaverse are instrumental in bridging the digital divide. They ensure that quality education is economically accessible to everyone, regardless of geographical location, socio-economic status, or disability (Memon & Memon, 2025). Further, those inclusive design principles embedded in these technologies create a culture of belonging and respect for diversity, which is critical for the well-being and success of students in the digital age.

Both AI and immersive technologies have shown potential for enhancing educational inclusivity, but current research often examines them in isolation. There is a need for a more integrated approach that investigates how their combined capabilities can support diverse learners and promote equitable learning experiences.

2.4 Collaborative Virtual Learning Spaces

Metaverse platforms facilitate collaboration between learners in real time, regardless of their location. Using avatars and immersive 3D interfaces, students can collaborate on virtual group projects, simulations, design challenges, or real-time scenarios that require problem-solving. These environments go beyond traditional video conferencing technology by allowing for physical interaction, co-presence, and spatial awareness, which are essential to fostering mutual engagement and authentic communication (Zhang et al., 2024). Students in metaverse environments can engage together in shared virtual laboratories, design studios, and role-playing, where collaborative input, decision-making, and reflection are required (Illi & El-hassouny, 2025). Such experiences are especially productive for the development of critical soft skills like teamwork, leadership, cross-cultural competence, and emotional intelligence (Onu et al., 2024). Learners not only consume content but also co-construct knowledge in a shared digital space (Shaofeng Wang & Zhang, 2024).

Such collaborative environments mimic several features of face-to-face classroom interactions and bring them to a global scale. Educational institutions are also testing virtual campuses, metaverse-based seminars, and immersive academic conferences, where students can engage socially and academically in clearly designed digital ecosystems (Yeganeh et al., 2025). These spaces accommodate synchronous and asynchronous interactions, peer tutoring, and cross-institutional collaborations, and thus, improve cognitive presence and social connectedness (Al-kfairy, Sendaba, et al., 2025; Oh et al., 2023). Moreover, the metaverse provides structured opportunities for collaboration across different fields. For instance, learners from engineering, business, and design backgrounds can come together in a shared metaverse platform to create virtual prototypes or participate in simulated business negotiations. AI integration adds to the capabilities of these spaces in helpful agents, real-time translation, and intelligent feedback to promote equal and effective communication (Dong, Liu, & Abbas, 2024).

In addition to that, collaborative learning provided in the metaverse enhances inclusive participation with various modes of participation that include voice, text, gesture, and visual expression, which accommodate various learning styles and accessibility needs (Yenduri et al., 2023). Such features not only ensure that learners with any form of disability or language barrier do not fall behind, but they can also actively participate in collaborative learning activities (Dudley, Yin, Garaj, & Kristensson, 2023).

While collaboration in virtual spaces is widely discussed, the role of AI in managing group dynamics, providing peer feedback, and creating adaptive collaboration paths is often overlooked. This intersection presents a critical opportunity to advance intelligent group learning environments.

2.5 Real-Time Learning Analytics and Feedback

AI technologies can continuously collect, extract, interpret, and visualise learner data, producing actionable insights that drive personalised learning. These systems track a wide range of metrics, including interaction patterns, learning behaviors, engagement levels, time spent on tasks, and quiz performance (Sajja, Sermet, & Demir, 2025). Real-time dashboards allow educators to monitor individual and group progress, detect misconceptions as they arise, and flag at-risk students early enough to allow adjustments to their instructional plan or differentiated support. Such data-driven insights, more than making instruction responsive, also inform higher-level strategic decisions like curriculum improvement, instructional design, and resource allocation (Wiedbusch et al., 2021). For example, cumulative analytics can identify topics that consistently hinder learners and equip teachers to adjust their pace, teaching style, or additional support (Esqueda, 2024).

From the learner's point of view, AI-enabled feedback systems provide instant and one-on-one feedback to their queries, formative assessments, and recommendations regarding their further learning. These systems can suggest further resources, mark where weakness was observed, and celebrate achievement, providing an even more autonomous and encouraging self-directed learning experience (Kanthimathi, Nanda, Venkatraman, Renganayagan, & Eswaran, 2025). This is a type of feedback loop which enhances mastery in learning and development of a growth mindset since it helps student understand their learning pattern and take ownership of their progress (Al-Zahrani & Alasmari, 2025; Zawacki-Richter et al., 2019). Moreover, AI-powered analytics tools often incorporate predictive modeling, which involves forecasting students' outcomes and alerting educators to those who may drop out or disengage from the educational process significantly in advance. These predictive insights enable proactive as opposed to reactive instructional support, improving retention rates and academic success rates across different educational settings (Shoaib et al., 2024).

The potential of AI for real-time analytics is promising; however, few studies explore how these insights function within continuous, immersive virtual environments. A cohesive framework for interpreting and responding to learner data in the metaverse is still essential.

2.6 Gamification and Motivation

The incorporation of gamification features, such as badges, leaderboards, progress bars, and reward systems, in AI-powered and metaverse-based educational platforms is transforming the way learners interact with content. By integrating game mechanics into learning practices, these technologies provide a more interactive, competitive, and goal-oriented experience that increases intrinsic and extrinsic motivation (Liu, Lin, Lo, Chang, & Lin, 2025). Learners are encouraged to accomplish tasks, to learn new skills, and to work with peers in enjoyable and pedagogically effective ways. AI is critical in **personalizing gamified learning experiences**. By applying learner analytics, AI systems track learner preferences, patterns of engagement, and mastery of skills to tailor the difficulty of games and the means of feedback in a dynamic way (Yang, Fang, Xu, Zhang, & Pan, 2024). For example, AI can adapt to the difficulty of a challenge or provide additional support based on the learner's current proficiency or struggle to balance challenge and skill, often referred to as the "flow state." (Bansal et al., 2024; Zainuddin, Chu, & Perera, 2024a). This responsive gamification increases satisfaction and dropout mitigation as learner retention is at optimal levels (Zainuddin, Chu, & Perera, 2024b).

The metaverse is an even greater magnifier of the effects of gamification, as it embeds **game-like narratives and immersive scenarios** in the learning setting (Thomas, Baral, Crocco, & Mohanan, 2023). Students can take quests, act out as historical and scientific characters, and engage in mission-based simulations that mimic real-world problems. Such experiences exploit the utilisation of 3D avatars, spatial environments, and interactive objects to raise a presence, urgency, and immersion that cannot be achieved in conventional platforms (Yang et al., 2024). These immersive gamified settings can contribute to critical soft skills development areas such as strategic thinking, collaboration, and decision-making (Thomas et al.,

2023). For instance, in a virtual business simulation, students can take control of a virtual business, participate in a challenge, or collaborate with peers from around the world in real time. AI agents present in the simulation can perform as coaches or competitors, tailoring their responses according to learner action, in order to generate realistic workplace interactions.

Furthermore, gamification helps with **formative assessment** by offering real-time and non-disruptive feedback regarding points, available content, or performance (Cigdem et al., 2024). Immediate attention for the learner's efforts is provided, which encourages achievement and stimulates further engagement. These micro-rewards over time lead to a general positive effect on motivation and learning persistence for the young and inexperienced learners (Matthews, Cumings, De Los Santos, Feng, & Mouloua, 2025).

The emerging synergy between AI and metaverse technologies is paving the way for a new generation of adaptive, immersive, and motivational learning environments. Gamification has evolved beyond just offering surface-level rewards; it is now closely integrated with pedagogical design, transforming education into a more engaging, individualized, and meaningful experience. However, while gamification is widely used to enhance engagement, its integration with AI-driven personalization in immersive learning contexts remains largely unexplored. By advancing this synergy, where adaptive AI customizes game mechanics for individual learners, we can provide deeper and more sustained motivation in virtual educational settings. Figure 1 illustrates how AI and the Metaverse enable new educational opportunities across different learning environments.

Figure 1. Educational opportunities enabled by AI and metaverse

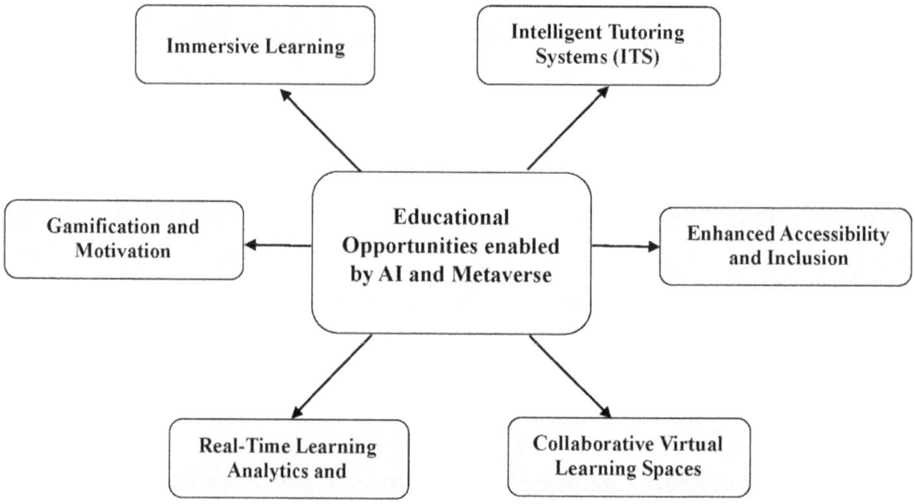

3. CHALLENGES AND LIMITATIONS OF INTEGRATING AI AND THE METAVERSE IN EDUCATION

Despite the transformative potential of AI and the metaverse in education, their integration presents several challenges and limitations that must be critically addressed. These include ethical considerations, unequal access to technology (the digital divide), and concerns about data privacy and governance. Understanding these limitations is crucial for developing responsible and inclusive educational ecosystems.

3.1 Ethical Concerns

Using algorithms and virtual worlds ethically in education is one of the main difficulty areas (Al-Kfairy, Alrabaee, Alfandi, Mohamed, & Khaddaj, 2025). Most often, the algorithms used to personalise, assess, and provide feedback to learners operate in a non-transparent manner. Neither educators nor students typically understand how these systems collect data, choose learning routes, or offer suitable interventions. This opacity raises legitimate concerns about algorithmic bias, fairness, and accountability, especially when such decisions affect grading, learning opportunities, or student evaluation (Adel, 2025). Biases present in how data is collected or an algorithm is designed can help maintain existing educational imbalances, especially among marginalised groups.

Besides, because avatars and immersive simulation are used in the metaverse, they raise new issues about identity, proper behaviour, and maintaining psychological safety (Al-Kfairy, Alrabaee, & Alfandi, 2024). While online, learners might come across cases of identity fraud, forms of discrimination in their avatar, or unwanted behaviour in spaces where there is no real-time monitoring. Because metaverse experiences are so realistic, users can become disoriented or lose touch with the real world unless significant safeguards are put in place. Many studies have raised concerns about the long-term psychological effects of prolonged interaction in highly immersive digital environments, and yet this subject is explored only rarely (Eltanbouly, Halabi, & Qadir, 2025). If ethics and usage guidelines are unclear, these technologies might threaten students' well-being, cause people to doubt their use, and inadvertently exacerbate educational and social disparities.

3.2 Pedagogical Readiness and Teacher Training

One of the most pressing challenges for education to integrate AI and the metaverse is the lack of pedagogical readiness and digital competence among educators. They lack the knowledge of how to use AI tools and design learning activities because they are unfamiliar with the theories behind such technologies (Lui, Not, & Wong, 2023). Consequently, they typically use AI for grading or try out VR, with little regard to setting clear goals or learning outcomes for their students (Johnson-Glenberg, 2018). This gap is particularly concerning in disciplines that require complex instructional design or ethical sensitivity, such as healthcare, humanities, or social sciences (Beck, Morgado, & O'Shea, 2023). Educators may have little knowledge about anything related to algorithmic bias, data rights, and proper behavior in the metaverse (Illi & Elhassouny, 2025). If they do not receive the proper training, they cannot help students appropriately use technology. In addition, since AI and XR technologies change rapidly, it could be problematic for educators to follow these changes without help from institutions (Yeganeh et al., 2025). To overcome this challenge, institutions must introduce **professional development programs** and training that address digital teaching methods, ethical topics in AI, best curriculum methods, and ways of working in various fields (Adel, 2025). Faculty should also be involved in the early stages of technology planning and policy formation to ensure their needs and insights shape implementation practices (Al-Kfairy, Alrabaee, et al., 2025).

3.3 Technical Complexity and Interoperability

The implementation of AI and metaverse technologies requires sophisticated technical skills and infrastructure, which many educational institutions find challenging to provide. Schools with limited funding frequently do not possess the essential processing capabilities, secure internet access, and compatible devices needed to effectively utilize these systems (Jagatheesaperumal, Ahmad, Al-Fuqaha, & Qadir, 2024). Dealing with such technical complexity, ensuring updates, and fixing any issues on these platforms can be so complex that IT departments may face difficulties, leading to implementation delays or inconsistencies (Chen, Zhong, & Wu, 2023). A key issue is interoperability. While AI can be beneficial in digital education, numerous AI-driven tools and metaverse platforms function as isolated systems, which restricts their capacity to connect with current learning management systems (LMS), research, digital libraries, and analytics tools (Almeman, EL Ayeb, Berrima, Issaoui, & Morsy, 2025). The consequence of this is distinct regions for education, challenges in exchanging information across various platforms, and costs incurred due to the use of multiple licenses, software, and support teams (Adel, 2025). In addition, creating high-quality immersive content, such as VR simulations, interactive 3D models, or gamified experiences, necessitates specific expertise in instructional design, 3D graphics development, programming, and user experience design.(UX) (Pellas, Mystakidis, & Christopoulos, 2021). Since developing and adjusting content usually requires many resources, smaller institutions find it hard to develop or customize their content (Damaševičius & Sidekerskienė,

2024). Furthermore, constraints related to hardware, including old devices, restricted availability of VR headsets, or inadequate bandwidth, can significantly diminish user experience and hinder the scalability of AI and metaverse applications. In the absence of dependable and scalable technical infrastructure, the advantages of these technologies for education remain more theoretical than practical. (Safikhani, Keller, Schweiger, & Pirker, 2022).

3.4 Digital Divide

The integration of advanced technologies such as AI and the metaverse in educational settings may heighten the existing digital divide. While these technologies facilitate the development of innovative services, they also widen the chasm between individuals who have access to the requisite infrastructure and those who do not. Students in rural areas, those from low-income backgrounds, and those attending schools or universities without sufficient technology frequently struggle to engage fully in AI-driven or immersive learning experiences (Memon & Memon, 2025). Moreover, the digital divide extends beyond hardware access to include disparities in digital literacy. When learners do not know how to use virtual platforms, AI programmes, or simulations, they may struggle more in learning than others (Zou, Kuek, Feng, & Cheng, 2025). Similarly, when educators teach in unfavourable conditions, they may lack the training, backup, or other resources needed to use these technologies effectively. Because of this, only students and educators using the latest technology can enjoy innovative learning opportunities (Onu et al., 2024). Without intervention, the unequal use of AI and the metaverse may unintentionally reinforce systemic inequities in education. This may increase the disparity between privileged and marginalized groups in securing an education that equips them for the future. Closing this divide across all communities demands more than merely providing equipment. Accomplishing this necessitates significant investment in digital infrastructure, utilizing inclusive software, ensuring everyone has internet access, and fostering the development of skilled professionals. To ensure that AI and the metaverse are accessible to all societal segments, it's crucial to create policies that promote equitable access, tailor content for all communities, and encourage local e-activities (Bucci, Fani, & Bandinelli, 2024).

3.5 Data Privacy and Governance

The integration of AI and metaverse technologies in educational settings, particularly in higher education, presents major worries about data privacy, consent, and governance. These platforms often gather and handle substantial volumes of sensitive information about learners, including biometric data. In the absence of adequate protections, sensitive information such as eye movement data, voice recordings, login history, geographical tracking, and behavioral trends could be exploited or result in unauthorized profiling (Jagatheesaperumal et al., 2024). The lack of standardised ethical guidelines in educational technologies increases these risks. Many AI models, mainly deep learning systems, are "black boxes" that do not allow users to see how their systems work (Chaudhary, 2024). Because of transparency issues, it is difficult for educators and institutions to verify if automated feedback and assessments are fair and accurate (Adadi & Berrada, 2018; Busuioc, 2021). At the same time, metaverse platforms often integrate third-party services and vendors, introducing additional vulnerabilities related to cross-border data transfer, commercial surveillance, and long-term storage or ownership of learner-generated content (Alkaeed, Qayyum, & Qadir, 2024).To mitigate these issues, it is essential for educational institutions to prioritize data protection, algorithmic transparency, and compliance with international legal frameworks such as the General Data Protection Regulation (GDPR) (Temme, 2017). Clear institutional policies must be established on data collection, retention, and sharing, ensuring that learners and educators understand what data is being used, for what purposes, and by whom (Onu et al., 2024). Additionally, empowering students with greater control over their digital identities, including options to access, edit, or delete their data, can foster a more ethical and trustworthy digital learning environment (Yingsoon et al., 2025).

4. IMPLICATIONS FOR STAKEHOLDERS

The adoption of AI and the metaverse in education carries wide-ranging implications for all stakeholders involved in the teaching and learning ecosystem. These technologies not only alter instructional methods but also reshape institutional strategies, student experiences, and policy considerations. Understanding the specific implications for educators, institutions, and learners is critical for maximizing the benefits and mitigating the risks associated with this digital transformation.

4.1 Educators

For educators, integrating AI and metaverse platforms requires a significant shift in both pedagogy and professional practice(Metaverse, 2025). Educators are now tasked with promoting learning through digital methods. They must choose appropriate AI-supported content, manage students' experiences, and oversee immersive virtual environments. Additionally, they need to understand real-time learning analytics, design assessments compatible with AI, and help students adopt ethical technology practices (Onu et al., 2024). This transformation requires continuous professional development in digital pedagogy, AI literacy, data interpretation, and XR instructional design. Without adequate support, educators may become confused or reluctant to integrate EdTech, which can impact their usage (Alfaisal, Hashim, & Azizan, 2024). Thus, educational institutions should make sure educators are trained effectively so they feel confident using AI and the metaverse in their classes (Almeman et al., 2025).

4.2 Institutions

The effective deployment of AI tools and immersive platforms in higher education necessitates strong collaboration among different departments, especially between IT services, academic leaders, and instructional design teams (Mariam, Adil, & Zakaria, 2024). This teamwork is crucial to ensure the interoperability of systems, adherence to data governance, and alignment with educational goals (Mariam, Adil, & Zakaria, 2024). Beyond technical integration, institutions of higher learning must proactively create thorough guidelines concerning the ethical management of student data, algorithmic decision-making, avatar representation, and acceptable behavior within the metaverse (Chawki, Basu, & Choi, 2024). These policies should comply with international data protection regulations, like the GDPR, while also being adapted to fit the cultural and regulatory contexts of local educational frameworks. Moreover, higher education institutions bear a societal obligation to bridge access gaps by investing in solid digital infrastructure and advocating for inclusive technology design. This strategy guarantees that the advantages of AI and metaverse technologies are shared fairly, enabling students from various socioeconomic backgrounds to access and participate fully in these developing learning environments (Memon & Memon, 2025).

4.3 Learners

This development has both benefits and drawbacks for students. On the plus side, AI and the metaverse provide flexible, engaging, and personalized learning experiences. Students can receive instant feedback, explore different learning styles, participate in computer simulations, and collaborate globally (Al-kfairy, Alrabaee, & Alfandi). However, they also need to develop new digital skills, such as interacting with AI tools, navigating various digital environments, analyzing dashboard analytics, and protecting their online identities. As technology advances, more students will need to understand the ethical and social challenges of AI, like bias, login surveillance, and decision-making (McStay, 2023). Additionally, extensive online time can cause information overload, digital fatigue, or reduced face-to-face interaction. Therefore, supporting students in online safety, time management, and digital health should be a key focus for institutions and educators (Memon & Memon, 2025; Zou et al., 2025).

4.4 Blended Learning Implications of AI–Metaverse Integration

While earlier sections highlighted the independent uses of AI and metaverse technologies, their combination presents considerable opportunities to enhance blended learning settings. AI enables customized instruction, responsive feedback, and immediate tracking of progress. At the same time, the metaverse offers immersive and engaging experiences that replicate real-world collaboration and active involvement. Together, these technologies form adaptable hybrid models that merge physical and virtual environments. This combined approach improves accessibility, supports various learning styles, and encourages deeper engagement, especially for students dealing with geographical, physical, or time-related obstacles. Moreover, the integration of AI and metaverse tools allows educators to track student performance, carry out formative assessments, and deliver prompt, tailored interventions. To effectively harness these advantages equitably, institutions must tackle infrastructure preparedness, encourage digital literacy, and provide continuous professional development for teachers. When implemented with care, this integration can contribute to the creation of inclusive, flexible, and future-ready learning ecosystems.

5. CONCEPTUAL FRAMEWORK FOR INTEGRATING AI AND THE METAVERSE IN EDUCATION

This research proposes a three-pillar framework for the meaningful and sustainable inclusion of AI and the metaverse in education. It organizes key elements into three domains: Pedagogical Integration, Technological Infrastructure and Access, and Ethical and Data Governance. This framework consolidates prior components like curriculum alignment, teacher education, and policy into broader, actionable categories for practical implementation in learning environments.(Akour, Al-Maroof, Alfaisal, & Salloum, 2022; Pachoulas, Christopoulos, & Stylios, 2024; M. Wang, Yu, Bell, & Chu, 2022). Having all of this information consolidated simplifies educational planning and enhances transparency for planners and institutions. All the information in one place makes educational planning easier and more transparent for planners and institutions.

5.1 Pedagogical Integration

The educational framework emphasizes the integration of AI and metaverse technologies with educational goals. AI enables personalized learning pathways, providing real-time feedback and formative assessments that adjust based on student performance. Meanwhile, the metaverse offers immersive, three-dimensional simulations that enhance experiential learning. This virtual environment fosters collaboration and social interaction among students, encouraging engagement and active knowledge construction through exploration and experimentation(Onu et al., 2024; Yeganeh et al., 2025). Educators play a crucial role in this integration process as they act as facilitators and guides throughout the learning journey. However, meaningful incorporation of these technologies requires that educators be thoroughly prepared with comprehensive digital pedagogy. This encompasses skills in designing and implementing effective AI- and metaverse-based learning activities, along with assessing student engagement and learning outcomes within these novel environments (Dong et al., 2024; Maghaydah et al., 2024).

To achieve a high level of knowledge in education, continuous professional development is crucial. Training programs should enhance technical skills related to AI tools and metaverse platforms, while also fostering transformative teaching practices. By focusing on both technological expertise and innovative instructional methods, educators can better utilize AI and the metaverse to improve student learning.

5.2 Technological Infrastructure and Access

The success of AI and VR applications hinges on a comprehensive and robust technological infrastructure. This encompasses not only access to essential hardware, such as cutting-edge VR headsets, high-performance computers, and mobile devices, but also a reliable, high-speed internet connectivity capable of supporting bandwidth-intensive applications. Additionally, compatibility across diverse platforms and learning management systems is crucial for seamless integration and user experience (Christopoulos, Conrad, & Shukla, 2018; Dong et al., 2024; Dudley et al., 2023). To ensure equitable access for all learners and prevent the exacerbation of the digital divide, educational institutions must proactively address disparities in access to technology, particularly for underserved communities. This can involve implementing initiatives to provide devices and internet access, as well as offering training to both students and educators on the effective use of these technologies. Beyond the infrastructure, institutions must also be equipped to support the implementation of AI and VR technologies with skilled technical staff who can provide ongoing support and maintenance. Furthermore, the availability of tailored digital tools and local, culturally relevant content is vital in addressing the varied learning contexts and needs of students. The text emphasizes a holistic approach to education that utilizes AI and VR to create an inclusive and effective learning environment. It highlights the importance of technical staff, digital tools, and local content tailored to various learning contexts (Chen et al., 2023; Wellings & Levine, 2009).

5.3 Ethical and Data Governance

The integration of AI and metaverse technologies also brings pressing concerns related to ethics, data privacy, and algorithmic accountability (Adadi & Berrada, 2018; Busuioc, 2021; Shan Wang et al., 2024; Yingsoon et al., 2025). These systems collect extensive learner data, including behavioral patterns, engagement metrics, and potentially biometric information, raising critical questions about informed consent, data ownership, transparency, and compliance with legal standards such as the General Data Protection Regulation (GDPR) (Diao & Su, 2025; Maghaydah et al., 2024; Memon & Memon, 2025; Yeganeh et al., 2025). Institutions must therefore establish clear governance frameworks that outline how data is collected, used, stored, and shared. Ethical principles must also guide the design and deployment of AI algorithms and virtual learning environments to avoid reinforcing bias, exclusion, or psychological harm (Mariam et al., 2024; McStay, 2023). This conceptual framework highlights a learner-centric approach to education by incorporating AI and the metaverse through three interconnected pillars: Pedagogical Integration, Technological Infrastructure and Access, and Ethical and Data Governance.

- **Pedagogical Integration** emphasizes the alignment of instructional design with tools from AI and the metaverse. It prioritizes curriculum alignment, the training of instructors, and immersive learning experiences.
- **Technological Infrastructure and Access** guarantee that students have sufficient hardware, reliable high-speed internet, compatible platforms, and technical assistance to promote equitable access for everyone.
- **Ethical and Data Governance** sets forth guidelines related to privacy, transparency in algorithms, data consent, and adherence to regulations.

At the core of these pillars is a commitment to addressing the needs and rights of learners, ensuring that technology effectively supports students. This framework is illustrated in Figure 2.

Figure 2. Conceptual Framework for Integrating AI and Metaverse

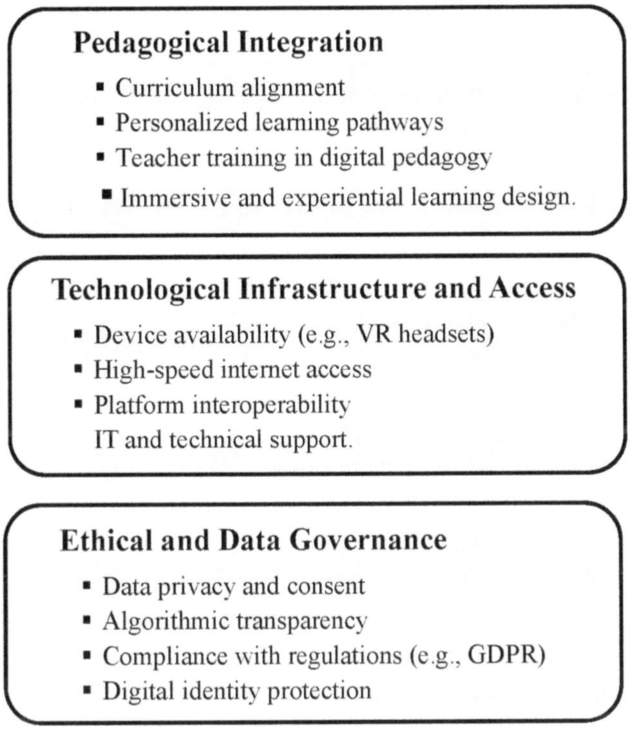

6. CONCLUSION

This chapter has explored how AI and the metaverse can be integrated into education, particularly in higher education. By conducting a thorough review of trends in adoption, educational prospects, challenges, and a proposed conceptual framework, the chapter has underscored the transformative potential of these technologies in shaping future educational environments. AI facilitates personalized learning and provides immediate feedback, whereas the metaverse delivers immersive, interactive experiences that enhance both engagement and collaboration. The conceptual framework presented in this chapter is structured around three main pillars: Pedagogical Integration, Technological Infrastructure and Access, and Ethical and Data Governance. These pillars, founded on a learner-centered perspective, offer a strategic basis for guiding institutional implementation and ensuring that technology promotes inclusive, responsible, and equitable educational objectives. The chapter also highlights the significance of the convergence of AI and the metaverse within blended learning contexts, where their integration supports hybrid teaching models, encourages flexible learner engagement, and improves accessibility. Furthermore, the discussion touches on underexamined yet crucial topics such as identity formation, emotional health, and the practical implementation challenges, including preparedness of digital infrastructure, faculty training, and institutional pushback. By integrating current literature with conceptual ideas, this chapter enhances the understanding of how AI and the metaverse can be effectively incorporated into higher education environments. It also lays the groundwork for future empirical research and interdisciplinary collaboration aimed at creating adaptive, ethical, and human-centered digital learning ecosystems.

Future research should explore the lasting impacts of AI and metaverse integration on educational outcomes, learner identity, and emotional resilience in diverse higher education settings. More empirical studies are needed to understand how students, instructors, and administrators engage with these technologies in blended learning. Additionally, emerging topics like AI-generated content, avatar ethics, and cross-platform data governance require further investigation. Research must also examine the adaptability of frameworks in various institutional contexts, considering costs, technical readiness, and organizational culture. Ultimately, interdisciplinary collaboration is crucial for ensuring that AI and the metaverse foster educational innovation in a human-centric and sustainable way.

REFERENCES

Adadi, A., & Berrada, M. (2018). Peeking inside the black-box: A survey on explainable artificial intelligence (XAI). *IEEE Access : Practical Innovations, Open Solutions*, *6*, 52138–52160. DOI: 10.1109/ACCESS.2018.2870052

Adel, M. M. (2025). Challenges and Opportunities of Educational AI in the Metaverse Era. *Innovations in Educational Robotics: Advancing AI for Sustainable Development*, 1–20.

Akour, I. A., Al-Maroof, R. S., Alfaisal, R., & Salloum, S. A. (2022). A conceptual framework for determining metaverse adoption in higher institutions of the Gulf area: An empirical study using a hybrid SEM-ANN approach. *Computers and Education: Artificial Intelligence*, *3*, 100052. DOI: 10.1016/j.caeai.2022.100052

Al-Emran, M. (2024). Unleashing the role of ChatGPT in Metaverse learning environments: Opportunities, challenges, and future research agendas. *Interactive Learning Environments*, *32*(10), 7497–7506. DOI: 10.1080/10494820.2024.2324326

Al-Kfairy, M., Alrabaee, S., & Alfandi, O. (2024). *Ethical Pathways in VR and the Metaverse: Frameworks for Responsible Innovation.* Paper presented at the 2024 2nd International Conference on Intelligent Metaverse Technologies & Applications (iMETA). DOI: 10.1109/iMETA62882.2024.10807903

Al-kfairy, M., Alrabaee, S., & Alfandi, O. Navigating the Ethical Landscape of Metaverse: Challenges, Solutions and Governance Initiatives. *Solutions and Governance Initiatives.*

Al-Kfairy, M., Alrabaee, S., Alfandi, O., Mohamed, A. T., & Khaddaj, S. (2025). Navigating Ethical Dimensions in the Metaverse: Challenges, Frameworks, and Solutions. *IEEE Access : Practical Innovations, Open Solutions*, *13*, 79996–80018. DOI: 10.1109/ACCESS.2025.3564498

Al-kfairy, M., Sendaba, O., & Alfandi, O. (2025). Understanding trust in educational Metaverse: The role of social cognitive theory constructs and perceived risks. *Kybernetes*. Advance online publication. DOI: 10.1108/K-11-2024-3057

Al-Sharafi, M. A., Al-Emran, M., Al-Qaysi, N., Iranmanesh, M., & Ibrahim, N. (2024). Drivers and barriers affecting metaverse adoption: A systematic review, theoretical framework, and avenues for future research. *International Journal of Human-Computer Interaction*, *40*(22), 7043–7064. DOI: 10.1080/10447318.2023.2260984

Al-Zahrani, A. M., & Alasmari, T. M. (2025). A comprehensive analysis of AI adoption, implementation strategies, and challenges in higher education across the Middle East and North Africa (MENA) region. *Education and Information Technologies*, *30*(8), 1–51. DOI: 10.1007/s10639-024-13300-y

Alfaisal, R., Hashim, H., & Azizan, U. H. (2024). *Empowering the Metaverse in Education: ChatGPT's Role in Transforming Learning Experiences.* Paper presented at the International Conference on Breaking Barriers with Generative Intelligence. DOI: 10.1007/978-3-031-65996-6_2

Alkaeed, M., Qayyum, A., & Qadir, J. (2024). Privacy preservation in Artificial Intelligence and Extended Reality (AI-XR) metaverses: A survey. *Journal of Network and Computer Applications*, *231*, 103989. DOI: 10.1016/j.jnca.2024.103989

Almeman, K. E. L., Ayeb, F., Berrima, M., Issaoui, B., & Morsy, H. (2025). The Integration of AI and Metaverse in Education: A Systematic Literature Review. *Applied Sciences (Basel, Switzerland)*, *15*(2), 863. DOI: 10.3390/app15020863

Bahroun, Z., Anane, C., Ahmed, V., & Zacca, A. (2023). Transforming education: A comprehensive review of generative artificial intelligence in educational settings through bibliometric and content analysis. *Sustainability (Basel)*, *15*(17), 12983. DOI: 10.3390/su151712983

Bansal, G., Chamola, V., Hussain, A., Guizani, M., & Niyato, D. (2024). Transforming conversations with AI—A comprehensive study of ChatGPT. *Cognitive Computation*, *16*(5), 2487–2510. DOI: 10.1007/s12559-023-10236-2

Beck, D., Morgado, L., & O'Shea, P. (2023). Educational practices and strategies with immersive learning environments: Mapping of reviews for using the metaverse. *IEEE Transactions on Learning Technologies*, *17*, 319–341. DOI: 10.1109/TLT.2023.3243946

Bucci, I., Fani, V., & Bandinelli, R. (2024). Towards Human-Centric Manufacturing: Exploring the Role of Human Digital Twins in Industry 5.0. *Sustainability (Basel)*, *17*(1), 129. DOI: 10.3390/su17010129

Busuioc, M. (2021). Accountable artificial intelligence: Holding algorithms to account. *Public Administration Review*, *81*(5), 825–836. DOI: 10.1111/puar.13293 PMID: 34690372

Chaudhary, G. (2024). Unveiling the black box: Bringing algorithmic transparency to AI. *Masaryk University Journal of Law and Technology*, *18*(1), 93–122. DOI: 10.5817/MUJLT2024-1-4

Chawki, M., Basu, S., & Choi, K.-S. (2024). Redefining boundaries in the Metaverse: Navigating the challenges of virtual harm and user safety. *Laws*, *13*(3), 33. DOI: 10.3390/laws13030033

Chen, X., Zhong, Z., & Wu, D. (2023). Metaverse for education: Technical framework and design criteria. *IEEE Transactions on Learning Technologies*, *16*(6), 1034–1044. DOI: 10.1109/TLT.2023.3276760

Christopoulos, A., Conrad, M., & Shukla, M. (2018). Increasing student engagement through virtual interactions: How? *Virtual Reality (Waltham Cross)*, *22*(4), 353–369. DOI: 10.1007/s10055-017-0330-3

Cigdem, H., Ozturk, M., Karabacak, Y., Atik, N., Gürkan, S., & Aldemir, M. H. (2024). Unlocking student engagement and achievement: The impact of leaderboard gamification in online formative assessment for engineering education. *Education and Information Technologies*, *29*(18), 1–26. DOI: 10.1007/s10639-024-12845-2

Damaševičius, R., & Sidekerskienė, T. (2024). Virtual worlds for learning in the metaverse: A narrative review. *Sustainability (Basel)*, *16*(5), 2032. DOI: 10.3390/su16052032

Diao, Y., & Su, Y.-S. (2025). Exploring the Impact of the Metaverse on Promoting Students' Access to Quality Education: A Meta-Analysis. *IEEE Transactions on Learning Technologies*, *18*, 321–334. DOI: 10.1109/TLT.2025.3550714

Dong, S., Liu, M., & Abbas, K. (2024). The Metaverse Review: Exploring the Boundless Ream of Digital Reality. *Computers, Materials & Continua*, *81*(3), 3451–3498. DOI: 10.32604/cmc.2024.055575

Dudley, J., Yin, L., Garaj, V., & Kristensson, P. O. (2023). Inclusive Immersion: A review of efforts to improve accessibility in virtual reality, augmented reality and the metaverse. *Virtual Reality (Waltham Cross)*, *27*(4), 2989–3020. DOI: 10.1007/s10055-023-00850-8

Dwivedi, Y. K., Hughes, L., Ismagilova, E., Aarts, G., Coombs, C., Crick, T., & Eirug, A. (2021). Artificial Intelligence (AI): Multidisciplinary perspectives on emerging challenges, opportunities, and agenda for research, practice and policy. *International Journal of Information Management*, *57*, 101994. DOI: 10.1016/j.ijinfomgt.2019.08.002

Eltanbouly, S., Halabi, O., & Qadir, J. (2025). Avatar privacy challenges in the metaverse: A comprehensive review and future directions. *International Journal of Human-Computer Interaction*, *41*(4), 1967–1984. DOI: 10.1080/10447318.2024.2374091

Esqueda, D. (2024). *From Data-Driven to Data-Informed: How Principals, Counselors, and Teachers Use Collaborative Practices to Support Student Achievement in an Urban High School*. University of California.

Gadekallu, T. R., Yenduri, G., Kaluri, R., Rajput, D. S., Lakshmanna, K., Fang, K., Chen, J., & Wang, W. (2025). The role of GPT in promoting inclusive higher education for people with various learning disabilities: A review. *PeerJ. Computer Science*, *11*, e2400. DOI: 10.7717/peerj-cs.2400 PMID: 40062249

Gilbert, C., & Gilbert, M. A. (2024). The Role of Artificial Intelligence (AI) in Combatting Deepfakes and Digital Misinformation. *International Research Journal of Advanced Engineering and Science (ISSN: 2455-9024), 9*(4), 170-181.

Holmes, W., Bialik, M., & Fadel, C. (2019). *Artificial intelligence in education promises and implications for teaching and learning*. Center for Curriculum Redesign.

Huawei, S., & Aryadoust, V. (2023). A systematic review of automated writing evaluation systems. *Education and Information Technologies*, *28*(1), 771–795. DOI: 10.1007/s10639-022-11200-7

Ilieva, G., Yankova, T., Klisarova-Belcheva, S., Dimitrov, A., Bratkov, M., & Angelov, D. (2023). Effects of generative chatbots in higher education. *Information (Basel)*, *14*(9), 492. DOI: 10.3390/info14090492

Illi, C., & Elhassouny, A. (2025). Edu-Metaverse: A Comprehensive Review of Virtual Learning Environments. *IEEE Access : Practical Innovations, Open Solutions*, *13*, 30186–30211. DOI: 10.1109/ACCESS.2025.3540944

Jagatheesaperumal, S. K., Ahmad, K., Al-Fuqaha, A., & Qadir, J. (2024). Advancing education through extended reality and internet of everything enabled metaverses: Applications, challenges, and open issues. *IEEE Transactions on Learning Technologies*, *17*, 1120–1139. DOI: 10.1109/TLT.2024.3358859

Jin, Y., Yan, L., Echeverria, V., Gašević, D., & Martinez-Maldonado, R. (2025). Generative AI in higher education: A global perspective of institutional adoption policies and guidelines. *Computers and Education: Artificial Intelligence*, *8*, 100348. DOI: 10.1016/j.caeai.2024.100348

Johnson-Glenberg, M. C. (2018). Immersive VR and education: Embodied design principles that include gesture and hand controls. *Frontiers in Robotics and AI*, *5*, 375272. DOI: 10.3389/frobt.2018.00081 PMID: 33500960

Joksimovic, S., Ifenthaler, D., Marrone, R., De Laat, M., & Siemens, G. (2023). Opportunities of artificial intelligence for supporting complex problem-solving: Findings from a scoping review. *Computers and Education: Artificial Intelligence*, *4*, 100138. DOI: 10.1016/j.caeai.2023.100138

Kanthimathi, S., Nanda, P., Venkatraman, S., Renganayagan, V., & Eswaran, S. (2025). *Transforming Education through AI-Powered Personalized Assessment Models Adopting Artificial Intelligence Tools in Higher Education*. CRC Press.

Kasneci, E., Seßler, K., Küchemann, S., Bannert, M., Dementieva, D., Fischer, F., & Hüllermeier, E. (2023). ChatGPT for good? On opportunities and challenges of large language models for education. *Learning and Individual Differences*, *103*, 102274. DOI: 10.1016/j.lindif.2023.102274

Li, Y. F., Guan, J. Q., Wang, X. F., Chen, Q., & Hwang, G. J. (2024). Examining students' self-regulated learning processes and performance in an immersive virtual environment. *Journal of Computer Assisted Learning*, *40*(6), 2948–2963. DOI: 10.1111/jcal.13047

Liu, C.-C., Lin, Y.-Y., Lo, F.-y., Chang, C.-H., & Lin, H.-M. (2025). From readers to players: Exploring student engagement in a gamified metaverse and its effect on reading interest. *Education and Information Technologies*, *30*(1), 421–447. DOI: 10.1007/s10639-024-13068-1

Luckin, R., & Holmes, W. (2016). Intelligence unleashed: An argument for AI in education.

Lui, A. L., Not, C., & Wong, G. K. (2023). Theory-based learning design with immersive virtual reality in science education: A systematic review. *Journal of Science Education and Technology*, *32*(3), 390–432. DOI: 10.1007/s10956-023-10035-2

Maas, M. J., & Hughes, J. M. (2020). Virtual, augmented and mixed reality in K–12 education: A review of the literature. *Technology, Pedagogy and Education*, *29*(2), 231–249. DOI: 10.1080/1475939X.2020.1737210

Maghaydah, S., Al-Emran, M., Maheshwari, P., & Al-Sharafi, M. A. (2024). Factors affecting metaverse adoption in education: A systematic review, adoption framework, and future research agenda. *Heliyon*, *10*(7), e28602. DOI: 10.1016/j.heliyon.2024.e28602 PMID: 38576548

Mariam, G., Adil, L., & Zakaria, B. (2024). The integration of artificial intelligence (ai) into education systems and its impact on the governance of higher education institutions. *International Journal of Professional Business Review: Int. J. Prof. Bus. Rev.*, *9*(12), 13.

Matthews, G., Cumings, R., De Los Santos, E. P., Feng, I. Y., & Mouloua, S. A. (2025). A new era for stress research: Supporting user performance and experience in the digital age. *Ergonomics*, *68*(6), 913–946. DOI: 10.1080/00140139.2024.2425953 PMID: 39520089

McStay, A. (2023). The metaverse: Surveillant physics, virtual realist governance, and the missing commons. *Philosophy & Technology*, *36*(1), 13. DOI: 10.1007/s13347-023-00613-y

Memon, F. N., & Memon, S. N. (2025). *Digital Divide and Equity in Education: Bridging Gaps to Ensure Inclusive Learning Impact of Digitalization on Education and Social Sustainability*. IGI Global.

Metaverse, I. (2025). Exploring the Future of Education: Integrating Metaverse and AI Tools to Enhance Learning Experiences.

Mitani, H., Honda, Y., Narita, K., Nakamura, Y., Morishita, S., Kondo, S., & Higaki, T. (2025). Effectiveness of a virtual reality-based interventional radiology simulator for medical student education. *Japanese Journal of Radiology*, *43*(8), 1–7. DOI: 10.1007/s11604-025-01771-z PMID: 40156739

Oh, H. J., Kim, J., Chang, J. J., Park, N., & Lee, S. (2023). Social benefits of living in the metaverse: The relationships among social presence, supportive interaction, social self-efficacy, and feelings of loneliness. *Computers in Human Behavior*, *139*, 107498. DOI: 10.1016/j.chb.2022.107498

Onu, P., Pradhan, A., & Mbohwa, C. (2024). Potential to use metaverse for future teaching and learning. *Education and Information Technologies*, *29*(7), 8893–8924. DOI: 10.1007/s10639-023-12167-9

Orynbay, L., Razakhova, B., Peer, P., Meden, B., & Emeršič, Ž. (2024). Recent advances in synthesis and interaction of speech, text, and vision. *Electronics (Basel)*, *13*(9), 1726. DOI: 10.3390/electronics13091726

Ouyang, F., Zheng, L., & Jiao, P. (2022). Artificial intelligence in online higher education: A systematic review of empirical research from 2011 to 2020. *Education and Information Technologies*, *27*(6), 7893–7925. DOI: 10.1007/s10639-022-10925-9

Pachoulas, G., Christopoulos, A., & Stylios, C. (2024). *A Conceptual Framework for Educational Metaverse*. Paper presented at the 2024 2nd International Conference on Intelligent Metaverse Technologies & Applications (iMETA). DOI: 10.1109/iMETA62882.2024.10807878

Pellas, N., Mystakidis, S., & Christopoulos, A. (2021). A systematic literature review on the user experience design for game-based interventions via 3D virtual worlds in K-12 education. *Multimodal Technologies and Interaction*, *5*(6), 28. DOI: 10.3390/mti5060028

Rekha, K., Gopal, K., Satheeskumar, D., Anand, U. A., Doss, D. S. S., & Elayaperumal, S. (2024). *Ai-Powered Personalized Learning System Design: Student Engagement and Performance Tracking System*. Paper presented at the 2024 4th International Conference on Advance Computing and Innovative Technologies in Engineering (ICACITE). DOI: 10.1109/ICACITE60783.2024.10617155

Rodway, P., & Schepman, A. (2023). The impact of adopting AI educational technologies on projected course satisfaction in university students. *Computers and Education: Artificial Intelligence*, *5*, 100150. DOI: 10.1016/j.caeai.2023.100150

Safikhani, S., Keller, S., Schweiger, G., & Pirker, J. (2022). Immersive virtual reality for extending the potential of building information modeling in architecture, engineering, and construction sector: Systematic review. *International Journal of Digital Earth*, *15*(1), 503–526. DOI: 10.1080/17538947.2022.2038291

Sajja, R., Sermet, Y., & Demir, I. (2025). End-to-end deployment of the educational AI hub for personalized learning and engagement: A case study on environmental science education. *IEEE Access : Practical Innovations, Open Solutions*, *13*, 55169–55186. DOI: 10.1109/ACCESS.2025.3554222

Shoaib, M., Sayed, N., Singh, J., Shafi, J., Khan, S., & Ali, F. (2024). AI student success predictor: Enhancing personalized learning in campus management systems. *Computers in Human Behavior*, *158*, 108301. DOI: 10.1016/j.chb.2024.108301

Singh, M. (2024). Exploring the possibilities to implement metaverse in higher education institutions of India. *Education and Information Technologies*, *29*(15), 20715–20728. DOI: 10.1007/s10639-024-12691-2

Temme, M. (2017). Algorithms and transparency in view of the new general data protection regulation. *Eur. Data Prot. L. Rev.*, *3*(4), 473–485. DOI: 10.21552/edpl/2017/4/9

Thomas, N. J., Baral, R., Crocco, O. S., & Mohanan, S. (2023). A framework for gamification in the metaverse era: How designers envision gameful experience. *Technological Forecasting and Social Change*, *193*, 122544. DOI: 10.1016/j.techfore.2023.122544

Villegas-Ch, W., García-Ortiz, J., & Sánchez-Viteri, S. (2024). Educational advances in the metaverse: Boosting learning through virtual and augmented reality and artificial intelligence. *IEEE Access : Practical Innovations, Open Solutions, 12*, 59093–59112. DOI: 10.1109/ACCESS.2024.3393776

Wang, M., Yu, H., Bell, Z., & Chu, X. (2022). Constructing an edu-metaverse ecosystem: A new and innovative framework. *IEEE Transactions on Learning Technologies, 15*(6), 685–696. DOI: 10.1109/TLT.2022.3210828

Wang, S., Wang, F., Zhu, Z., Wang, J., Tran, T., & Du, Z. (2024). Artificial intelligence in education: A systematic literature review. *Expert Systems with Applications, 252*, 124167. DOI: 10.1016/j.eswa.2024.124167

Wang, S., & Zhang, H. (2024). Digital capabilities and metaverse entrepreneurial performance: Role of entrepreneurial orientation. *Journal of Innovation & Knowledge, 9*(4), 100617. DOI: 10.1016/j.jik.2024.100617

Wellings, J., & Levine, M. H. (2009). *The digital promise: Transforming learning with innovative uses of technology.* Paper presented at the New York: Joan Ganz Cooney Center at Sesame Workshop.

Wiedbusch, M. D., Kite, V., Yang, X., Park, S., Chi, M., Taub, M., & Azevedo, R. (2021). *A theoretical and evidence-based conceptual design of metadash: An intelligent teacher dashboard to support teachers' decision making and students' self-regulated learning.* Paper presented at the Frontiers in education. DOI: 10.3389/feduc.2021.570229

Woolf, B. P. (2010). *Building intelligent interactive tutors: Student-centered strategies for revolutionizing e-learning*. Morgan Kaufmann.

Yang, W., Fang, M., Xu, J., Zhang, X., & Pan, Y. (2024). Exploring the mediating role of different aspects of learning motivation between metaverse learning experiences and gamification. *Electronics (Basel), 13*(7), 1297. DOI: 10.3390/electronics13071297

Yeganeh, L. N., Fenty, N. S., Chen, Y., Simpson, A., & Hatami, M. (2025). The Future of Education: A Multi-Layered Metaverse Classroom Model for Immersive and Inclusive Learning. *Future Internet, 17*(2), 63. DOI: 10.3390/fi17020063

Yenduri, G., Kaluri, R., Rajput, D. S., Lakshmanna, K., Gadekallu, T. R., Mahmud, M., & Brown, D. J. (2023). From assistive technologies to metaverse—Technologies in inclusive higher education for students with specific learning difficulties: A review. *IEEE Access : Practical Innovations, Open Solutions, 11*, 64907–64927. DOI: 10.1109/ACCESS.2023.3289496

Yingsoon, G. Y., Chua, N. A., Suyan, Z., Yiming, C., Haiyan, Z., & Xiaoyao, T. (2025). *Empowering Digital Citizens: Navigating AI Ethics, Engagement, and Privacy in the Era of Advanced Education Digital Citizenship and the Future of AI Engagement, Ethics, and Privacy*. IGI Global Scientific Publishing. DOI: 10.4018/979-8-3693-9015-3.ch003

Zainuddin, Z., Chu, S. K. W., & Perera, C. J. (2024a). *Gamification in Education Gamification in A Flipped Classroom: Pedagogical Methods and Best Practices*. Springer. DOI: 10.1007/978-981-97-2219-8

Zainuddin, Z., Chu, S. K. W., & Perera, C. J. (2024b). *Gamification in the Flipped Classroom Gamification in A Flipped Classroom: Pedagogical Methods and Best Practices*. Springer. DOI: 10.1007/978-981-97-2219-8

Zawacki-Richter, O., Marín, V. I., Bond, M., & Gouverneur, F. (2019). Systematic review of research on artificial intelligence applications in higher education–where are the educators? *International Journal of Educational Technology in Higher Education*, *16*(1), 1–27. DOI: 10.1186/s41239-019-0171-0

Zhang, L., Jiang, Q., Xiong, W., & Zhao, W. (2024). Effects of ChatGPT-Based Human–Computer Dialogic Interaction Programming Activities on Student Engagement. *Journal of Educational Computing Research*, 07356331251333874.

Zou, Y., Kuek, F., Feng, W., & Cheng, X. (2025). *Digital learning in the 21st century: trends, challenges, and innovations in technology integration.* Paper presented at the Frontiers in Education.

Chapter 11
Crafting Education Policies and Governance: Factoring the Eclipse of Artificial Intelligence

K. S. Shibani Shankar Ray
https://orcid.org/0009-0009-5890-0814
Rajiv Gandhi National Aviation University, Fursatganj, India

Durga Madhab Mahapatra
https://orcid.org/0000-0003-1272-7285
North Eastern Hill University, Shillong, India

Zakir Hossen Shaikh
https://orcid.org/0000-0003-4733-4166
Kingdom University, Baharin

Srabani Priyadarsini Dash
Maa Manikeshwari University, Bhawanipatana, India

Rohit Kumar Rawat
https://orcid.org/0009-0009-1789-0533
Rajiv Gandhi National Aviation University, Fursatganj, India

ABSTRACT

Integrating Artificial Intelligence (AI) into blended learning systems can make education more equitable, personalized, and inclusive. However, this promise can only be fulfilled through coherent, context-sensitive policies that address infrastructure, ethics, curriculum, teacher capacity, and data protection. Examples from across the Global South demonstrate that with the right policy instruments, AI-infused

DOI: 10.4018/979-8-3373-3815-6.ch011

yright © 2026, IGI Global Scientific Publishing. Copying or distributing in print or electronic forms without written permission of IGI Global Scientific Publishing is prohibited. Use of this chapter to ain generative artificial intelligence (AI) technologies is expressly prohibited. The publisher reserves all rights to license its use for generative AI training and machine learning model development.

blended learning can close the educational gap. The chapter is thus divided into three sections: Section A deals with Rising Interest in AI in Education and Reasons to Address AI in Education Section B covers Policies for AI in Education The Role of AI in Shaping Future Educational Policies and How AI is Transforming Education Systems and Governance Section C talks about Building Ethical, Equitable Policies. Section D unravels The Challenges of Implementing AI in Educational Policy. Finally, a concluding section develops a comprehensive AI governance framework that balances the potential of Generative AI with the ethical considerations of its use.

1. INTRODUCTION

Artificial Intelligence (AI) continues to reshape the educational landscape, offering opportunities to personalise learning, automate administrative tasks, and democratize access to resources. However, to truly harness AI's potential, it must be embedded within inclusive educational frameworks such as blended learning- an approach combining digital tools with traditional classroom methods (Kaur & Singh, 2023; Alharthi et al., 2024). Blended learning provides a natural conduit for AI, enabling flexible pedagogical strategies and enhancing student engagement across various socio-economic backgrounds (Chen et al., 2023; Gupta & Patel, 2023). In regions of the Global South, where infrastructure and teaching capacity are uneven, integrating AI into blended models allows for scalable, context-responsive interventions (Tshabalala et al., 2024; Mendes & Jorge, 2023). This synergy calls for policies that not only regulate AI technologies but also foster ecosystems where blended learning thrives. AI-powered personalisation in blended learning environments can significantly enhance student outcomes by tailoring content to individual learning styles, pace, and proficiency (Johnson & Sato, 2023; Lam et al., 2024). Adaptive learning platforms like Squirrel AI and Century Tech have demonstrated the efficacy of AI in diagnosing knowledge gaps and customising pathways, particularly in STEM education (O'Brien et al., 2023; Narayanan & Luo, 2024). When combined with teacher-led instruction, these tools can bridge gaps in understanding, especially in resource-constrained settings (Mhlanga, 2023; Ahmed & El-Gohary, 2023). However, equity must guide personalisation efforts; without culturally adaptive algorithms and policy oversight, such tools may reinforce existing disparities (Singh & Iyer, 2023; Weller et al., 2024). Blended learning's success hinges on reliable infrastructure and equitable access to technology. While AI can optimise learning experiences, these benefits remain inaccessible to many in under-connected regions (Patra & Kumar, 2024; Zhou & Raj, 2023). Policies must prioritise internet penetration, device availability, and maintenance support to ensure the effectiveness of AI-infused blended models (Srinivasan et al., 2023; Adusei & Boateng, 2023).

Programs like India's PM eVidya and Kenya's Digital Literacy Programme illustrate how blended learning, supported by AI, can serve as an equalizer in education (Mwangi & Karanja, 2023; Bansal et al., 2023). Policymakers must incentivise public-private partnerships that expand digital infrastructure and create localised solutions (Reyes & Torres, 2024; Bello et al., 2023). Teachers play a central role in the integration of AI in blended learning, yet many educators lack training in both domains. Policy frameworks must emphasise continuous professional development, enabling teachers to understand and use AI tools effectively within blended models (Nguyen & Liu, 2023; Choudhury & Farooq, 2024). Initiatives such as Ghana's AI4Ed and Malaysia's MyDigitalEducator program showcase the value of equipping educators with AI literacy and blended learning pedagogies (Ofori & Asare, 2023; Zulkifli et al., 2024). AI should augment, not replace, teachers; supporting them in lesson planning, grading, and identifying struggling students (Moyo & Banda, 2024; Hassan & Noor, 2023). The ethical dimensions of AI in blended learning demand urgent attention. AI algorithms, if unchecked, can encode and perpetuate biases, particularly against marginalised learners (Khanna & Bhatia, 2024; Silva et al., 2023). Effective policies must mandate transparency, accountability, and fairness in algorithm design, ensuring that blended learning environments uphold the principles of justice and inclusion (Das & Basu, 2023; Rani & Prasad, 2024). Ethical AI practices should be embedded into procurement processes and curriculum development to mitigate risks and foster trust (Ncube & Hlongwane, 2023; Menon & Patel, 2024). Integrating AI into blended learning requires a curriculum that reflects local cultures, languages, and pedagogical values. Generic AI content may alienate learners if it fails to resonate with their lived experiences (Yamamoto & Singh, 2023; Otieno & Wekesa, 2024). Education policies should support the co-design of localized AI-blended curricula with input from educators, technologists, and communities (Peters & Adebayo, 2023; Kavita et al., 2024). Initiatives like South Africa's Smart Classroom Pilot and Indonesia's Merdeka Belajar reform are examples of grounded innovation that bridge global technology with local relevance (Nyathi & Zondi, 2023; Santoso & Wulandari, 2024). Blended learning powered by AI can significantly enhance inclusivity, particularly for students with disabilities. Tools such as speech-to-text, personalised learning dashboards, and emotion recognition systems support differentiated instruction (Rajkumar & Fernandez, 2023; Islam & Chowdhury, 2024). Policies must require accessibility standards in AI tools and allocate funding for inclusive educational technologies (Mitra & Rajan, 2024; Lekota & Mthembu, 2023).

Figure 1. AI Integration in Blended Learning

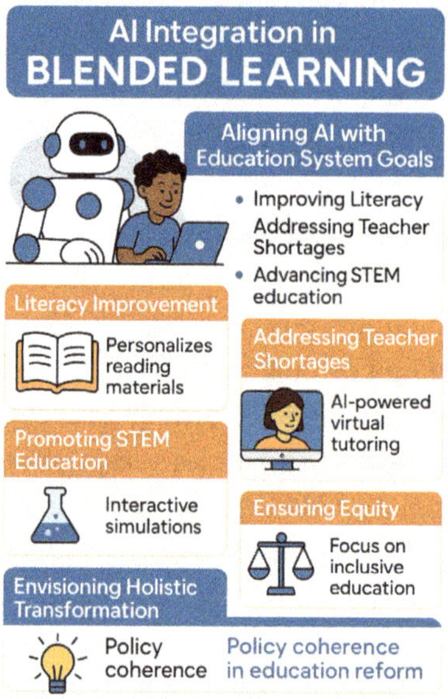

(Source: Author's compilation)

For instance, Brazil's EDUCA-AI initiative integrates AI to support learners with visual and auditory impairments in hybrid classroom settings (Silva et al., 2024; Rocha & Almeida, 2023).

Robust monitoring and evaluation mechanisms are essential for scaling AI in blended learning. Governments need real-time data on student progress, system performance, and implementation barriers to refine policy in an agile manner (Lee & Park, 2023; Thakur & Jain, 2024). Learning analytics platforms can support adaptive policymaking, but must also protect student data privacy and adhere to cybersecurity norms (Obi & Nnaji, 2023; Banerjee & Ray, 2024). Policymakers should adopt sandbox approaches to test innovations, enabling iterative improvements based on empirical evidence (Uddin & Rahman, 2023; Gómez & Martínez, 2024). AI and blended learning present global challenges and opportunities, requiring cross-border cooperation. International organisations, NGOs, and regional networks should share policy models, research, and best practices (Tiwari & Sharma, 2023; Bello et al., 2024). South-South cooperation, such as between Brazil and India or Kenya and Rwanda, can foster regional AI policy frameworks that support scalable blended learning solutions (Kabir & Olawale, 2024; Pérez & Santiago, 2023). However, policy borrowing must be contextualised to prevent top-down impositions that fail to meet local needs (Basu & Chatterjee, 2023; Fadel & Zaki, 2024). Integrating AI into blended learning systems holds the potential to make education more equitable, personalised, and inclusive. But this promise can only be fulfilled through coherent, context-sensitive policies that address infrastructure, ethics, curriculum, teacher capacity, and data protection (Chowdhury & Hassan, 2024; Onyango & Akinyi, 2024). Examples from across the Global South demonstrate that with the right policy instruments, AI-infused blended learning can close, not widen the educational gap (Ibrahim & Adeyemi, 2023; Raj & Das, 2024). By viewing AI as a tool for transformation rather than disruption, governments can chart a course toward a more just and empowered educational future.

2. INCLUSIVE POLICY DESIGN: STAKEHOLDERS AT THE CENTRE- WITH BLENDED LEARNING AS A BRIDGE

A central theme emerging from discussions on AI governance in education is the critical need for inclusive and participatory policy design. Effective AI policy must not be crafted in isolation by governmental or technical elites but through the active engagement of diverse stakeholders, particularly those directly impacted by educational technologies. Inclusive policy-making, where the voices of all relevant parties are considered, is crucial to avoid technology imposition that might be disconnected from the real needs of educators, students, and communities (Binns, 2020). One vital strategy to foster this inclusivity is the integration of blended learning models into national education strategies. Blended learning provides a tangible, adaptable pathway for stakeholders to co-create AI-enhanced learning environments that balance technological tools with human interaction, making innovations more relevant to local teaching and learning practices (Kaur & Singh, 2023). Chile serves as a compelling model for such an approach. In developing their national AI policy, Chile convened a working group of over 300 experts from fields including pedagogy, educational technology, ethics, and data science. This broad consultation ensured that a variety of professional and academic perspectives shaped the policy framework, preventing the policy from being solely dictated by one sector (Ministerio de Ciencia, Technología, Conocimiento e Innovación, 2021). Importantly, Chile's model of AI policy development was not confined to expert consultation alone. The country conducted extensive public consultations, which included input from teachers, students, parents, and broader community members through both in-person forums and online platforms. In these consultations, stakeholders consistently highlighted not only issues such as equitable access to AI tools and the ethical use of student data, but also the importance of pedagogical flexibility and blended instructional models. Blended learning was viewed as a practical compromise, especially in underserved and rural regions, where full-scale digital transformation may be limited by infrastructure or training gaps (Greer & Craddock, 2020). By incorporating blended learning frameworks into policy discussions, Chile created room for solutions that leverage AI's potential while preserving teacher agency and ensuring that students continue to benefit from social, collaborative, and contextually grounded education (Floridi et al., 2018). These consultations also surfaced critical concerns such as the digital divide and unequal access to AI infrastructure, which blended learning models can partially mitigate. Offline or low-bandwidth-compatible tools used in hybrid classrooms allow for a broader reach, ensuring that innovations are not restricted to urban or well-resourced schools (Gupta & Patel, 2023). By allowing stakeholders to shape policy from its earliest stages- including the modes of AI application such as blended learning- Chile ensured that the resulting framework was more relevant to the lived realities of its users.

Table 1. Strategic Dimensions for Equitable AI Integration in Blended Learning

Dimension	Strategy	Outcome
Governance	Multi-sectoral AI-education steering committees	Coordinated, multi-stakeholder policy leadership
Curriculum Development	Co-design of AI and ethics modules + blended pedagogy	Relevant, localized, future-ready curricula
Technology Implementation	Public-private partnerships for AI tool deployment in blended contexts	Scalable, sustainable, and inclusive tech rollouts
Monitoring & Evaluation	Mixed-methods impact assessments; user-centered indicators	Evidence-based policy refinement
Sustainability Planning	Integrate with SDGs; phased funding models	Long-term education system resilience and innovation

(Source: Author's compilation)

This approach is particularly relevant in the context of AI governance for education, where issues of equity, access, and cultural context are paramount. The educational landscape in different regions can vary significantly, with unique challenges faced by urban, rural, and underserved communities (Zhang & Wang, 2020). Participatory models like the one used in Chile not only bring diverse perspectives to the table but also allow for greater customisation of AI solutions that consider the socio-economic, cultural, and pedagogical goals of local communities. Moreover, blended learning acts as a customizable template; adaptable across contexts and responsive to local capacities, making it a vital bridge in global education policy discourse (Adusei & Boateng, 2023).

Table 2. Stakeholder Roles in Policy Formation and Blended Learning Integration

Stakeholder	Role in Policy Formation	Role in Blended Learning Integration
Government	Regulatory frameworks, infrastructure funding	Enable platforms and standards for blended delivery
Educators	Curricular input, pedagogical innovation	Design and implement hybrid learning environments
Students	User feedback, testing of tools	Adapt learning preferences across modalities
Parents/ Communities	Cultural validation, equity watchdogs	Support home-based components of blended learning
Tech Developers	AI tool design and compliance	Ensure compatibility with blended pedagogical models
NGOs/CSOs	Advocacy, research, community mobilization	Assist in outreach and digital inclusion programs
Academia	Research, teacher education, policy analysis	Evaluate effectiveness and impact of AI in blended setups

(Source: Author's compilation)

Additionally, such engagement fosters greater public trust in AI systems, as stakeholders are more likely to support initiatives they had a hand in shaping. This increases the likelihood of effective implementation and reduces resistance to change, particularly in systems where there is scepticism about AI's role. Furthermore, Chile's participatory approach aligns with best practices in AI governance, as outlined by international bodies such as UNESCO (2021) and the OECD (2020), which advocate for a bottom-up approach in designing policies around AI technologies. Blended learning reinforces these frameworks by offering a tangible mode of implementation that is inherently adaptable and rooted in teacher-student interaction; elements essential for community acceptance and long-term sustainability (Brynjolfsson & McAfee, 2017). Chile's approach also exemplifies the power of collaborative policy design, which can foster greater accountability among all parties involved. By including a wide range of stakeholders, from teachers and students to tech companies and civil society, policy becomes more democratic and transparent. These stakeholders can shape how AI is implemented- such as selecting which AI-enabled platforms should be integrated into blended classrooms or deciding how much autonomy should be granted to algorithms in lesson planning. This not only ensures technical relevance but also reinforces pedagogical and ethical alignment with local values (Weller, 2020).

2.1. 2x2 Model: AI and Blended Learning Integration

This matrix helps policymakers conceptualise the balance between AI integration and blended learning. The top-left quadrant, *Innovative & Inclusive,* is the ideal zone where blended learning supports equitable, AI-enhanced education. It contrasts with the lower-left (*AI-Centric Risk*) and lower-right (*Status Quo*) zones that highlight the pitfalls of poor alignment or lack of innovation.

Figure 2. Inclusive AI policy in Learning

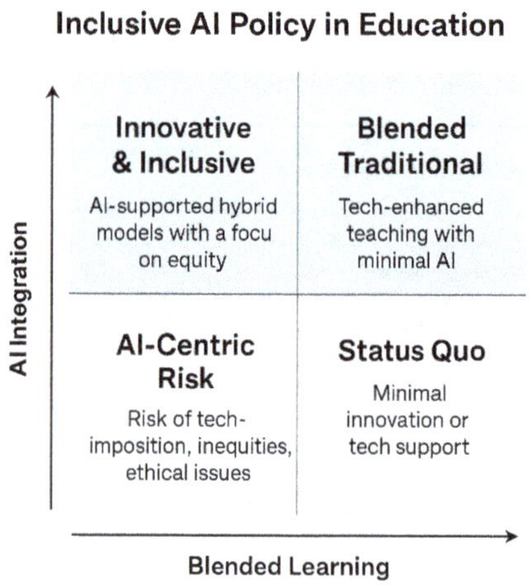

(Source: Author's compilation)

Moreover, the participatory process supports capacity-building by giving educators and learners hands-on experience with hybrid instructional models, allowing them to engage with AI tools in meaningful ways. Blended learning environments serve as testbeds for stakeholder feedback, where AI applications can be trialled, evaluated, and iteratively improved based on actual classroom experience (Brock, 2019). This fosters a more informed and empowered user base, capable of engaging critically with AI technologies and contributing to ongoing policy refinement (Bell, 2020). Chile's participatory model for AI policy development in education is a powerful example of how inclusive, stakeholder-driven approaches can lead to more relevant, ethical, and effective governance frameworks. The integration of blended learning into such models further enhances their potential by offering scalable, flexible, and context-sensitive solutions. As AI continues to be integrated into educational systems worldwide, the lessons learned from Chile and similar initiatives must be adopted by other nations, particularly in the Global South. By ensuring that all voices are heard and that policies reflect local needs, while also embedding blended learning as a pedagogical pillar, countries can pave the way for an AI-powered education system that benefits all learners, regardless of their background or geographical location.

Figure 3. Participatory Approach in Policy Development

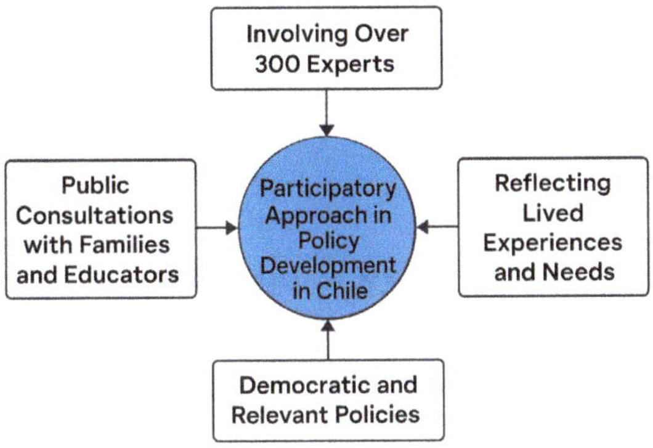

(Source: Author's compilation)

3. CROSS-SECTOR COLLABORATION: THE PUBLIC-PRIVATE-ACADEMIC TRIAD

Figure 4. Cross-Sector Collaboration

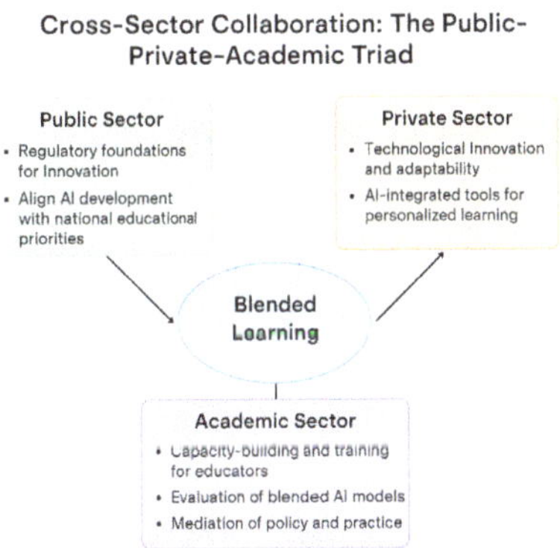

(Source: Author's Compilation)

In Latin America, particularly in regions like Paraná, Brazil, cross-sector collaboration among public agencies, private technology companies, and academic institutions has proven to be a vital model for driving innovation in AI-based educational policy. These partnerships enable rapid experimentation, real-time evaluation, and context-aware deployment of AI tools in classrooms, fostering policies that are both cutting-edge and grounded in the lived realities of teachers and learners (Alvarado et al., 2020; Garcia et al., 2021). A central feature of these tri-sectoral partnerships is the co-creation of blended learning ecosystems that utilise AI to enhance, not replace, human-led education. Blended learning provides a scaffolded approach for integrating AI technologies in ways that allow for flexibility, personalisation, and teacher guidance; an essential feature in environments marked by educational inequality and infrastructural disparity (Fernandes & Nunes, 2023; Silva, Oliveira, & Batista, 2022).

3.1. Public Sector: Regulatory Foundations for Innovation

The public sector, through ministries of education and innovation councils, provides the essential regulatory backbone. Government agencies in Brazil have emphasised the need to align AI development with national education strategies and digital inclusion plans, particularly through initiatives like EduTec Paraná, which aims to modernise teaching through blended and adaptive learning supported by AI tools (Ferreira & Pereira, 2019; Sousa et al., 2021). In these public-led initiatives, blended learning serves as a policy bridge: it allows gradual integration of AI tools within traditional school structures, ensuring that new technologies are piloted in safe, measurable, and inclusive environments (Costa & Silva, 2020; Santos & Lima, 2021). Notably, the Ministry of Education has supported low-bandwidth blended solutions, ensuring that rural and low-income communities are not excluded from innovation (Camargo & Reis, 2023).

3.2. Private Sector: Driving Technological Innovation and Adaptability

Private technology firms contribute critical technical expertise and scalable AI solutions that power blended learning platforms, ranging from intelligent tutoring systems to AI-powered learning analytics (Pereira et al., 2021; Carvalho et al., 2020). These tools allow teachers to customize content delivery based on real-time data, enabling personalized learning paths and timely interventions. Importantly, companies benefit from this ecosystem by gaining actionable feedback from educators and students who use their tools in blended classrooms. This feedback loop allows for agile development and contextual adaptation, helping products evolve in tandem with pedagogical needs (Silva et al., 2019; Dias & Costa, 2018). More recently, companies like *EducaAI Brasil* have partnered with regional governments to roll out AI-integrated blended learning in public schools, focusing on personalized literacy and numeracy support (Lopes & Andrade, 2023).

3.3. Academic Sector: Capacity-Building and Policy Mediation

Academic institutions act as mediators between technological innovation and educational practice. Universities in Paraná have developed professional development programs that prepare teachers to adopt AI tools within blended frameworks, ensuring a strong pedagogical foundation before full-scale implementation (Lima & Torres, 2021; Tavares et al., 2020). They also play a crucial evaluative role; assessing the impact of blended AI models on learning outcomes, identifying ethical issues such as algorithmic bias, and offering recommendations for curriculum adaptation (Souza & Santos, 2020; Cruz et al., 2021). Through initiatives like *LabAI Educação* at the Federal University of Paraná, researchers have piloted blended AI curricula in both urban and rural schools, adapting learning models to local language, cultural context, and infrastructure capacity (Ribeiro et al., 2021; Martins & Lima, 2021). Moreover, universities serve as knowledge translators, converting complex AI terminologies into actionable policy insights for decision-makers and fostering a more AI-literate education workforce. In this way, they help bridge technical and policy divides, particularly through community-based action research and open-source blended learning pilots (Medeiros & Almeida, 2019; Navarro et al., 2023). Here's a structured table that summarises and integrates the concept of Cross-Sector Collaboration with Blended Learning as a key pillar in AI educational policy, particularly drawing on the case of Paraná, Brazil:

Table 3. Stakeholder Roles and Contributions to Equitable AI-Enabled Blended Learning

Stakeholder	Role in AI Policy & Implementation	Contribution to Blended Learning	Key Benefits
Public Sector (Government Agencies)	Provide regulation, funding, national standards, and oversight	Develop policy frameworks that formally integrate blended learning models	Ensures equity, access, and alignment with national education goals
Private Sector (Tech Companies)	Supply AI tools, technical infrastructure, and real-time innovations	Design AI-compatible tools for blended environments (e.g., offline features)	Accelerates innovation and customizes solutions for diverse classroom needs
Academic Institutions (Universities, Research Centers)	Conduct training, research, and evaluation of AI tools	Train educators on blended models, assess impact on learning outcomes	Bridges theory and practice; contextualizes technology for local implementation

continued on following page

Table 3. Continued

Stakeholder	Role in AI Policy & Implementation	Contribution to Blended Learning	Key Benefits
Educators (Teachers & School Leaders)	Implement AI and blended learning in classrooms; provide user feedback	Customize AI applications to fit blended instructional approaches	Ensures relevance and usability; enhances pedagogical quality
Students and Families	Experience AI-enabled blended learning firsthand; offer lived-experience insights	Co-create feedback loops to adapt blended models to cultural and contextual needs	Strengthens inclusivity and local engagement

(*Source: Author's compilation*)

3.4. Integrative Impact of Blended Learning in the Tri-Sector Model

The integration of blended learning within this tri-sectoral collaboration enhances adaptability, democratisation, and relevance of AI in education. It allows stakeholders to co-develop solutions that:

- Prioritise equity through low-cost hybrid models accessible to marginalised communities (**Moreira & Cunha, 2023**).
- Encourage innovation by serving as a real-world testing ground for AI applications before nationwide scaling.
- Build teacher capacity through iterative learning and feedback loops supported by both universities and tech developers.
- Align with global frameworks, such as UNESCO's Recommendation on the Ethics of AI, which highlights the need for human-centric, inclusive, and context-responsive education systems **(UNESCO, 2023).**

As AI continues to transform educational systems worldwide, the Paraná model demonstrates that cross-sector partnerships, grounded in blended learning strategies, can help ensure that innovation is both inclusive and pedagogically sound. By combining the governance strength of the public sector, the agility of the private sector, and the reflective expertise of the academic community, Brazil is crafting a responsive AI policy landscape that holds promise for broader adoption across the Global South.

4. AGILE AND ITERATIVE POLICY FRAMEWORKS

The concept of "AI sandboxes" in Brazil represents a forward-thinking approach to AI policy, offering a flexible and adaptive framework for testing AI technologies in real educational environments. Unlike traditional, static policymaking, which often struggles to keep pace with the rapid evolution of technology, AI sandboxes allow for continuous feedback and real-time evaluation (Pereira & Costa, 2018; Martins & Lima, 2020). These experimental zones provide an opportunity to test AI tools in actual classrooms, where their effectiveness can be assessed based on a variety of factors such as student outcomes, teacher feedback, and system performance metrics (Alvarado et al., 2020; Rocha & Silva, 2021).

Figure 5. Interactive Policy Framework

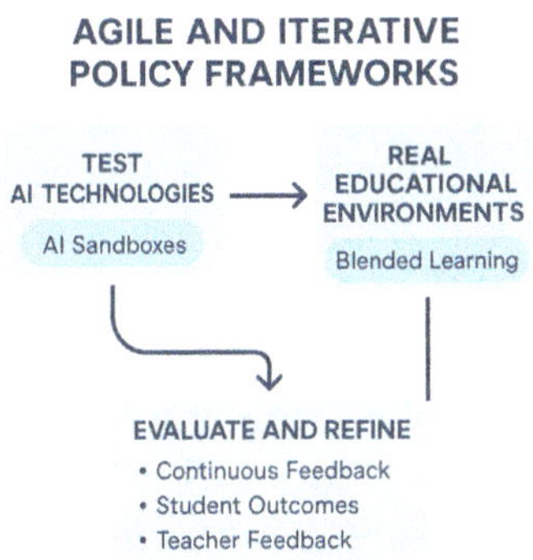

(Source: Author's compilation; Tool: Canva)

Recent innovations have further integrated blended learning models into these sandboxes, enabling a hybrid approach that combines face-to-face instruction with AI-driven digital learning platforms (Nascimento et al., 2023; Ferreira & Alves, 2024). This model supports differentiated instruction, allowing students to progress at their own pace while providing teachers with real-time data to tailor interventions. By embedding AI tools into blended learning contexts, sandboxes can evaluate not just the effectiveness of AI alone, but its contribution to hybrid pedagogies that reflect today's diverse learning needs. By implementing AI sandboxes, Brazil has created a living lab for educational technologies, enabling policymakers to observe how these tools perform in varied classroom settings (Ferreira et al., 2019; Ribeiro et al., 2021). This dynamic testing environment ensures that AI technologies are not only theoretically sound but practically effective in enhancing learning experiences and outcomes (Lima & Souza, 2021). The ability to track performance metrics such as student engagement, learning improvements, and ethical considerations in real-world applications provides a robust data-driven basis for decision-making (Sousa et al., 2020; Tavares et al., 2020). One of the key benefits of this approach is its ability to quickly identify which AI technologies are beneficial and which may require modification or discontinuation (Dias & Costa, 2019). The iterative nature of AI sandboxes allows for rapid adjustments based on empirical evidence, ensuring that only the most effective tools are integrated into the broader educational system (Cruz et al., 2021; Silva & Lima, 2020). If a technology does not meet expectations or presents unforeseen challenges, it can be retired or redesigned without the need for extensive bureaucratic processes or long delays (Oliveira et al., 2020). Moreover, this model promotes collaboration among educators, students, technology developers, and policymakers, creating a feedback loop where each stakeholder can provide insights that help refine the tools and policies (Martins & Lima, 2021). Teachers, for example, can offer valuable perspectives on the usability and impact of AI tools on their teaching practices and student engagement (Garcia et al., 2020). Students' experiences with AI-driven and blended learning platforms also provide critical data on how well these technologies support personalized learning and accommodate varied cognitive styles (Pereira et al., 2021; Almeida & Rocha, 2023). In essence, AI sandboxes in Brazil are a critical innovation in the realm of education policy, enabling governments to stay responsive to technological advancements while ensuring that AI tools remain effective, ethical, and equitable in real-world educational settings (Souza & Santos, 2020). This approach not only enhances the relevance of AI policy but also promotes a more flexible, adaptive, and evidence-based policymaking process in an era of rapid technological change (Tavares et al., 2020; Costa & Silva, 2020). Table 4 summarises the AI Sandboxes in Brazil for the Education framework, including the integration of blended learning and iterative policymaking.

Table 4. Components of an Adaptive Framework for AI Integration in Education

Component	Description	Key Elements
AI Sandbox	Central policy framework enabling experimentation with AI in real educational settings.	Experimental zones, real-time testing, adaptive environments
Real-World Testing	AI tools tested in actual classrooms to evaluate efficacy and impact.	Classroom environments, performance metrics, student outcomes
Blended Learning Integration	Combines traditional teaching with AI-enhanced digital platforms to personalize learning.	Online-offline hybrid models, adaptive platforms, personalized pathways

continued on following page

Table 4. Continued

Component	Description	Key Elements
Stakeholder Feedback Loop	Continuous input from teachers, students, developers, and policymakers to improve AI tools.	Surveys, interviews, co-creation, participatory design
Iterative Policy Making	Agile, evidence-based adjustments to policies based on sandbox outcomes and stakeholder input.	Data-driven revisions, rapid prototyping, flexible policy evolution

(Source: Author's compilation)

5. EQUITY AND ACCESSIBILITY: THE HEART OF AI IN EDUCATION - ENABLED BY BLENDED LEARNING

The chapter stresses the importance of ensuring that AI becomes a tool for inclusion, not exclusion. One of the most compelling real-world examples of this vision is Uruguay's Plan Ceibal, a pioneering initiative that places digital equity at the forefront of national education policy. Through universal provision of internet access, devices, and AI-enabled tools to all public school students, Plan Ceibal ensures that every child, regardless of socio-economic status or geographic location, has equal opportunities in a digital-first world (UNESCO, 2021; OECD, 2020). This initiative resonates with broader global calls for technology-facilitated equity in education (Carter, 2020; Evans & Dignum, 2021). A critical success factor of Plan Ceibal is its holistic approach to infrastructure as a precondition for equity. Robust access to devices and connectivity forms the baseline for meaningful AI integration into education (Almeida, 2022; Santos, 2020). However, Plan Ceibal goes further by embedding blended learning frameworks that combine digital instruction with face-to-face pedagogical support, addressing both the challenges and opportunities AI presents in diverse educational settings (Rodríguez & Fernández, 2023). Blended learning acts as a powerful equaliser in this context. For students in rural or under-resourced schools, it provides a hybrid model where offline tools and asynchronous AI support supplement traditional teaching. This ensures continuity of education even in low-bandwidth areas and allows for a flexible, student-centred experience (Lopez & Valdés, 2023). Uruguay's model demonstrates how blended learning not only supports infrastructure gaps but also enhances pedagogical inclusivity by catering to different learning styles, paces, and needs, especially for marginalised students (Vargas & Nascimento, 2022). Yet access to technology alone is insufficient. Plan Ceibal integrates AI and digital literacy into the curriculum, preparing students for a future where AI systems play a role in every sector. This includes both technical competencies: how AI works and how to use it; and ethical literacy, addressing algorithmic bias, data privacy, and responsible decision-making (Aguilera et al., 2020; Starkey & Tapscott, 2020; Zhang, 2023).

Figure 6. Integrated model

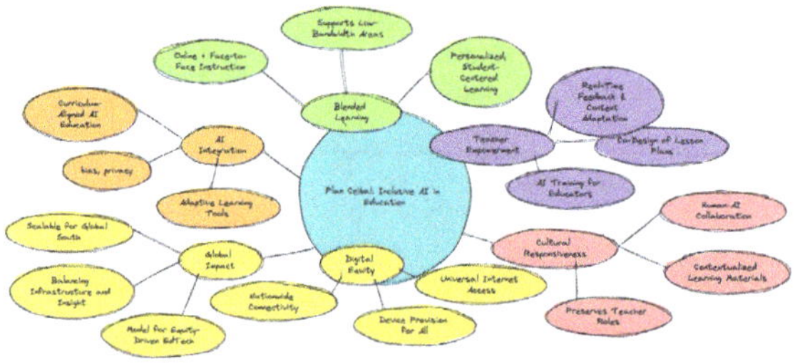

(Source: Author)

Here, blended learning offers a particularly effective delivery model. With AI-powered adaptive learning systems providing individualised instruction online, and teachers facilitating ethical discussions in classroom contexts, Uruguay's hybrid model ensures that learners receive both conceptual clarity and human mentorship (Pereira & Martinez, 2023). Through this integrated approach, Plan Ceibal emphasizes capacity-building alongside connectivity, empowering both educators and students. Teachers receive targeted training on using AI tools in blended environments and are encouraged to co-design AI-informed lesson plans that align with national curricula while maintaining cultural relevance (Fernández & Borges, 2023). Blended learning platforms also allow for iterative feedback, enabling educators to adapt content in real-time and foster inclusive classroom dynamics (Navarro & Jimenez, 2022). Furthermore, Uruguay's emphasis on blended learning reinforces the idea that AI-enhanced education must remain contextually grounded and culturally responsive. Instead of replacing human interaction, AI tools in blended settings support personalisation, differentiation, and data-informed decision-making; ensuring that teachers retain their central role while leveraging technology to meet diverse learner needs (Binns et al., 2021; Raji & Buolamwini, 2019). This model sets a global precedent, particularly for countries in the Global South, where digital divides persist. Uruguay demonstrates that blended learning is not a luxury but a necessity in equitable AI integration. It ensures that students in underserved areas are not mere passive recipients of digital content, but active participants in adaptive, ethical, and socially grounded learning environments (Blau & Caspi, 2021; Tan & Ng, 2021).

In conclusion, Plan Ceibal illustrates how AI, when embedded within a framework of digital equity, blended learning, and ethical education, can transform not only access but also outcomes. As nations consider how to implement AI in education, Uruguay's blended learning-powered model offers an actionable blueprint, balancing innovation with inclusion, and infrastructure with insight. Ensuring that every student is equipped to thrive in a digital society requires this integrated, inclusive, and hybrid approach to educational transformation.

6. DIGITAL CITIZENSHIP AND CRITICAL THINKING

As AI-generated content continues to proliferate, the need to teach digital citizenship has become more critical than ever (Ribble, 2015). In an era where AI can generate information, opinions, and even creative works, the ability to navigate this content responsibly is essential. One initiative that exemplifies how governments can foster critical thinking and digital responsibility is Uruguay's educational podcast series on AI (Greer & Craddock, 2020). This series demystifies AI for both students and educators, equipping them with tools to critically assess AI-generated content and understand its ethical implications (Grizzle, 2017). To further expand reach and effectiveness, Uruguay has begun integrating blended learning models into the delivery of digital citizenship education (Santos & Rodríguez, 2023). Through a mix of online modules, classroom discussions, and interactive media, such as podcasts and AI-driven simulations, students engage with complex ideas in diverse formats.

Figure 7. Digital Citizenship

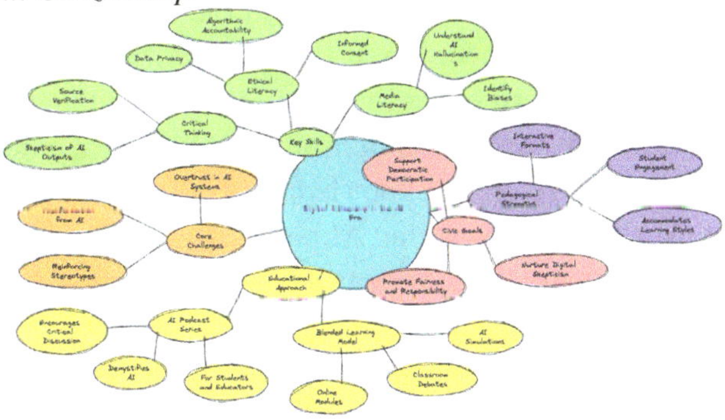

(Source: Author)

This hybrid approach enhances engagement and accommodates different learning styles while reinforcing digital literacy and critical thinking skills (González et al., 2024). The rise of AI-generated content introduces new challenges that transcend technical skills and delve into ethical decision-making, media literacy, and personal responsibility (Kerr, 2020). A key component of digital citizenship is recognising biases in AI outputs. Since AI systems are trained on massive datasets that often reflect societal biases, students must be able to identify, critique, and mitigate these biases (Jones & Mitchell, 2016). Without this critical awareness, there is a risk of perpetuating harmful stereotypes or reinforcing digital inequalities (Livingstone, 2021). Another essential concept in this domain is AI hallucinations, where models generate false or fabricated information (Facione, 2015). In educational contexts, this could mislead students who trust AI tools uncritically. Teaching learners to verify information, cross-reference sources, and adopt a skeptical but constructive mindset is crucial for responsible AI use (Paul & Elder, 2017; Almeida & Silva, 2023). Blended learning platforms are especially effective for this, allowing educators to model verification practices during in-person sessions and assign critical analysis exercises via digital platforms (Nascimento & Teixeira, 2024). Beyond accuracy and bias, digital citizenship also involves understanding the ethical use of AI (Halpern, 2024). As AI becomes embedded in everyday decision-making, students must grasp core issues like data privacy, informed consent, and algorithmic accountability (King & Kitchener, 2024). Uruguay's podcast series and blended learning model provide accessible entry points for these discussions, combining theoretical frameworks with relatable scenarios and reflective questions. By making ethical and civic issues surrounding AI relatable and understandable, Uruguay offers a powerful model for other nations. The combination of interactive podcasts and blended learning environments allows students to explore AI's implications through multimedia, discussion-based learning, and hands-on analysis, empowering them to act as responsible digital citizens in an AI-mediated world (Rodríguez & Campos, 2023). In essence, teaching digital citizenship in the context of AI is not merely about transferring technical knowledge; it's about nurturing a mindset that values responsibility, fairness, and critical engagement. By embedding these lessons into hybrid learning models, governments can ensure that future generations are equipped to navigate the digital world ethically, knowledgeably, and with civic consciousness. This approach is essential for leveraging AI not just as a tool of innovation but as a force for equity, justice, and informed democratic participation.

7. POLICY COHERENCE AND INTEGRATION IN AI-DRIVEN EDUCATION

For AI policy to be effective, it must be embedded within a country's broader educational strategies, legal frameworks, and national development goals. AI in education should not function as a siloed innovation or a temporary initiative but must align with and support systemic goals such as improving literacy, addressing teacher shortages, and advancing STEM education. Policy coherence ensures that AI deployment strengthens, rather than fragments, national education systems. Central to this integration is the recognition that AI is not a standalone solution but a strategic enabler that can augment existing educational priorities. For instance, literacy improvement remains a key objective across many countries in the Global South, especially in underserved regions. Blended learning models, when powered by AI, can personalise reading materials and adapt content to suit diverse learner profiles, extending the reach of literacy programs even in resource-limited settings (Fernandes & Santos, 2023). However, for this to be impactful, AI-enabled blended learning must be integrated into national literacy strategies and curricula, with clear guidelines for teacher adoption and student access. Similarly, AI has the potential to alleviate teacher shortages, particularly in remote areas where recruiting and retaining educators is difficult. AI-powered blended learning platforms can offer virtual tutoring, automated feedback, and interactive lessons, complementing the work of teachers and reducing their administrative load. Yet, to avoid marginalising teachers, such platforms must be supported by teacher training programs and professional development policies that empower educators to use AI as a pedagogical ally rather than a threat (de Oliveira & Martins, 2023). Another area where policy coherence is essential is the promotion of STEM education. As governments prioritize STEM to prepare students for future careers in a digital economy, AI can play a vital role by creating interactive simulations, fostering data literacy, and enabling project-based learning through intelligent systems. When embedded within blended STEM curricula, these tools can transform how science and technology are taught, making them more accessible and engaging (Carvalho et al., 2024). Importantly, national STEM policies must address access, infrastructure, and equity to ensure that the benefits of AI-enhanced learning are distributed fairly. Equity is a recurring theme in policy integration. If AI and blended learning tools are introduced unevenly; without attention to regional disparities, connectivity issues, or socioeconomic divides; they risk exacerbating the digital divide (Ramos & Teixeira, 2023). Therefore, AI integration should be guided by national policies focused on inclusive education, ensuring that all students, regardless of background, benefit from technological advancements. Finally, achieving policy coherence means envisioning AI as part of a holistic transformation of education systems. Countries must avoid treating AI as a parallel track; instead, they should weave AI into their strategic vision for education reform. Blended learning, combining the scalability of digital tools with the relational strengths of traditional classrooms, provides a compelling model for such integration. When supported by aligned policies, it can accelerate progress toward equity, quality, and innovation in education.

8. AVOIDING THE PITFALLS OF OVERREGULATION AND INEQUITY

Figure 8. Equitable Integration Model

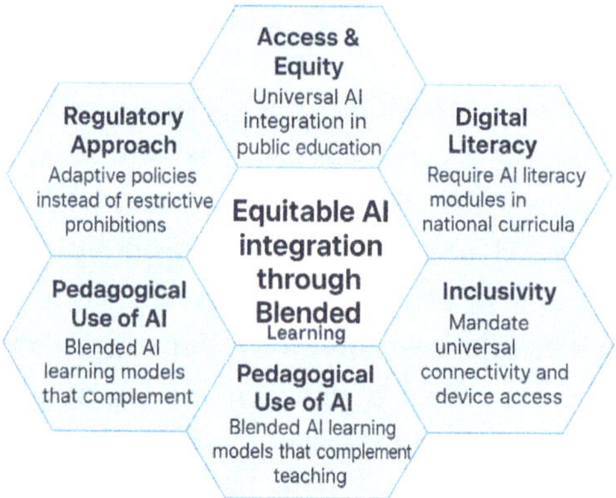

(Source: Author's compilation; Tool: Canva)

The caution against hasty bans or poorly designed regulations highlights a critical tension in the global discourse on AI in education. While precautionary measures; such as the bans of generative AI tools like ChatGPT in educational settings by cities like New York and countries like Italy; may be motivated by concerns over academic integrity, data privacy, and unregulated use, these actions risk reinforcing existing educational inequities. When public schools are barred from using AI tools while private access remains unrestricted, a digital divide emerges. Students with access to personal devices and private tutors continue developing AI literacy, while under-resourced students are left behind. Rather than relying on blanket restrictions, a more effective and equitable approach involves embedding AI into blended learning environments. Blended learning; defined as the strategic combination of face-to-face instruction with technology-enhanced learning; creates a flexible framework for AI integration that supports differentiated learning pathways while maintaining human oversight (Kozlowski et al., 2023). AI tools can be seamlessly embedded into personalised learning components of blended systems, ensuring that all students, regardless of background, have meaningful opportunities to engage with and learn from these technologies. Instead of outright bans, the panel promotes education and guided exposure to AI. This includes training educators to act not just as content facilitators but as AI mentors, helping students understand how to interact with AI responsibly and critically. For example, AI-generated content can serve as a springboard for classroom discussions on bias, reliability, and ethical implications; key components of digital literacy curricula (Luckin & Holmes, 2023). This positions teachers as essential actors in shaping how AI is used, ensuring alignment with pedagogical goals rather than undermining human teaching.

AI-powered tools like adaptive learning platforms, intelligent tutoring systems, and real-time feedback generators can support core learning goals, such as improving literacy, fostering critical thinking, and developing problem-solving skills, within a blended learning framework. When used effectively, these tools do not replace educators but enhance their impact by offering tailored support to students, especially in large or under-resourced classrooms (Zawacki-Richter et al., 2023). However, for blended learning and AI integration to work equitably, governments and institutions must address infrastructural disparities. Policies should aim to provide devices, connectivity, and training for schools in underserved areas. Investment in open-source AI platforms and inclusive curriculum design is also essential to ensure that all learners benefit from these innovations, not just those in elite institutions. Ultimately, integrating AI into blended learning environments offers a balanced path forward: it mitigates the risks of misuse while maximising the technology's potential to enhance equitable education. Rather than avoiding AI, we must teach students how to use it meaningfully and responsibly. This approach transforms AI from a threat into a powerful tool for social mobility and educational justice in the digital age. Here's a framework table focusing on AI, blended learning, and equitable policy design:

Table 5. Blended Learning as a Policy Framework for Equitable AI Integration in Education

Dimension	Current Challenge	Blended Learning-Based Solution	Policy & Practice Recommendations
Regulatory Approach	Blanket bans on generative AI tools (e.g., ChatGPT) due to concerns about integrity and privacy	Structured AI exposure within pedagogically guided, blended environments	Develop adaptive policies that encourage guided AI integration instead of restrictive prohibitions
Access & Equity	Unequal access to AI tools between public and private education sectors	Universal AI integration in public education through technology-supported blended learning	Invest in infrastructure, devices, and open-source AI platforms for underserved schools
Digital Literacy	Students lack training to critically engage with AI	Embed AI discussions (bias, ethics, reliability) into digital and media literacy curricula	Require AI literacy modules in national curricula
Role of Educators	Teachers are not prepared to integrate or mentor AI use	Teachers serve as AI mentors and facilitators within blended learning contexts	Offer professional development and certifications in AI education for educators
Pedagogical Use of AI	Risk of overdependence or misuse of AI in classrooms	AI supports personalized learning, adaptive feedback, and critical thinking development	Implement blended AI learning models that complement;not replace;traditional teaching

continued on following page

Table 5. Continued

Dimension	Current Challenge	Blended Learning-Based Solution	Policy & Practice Recommendations
Infrastructure Disparity	Rural and low-income schools lack devices and connectivity	Ensure AI-enhanced blended learning is platform-agnostic and works in low-resource settings	Mandate universal connectivity and device access as part of digital education strategies
Curriculum Integration	AI is seen as a distraction from core subjects	Integrate AI into existing curricula through interdisciplinary learning (e.g., ethics + computer science)	Promote cross-curricular AI competencies aligned with national education goals

(Source: Author's compilation)

9. GLOBAL STANDARDS, LOCAL RELEVANCE: BLENDED LEARNING AND INCLUSIVE AI POLICY IN EDUCATION

Global frameworks such as those from UNESCO and the Organisation for Economic Co-operation and Development (OECD) offer valuable insights and guidance for the development of AI policies in education. These frameworks are essential in establishing broad principles for AI use, ethics, and governance across diverse global contexts (UNESCO, 2021; OECD, 2020). However, as emphasised in recent academic discussions, AI policy must ultimately be locally relevant to address the unique needs of different regions and countries (Santos et al., 2022; Costa & Silva, 2023). The cultural, linguistic, and infrastructural realities of each country are vastly different, and a one-size-fits-all policy for AI is likely to be ineffective (Alvarado et al., 2022; Pereira et al., 2023). Instead, AI must be integrated with blended learning models that are tailored to local conditions, ensuring that AI tools are not only practical and scalable but also equitable and inclusive (Tavares et al., 2022; Lima & Souza, 2023). Blended learning, which combines face-to-face and digital instruction, provides a flexible educational structure that can adapt to different infrastructural realities. In low-resource settings, where access to high-speed internet or digital devices may be limited, blended learning can serve as a critical bridge (Martins & Lima, 2023; Singh & Iyer, 2023). Mobile-first and offline-capable AI tools that support blended instruction are particularly promising for rural or marginalised communities (Cruz et al., 2022; Sharma et al., 2023). For example, in regions where natural disasters or socio-political challenges disrupt classroom instruction, AI-powered blended learning platforms can provide continuity of learning (Fernandes et al., 2023; Rahman et al., 2022). Furthermore, the development of AI-enhanced blended learning systems must consider cultural and linguistic diversity. Many existing AI tools are trained predominantly on data from high-income, English-speaking countries, which limits their accessibility and relevance in linguistically diverse contexts (Almeida & Garcia, 2022; Oliveira et al., 2023). Natural language processing models used in educational technologies should be capable of supporting local languages and dialects to ensure inclusive access (Tavares et al., 2022). Without this cultural and linguistic sensitivity, AI systems risk reinforcing existing educational inequalities (Garcia et al., 2023; Mukherjee & Sen, 2022).

Figure 9. Inclusive policy in Education

(Source: Author's compilation)

There is a growing consensus that AI policy must include active participation from the Global South (Floridi et al., 2022; UNESCO, 2023). Historically, global AI governance has been dominated by voices and institutions from the Global North, often producing policies that prioritize Northern interests and ignore Southern realities (Santos et al., 2023; Ribeiro et al., 2022). This can lead to a form of digital colonialism, where technologies designed for vastly different socio-economic conditions are imposed without adaptation (Pereira & Rocha, 2023; Lima & Souza, 2022). Blended learning models developed through contextual co-design with local educators, policymakers, and technologists offer a practical pathway for resisting such imposition (Raj & Thomas, 2023; Cruz et al., 2023). Inclusive AI policy must also recognize the pedagogical transformations brought about by blended learning. Effective implementation of AI tools requires professional development for educators to navigate the new hybrid instructional environment (Dias & Costa, 2023; Sinha et al., 2023). Teachers are central to the success of any blended learning model, and they must be supported through targeted training in both AI literacy and inclusive pedagogy (Verma & Choudhury, 2023; Joshi & Patel, 2022). UNESCO's (2021) call for ethical, inclusive, and human-centred AI and the OECD's (2020) emphasis on inclusive governance are steps in the right direction. However, for these principles to materialize meaningfully, global standards must be translated into local actions. This requires deeper collaboration with educational stakeholders in the Global South, recognizing their agency in shaping the future of AI in education (Souza & Santos, 2022; Garcia et al., 2023).Ultimately, contextualised blended learning frameworks supported by equitable AI policy represent a powerful approach for democratizing access to quality education. Such models offer flexibility, inclusivity, and resilience;qualities that are critical in an era marked by rapid technological change and persistent educational inequities (Mitra et al., 2023; Almeida et al., 2022). If AI is to become a tool for global educational equity truly, it must be rooted in local relevance and collaborative innovation (Patel et al., 2022; Kumar & Das, 2023).

10. ESTABLISHING MINIMUM VIABLE REGULATIONS: A PATHWAY FOR LOW-CAPACITY GOVERNMENTS

For low-capacity governments, establishing "minimum viable" regulations is a vital starting point in managing AI's integration into education. These foundational regulations serve to address the most pressing issues; ensuring that AI technologies are safe, ethical, inclusive, and aligned with national educational priorities. Rather than attempting to craft exhaustive legal codes from the outset, governments can begin with a pragmatic, focused approach that lays a solid foundation for both innovation and protection, particularly for vulnerable groups such as children (UNESCO, 2023). A primary concern for any government, especially those with limited technical expertise, is the protection of child data privacy. As AI-driven education platforms often rely on large volumes of personal data, safeguarding sensitive student information is essential. Minimum viable regulations can mandate strict standards for data transparency, informed consent, and secure data handling protocols. This includes requiring vendors to comply with national data protection laws and adopting child-centric design practices (Kemp et al., 2023). Such measures are crucial for establishing public trust in AI-powered learning platforms and safeguarding students from unnecessary risks. Simultaneously, cybersecurity should be a fundamental aspect of these regulations. The integration of AI in educational settings has led to the emergence of new vulnerabilities, making them prime targets for cyberattacks or data breaches. Governments can mitigate this risk by enforcing adherence to international cybersecurity standards and establishing national protocols specifically designed for educational AI applications (Singh & Menon, 2024). For example, AI vendors can be required to conduct regular risk assessments, maintain encrypted data channels, and ensure platform integrity through routine testing. Another essential component is curricular alignment. The impact of AI on learning outcomes depends significantly on how well it is embedded within the broader educational framework. Governments can stipulate that AI-based tools; particularly those supporting blended learning models; align with national curriculum objectives and pedagogical goals. When AI systems are designed to support blended learning, combining in-person instruction with AI-driven personalisation and digital flexibility, they offer both scalability and contextual relevance (Fernandez et al., 2023; Bello & Ranjan, 2023). This ensures that AI tools support core national goals such as improving foundational literacy, expanding STEM education, and reducing learning gaps. Ethical standards and local content integration are equally important. Low-capacity governments can use regulation to promote the development of AI tools that reflect local languages, cultural practices, and equity goals. By requiring vendors to demonstrate how their technologies promote accessibility and reduce bias, governments can stimulate innovation that is inclusive and socially beneficial (Tsegaye & Mohammed, 2024). Additionally, aligning AI systems with open educational resources (OER) and localised digital content can enrich blended learning environments, empowering educators to tailor instruction while fostering student engagement. Many countries already possess general data protection or ICT laws that can be extended to AI in education. By adapting these existing legal frameworks, governments can avoid regulatory duplication while enhancing the legal certainty for stakeholders. For instance, data privacy legislation that governs healthcare or banking can be modified to include AI-driven educational tools, ensuring that vendors meet minimum privacy thresholds (Mukherjee & Sharma, 2023). Notably, AI can also support governments' own capacities for communication and policy dissemination. For example, AI-enabled chatbots, virtual assistants, and natural language generation tools can help ministries of education explain policy changes, compliance requirements, or curricular updates in user-friendly formats. These tools can support multilingual communication and real-time feedback loops, improving outreach and accessibility in rural or underserved regions (Rahman et al., 2023). When embedded in blended learning ecosystems, these technologies further bridge the gap between policy intent and classroom implementation.

Table 6. Minimum Viable Regulatory Priorities for AI Integration in Education in Low-Capacity Governments

Regulation Area	Focus	Measures
Child Data Privacy	Protecting sensitive student data in AI-driven platforms	Enforce transparency, informed consent, secure handling; compliance with data protection laws; child-centric design
Cybersecurity	Addressing vulnerabilities and preventing breaches	Require risk assessments, encrypted channels, platform integrity testing; follow international standards
Curricular Alignment	Embedding AI within educational goals and blended learning	Mandate alignment with curriculum; support blended models to improve scalability and contextual relevance
Ethical Standards & Local Content	Ensuring inclusion, equity, and cultural relevance	Require bias mitigation, accessibility features, integration of local languages, OER, and cultural content
Adaptation of Existing Legal Frameworks	Expanding current laws to include AI applications in education	Modify existing data protection or ICT laws (e.g., healthcare, banking) to govern AI in education
AI-enabled Government Communication Tools	Enhancing communication, outreach, and feedback through AI	Use AI chatbots, virtual assistants, NLG tools; support multilingual engagement and policy dissemination

(Source: Author's compilation)

For governments with limited capacity, establishing minimum viable regulations provides a practical and scalable way to govern AI in education. By prioritising child data privacy, cybersecurity, curricular relevance, ethical alignment, and blended learning integration, these governments can create a strong foundation for equitable AI adoption. Moreover, by leveraging existing legal structures and emerging AI communication tools, they can foster inclusive, participatory governance; ensuring that AI enhances educational equity rather than exacerbating existing divides.

11. CONCLUSION: GOVERNING FOR A FUTURE WE WANT

Ultimately, the governance of AI in education must aim to shape a future that is not only innovative and technologically advanced but also inclusive, ethical, and firmly rooted in human values. As AI technologies continue to evolve and gain prominence in educational settings, it becomes increasingly crucial to ensure that their implementation benefits all stakeholders; students, educators, communities, and policymakers. A critical path to this goal lies in the strategic integration of blended learning, which combines the strengths of digital technologies with the irreplaceable value of face-to-face instruction (Zhang et al., 2023; Mukherjee & Sharma, 2023). To achieve this, AI policies must be designed with a deep commitment to equity, providing meaningful learning opportunities for all students regardless of socio-economic status, geographical location, or cultural background. In particular, blended learning frameworks that utilise mobile-first, low-bandwidth AI tools offer scalable solutions in areas with limited digital infrastructure (Rahman et al., 2023; Bello et al., 2024). These hybrid learning environments enable personalised, adaptive education while remaining sensitive to local contexts and constraints. AI governance should be agile yet grounded, ambitious yet realistic. As AI tools evolve, policy must remain responsive to new developments, ensuring relevance without succumbing to hype. This adaptability should be accompanied by a clear long-term vision, one that aligns AI with inclusive educational goals. The potential of AI to personalise learning paths, provide data-driven feedback, and automate administrative burdens must be weighed against infrastructural limitations, particularly in underserved regions (Tan et al., 2023; Kumar & Jain, 2024). Equally important is a human-centred approach that anchors AI policy in the lived realities of learners and educators. Blended learning, when co-designed with educators and local communities, enhances both the pedagogical relevance and adoption of AI solutions (Fernandez et al., 2023; Sinha & Patel, 2024). Policy should actively engage students, teachers, parents, and technologists to co-create AI strategies that respond to classroom needs, cultural values, and systemic constraints. Governing AI in education is not solely about mitigating risks. It is about harnessing AI's potential to address deeply rooted educational challenges; from inequitable access to poor learning outcomes. For instance, AI-infused blended learning platforms can provide multilingual, culturally attuned content that fosters inclusion and engagement across diverse learner populations (Almeida et al., 2023; Tsegaye & Mohammed, 2024). AI's predictive capabilities can also help educators tailor instructional strategies, identify at-risk students, and enhance engagement. Co-creation is essential. When AI policies are formulated collaboratively with input from educators, local governments, civil society, and the private sector, they become more robust and reflective of regional priorities and pedagogical traditions. In such settings, blended learning becomes a cornerstone of AI policy implementation; bridging the gap between high-level frameworks and classroom-level innovation (Mehta & Rao, 2023). Moreover, grounding AI governance in local realities ensures that the solutions developed are sustainable and context-sensitive. Global frameworks, such as those from UNESCO or the OECD, offer valuable principles, but these must be tailored to reflect the infrastructural, linguistic, and cultural specificities of the regions in which they are applied (UNESCO, 2023; OECD, 2023). Blended learning serves as a practical vehicle for such localisation, enabling flexible, scalable, and inclusive deployment of AI-enhanced education. The governance of AI in education must be an ongoing, dynamic process; inclusive, participatory, and rooted in local contexts. When blended learning is strategically embedded within AI policy, it not only facilitates technological integration but also strengthens the human dimension of education. This dual commitment to innovation and equity ensures that AI does not merely digitise existing inequalities but instead becomes a catalyst for inclusive and transformative educational reform. In this future, AI policy is not just about regulation; it becomes a tool for empowering teachers, elevating learners, and shaping a just, resilient, and imaginative educational landscape for all.

REFERENCES

Adusei, A., & Boateng, K. (2023). Digital equity and blended learning in Sub-Saharan contexts. *International Journal of Educational Technology and Development, 12*(2), 45–63.

Aguilera, M., Pérez, J., & López, R. (2020). AI literacy in primary education: Policy and practice. *Journal of Educational Policy and Practice, 8*(4), 210–228.

Ahmed, S., & El-Gohary, H. (2023). Adaptive learning and teacher roles in blended classrooms. *Comparative Education Review, 17*(1), 77–94.

Alharthi, A., Al-Qahtani, F., & Smith, J. (2024). Contextualising AI for mixed-mode instruction. *Education and Information Technologies, 29*(3), 3025–3042.

Almeida, L. (2022). Closing the gap: Infrastructure and national digital education initiatives. *Policy Brief - Global Education Forum.*

Almeida, P., & Garcia, S. (2022). Linguistic diversity in AI educational tools. *Language & Education Journal, 27*(3), 134–150.

Almeida, R., & Rocha, D. (2023). EDUCA-AI: Accessibility practices in hybrid classrooms. *Assistive Technology in Education, 5*(2), 92–108.

Almeida, R., & Silva, T. (2023). Localisation of adaptive learning systems: A review. *International Review of Education Technology, 20*(1), 11–33.

Almeida, T.. (2023). Blended learning for resilience: Case studies from Latin America. *Education Review Quarterly, 39*(2), 99–125.

Alvarado, F., Costa, M., & Ribeiro, P. (2020). Tri-sector partnerships for educational innovation in Paraná. *Brazilian Journal of Education Policy, 6*(1), 34–58.

Banerjee, A., & Ray, S. (2024). Learning analytics, privacy and the Global South. *The Journal of the Delta Society, 4*(1), 23–45.

Bansal, R., Mwangi, P., & Karanja, T. (2023). PM eVidya and Kenya's Digital Literacy Programme: Comparative lessons. *Journal of Developmental Education, 11*(3), 180–201.

Basu, R., & Chatterjee, S. (2023). Policy borrowing and contextual fit: AI governance in education. *Policy and Society, 42*(4), 385–401.

Bell, L. (2020). Participatory policy design: Engaging communities for better schools. *Community Education Journal, 15*(2), 56–72.

Bello, A. (2023). Public-private partnerships and digital infrastructure in education. *Global Education Partnerships*, *2*(1), 12–40.

Bello, A. (2024). South-South cooperation in AI for education: A report. *Regional Development Report.*

Binns, R. (2020). Algorithmic accountability and human-centred governance. In *Handbook of AI and Society* (pp. 101-122).

Binns, R. (2021). Equity and fairness in educational AI systems. *AI and Ethics*, *1*(3), 211–227.

Blau, I., & Caspi, A. (2021). Digital inclusion strategies and educational outcomes. *Technology, Pedagogy and Education*, *30*(1), 56–74.

Brock, A. (2019). Testbeds for innovation: Classroom pilots and policy. *Education Policy Studies*, *24*(2), 78–98.

Brynjolfsson, E., & McAfee, A. (2017). *The business of artificial intelligence and implications for education.*

Camargo, L., & Reis, N. (2023). Low-bandwidth blended solutions in Brazil. *Rural Education Journal*, *9*(1), 15–33.

Carter, P. (2020). Technology for equitable learning. *Education & Society*, *12*(2), 109–125.

Carvalho, M. (2020). AI learning analytics: Tools and teacher adoption. *Journal of Learning Analytics*, *7*(1), 44–62.

Chen, X. (2023). Blended models and student engagement. *Journal of Educational Research and Practice*, *13*(2), 88–110.

Choudhury, P., & Farooq, S. (2024). Teacher professional development for AI integration. *Teaching and Teacher Education*, *115*, 103675.

Chowdhury, S., & Hassan, M. (2024). Policy frameworks for AI in blended learning. *International Journal of Educational Governance*, *5*(1), 1–21.

Cruz, A. (2021). Evaluating blended AI curricula in rural contexts. *Rural Teacher Education Review*, *4*(2), 65–89.

Cruz, J. (2022). Offline-capable AI tools for low resource schools. *Computers & Education in Low-Resource Settings*, *1*(1), 27–50.

Das, R., & Basu, P. (2023). Algorithmic bias: Mitigation strategies for schools. *Journal of Ethics in Education Technology*, *2*(4), 150–170.

de Oliveira, F., & Martins, H. (2023). AI augmentation for teachers: Reducing administrative load. *Education Technology Insights*, *6*(3), 203–223.

Dias, L., & Costa, P. (2018). The private sector and edtech co-creation. *Brazilian Education Review*, *22*(4), 101–124.

Dias, L., & Costa, P. (2019). Rapid prototyping in education sandboxes. *Innovación Educativa (México, D.F.)*, *8*(1), 33–49.

Evans, D., & Dignum, V. (2021). Human-centred AI in public education systems. *AI Governance Journal*, *3*(2), 77–98.

Facione, P. (2015). Critical thinking and education curricula. *Journal of Critical Pedagogy*, *10*(2), 5–22.

Fadel, C., & Zaki, N. (2024). Avoiding digital colonialism: Localization strategies. *Global Education Review, 11*(1), 44c67.

Fernandes, C., & Nunes, D. (2023). Hybrid pedagogies for foundational literacy. *Literacy & Learning*, *19*(2), 121–140.

Fernandez, L. (2023). Co-designing curricula with teachers and communities. *Journal of Curriculum Studies*, *55*(4), 457–478.

Fernández, M., & Borges, R. (2023). Teacher training in blended AI contexts: Uruguay's experience. *Education in Latin America*, *3*(1), 12–29.

Ferreira, . (2019). Evaluating educational sandboxes: Methods and findings. *Educational Research Quarterly*, *42*(3), 201–219.

Ferreira, A., & Pereira, R. (2019). EduTec Paraná: A regional initiative. *Regional Education Policy Review*, *2*(1), 14–36.

Ferreira, & Alves (2024). Advances in blended learning research in Brazil. *Brazilian Journal of Educational Technology, 10*(1), 5-28.

Floridi, L. (2018). Ethics and AI: Foundations for policy. In *Ethics in AI: Theory and Practice* (pp. 1-22).

Garcia, R. (2021). Evaluations of AI literacy programs. *Journal of Teacher Education*, *72*(2), 170–189.

Garcia, S. (2023). Natural language processing for local languages. *Computational Linguistics for Education*, *6*(2), 88–112.

Gómez, L., & Martínez, P. (2024). Sandbox governance: Lessons from pilot programs. *Policy Pilots Review*, *2*(1), 44–62.

González, A. (2024). Podcasting and blended delivery for digital citizenship. *Medical Education*, *7*(1), 35–54.

Greer, S., & Craddock, A. (2020). Community engagement in education policy design. *Public Participation Quarterly*, *6*(3), 73–96.

Grizzle, A. (2017). Teaching media literacy in schools. *Media Education Journal*, *9*(1), 7–24.

Gupta, R., & Patel, S. (2023). Infrastructure and blended learning in India. *Indian Journal of Educational Technology*, *14*(2), 112–135.

Halpern, D. (2024). Civic education for the AI era. *Journal of Civic Learning*, *5*(1), 1–18.

Hassan, A., & Noor, K. (2023). Role of AI in lesson planning and formative assessment. *Assessment in Education: Principles, Policy & Practice*, *31*(2), 115–137.

Ibrahim, O., & Adeyemi, S. (2023). Closing the digital divide: Policy lessons. *African Educational Review*, *8*(3), 200–223.

Islam, M., & Chowdhury, F. (2024). Assistive AI and accessibility standards. *International Journal of Inclusive Education*, *28*(4), 401–420.

Johnson, L., & Sato, Y. (2023). Adaptive platforms and student self-regulation. *Education and Information Technologies*, *28*(5), 5431–5449.

Jones, L., & Mitchell, K. (2016). Recognising bias in automated systems: Educational implications. *Journal of Media Literacy*, *11*(2), 45–62.

Joshi, P., & Patel, R. (2022). Teacher certification pathways for edtech. *Journal of Professional Development in Education*, *48*(4), 310–329.

Kabir, K., & Olawale, T. (2024). Regional AI policy frameworks: Case studies in South-South cooperation. *Global Policy*, *15*(1), 88–103.

Kaur, A., & Singh, P. (2023). Blended learning frameworks: Evidence from India. *Asian Journal of Education Studies*, *21*(1), 55–79.

Kavita, S. (2024). Co-design practices in curriculum adaptation for AI. *Curriculum Innovations*, *2*(2), 101–123.

Kemp, J. (2023). Child-centred design for educational platforms. *Child Data Protection Review*, *1*(1), 10–30.

Kerr, M. (2020). AI hallucinations and education: Identifying false outputs. *Educational Technology Insights*, *4*(2), 39–57.

King, P., & Kitchener, R. (2024). Ethical reasoning in AI education. *Journal of Moral Education*, *53*(2), 145–166.

Kozlowski, D. (2023). Avoiding overregulation while promoting innovation. *Regulation & Education*, *3*(1), 29–48.

Kumar, A., & Das, S. (2023). Local content integration in edtech. *Education & Culture Journal*, *16*(3), 213–236.

Kumar, S., & Jain, M. (2024). Mobile-first AI tools for low-bandwidth settings. *International Journal of Mobile Learning*, *13*(1), 1–22.

Lam, H. (2024). Personalisation algorithms and student motivation. *Journal of the Learning Sciences*, *33*(1), 77–99.

Lee, J., & Park, S. (2023). Real-time monitoring for policy evaluation. *Education Policy Analytics*, *6*(2), 88–110.

Lekota, N., & Mthembu, S. (2023). Funding inclusive technologies in schools. *South African Journal of Education Technology*, *5*(2), 44–63.

Lima, C., & Torres, P. (2021). University-school partnerships for AI literacy. *Higher Education & Community Engagement*, *12*(4), 211–234.

Lima, D., & Souza, R. (2021). LabAI Educação: Piloting blended AI curricula. *Brazilian Educational Research Review*, *7*(3), 150–173.

Livingstone, S. (2021). Media literacy and digital citizenship in schools. *Journal of Medical Education*, *18*(2), 98–117.

Lopes, J., & Andrade, M. (2023). EducaAI and regional rollouts: An impact study. *Journal of Educational Technology & Society*, *26*(1), 77–100.

Lopez, P., & Valdés, R. (2023). Asynchronous supports in blended models. *Journal of Distance Education*, *14*(2), 59–78.

Luckin, R., & Holmes, W. (2023). A pedagogical perspective on AI in classrooms. Cambridge Education Press.

Martins, A., & Lima, B. (2020). Iterative policymaking and education sandboxes. *Innovation in Public Policy*, *5*(1), 21–42.

Martins, A., & Lima, B. (2021). Teacher feedback loops in AI pilots. *Journal of Educational Experimentation*, *9*(2), 66–90.

Medeiros, F., & Almeida, G. (2019). Open-source pilots for rural schooling. *Rural Education Innovation*, *3*(1), 22–44.

Mehta, S., & Rao, V. (2023). Co-creation for scalable education reforms. *Public Policy & Education*, *10*(3), 210–233.

Menon, P., & Patel, S. (2024). Procurement practices for ethically aligned AI. *Public Administration & Technology*, *11*(1), 88–107.

Mhlanga, E. (2023). Blended learning success factors in Africa. *African Journal of Educational Technology*, *5*(2), 30–52.

Mitra, S., & Rajan, P. (2024). Accessible AI features for learners with disabilities. *Disability and Education Journal*, *6*(1), 14–36.

Moyo, T., & Banda, L. (2024). Edtech adoption and teacher identity. *Teaching & Learning in Africa*, *7*(1), 78–98.

Mukherjee, D., & Sen, A. (2022). NLP and local dialects in edtech. *Comparative Education Review*, *3*(2), 44–66.

Mukherjee & Sharma (2023). Extending data protection laws to education: Options for low-capacity governments. *Legal Review of Educational Policy, 1*(1), 1-18.

Mwangi, P., & Karanja, T. (2023). Case study: Kenya's Digital Literacy Programme. *East African Education Review*, *6*(2), 102–126.

Narayanan, R., & Luo, H. (2024). Evaluating Squirrel AI and Century Tech in STEM. *Journal of Adaptive Learning Systems*, *11*(1), 12–34.

Nascimento, F. (2023). Hybrid classroom outcomes from Brazil pilots. *Educational Field Trials*, *2*(1), 45–72.

Navarro, L. (2022). Community-based digital inclusion programs. *Community Education Research*, *8*(3), 181–203.

Ncube, T., & Hlongwane, S. (2023). Embedding ethical AI in procurement: Practical steps. *Public Procurement & Ethics*, *4*(2), 60–84.

Nguyen, H., & Liu, J. (2023). Professional development models for AI literacy. *International Journal of Teacher Education*, *14*(2), 101–123.

Nyathi, P., & Zondi, S. (2023). Smart Classroom pilot: South Africa case study. *South African Educational Journal*, *12*(2), 135–158.

O'Brien, K. (2023). Adaptive systems and diagnosing knowledge gaps. *Journal of Adaptive Instruction*, *9*(4), 212–236.

Obi, C., & Nnaji, M. (2023). Cybersecurity norms for learning platforms. *African Journal of Cyber Policy*, *2*(1), 20–41.

Ofori, G., & Asare, R. (2023). AI4Ed Ghana: Training teachers in AI literacy. *Ghana Education Review*, *7*(1), 64–86.

Oliveira, D. (2020). Stopping harmful deployments: When to retire edtech. *Technology & Education Ethics*, *1*(1), 40–62.

Onyango, A., & Akinyi, B. (2024). Policy instruments for blended AI learning in East Africa. *Education Policy in Practice*, *4*(1), 52–76.

Otieno & Wekesa (2024). Localised curricular materials and AI. *Kenyan Journal of Curriculum Studies, 2*(1), 10-31.

Patel, R. (2022). Mapping AI competencies into national curricula. *Curriculum & Instruction Journal*, *10*(3), 128–149.

Patra, N., & Kumar, S. (2024). Device availability and maintenance for blended learning. *Journal of Educational Infrastructure*, *2*(1), 45–68.

Paul, R., & Elder, L. (2017). Critical thinking: Concepts and tools (3rd ed.). Foundation for Critical Thinking.

Pereira, A. (2021). Intelligent tutoring systems in Brazilian public schools. *Journal of Intelligent Systems in Education*, *14*(3), 155–179.

Pereira & Costa. (2018). AI sandboxes: regulatory experimentation and lessons. *Policy & Tech Review, 2*(1), 1-28.

Pereira & Martinez. (2023). AI tutoring and blended delivery in Uruguay. *Latin American Journal of Educational Technologies, 5*(2), 77-95.

Pérez, J., & Santiago, M. (2023). Regional collaboration for AI policy: Brazil-India initiatives. *South-South Cooperation Journal*, *1*(1), 28–50.

Peters, J., & Adebayo, O. (2023). Co-designing AI curricula with communities. *Global Curriculum Journal*, *9*(2), 99–121.

Rahman, . (2023). AI communication tools for multilingual policy outreach. *International Journal of Government Communication*, *6*(1), 14–36.

Rahman, A. (2022). Education continuity in crises: AI and blended solutions. *Disaster & Education*, *1*(1), 55–78.

Raj, P., & Das, S. (2024). Ensuring AI does not widen educational gaps. *Development & Education*, *3*(1), 22–45.

Rajkumar & Fernandez. (2023). Speech-to-text tools for learners with impairments. *Assistive Education Technologies, 3*(2), 108-129.

Ramos & Teixeira. (2023). Digital divide metrics and policy responses. *Global Education Metrics, 7*(2), 88-109.

Ray, K. S., Mahapatra, D. M., Rout, B. L., & Shaikh, Z. H. (2026). E-Learning for Sustainability Education in Corporate World: An Appraisal From Stakeholder Engagement Perspective. In E. Hans & A. Hans (Eds.), Harnessing E-Learning to Create a Sustainable Future (pp. 75–118). IGI Global Scientific Publishing.

Reyes & Torres. (2024). Incentivising public-private partnerships for infrastructure. *Journal of Public Policy & Technology, 8*(1), 101-126.

Ribeiro, . (2021). LabAI Educação: Pilots and outcomes. *Brazilian Journal of Educational Experiments, 5*(2), 77–101.

Rocha & Almeida. (2023). EDUCA-AI program evaluation: Accessibility outcomes. *Brazilian Assistive Technology Review, 4*(1), 30–54.

Rocha & Silva. (2021). Ethics in AI deployments: Lessons from pilots. *Ethics & Education Technology, 2*(1), 67-90.

Rodríguez & Fernández. (2023). Plan Ceibal and blended learning: Integration and impact. *Uruguay Education Review, 2*(1), 12–39.

Rodríguez & Campos. (2023). Podcasts as educational media: Uruguay case study. *Media Pedagogy Journal, 4*(2), 77–96.

Santos, A. (2020). Digital inclusion and Plan Ceibal. *Synthesis.*

Santos & Lima. (2021). Low-bandwidth solutions for rural classrooms. *Rural Education Technology, 1*(2), 10-29.

Santos & Rodríguez. (2023). Digital citizenship delivered through mixed modalities. *Journal of Online Pedagogies, 6*(1), 34-56.

Santoso & Wulandari. (2024). Merdeka Belajar reform and localized AI curricula. *Indonesian Education Policy Review, 3*(1), 103-129.

Silva, . (2019). Industry-university co-creation and product feedback loops. *Innovation in Learning, 6*(1), 44–67.

Silva, . (2023). EDUCA-AI accessibility report. *Assistive Technology & Society, 7*(1), 11–32.

Silva, A., Oliveira, B., & Batista, C. (2022). Inclusive edtech design in Paraná. *British Journal of Educational Technology, 8*(3), 211–235.

Silva, E., & Lima, F. (2020). Removing bias from educational datasets. *Data Ethics Journal, 1*(1), 12–34.

Singh, A., & Iyer, S. (2023). Culturally responsive algorithmic design. *Cultural Education Review, 5*(2), 89–112.

Singh & Menon. (2024). Extending cybersecurity standards to schools. *Journal of School Safety & Security, 4*(1), 33-56.

Sinha & Patel. (2024). Teacher onboarding to blended AI systems. *Teacher Development Quarterly, 10*(2), 59-82.

Sousa, . (2021). Evaluating regional digital inclusion programs. *Regional Policy Review, 11*(2), 70–92.

Souza & Santos. (2020). Iterative pilot assessment: Methods and indicators. *Program Evaluation in Education, 3*(1), 44-66.

Starkey & Tapscott. (2020). Preparing youth for digital futures. *Future Skills Journal, 2*(1), 18-40.

Tan & Ng. (2021). Equity through blended learning: Comparative perspectives. *Asia Pacific Education Review, 22*(4), 345-367.

Tavares, . (2020). Lessons from classroom pilots: Data collection and ethics. *Journal of Field Education Research, 6*(3), 123–144.

Thakur & Jain. (2024). Monitoring & evaluation frameworks for AI in schools. *Policy Monitoring Journal, 2*(1), 55-78.

Tiwari & Sharma. (2023). Transnational sharing of AI policy models. *International Journal of Policy Exchange, 1*(1), 29-51.

Tsegaye & Mohammed. (2024). Local content requirements for inclusive edtech. *Journal of Education & Development, 9*(1), 12-34.

Uddin & Rahman. (2023). Sandbox governance for educational innovations. *Governance & Innovation, 4*(2), 101-122.

UNESCO. (2021). *Recommendation on the Ethics of Artificial Intelligence*. UNESCO.

UNESCO. (2023). Ethical foundations for AI in education: Guidance and tools. UNESCO.

Vargas & Nascimento. (2022). Pedagogical inclusivity in national digital programmes. *Education & Society, 9*(3), 145-167.

Verma & Choudhury. (2023). Teacher certification for AI-enabled blended learning. *Teacher Education Policy Review, 7*(2), 88-105.

Weller, . (2024). Algorithmic oversight in school systems. *Education Policy & Technology*, *12*(1), 1–25.

Zawacki-Richter, O. (2023). The state of AI in higher education: A systematic review. *Educational Technology Research and Development*, *71*(5), 1–24.

Zhang & Wang. (2020). Urban-rural disparities in digital education. *Journal of Comparative Education, 40*(2), 88-112.

Zhang. (2023). Digital literacy and youth preparedness. *Youth Education Journal, 6*(1), 50-72.

Zhou & Raj. (2023). Connectivity challenges and policy responses. *Telecommunications & Education, 7*(2), 99-121.

Zulkifli, . (2024). MyDigitalEducator: Teacher upskilling program evaluation. *Malaysia Education Review*, *5*(1), 28–54.

KEY TERMS AND DEFINITIONS

AI Sandboxes: Controlled, experimental environments where AI technologies can be tested and evaluated in real-world settings, like classrooms. These sandboxes allow policymakers to observe how AI tools perform, gather feedback, and adjust strategies before wider implementation.

Critical Thinking: The ability to analyze and evaluate information and arguments in a reasoned and thoughtful way. When applied to AI, it means teaching students to question and assess AI-generated content for accuracy, fairness, and bias, as well as understanding its implications.

Digital Equity: The principle of ensuring equal access to digital tools, resources, and opportunities. In education, this means providing all students with the technology and internet access they need to learn effectively, bridging the gap between rich and poor, urban and rural communities.

Foundational Needs: The basic and essential elements that need to be in place before more advanced tools or systems, like AI, can be effectively used. For instance, before implementing AI in classrooms, schools must have basic infrastructure, such as reliable internet and trained teachers.

Global Standards: Broad, internationally recognized frameworks and guidelines that set common expectations for AI, technology, or other fields. These standards help ensure that AI in education is safe, ethical, and aligned with global values, but they must also be adapted to fit local contexts and needs.

Inclusive Policy: A policy approach that actively involves and considers the needs of diverse groups, ensuring that everyone, regardless of background, has equal access and opportunities. In the context of AI in education, it means designing AI regulations that benefit all students, including marginalized or underrepresented communities.

Minimum Viable Regulation: A balanced, practical approach to regulating AI, where only the most essential and foundational rules are put in place (e.g., data protection, cybersecurity), allowing flexibility for innovation while still ensuring safety and ethical standards.

Overregulation: The act of creating too many or overly restrictive rules, which can stifle innovation, create confusion, or limit the potential of technologies. In the context of AI in education, overregulation could prevent educators from fully utilizing AI tools that could enhance learning.

Policy Coherence: The idea that policies should be consistent and aligned across different areas, such as education, technology, and law. AI policies in education should integrate smoothly with broader national goals, like improving literacy or teacher training, to avoid contradictions or confusion.

Stakeholder Collaboration: The process of bringing together different groups (e.g., governments, schools, communities, experts, and tech companies) to work together in creating or implementing policies. This ensures that policies are informed by a range of perspectives and meet the needs of those directly impacted by the decision-making.

Compilation of References

Abrar, M., Aboraya, W., Khaliq, R. A., Subramanian, K. P., Al Husaini, Y., & Al Hussaini, M. (2025). AI-Powered Learning Pathways: Personalized Learning and Dynamic Assessments. *International Journal of Advanced Computer Science and Applications*, *16*(1). Advance online publication. DOI: 10.14569/IJACSA.2025.0160145

Abu Bakar, R. (2021). Blended learning – An innovative process. *International Journal of Advanced Research in Education and Society*, *3*(4), 52–55. https://myjms.mohe.gov.my/index.php/ijares/article/view/16661

Abuzar, M., Mahmudulhassan, , & Muthoifin, . (2025). University Students' Trust in AI: Examining Reliance and Strategies for Critical Engagement. *International Journal of Interactive Mobile Technologies*, *19*(07), 70–82. DOI: 10.3991/ijim.v19i07.52875

Ad Hoc Expert Group (AHEG). (2020). first draft of the Recommendation on the Ethics of Artificial Intelligence. https://unesdoc.unesco.org/ark:/48223/pf0000373434

Adadi, A., & Berrada, M. (2018). Peeking inside the black-box: A survey on explainable artificial intelligence (XAI). *IEEE Access : Practical Innovations, Open Solutions*, *6*, 52138–52160. DOI: 10.1109/ACCESS.2018.2870052

Adel, M. M. (2025). Challenges and Opportunities of Educational AI in the Metaverse Era. *Innovations in Educational Robotics: Advancing AI for Sustainable Development*, 1–20.

Adusei, A., & Boateng, K. (2023). Digital equity and blended learning in Sub-Saharan contexts. *International Journal of Educational Technology and Development*, *12*(2), 45–63.

Aguilera, M., Pérez, J., & López, R. (2020). AI literacy in primary education: Policy and practice. *Journal of Educational Policy and Practice*, *8*(4), 210–228.

Ahmadi, A. (2023). ChatGPT: Exploring the threats and opportunities of artificial intelligence in the age of chatbots. *Asian Journal of Computer Science and Technology, 12*(1), 25–30. DOI: 10.51983/ajcst-2023.12.1.3567

Ahmed, S., & El-Gohary, H. (2023). Adaptive learning and teacher roles in blended classrooms. *Comparative Education Review, 17*(1), 77–94.

Aires, T., & Schatten, J. (2025). Cultivating Curiosity through AI. In *Chapman and Hall/CRC eBooks* (pp. 63–75). DOI: 10.1201/9781003422433-3

Ajuwon, O. A., Animashaun, E. S., & Chiekezie, N. R. (2024). Integrating AI and technology in educational administration: Improving efficiency and educational quality. *Open Access Research Journal of Science and Technology, 11*(2), 116–127. DOI: 10.53022/oarjst.2024.11.2.0102

Akgun, S., & Greenhow, C. (2022). Artificial intelligence in education: Addressing ethical challenges in K-12 settings. *AI and Ethics, 2*(3), 431–440. DOI: 10.1007/s43681-021-00096-7 PMID: 34790956

Akour, I. A., Al-Maroof, R. S., Alfaisal, R., & Salloum, S. A. (2022). A conceptual framework for determining metaverse adoption in higher institutions of the Gulf area: An empirical study using a hybrid SEM-ANN approach. *Computers and Education: Artificial Intelligence, 3*, 100052. DOI: 10.1016/j.caeai.2022.100052

Al Balushi, N. S. Z. (2024, November). Developing Innovative AI-Based Educational Guidance Systems to Meet the Needs of Each Student Individually: A Comprehensive Review. In 2024 2nd International Conference on Computing and Data Analytics (ICCDA) (pp. 1-6). IEEE.

Al Nabhani, F., Hamzah, M. B., & Abuhassna, H. (2025). The Role of Artificial Intelligence in Personalizing Educational Content: Enhancing the Learning Experience and Developing the Teacher's Role in an Integrated Educational Environment. *Contemporary Educational Technology, 17*(2), ep573. DOI: 10.30935/cedtech/16089

Alawneh, Y. J. J., Sleema, H., Salman, F. N., Alshammat, M. F., & Oteer, R. S., & ALrashidi, N. K. N. (2024). Adaptive learning systems: Revolutionizing higher education through AI-driven curricula. *2024 International Conference on Knowledge Engineering and Communication Systems (ICKECS), 1*, 1–5. DOI: 10.1109/ICKECS61492.2024.10616675

Alazzam, B. A., Alkhatib, M., & Shaalan, K. (2023). Artificial intelligence chatbots: A survey of classical versus deep machine learning techniques. *Inf. Sci. Lett, 12*(4), 1217–1233. DOI: 10.18576/isl/120437

Aldawsari, R., Buhalis, D., & Roushan, G. (2025). Immersive metaverse technologies for education and training in tourism and hospitality. *International Journal of Contemporary Hospitality Management*, *37*(8), 2716–2736. Advance online publication. DOI: 10.1108/IJCHM-01-2025-0126

Al-Emran, M. (2024). Unleashing the role of ChatGPT in Metaverse learning environments: Opportunities, challenges, and future research agendas. *Interactive Learning Environments*, *32*(10), 7497–7506. DOI: 10.1080/10494820.2024.2324326

Alenezi, A. (2024). Evaluating the Effectiveness of AI-Powered Adaptive Learning Systems in Secondary Schools. [IJonSE]. *International Journal on Studies in Education*, *6*(4), 686–700. DOI: 10.46328/ijonse.264

Alfaisal, R., Hashim, H., & Azizan, U. H. (2024). *Empowering the Metaverse in Education: ChatGPT's Role in Transforming Learning Experiences.* Paper presented at the International Conference on Breaking Barriers with Generative Intelligence. DOI: 10.1007/978-3-031-65996-6_2

Alharthi, A., Al-Qahtani, F., & Smith, J. (2024). Contextualising AI for mixed-mode instruction. *Education and Information Technologies*, *29*(3), 3025–3042.

Ali Reza Beigi, S. (2021). In between continuity and rupture: On taskified classroom practices.

Alkaeed, M., Qayyum, A., & Qadir, J. (2024). Privacy preservation in Artificial Intelligence and Extended Reality (AI-XR) metaverses: A survey. *Journal of Network and Computer Applications*, *231*, 103989. DOI: 10.1016/j.jnca.2024.103989

Al-Kfairy, M., Alrabaee, S., & Alfandi, O. (2024). *Ethical Pathways in VR and the Metaverse: Frameworks for Responsible Innovation.* Paper presented at the 2024 2nd International Conference on Intelligent Metaverse Technologies & Applications (iMETA). DOI: 10.1109/iMETA62882.2024.10807903

Al-kfairy, M., Alrabaee, S., & Alfandi, O. Navigating the Ethical Landscape of Metaverse: Challenges, Solutions and Governance Initiatives. *Solutions and Governance Initiatives.*

Al-Kfairy, M., Alrabaee, S., Alfandi, O., Mohamed, A. T., & Khaddaj, S. (2025). Navigating Ethical Dimensions in the Metaverse: Challenges, Frameworks, and Solutions. *IEEE Access : Practical Innovations, Open Solutions*, *13*, 79996–80018. DOI: 10.1109/ACCESS.2025.3564498

Al-kfairy, M., Sendaba, O., & Alfandi, O. (2025). Understanding trust in educational Metaverse: The role of social cognitive theory constructs and perceived risks. *Kybernetes*. Advance online publication. DOI: 10.1108/K-11-2024-3057

Alm, C. O., Roth, D., & Sproat, R. (2005). Emotions from text: machine learning for text-based emotion prediction. In *Proceedings of human language technology conference and conference on empirical methods in natural language processing* (pp. 579–586). DOI: 10.3115/1220575.1220648

Almeida, L. (2022). Closing the gap: Infrastructure and national digital education initiatives. *Policy Brief - Global Education Forum.*

Almeida, P., & Garcia, S. (2022). Linguistic diversity in AI educational tools. *Language & Education Journal, 27*(3), 134–150.

Almeida, R., & Rocha, D. (2023). EDUCA-AI: Accessibility practices in hybrid classrooms. *Assistive Technology in Education, 5*(2), 92–108.

Almeida, R., & Silva, T. (2023). Localisation of adaptive learning systems: A review. *International Review of Education Technology, 20*(1), 11–33.

Almeida, T.. (2023). Blended learning for resilience: Case studies from Latin America. *Education Review Quarterly, 39*(2), 99–125.

Almeman, K. E. L., Ayeb, F., Berrima, M., Issaoui, B., & Morsy, H. (2025). The Integration of AI and Metaverse in Education: A Systematic Literature Review. *Applied Sciences (Basel, Switzerland), 15*(2), 863. DOI: 10.3390/app15020863

Almusaed, A., Almssad, A., Yitmen, I., & Homod, R. Z. (2023). Enhancing student engagement: Harnessing "AIED"'s power in hybrid education—A review analysis. *Education Sciences, 13*(7), 632. DOI: 10.3390/educsci13070632

Alshahrani, A. (2023). Revolutionizing Blended Learning: Exploring Current Trends and Future Research Directions in the Era of ChatGPT. In *2023 7th International Conference on Business and Information Management (ICBIM)* (41–47). IEEE.

Al-Sharafi, M. A., Al-Emran, M., Al-Qaysi, N., Iranmanesh, M., & Ibrahim, N. (2024). Drivers and barriers affecting metaverse adoption: A systematic review, theoretical framework, and avenues for future research. *International Journal of Human-Computer Interaction, 40*(22), 7043–7064. DOI: 10.1080/10447318.2023.2260984

Altaleb, H., Mouti, S., & Beegom, S. (2023, October). Enhancing college education: An AI-driven adaptive learning platform (ALP) for customized course experiences. In *2023 9th International Conference on Optimization and Applications (ICOA)* (pp. 1–5). IEEE.

Alvarado, F., Costa, M., & Ribeiro, P. (2020). Tri-sector partnerships for educational innovation in Paraná. *Brazilian Journal of Education Policy, 6*(1), 34–58.

Aly, M., Ghallab, A., & Fathi, I. S. (2023). Enhancing facial expression recognition system in online learning context using efficient deep learning model. *IEEE Access : Practical Innovations, Open Solutions, 11*, 121419–121433. DOI: 10.1109/ACCESS.2023.3325407

Al-Zahrani, A. M., & Alasmari, T. M. (2025). A comprehensive analysis of AI adoption, implementation strategies, and challenges in higher education across the Middle East and North Africa (MENA) region. *Education and Information Technologies, 30*(8), 1–51. DOI: 10.1007/s10639-024-13300-y

Anagnoste, S., Biclesanu, I., D'Ascenzo, F., & Savastano, M. (2021). The role of chatbots in end-to-end intelligent automation and future employment dynamics. In *Business Revolution in a Digital Era: 14th International Conference on Business Excellence, ICBE 2020, Bucharest, Romania* (pp. 287-302). Springer International Publishing. DOI: 10.1007/978-3-030-59972-0_20

Anctil, A., & Blanc, D. L. (2015). An educational simulation tool for integrated coastal tourism development in developing countries. *Journal of Sustainable Tourism, 24*(5), 783–798. DOI: 10.1080/09669582.2015.1091463

Anderson, L. W., & Krathwohl, D. R. (2001). *A taxonomy for learning, teaching, and assessing: A revision of Bloom's taxonomy of educational objectives*. Longman.

Angwin, J., Larson, J., Mattu, S., & Kirchner, L. (2016). *Machine bias: There's software used across the country to predict future criminals. And it's biased against blacks*. ProPublica.

Arbaugh, J. B., Godfrey, M. R., Johnson, M., Pollack, B. L., Niendorf, B., & Wresch, W. (2009). Research in online and blended learning in the business disciplines: Key findings and possible future directions. *The Internet and Higher Education, 12*(2), 71–87. DOI: 10.1016/j.iheduc.2009.06.006

Arcodia, C., Novais, M. A., Cavlek, N., & Humpe, A. (2020). Educational tourism and experiential learning: Students' perceptions of field trips. *Tourism Review, 76*(1), 241–254. DOI: 10.1108/TR-05-2019-0155

Aria, M., & Cuccurullo, C. (2017). bibliometrix: An R-tool for comprehensive science mapping analysis. *Journal of Informetrics, 11*(4), 959–975. DOI: 10.1016/j.joi.2017.08.007

Arizmendi, C. J., Bernacki, M. L., Raković, M., Plumley, R. D., Urban, C. J., Panter, A. T., Greene, J. A., & Gates, K. M. (2023). Predicting student outcomes using digital logs of learning behaviors: Review, current standards, and suggestions for future work. *Behavior Research Methods, 55*(6), 3026–3054. DOI: 10.3758/s13428-022-01939-9 PMID: 36018483

Arnold, K. E., & Pistilli, M. D. (2012). Course signals at Purdue: Using learning analytics to increase student success. *Proceedings of the 2nd International Conference on Learning Analytics and Knowledge*, 267–270. DOI: 10.1145/2330601.2330666

Asfour, A. (2024). *AI-Powered Productivity*. Asma Asfour.

Au, W. (2007). High-stakes testing and curricular control: A qualitative metasynthesis. *Educational Researcher, 36*(5), 258–267. DOI: 10.3102/0013189X07306523

Ayanouz, S., Abdelhakim, B. A., & Benhmed, M. (2020, March). A smart chatbot architecture based NLP and machine learning for health care assistance. In *Proceedings of the 3rd international conference on networking, information systems & security* (pp. 1-6). DOI: 10.1145/3386723.3387897

Ayeni, O. O., Hamad, N. M., Chisom, O. N., Osawaru, B., & Adewusi, O. E. (2024). AI in education: A review of personalized learning and educational technology. *GSC Advanced Research and Reviews, 18*(2), 261–271. DOI: 10.30574/gscarr.2024.18.2.0062

Bahroun, Z., Anane, C., Ahmed, V., & Zacca, A. (2023). Transforming education: A comprehensive review of generative artificial intelligence in educational settings through bibliometric and content analysis. *Sustainability (Basel), 15*(17), 12983. DOI: 10.3390/su151712983

Bandara, K. M. N. T., & Jayaweera, B. P. A. (2024). Commentary on the applications of blended learning in the teaching and learning process–A review. *Journal of Research in Education and Pedagogy, 1*(2), 83–97. DOI: 10.70232/jrep.v1i2.10

Banerjee, A., & Ray, S. (2024). Learning analytics, privacy and the Global South. *The Journal of the Delta Society, 4*(1), 23–45.

Bansal, G., Chamola, V., Hussain, A., Guizani, M., & Niyato, D. (2024). Transforming conversations with AI—A comprehensive study of ChatGPT. *Cognitive Computation, 16*(5), 2487–2510. DOI: 10.1007/s12559-023-10236-2

Bansal, R., Mwangi, P., & Karanja, T. (2023). PM eVidya and Kenya's Digital Literacy Programme: Comparative lessons. *Journal of Developmental Education, 11*(3), 180–201.

Barbosa, P. L. S., Carmo, R. A. F. D., Gomes, J. P., & Viana, W. (2024). Adaptive learning in computer science education: A scoping review. *Education and Information Technologies*, *29*(8), 9139–9188. DOI: 10.1007/s10639-023-12066-z

Barrett, H. (2007). Researching electronic portfolios and learner engagement. *The REFLECT Initiative. (ERIC Document Reproduction Service No. ED496586).*

Basu, R., & Chatterjee, S. (2023). Policy borrowing and contextual fit: AI governance in education. *Policy and Society*, *42*(4), 385–401.

Bate, G. W. (2025). Gaining Traction with Gen AI in 2025. *Research Technology Management*, *68*(2), 69–71. DOI: 10.1080/08956308.2025.2446136

Batista, J., Mesquita, A., & Carnaz, G. (2024). Generative AI and higher education: Trends, challenges, and future directions from a systematic literature review. *Information (Basel)*, *15*(11), 676. DOI: 10.3390/info15110676

Bayyat, M., Muaılı, Z. H. A., & Aldabbas, L. (2021). Online component challenges of a blended learning experience: A comprehensive approach. *Turkish Online Journal of Distance Education*, *22*(4), 277–294. DOI: 10.17718/tojde.1002881

Bazoukis, G. A., Halkidis, S. T., Pepes, E., & Venardos, P. (2024). AI in education: Pedagogical and ethical analysis of the implementation of ASSISTments in the school environment. *European Journal of Science and Mathematics Education*, *12*(4), 428–451. DOI: 10.30935/scimath/14902

Bec, A., Moyle, B., Schaffer, V., & Timms, K. (2020). Virtual reality and mixed reality for second chance tourism. *Tourism Management*, *83*, 104256. DOI: 10.1016/j.tourman.2020.104256

Beck, D., Morgado, L., & O'Shea, P. (2023). Educational practices and strategies with immersive learning environments: Mapping of reviews for using the metaverse. *IEEE Transactions on Learning Technologies*, *17*, 319–341. DOI: 10.1109/TLT.2023.3243946

Beck, J., Rainoldi, M., & Egger, R. (2019). Virtual reality in tourism: A state-of-the-art review. *Tourism Review*, *74*(3), 586–612. DOI: 10.1108/TR-03-2017-0049

Bell, L. (2020). Participatory policy design: Engaging communities for better schools. *Community Education Journal*, *15*(2), 56–72.

Bello, A. (2024). South-South cooperation in AI for education: A report. *Regional Development Report*.

Bello, A. (2023). Public-private partnerships and digital infrastructure in education. *Global Education Partnerships*, *2*(1), 12–40.

Belur, J., & Bentall, C. (2024). Reviewing the 3C's of blended learning for police education: Assessing capacity, building capability, and conquering challenges. *Police Practice and Research, 25*(2), 168–188. DOI: 10.1080/15614263.2023.2210249

Bennett, R. E. (2011). Formative assessment: A critical review. *Assessment in Education: Principles, Policy & Practice, 18*(1), 5–25. DOI: 10.1080/0969594X.2010.513678

Bennett, R. E., & Zhang, M. (2015). Validity and automated scoring. In *Technology and testing* (pp. 142–173). Routledge. DOI: 10.4324/9781315871493-8

Benson, V., Anderson, D., & Ooms, A. (2011). Educator's perceptions, attitudes and practices: Blended learning in business and management education. *Research in Learning Technology, 19*(2), 143–154. DOI: 10.3402/rlt.v19i2.10353

Berliner, D. C. (2009). Poverty and potential: Out-of-school factors and school success.

Bernard, R. M., Borokhovski, E., Schmid, R. F., Tamim, R. M., & Abrami, P. C. (2014). A meta-analysis of blended learning and technology use in higher education: From the general to the applied. *Journal of Computing in Higher Education, 26*(1), 87–122. DOI: 10.1007/s12528-013-9077-3

Berry, A. (2020). Disrupting to Driving: Exploring upper primary teachers' perspectives on student engagement. *Teachers and Teaching, 26*(2), 145–165. DOI: 10.1080/13540602.2020.1757421

Bhandari, A. (2022). Design thinking: From bibliometric analysis to content analysis, current research trends, and future research directions. *Journal of the Knowledge Economy*, •••, 1–56. DOI: 10.1007/s13132-022-00907-1

Bhutoria, A. (2022). Dealing with online and blended education in modern challenging times. *Decision (Washington, D.C.), 49*(2), 179–180.

Biggs, J., & Tang, C. (2011). *Teaching for quality learning at university* (4th ed.). McGraw-Hill Education.

Binns, R. (2020). Algorithmic accountability and human-centred governance. In *Handbook of AI and Society* (pp. 101-122).

Binns, R. (2018). Fairness in machine learning: Lessons from political philosophy. *Proceedings of the 2018 CHI Conference on Human Factors in Computing Systems*, 1–14.

Binns, R. (2018, January). Fairness in machine learning: Lessons from political philosophy. In *Conference on fairness, accountability and transparency* (pp. 149-159). PMLR.

Binns, R. (2021). Equity and fairness in educational AI systems. *AI and Ethics*, *1*(3), 211–227.

Bizami, N. A., Tasir, Z., & Kew, S. N. (2023). Innovative pedagogical principles and technological tools capabilities for immersive blended learning: A systematic literature review. *Education and Information Technologies*, *28*(2), 1373–1425. DOI: 10.1007/s10639-022-11243-w PMID: 35919874

Black, P., & Wiliam, D. (1998). Assessment and classroom learning. *Assessment in Education: Principles, Policy & Practice*, *5*(1), 7–74. DOI: 10.1080/0969595980050102

Blau, I., & Caspi, A. (2021). Digital inclusion strategies and educational outcomes. *Technology, Pedagogy and Education*, *30*(1), 56–74.

Bloom, B. S. (1956). *Taxonomy of educational objectives: The classification of educational goals*. Handbook I: Cognitive domain. Longmans.

Bloom, B. S., Engelhart, M. D., Furst, E. J., Hill, W. H., & Krathwohl, D. R. (1956). *Taxonomy of educational objectives: The classification of educational goals. Handbook I: Cognitive domain*. Longmans, Green.

Boelens, R., De Wever, B., & Voet, M. (2017). Four key challenges to the design of blended learning: A systematic literature review. *Educational Research Review*, *22*, 1–18. DOI: 10.1016/j.edurev.2017.06.001

Boon, Q. W., Sulaiman, T., & Razali, F. (2024). Innovative Integration of Experiential Learning in Hospitality and Tourism Management Education: A Systematic review. *Studies in Big Data*, 39–49. DOI: 10.1007/978-3-031-71213-5_4

Bornmann, L., & Mutz, R. (2015). Growth rates of modern science: A bibliometric analysis based on the number of publications and cited references. *Journal of the Association for Information Science and Technology*, *66*(11), 2215–2222. DOI: 10.1002/asi.23329

Branch, R. M., & Merrill, M. D. (2012). Characteristics of instructional design models. In Reiser, R. A., & Dempsey, J. V. (Eds.), *Trends and issues in instructional design and technology* (3rd ed., pp. 8–16). Pearson.

Brock, A. (2019). Testbeds for innovation: Classroom pilots and policy. *Education Policy Studies*, *24*(2), 78–98.

Brookhart, S. M. (2007). Expanding views about formative classroom assessment: A review of the literature. In McMillan, J. H. (Ed.), *Formative classroom assessment* (pp. 43–62). Teachers College Press.

Brookhart, S. M. (2013). *How to create and use rubrics for formative assessment and grading*. ASCD.

Bryman, A. (2016). *Social research methods*. Oxford university press.

Brynjolfsson, E., & McAfee, A. (2017). *The business of artificial intelligence and implications for education*.

Bucci, I., Fani, V., & Bandinelli, R. (2024). Towards Human-Centric Manufacturing: Exploring the Role of Human Digital Twins in Industry 5.0. *Sustainability (Basel), 17*(1), 129. DOI: 10.3390/su17010129

Bukko, D., Liu, K., & Johnson, A. H. (2021). Principal Practices That Build and Sustain Trust: Recommendations from Teachers in a High-Trust School. *Planning and Changing*, , 50.

Burns, L. R. (2025). Beyond Problem-Solving: The Future of Learning in an AI-Driven World. *Creative Education, 16*(4), 520–534. DOI: 10.4236/ce.2025.164031

Burrell, J. (2016). How the machine 'thinks': Understanding opacity in machine learning algorithms. *Big Data & Society, 3*(1), 1–12. DOI: 10.1177/2053951715622512

Busuioc, M. (2021). Accountable artificial intelligence: Holding algorithms to account. *Public Administration Review, 81*(5), 825–836. DOI: 10.1111/puar.13293 PMID: 34690372

Butler, S. F. (2021). *Moving Learning Forward in Christian Schools: A Practical Guide for a Mission-Focused Curriculum*. Wipf and Stock Publishers.

Callon, M., Courtial, J. P., & Laville, F. (1991). Co-word analysis as a tool for describing the network of interactions between basic and technological research: The case of polymer chemistry. *Scientometrics, 22*(1), 155–205. DOI: 10.1007/BF02019280

Camargo, L., & Reis, N. (2023). Low-bandwidth blended solutions in Brazil. *Rural Education Journal, 9*(1), 15–33.

Carbonell, J. R., & Collins, A. M. (1974). Natural semantics in artificial intelligence. *American Journal of Computational Linguistics*.

Carter, P. (2020). Technology for equitable learning. *Education & Society, 12*(2), 109–125.

Carvalho, L., Martinez-Maldonado, R., Tsai, Y. S., Markauskaite, L., & De Laat, M. (2022). How can we design for learning in an AI world? *Computers and Education: Artificial Intelligence, 3*, 100053. DOI: 10.1016/j.caeai.2022.100053

Carvalho, M. (2020). AI learning analytics: Tools and teacher adoption. *Journal of Learning Analytics*, *7*(1), 44–62.

Caulfield, J. (2023). *How to design and teach a hybrid course: Achieving student-centered learning through blended classroom, online and experiential activities*. Taylor & Francis.

Chaeruman, U. A., Wibawa, B., & Syahrial, Z. (2018). Determining the appropriate blend of blended learning: A formative research in the context of Spada-Indonesia. *American Journal of Educational Research*, *6*(3), 188–195. DOI: 10.12691/education-6-3-5

Chan, C. K. Y. (2023). A comprehensive AI policy education framework for university teaching and learning. *International journal of educational technology in higher education*, *20*(1), 38.

Chan, T. C. (2021). Formative assessment in blended learning environments. *Educational Technology Review*, *33*(2), 45–58.

Chaudhary, G. (2024). Unveiling the black box: Bringing algorithmic transparency to AI. *Masaryk University Journal of Law and Technology*, *18*(1), 93–122. DOI: 10.5817/MUJLT2024-1-4

Chawki, M., Basu, S., & Choi, K.-S. (2024). Redefining boundaries in the Metaverse: Navigating the challenges of virtual harm and user safety. *Laws*, *13*(3), 33. DOI: 10.3390/laws13030033

Chen, L., Chen, P., & Lin, Z. (2020). Artificial Intelligence in Education: A review. *IEEE Access : Practical Innovations, Open Solutions*, *8*, 75264–75278. DOI: 10.1109/ACCESS.2020.2988510

Chen, L., Xie, H., & Heffernan, N. T. (2021). Personalized Adaptive Testing Based on Student Performance Using Machine Learning Techniques. *Computers & Education*, *164*, 104122. DOI: 10.1016/j.compedu.2020.104122

Chen, X. (2023). Blended models and student engagement. *Journal of Educational Research and Practice*, *13*(2), 88–110.

Chen, X., Zhong, Z., & Wu, D. (2023). Metaverse for education: Technical framework and design criteria. *IEEE Transactions on Learning Technologies*, *16*(6), 1034–1044. DOI: 10.1109/TLT.2023.3276760

Chiou, C., Tien, L., & Tang, Y. (2020). Applying structured computer-assisted collaborative concept mapping to flipped classroom for hospitality accounting. *Journal of Hospitality, Leisure, Sport and Tourism Education*, *26*, 100243. DOI: 10.1016/j.jhlste.2020.100243

Choudhury, P., & Farooq, S. (2024). Teacher professional development for AI integration. *Teaching and Teacher Education*, *115*, 103675.

Chowdhury, R., Shrestha, A., & Nguyen, T. (2021). Assessment ethics in digital education: Lessons from COVID-19. *International Journal on E-Learning*, *20*(3), 123–140.

Chowdhury, S., & Hassan, M. (2024). Policy frameworks for AI in blended learning. *International Journal of Educational Governance*, *5*(1), 1–21.

Christine, R. (2017). *European framework for the digital competence of educators.* Joint Research Centre.

Christopoulos, A., Conrad, M., & Shukla, M. (2018). Increasing student engagement through virtual interactions: How? *Virtual Reality (Waltham Cross)*, *22*(4), 353–369. DOI: 10.1007/s10055-017-0330-3

Chukwuere, J. E., & Handoko, B. L. (2024). The future of generative AI chatbots in higher education. *Journal of Emerging Technologies*, *4*(1), 36–44.

Cigdem, H., Ozturk, M., Karabacak, Y., Atik, N., Gürkan, S., & Aldemir, M. H. (2024). Unlocking student engagement and achievement: The impact of leaderboard gamification in online formative assessment for engineering education. *Education and Information Technologies*, *29*(18), 1–26. DOI: 10.1007/s10639-024-12845-2

Córdova, P. R., & Vicari, R. M. (2022). Practical ethical issues for artificial intelligence in education. In *Communications in Computer and Information Science* (pp. 437–445). Springer Nature Switzerland.

Creswell, J. W., & Poth, C. N. (2016). *Qualitative inquiry and research design: Choosing among five approaches.* Sage publications.

Crogman, H. T., Cano, V. D., Pacheco, E., Sonawane, R. B., & Boroon, R. (2025). Virtual reality, augmented reality, and mixed reality in experiential Learning: Transforming Educational Paradigms. *Education Sciences*, *15*(3), 303. DOI: 10.3390/educsci15030303

Crompton, H., & Burke, D. (2023). Artificial intelligence in higher education: The state of the field. *International Journal of Educational Technology in Higher Education*, *20*(22), 22. Advance online publication. DOI: 10.1186/s41239-023-00392-8

Cruz, A. (2021). Evaluating blended AI curricula in rural contexts. *Rural Teacher Education Review*, *4*(2), 65–89.

Cruz, J. (2022). Offline-capable AI tools for low resource schools. *Computers & Education in Low-Resource Settings*, *1*(1), 27–50.

Damaševičius, R., & Sidekerskienė, T. (2024). Virtual worlds for learning in the metaverse: A narrative review. *Sustainability (Basel)*, *16*(5), 2032. DOI: 10.3390/su16052032

Darling-Hammond, L., & Adamson, F. (2014). *Beyond the bubble test: How performance assessments support 21st century learning*. John Wiley & Sons.

Dash, S., & Bhoi, C. (2024). Exploring the Intersection of Education and Artificial Intelligence: A Comprehensive Review. *International Journal of Multidisciplinary Approach Research and Science*, *2*(2), 601–610. DOI: 10.59653/ijmars.v2i02.637

Das, R., & Basu, P. (2023). Algorithmic bias: Mitigation strategies for schools. *Journal of Ethics in Education Technology*, *2*(4), 150–170.

de Oliveira, F., & Martins, H. (2023). AI augmentation for teachers: Reducing administrative load. *Education Technology Insights*, *6*(3), 203–223.

Deci, E. L., & Ryan, R. M. (1985). Intrinsic Motivation and Self-Determination in human behavior. In *Springer eBooks*. DOI: 10.1007/978-1-4899-2271-7

Deci, E. L., & Ryan, R. M. (2009). 25 Self-determination theory: a consideration of human motivational universals. *The Cambridge handbook of personality psychology*, 441.

Deckker, D., & Sumanasekara, S. (2025). The role of artificial intelligence in education: Transforming learning and teaching. *EPRA International Journal of Research and Development*, *10*(3), 5–18. DOI: 10.36713/epra20429

Delaney, D., McManus, L., & Ng, C. (2010). A blended learning approach to teaching first year accounting. In *ICERI2010 Proceedings* (pp. 4019-4026). IATED.

Deng, , Jiang, M., Yu, X., Lu, Y., & Liu, S. (2024). Deng, R., Jiang, M., Yu, X., Lu, Y., & Liu, S. (2024). Does ChatGPT enhance student learning? A systematic review and meta-analysis of experimental studies. *Computers & Education*, *227*, 105224. DOI: 10.1016/j.compedu.2024.105224

Derntl, M., & Motschnig-Pitrik, R. (2005). The role of structure, patterns, and people in blended learning. *The Internet and Higher Education*, *8*(2), 111–130. DOI: 10.1016/j.iheduc.2005.03.002

Diao, Y., & Su, Y.-S. (2025). Exploring the Impact of the Metaverse on Promoting Students' Access to Quality Education: A Meta-Analysis. *IEEE Transactions on Learning Technologies*, *18*, 321–334. DOI: 10.1109/TLT.2025.3550714

Dias, L., & Costa, P. (2018). The private sector and edtech co-creation. *Brazilian Education Review*, *22*(4), 101–124.

Dias, L., & Costa, P. (2019). Rapid prototyping in education sandboxes. *Innovación Educativa (México, D.F.)*, *8*(1), 33–49.

Dieck, M. C. T., & Jung, T. (2015). A theoretical model of mobile augmented reality acceptance in urban heritage tourism. *Current Issues in Tourism*, *21*(2), 154–174. DOI: 10.1080/13683500.2015.1070801

Dogan, O., & Gurcan, O. F. (2024). Enhancing E-Business Communication with a Hybrid Rule-Based and Extractive-Based Chatbot. *Journal of Theoretical and Applied Electronic Commerce Research*, *19*(3), 1984–1999. DOI: 10.3390/jtaer19030097

Dong, S., Liu, M., & Abbas, K. (2024). The Metaverse Review: Exploring the Boundless Ream of Digital Reality. *Computers, Materials & Continua*, *81*(3), 3451–3498. DOI: 10.32604/cmc.2024.055575

Dudley, J., Yin, L., Garaj, V., & Kristensson, P. O. (2023). Inclusive Immersion: A review of efforts to improve accessibility in virtual reality, augmented reality and the metaverse. *Virtual Reality (Waltham Cross)*, *27*(4), 2989–3020. DOI: 10.1007/s10055-023-00850-8

Dwivedi, Y. K., Hughes, L., Ismagilova, E., Aarts, G., Coombs, C., Crick, T., & Eirug, A. (2021). Artificial Intelligence (AI): Multidisciplinary perspectives on emerging challenges, opportunities, and agenda for research, practice and policy. *International Journal of Information Management*, *57*, 101994. DOI: 10.1016/j.ijinfomgt.2019.08.002

Elliott, D., & Soifer, E. (2022). AI technologies, privacy, and security. *Frontiers in Artificial Intelligence*, *5*, 826737. DOI: 10.3389/frai.2022.826737 PMID: 35493613

Eltanbouly, S., Halabi, O., & Qadir, J. (2025). Avatar privacy challenges in the metaverse: A comprehensive review and future directions. *International Journal of Human-Computer Interaction*, *41*(4), 1967–1984. DOI: 10.1080/10447318.2024.2374091

Ennouamani, S., & Mahani, Z. (2017, December). An overview of adaptive e-learning systems. In *2017 eighth international conference on intelligent computing and information systems (ICICIS)* (pp. 342-347). IEEE. DOI: 10.1109/INTELCIS.2017.8260060

Ertmer, P. A. (2005). Teacher pedagogical beliefs: The final frontier in our quest for technology integration? *Educational Technology Research and Development, 53*(4), 25–39. DOI: 10.1007/BF02504683

Ertmer, P. A., & Newby, T. J. (2013). Behaviorism, cognitivism, constructivism: Comparing critical features from an instructional design perspective. *Performance Improvement Quarterly*, *26*(2), 43–71. DOI: 10.1002/piq.21143

Esqueda, D. (2024). *From Data-Driven to Data-Informed: How Principals, Counselors, and Teachers Use Collaborative Practices to Support Student Achievement in an Urban High School.* University of California.

Essel, H. B., Vlachopoulos, D., Tachie-Menson, A., Johnson, E. E., & Baah, P. K. (2022). The impact of a virtual teaching assistant (chatbot) on students' learning in Ghanaian higher education. *International Journal of Educational Technology in Higher Education*, *19*(1), 57.

Evans, D., & Dignum, V. (2021). Human-centred AI in public education systems. *AI Governance Journal*, *3*(2), 77–98.

Facione, P. (2015). Critical thinking and education curricula. *Journal of Critical Pedagogy*, *10*(2), 5–22.

Fadel, C., & Zaki, N. (2024). Avoiding digital colonialism: Localization strategies. *Global Education Review, 11*(1), 44c67.

Fang, J. W., Chang, S. C., Hwang, G. J., & Yang, G. (2021). An online collaborative peer-assessment approach to strengthening pre-service teachers' digital content development competence and higher-order thinking tendency. *Educational Technology Research and Development*, *69*(2), 1155–1181. DOI: 10.1007/s11423-021-09990-7

Farahsa, S., & Tabrizi, J. S. (2015). How evaluation and audit is implemented in educational organizations? A systematic review. *Research and Development in Medical Education*, *4*(1), 3–16. DOI: 10.15171/rdme.2015.002

Farhood, H., Joudah, I., Beheshti, A., & Muller, S. (2024). Evaluating and enhancing artificial intelligence models for predicting student learning outcomes. *Informatics (MDPI)*, *11*(3), 46. DOI: 10.3390/informatics11030046

Farrokhnia, M., Banihashem, S. K., Noroozi, O., & Wals, A. (2024). A SWOT analysis of ChatGPT: Implications for educational practice and research. *Innovations in Education and Teaching International*, *61*(3), 460–474. DOI: 10.1080/14703297.2023.2195846

Fathahillah, F., Fakhri, M. M., & Ahmar, A. S. (2023). Analysis of artificial intelligence literacy in the blended learning model in higher education. *EduLine: Journal of Education and Learning Innovation, 3*(4), 566–575. DOI: 10.35877/454RI.eduline2049

Fazlul, I., Koedel, C., & Parsons, E. (2022). Using Predicted Academic Performance to Identify At-Risk Students in Public Schools. *Educational Evaluation and Policy Analysis*, , 01623737231212163.

Fernandes, C., & Nunes, D. (2023). Hybrid pedagogies for foundational literacy. *Literacy & Learning, 19*(2), 121–140.

Fernandez, L. (2023). Co-designing curricula with teachers and communities. *Journal of Curriculum Studies, 55*(4), 457–478.

Fernández, M., & Borges, R. (2023). Teacher training in blended AI contexts: Uruguay's experience. *Education in Latin America, 3*(1), 12–29.

Ferreira, & Alves (2024). Advances in blended learning research in Brazil. *Brazilian Journal of Educational Technology, 10*(1), 5-28.

Ferreira, . (2019). Evaluating educational sandboxes: Methods and findings. *Educational Research Quarterly, 42*(3), 201–219.

Ferreira, A., & Pereira, R. (2019). EduTec Paraná: A regional initiative. *Regional Education Policy Review, 2*(1), 14–36.

Ferrer, J., Ringer, A., Saville, K., Parris, M. A., & Kashi, K. (2020). Students' motivation and engagement in higher education: The importance of attitude to online learning. *Higher Education, 83*(2), 317–338. DOI: 10.1007/s10734-020-00657-5

Fleck, J. (2012). Blended learning and learning communities: Opportunities and challenges. *Journal of Management Development, 31*(4), 398–411. DOI: 10.1108/02621711211219059

Floridi, L. (2018). Ethics and AI: Foundations for policy. In *Ethics in AI: Theory and Practice* (pp. 1-22).

Floridi, L., Cowls, J., Beltrametti, M., Chatila, R., Chazerand, P., Dignum, V., Luetge, C., Madelin, R., Pagallo, U., Rossi, F., Schafer, B., Valcke, P., & Vayena, E. (2018). AI4People—An ethical framework for a good AI society: Opportunities, risks, principles, and recommendations. *Minds and Machines, 28*(4), 689–707. DOI: 10.1007/s11023-018-9482-5 PMID: 30930541

Fraile-Martinez, O., García-Montero, C., Fraile-Martinez, M., Pekarek, L., Barrena-Blázquez, S., López-González, L., Álvarez-Mon, M. A., Pekarek, T., Casanova, C., Álvarez-Mon, M., Saez, M. A., Diaz, R., & Ortega, M. A. (2025, March). From Greek paideia to modern educational systems: Evidence for the need to integrate physical activity into academic settings. []). Frontiers Media SA.]. *Frontiers in Education, 10*, 1541876. DOI: 10.3389/feduc.2025.1541876

Gadekallu, T. R., Yenduri, G., Kaluri, R., Rajput, D. S., Lakshmanna, K., Fang, K., Chen, J., & Wang, W. (2025). The role of GPT in promoting inclusive higher education for people with various learning disabilities: A review. *PeerJ. Computer Science, 11*, e2400. DOI: 10.7717/peerj-cs.2400 PMID: 40062249

Gao, R., Merzdorf, H. E., Anwar, S., Hipwell, M. C., & Srinivasa, A. (2023). Automatic assessment of text-based responses in post-secondary education: A systematic review. *Computers and Education: Artificial Intelligence, 6*, 100206. DOI: 10.1016/j.caeai.2024.100206

Gao, T. (2024). Research on the design of online gamified tourism education activities based on Moodle platform. *Entertainment Computing, 52*, 100823. DOI: 10.1016/j.entcom.2024.100823

Garcia, R. (2021). Evaluations of AI literacy programs. *Journal of Teacher Education, 72*(2), 170–189.

Garcia, S. (2023). Natural language processing for local languages. *Computational Linguistics for Education, 6*(2), 88–112.

Garrison, D. R., & Vaughan, N. D. (2008). *Blended learning in higher education: Framework, principles, and guidelines*. John Wiley & Sons.

Gašević, D., Dawson, S., & Siemens, G. (2015). Let's not forget: Learning analytics are about learning. *TechTrends, 59*(1), 64–71. DOI: 10.1007/s11528-014-0822-x

Ge, W., Sun, Y., Wang, Z., Zheng, H., He, W., Wang, P., . . . Wang, B. (2025). SRLAgent: Enhancing Self-Regulated Learning Skills through Gamification and LLM Assistance. arXiv preprint arXiv:2506.09968.

Gharkan, H. K., Radif, M. J., & Alsaeedi, A. H. (2025). Analysis of AI-empowered predictive models for predicting student performance in higher education. *Journal of Al-Qadisiyah for Computer Science and Mathematics, 17*(1), 103–121. DOI: 10.29304/jqcsm.2025.17.11967

Gikandi, J. W., Morrow, D., & Davis, N. E. (2011). Online formative assessment in higher education: A review of the literature. *Computers & Education, 57*(4), 2333–2351. DOI: 10.1016/j.compedu.2011.06.004

Gilbert, C., & Gilbert, M. A. (2024). The Role of Artificial Intelligence (AI) in Combatting Deepfakes and Digital Misinformation. *International Research Journal of Advanced Engineering and Science (ISSN: 2455-9024), 9*(4), 170-181.

Gkinko, L., & Elbanna, A. (2022). Hope, tolerance and empathy: Employees' emotions when using an AI-enabled chatbot in a digitalised workplace. *Information Technology & People, 35*(6), 1714–1743. DOI: 10.1108/ITP-04-2021-0328

Gligorea, I., Cioca, M., Oancea, R., Gorski, A. T., Gorski, H., & Tudorache, P. (2023). Adaptive learning using artificial intelligence in e-learning: A literature review. *Education Sciences, 13*(12), 1216. DOI: 10.3390/educsci13121216

Gobrecht, A., Tuma, F., Möller, M., Zöller, T., Zakhvatkin, M., Wuttig, A., Sommerfeldt, H., & Schütt, S. (2024). Beyond human subjectivity and error: A novel AI grading system Preprint. *arXiv*. https://doi.org//arXiv.2405.04323DOI: 10.48550

Goedhart, N. S., Blignaut-van Westrhenen, N., Moser, C., & Zweekhorst, M. B. (2019). The flipped classroom: Supporting a diverse group of students in their learning. *Learning Environments Research, 22*(2), 297–310. DOI: 10.1007/s10984-019-09281-2

Gökçearslan, S., Tosun, C., & Erdemir, Z. G. (2024). Benefits, challenges, and methods of artificial intelligence (AI) chatbots in education: A systematic literature review. *International Journal of Technology in Education, 7*(1), 19–39. DOI: 10.46328/ijte.600

Goldie, J. G. S. (2016). Connectivism: A knowledge learning theory for the digital age? *Medical Teacher, 38*(10), 1064–1069. DOI: 10.3109/0142159X.2016.1173661 PMID: 27128290

Gómez, L., & Martínez, P. (2024). Sandbox governance: Lessons from pilot programs. *Policy Pilots Review, 2*(1), 44–62.

González, A. (2024). Podcasting and blended delivery for digital citizenship. *Medical Education, 7*(1), 35–54.

González-Calatayud, V., Prendes-Espinosa, P., & Roig-Vila, R. (2021). Artificial intelligence for student assessment: A systematic review. *Applied Sciences (Basel, Switzerland), 11*(12), 5467. DOI: 10.3390/app11125467

González-Hernández, F., Zatarain-Cabada, R., Barrón-Estrada, M. L., & Rodríguez-Rangel, H. (2018). Recognition of learning-centered emotions using a convolutional neural network. *Journal of Intelligent & Fuzzy Systems, 34*(5), 3325–3336. DOI: 10.3233/JIFS-169514

Goodyear, P., & Retalis, S. (2010). *Technology-enhanced learning: Design patterns and pattern languages*. Brill. DOI: 10.1163/9789460910623

Graesser, A. C., Hu, X., Nye, B. D., VanLehn, K., Kumar, R., Heffernan, C., Heffernan, N., Woolf, B., Olney, A. M., Rus, V., Andrasik, F., Pavlik, P., Cai, Z., Wetzel, J., Morgan, B., Hampton, A. J., Lippert, A. M., Wang, L., Cheng, Q., & Baer, W. (2018). ElectronixTutor: An intelligent tutoring system with multiple learning resources for electronics. *International Journal of STEM Education*, *5*(1), 15. DOI: 10.1186/s40594-018-0110-y PMID: 30631705

Graham, C. R. (2013). Emerging practice and research in blended learning. In *Handbook of distance education* (pp. 333–350). Routledge. DOI: 10.4324/9780203803738.ch21

Greer, S., & Craddock, A. (2020). Community engagement in education policy design. *Public Participation Quarterly*, *6*(3), 73–96.

Gremsl, T., & Hödl, E. (2022). Emotional AI: Legal and ethical challenges1. *Information Polity*, *27*(2), 163–174. DOI: 10.3233/IP-211529

Grizzle, A. (2017). Teaching media literacy in schools. *Media Education Journal*, *9*(1), 7–24.

Grudin, J., & Jacques, R. (2019, May). Chatbots, humbots, and the quest for artificial general intelligence. In *Proceedings of the 2019 CHI conference on human factors in computing systems* (pp. 1-11). DOI: 10.1145/3290605.3300439

Guan, R., Raković, M., Chen, G., & Gašević, D. (2025). How educational chatbots support self-regulated learning? A systematic review of the literature. *Education and Information Technologies*, *30*(4), 4493–4518. DOI: 10.1007/s10639-024-12881-y

Gunawan, R. D., Sutisna, A., & Ana, E. F. (2024). Literature review: The role of learning management system (LMS) in improving the digital literacy of educators. *Jurnal Inovasi Teknologi Pendidikan*, *11*(2), 116–123.

Gunnam, G. R. (2024). *The Performance and AI Optimization Issues for Task-Oriented Chatbots* (Doctoral dissertation, The University of Texas at San Antonio).

Gupta, A., Lee, S., Mott, B., Chakraburty, S., Glazewski, K., Ottenbreit-Leftwich, A., Scribner, A., Hmelo-Silver, C. E., & Lester, J. (2024). Supporting upper elementary students in learning AI concepts with story-driven game-based learning. *Proceedings of the AAAI Conference on Artificial Intelligence*, *38*(21), 23092–23100. DOI: 10.1609/aaai.v38i21.30354

Gupta, R., & Patel, S. (2023). Infrastructure and blended learning in India. *Indian Journal of Educational Technology*, *14*(2), 112–135.

Guttentag, D. A. (2009). Virtual reality: Applications and implications for tourism. *Tourism Management*, *31*(5), 637–651. DOI: 10.1016/j.tourman.2009.07.003

Halpern, D. (2024). Civic education for the AI era. *Journal of Civic Learning*, *5*(1), 1–18.

Halverson, L. R., Spring, K. J., Huyett, S., Henrie, C. R., & Graham, C. R. (2023). Blended learning research in higher education and K-12 settings. In Learning, design, and technology: An international compendium of theory, research, practice, and policy (pp. 3107-3135). Cham: Springer international publishing.

Halverson, L. R., Graham, C. R., Spring, K. J., Drysdale, J. S., & Henrie, C. R. (2014). A thematic analysis of the most highly cited scholarship in the first decade of blended learning research. *The Internet and Higher Education*, *20*, 20–34. DOI: 10.1016/j.iheduc.2013.09.004

Harry, A. (2023). Role of AI in education. [INJURITY]. *Interdisciplinary Journal & Humanity*, *2*(3), 1–10.

Harsha, S., Chandrappa, S. R., Priyanga, P., & Bhavanishankar, K. (2024, December). Strategic teaching enhancement through predictive analysis for individuals (STEP.AI). In *2024 IEEE International Conference on Teaching, Assessment and Learning for Engineering (TALE)* (pp. 1–6). IEEE.

Hasal, M., Nowaková, J., Ahmed Saghair, K., Abdulla, H., Snášel, V., & Ogiela, L. (2021). Chatbots: Security, privacy, data protection, and social aspects. *Concurrency and Computation*, *33*(19), e6426. DOI: 10.1002/cpe.6426

Hassan, A., & Noor, K. (2023). Role of AI in lesson planning and formative assessment. *Assessment in Education: Principles, Policy & Practice*, *31*(2), 115–137.

Hassan, M., Fang, S., Malik, A. A., Lak, T. A., & Rizwan, M. (2023). Impact of perceived social support and psychological capital on university students' academic success: Testing the role of academic adjustment as a moderator. *BMC Psychology*, *11*(1), 340. DOI: 10.1186/s40359-023-01385-y PMID: 37849001

Hattie, J., & Timperley, H. (2007). The power of feedback. *Review of Educational Research*, *77*(1), 81–112. DOI: 10.3102/003465430298487

Haugeland, I. K. F., Følstad, A., Taylor, C., & Bjørkli, C. A. (2022). Understanding the user experience of customer service chatbots: An experimental study of chatbot interaction design. *International Journal of Human-Computer Studies, 161*, 102788. DOI: 10.1016/j.ijhcs.2022.102788

Haustein, S. (2016). Grand challenges in altmetrics: Heterogeneity, data quality and dependencies. *Scientometrics, 108*(1), 413–423. DOI: 10.1007/s11192-016-1910-9

Heffernan, N. T., & Heffernan, C. L. (2014). The ASSISTments ecosystem: Building a platform that brings scientists and teachers together for minimally invasive research on human learning and teaching. *International Journal of Artificial Intelligence in Education, 24*(4), 470–497. DOI: 10.1007/s40593-014-0024-x

He, T., Li, C., Wang, J., Wang, M., Wang, Z., & Jiao, C. (2022). An emotion analysis in learning environment based on theme-specified drawing by convolutional neural network. *Frontiers in Public Health, 10*, 958870. DOI: 10.3389/fpubh.2022.958870 PMID: 36408050

Hilton, M. L., & Pellegrino, J. W. (Eds.). (2012). *Education for life and work: Developing transferable knowledge and skills in the 21st century*. National Academies Press.

Hodges, C., Moore, S., Lockee, B., Trust, T., & Bond, A. (2020). The difference between emergency remote teaching and online learning. *EDUCAUSE Review, 27*(1), 1–9.

Hodgson, P., Lee, V. W. Y., Chan, J. C. S., Fong, A., Tang, C. S. Y., Chan, L., & Wong, C. (2019). Immersive Virtual Reality (IVR) in Higher Education: development and implementation. In *Progress in IS* (pp. 161–173). DOI: 10.1007/978-3-030-06246-0_12

Holmes, W., Bialik, M., & Fadel, C. (2019). Artificial Intelligence in Education: Promises and Implications for Teaching and learning. Center for Curriculum Redesign. https://circls.org/primers/artificial-intelligence-in-education-promises-and-implications-for-teaching-and-learning

Holmes, W., Bialik, M., & Fadel, C. (2019). *Artificial intelligence in education promises and implications for teaching and learning*. Center for Curriculum Redesign.

Holmes, W., Bialik, M., & Fadel, C. (2019). *Artificial intelligence in education: Promises and implications for teaching and learning*. Center for Curriculum Redesign.

Holmes, W., Bialik, M., & Fadel, C. (2019). *Artificial Intelligence in Education: Promises and Implications for Teaching and Learning*. Center for Curriculum Redesign.

Holmes, W., Persson, J., Chounta, I. A., Wasson, B., & Dimitrova, V. (2022). *Artificial intelligence and education: A critical view through the lens of human rights, democracy and the rule of law*. Council of Europe.

Holmes, W., Porayska-Pomsta, K., Holstein, K., Sutherland, E., Baker, T., Shum, S. B., Santos, O. C., Rodrigo, M. T., Cukurova, M., Bittencourt, I. I., & Koedinger, K. R. (2022). Ethics of AI in education: Towards a community-wide framework. *International Journal of Artificial Intelligence in Education*, *32*(3), 504–526. DOI: 10.1007/s40593-021-00239-1

Holmes, W., & Tuomi, I. (2022). State of the art and practice in AI in education. *European Journal of Education*, *57*(4), 542–570. DOI: 10.1111/ejed.12533

Holt, S. (2022). Virtual reality, augmented reality and mixed reality: For astronaut mental health; and space tourism, education and outreach. *Acta Astronautica*, *203*, 436–446. DOI: 10.1016/j.actaastro.2022.12.016

Hopfenbeck, T. N., Decristan, J., & Stoeckigt, G. (2023). Artificial intelligence and feedback: New tools for old problems. *Assessment in Education: Principles, Policy & Practice*, *30*(1), 10–28.

Hrastinski, S. (2008). Asynchronous and synchronous e-learning. *EDUCAUSE Quarterly*, *31*(4), 51–55.

Hsu, C. H. (2017). Tourism education on and beyond the horizon. *Tourism Management Perspectives*, *25*, 181–183. DOI: 10.1016/j.tmp.2017.11.022

Huang, A., De La Mora Velasco, E., & Haney, A. (2022). Examining Instructional Technologies in Hospitality and Tourism Education: A Systematic Review of literature. *Journal of Hospitality & Tourism Education*, *36*(2), 113–131. DOI: 10.1080/10963758.2022.2109480

Huang, H. M., Rauch, U., & Liaw, S. S. (2010). Investigating learners' attitudes toward virtual reality learning environments: Based on a constructivist approach. *Computers & Education*, *55*(3), 1171–1182. DOI: 10.1016/j.compedu.2010.05.014

Huang, X., Zou, D., Cheng, G., Chen, X., & Xie, H. (2023). Trends, research issues and applications of artificial intelligence in language education. *Journal of Educational Technology & Society*, *26*(1), 112–131.

Huawei, S., & Aryadoust, V. (2023). A systematic review of automated writing evaluation systems. *Education and Information Technologies*, *28*(1), 771–795. DOI: 10.1007/s10639-022-11200-7

Hwang, G.-J., Xie, H., Wah, B. W., & Gašević, D. (2020). Vision, challenges, roles and research issues of Artificial Intelligence in Education. *Computers and Education: Artificial Intelligence, 1*(100001), 100001. DOI: 10.1016/j.caeai.2020.100001

Hwang, S., & Kim, J. (2021). Toward a chatbot for financial sustainability. *Sustainability (Basel), 13*(6), 3173. DOI: 10.3390/su13063173

Ibrahim, O., & Adeyemi, S. (2023). Closing the digital divide: Policy lessons. *African Educational Review, 8*(3), 200–223.

Ifenthaler, D., & Yau, J. Y. K. (2020). Utilising learning analytics to support study success in higher education: A systematic review. *Educational Technology Research and Development, 68*(4), 1961–1990. DOI: 10.1007/s11423-020-09788-z

Ilieva, G., Yankova, T., Klisarova-Belcheva, S., Dimitrov, A., Bratkov, M., & Angelov, D. (2023). Effects of generative chatbots in higher education. *Information (Basel), 14*(9), 492. DOI: 10.3390/info14090492

Illi, C., & Elhassouny, A. (2025). Edu-Metaverse: A Comprehensive Review of Virtual Learning Environments. *IEEE Access : Practical Innovations, Open Solutions, 13*, 30186–30211. DOI: 10.1109/ACCESS.2025.3540944

Iqbal, A. I., Aamir, A., Hammad, A., Hafsa, H., Basit, A., Oduoye, M. O., Anis, M. W., Ahmed, S., Younus, M. I., & Jabeen, S. (2024). Immersive Technologies in Healthcare: An In-Depth exploration of virtual reality and augmented reality in enhancing patient care, medical education, and training paradigms. *Journal of Primary Care & Community Health, 15*, 21501319241293311. Advance online publication. DOI: 10.1177/21501319241293311 PMID: 39439304

Isaeva, R., Karasartova, N., Dznunusnalieva, K., Mirzoeva, K., & Mokliuk, M. (2025). Enhancing learning effectiveness through adaptive learning platforms and emerging computer technologies in education. *Jurnal Ilmiah Ilmu Terapan Universitas Jambi, 9*(1), 144–160. DOI: 10.22437/jiituj.v9i1.37967

Islam, M., & Chowdhury, F. (2024). Assistive AI and accessibility standards. *International Journal of Inclusive Education, 28*(4), 401–420.

ISTE. (2022). *ISTE Standards for educators*. International Society for Technology in Education. https://www.iste.org/standards/for-educators

Jagatheesaperumal, S. K., Ahmad, K., Al-Fuqaha, A., & Qadir, J. (2024). Advancing education through extended reality and internet of everything enabled metaverses: Applications, challenges, and open issues. *IEEE Transactions on Learning Technologies, 17*, 1120–1139. DOI: 10.1109/TLT.2024.3358859

Jahadakbar, M., & Yao, M. Z. (2025, January). The Routine: Enhancing Special Needs Education Through AI-Personalized Embodied Learning in Virtual Environments. In *2025 IEEE International Conference on Artificial Intelligence and eXtended and Virtual Reality (AIxVR)* (pp. 176-182). IEEE. DOI: 10.1109/AIxVR63409.2025.00034

Jennings, G., Cater, C. I., Hales, R., Kensbock, S., & Hornby, G. (2015). Partnering for real world learning, sustainability, tourism education. *Quality Assurance in Education, 23*(4), 378–394. DOI: 10.1108/QAE-03-2015-0010

Jin, S. H., Im, K., Yoo, M., Roll, I., & Seo, K. (2023). Supporting students' self-regulated learning in online learning using artificial intelligence applications. *International Journal of Educational Technology in Higher Education, 20*(1), 37. DOI: 10.1186/s41239-023-00406-5

Jin, Y., Yan, L., Echeverria, V., Gašević, D., & Martinez-Maldonado, R. (2025). Generative AI in higher education: A global perspective of institutional adoption policies and guidelines. *Computers and Education: Artificial Intelligence, 8*, 100348. DOI: 10.1016/j.caeai.2024.100348

Jobin, A., Ienca, M., & Vayena, E. (2019). The global landscape of AI ethics guidelines. *Nature Machine Intelligence, 1*(9), 389–399. DOI: 10.1038/s42256-019-0088-2

Johann, D. A., Nunes, A. D. F. P., Santos, G. B. D., Silva, D. J. C. D., Bresciani, S. A. T., & Lopes, L. F. D. (2020). Mapping of scientific production on design thinking as a tool for entrepreneurship education: A bibliometric study of a decade. *World Journal of Entrepreneurship, Management and Sustainable Development, 16*(4), 271–285. DOI: 10.1108/WJEMSD-05-2019-0028

Johnson-Glenberg, M. C. (2018). Immersive VR and education: Embodied design principles that include gesture and hand controls. *Frontiers in Robotics and AI, 5*, 375272. DOI: 10.3389/frobt.2018.00081 PMID: 33500960

Johnson, L., Becker, S. A., Cummins, M., Estrada, V., Freeman, A., & Hall, C. (2016). *NMC Horizon Report: 2016 Higher Education Edition*. The New Media Consortium.

Johnson, L., & Sato, Y. (2023). Adaptive platforms and student self-regulation. *Education and Information Technologies, 28*(5), 5431–5449.

Joksimovic, S., Ifenthaler, D., Marrone, R., De Laat, M., & Siemens, G. (2023). Opportunities of artificial intelligence for supporting complex problem-solving: Findings from a scoping review. *Computers and Education: Artificial Intelligence, 4*, 100138. DOI: 10.1016/j.caeai.2023.100138

Jonassen, D. H., & Rohrer-Murphy, L. (1999). Activity theory as a framework for designing constructivist learning environments. *Educational Technology Research and Development, 47*(1), 61–79. DOI: 10.1007/BF02299477

Jones, L., & Mitchell, K. (2016). Recognising bias in automated systems: Educational implications. *Journal of Media Literacy, 11*(2), 45–62.

Jose, B., Cherian, J., Verghis, A. M., Varghise, S. M., S, M., & Joseph, S. (2025). The cognitive paradox of AI in education: Between enhancement and erosion. *Frontiers in Psychology, 16*, 1550621. DOI: 10.3389/fpsyg.2025.1550621 PMID: 40297599

Jose, J., & Jose, B. J. (2024). Educators' academic insights on artificial intelligence: Challenges and opportunities. *Electronic Journal of e-Learning, 22*(2), 59–77. DOI: 10.34190/ejel.21.5.3272

Joshi, D., Zalte, S. M., Johny, K. R., & Mahajan, D. A. (2023). The impact of blended learning on student engagement in the digital era. *European Chemical Bulletin, 12*(1), 727–735.

Joshi, P., & Patel, R. (2022). Teacher certification pathways for edtech. *Journal of Professional Development in Education, 48*(4), 310–329.

Jovanović, J., Gašević, D., Dawson, S., Pardo, A., & Mirriahi, N. (2017). Learning analytics to unveil learning strategies in a flipped classroom. *The Internet and Higher Education, 33*, 74–85. DOI: 10.1016/j.iheduc.2017.02.001

Kabir, K., & Olawale, T. (2024). Regional AI policy frameworks: Case studies in South-South cooperation. *Global Policy, 15*(1), 88–103.

Kabudi, T., Pappas, I., & Olsen, D. H. (2021). AI-enabled adaptive learning systems: A systematic mapping of the literature. Computers and education. *Artificial Intelligence, 2*, 100017.

Kaliisa, R., & Dolonen, J. A. (2023). CADA: A teacher-facing learning analytics dashboard to foster teachers' awareness of students' participation and discourse patterns in online discussions. Technology. *Knowledge and Learning, 28*(3), 937–958. DOI: 10.1007/s10758-022-09598-7

Kalkstein, D. A., & Rheubert, R. A. (2024). Implementing weekly mastery quizzes in a blended learning environment. *Journal of Educational Technology, 45*(2), 145–162.

Kallou, S., & Kikilia, A. (2021). A transformative educational framework in tourism higher education through digital technologies during the COVID-19 pandemic. *Advances in Mobile Learning Educational Research, 1*(2), 37–47. DOI: 10.25082/AMLER.2021.01.005

Kanthimathi, S., Nanda, P., Venkatraman, S., Renganayagan, V., & Eswaran, S. (2025). *Transforming Education through AI-Powered Personalized Assessment Models Adopting Artificial Intelligence Tools in Higher Education*. CRC Press.

Karroum, S. Y. A., Elshaiekh, N. E. M., & Al-Hijji, K. Z. (2024). Exploring the role of artificial Intelligence in education: Assessing advantages and disadvantages for learning outcomes and pedagogical practices. *International Journal of Innovative Research in Engineering & Multidisciplinary Physical Sciences*, *12*(4), 231000. Advance online publication. DOI: 10.37082/IJIRMPS.v12.i4.231000

Kasneci, E., Seßler, K., Küchemann, S., Bannert, M., Dementieva, D., Fischer, F., Gasser, U., Groh, G., Günnemann, S., Hüllermeier, E., Krusche, S., Kutyniok, G., Michaeli, T., Nerdel, C., Pfeffer, J., Poquet, O., Sailer, M., Schmidt, A., Seidel, T., & Kasneci, G. (2023). ChatGPT for good? On opportunities and challenges of large language models for education. *Learning and Individual Differences*, *103*, 102274. DOI: 10.1016/j.lindif.2023.102274

Kaur, A., & Singh, P. (2023). Blended learning frameworks: Evidence from India. *Asian Journal of Education Studies*, *21*(1), 55–79.

Kaur, S., Budhraja, K., Pahuja, A., Nayyar, V., & Saluja, S. (2024). Leveraging artificial intelligence in education: Enhancing learning experience. In *Ethical AI and Data Management Strategies in Marketing* (pp. 140–155). IGI Global Scientific Publishing. DOI: 10.4018/979-8-3693-6660-8.ch010

Kavita, S. (2024). Co-design practices in curriculum adaptation for AI. *Curriculum Innovations*, *2*(2), 101–123.

Kayyali, M. (2024 a). Global Perspectives on Personalized Learning: Case Studies and Best Practices. In Transforming Education for Personalized Learning (pp. 66-84). IGI Global.

Kayyali, M. (2025 b). Digital Literacy for Sustainability: Preparing Students for the AI-Driven World. In Rethinking the Pedagogy of Sustainable Development in the AI Era (pp. 197-224). IGI Global Scientific Publishing.

Kayyali, M. (2026 a). Online and Blended Learning in Doctoral Studies: Opportunities and Challenges. Improving Doctoral Education and Research Development for Sustainability, 103-138.

Kayyali, M. (2026 b). Ethical AI and Automation in the Workplace. In Leading Inclusive Workplaces Through Digital Transformation and Organizational Change (pp. 103-138). IGI Global Scientific Publishing.

Kayyali, M. (2026 c). AI in Higher Education: The Risk of Excluding Vulnerable Learners. In AI and New Forms of Exclusion (pp. 57-82). IGI Global Scientific Publishing.

Kayyali, M. (2026 d). The Impact of AI on Classroom Dynamics in Higher Education: Shifting Roles for Professors and Students. In Responsible AI Integration in Education (pp. 151-180). IGI Global Scientific Publishing.

Kayyali, M. (2024 b). Quality Assurance in Online and Blended Learning Environments. In *Quality Assurance and Accreditation in Higher Education: Issues, Models, and Best Practices* (pp. 227–292). Springer Nature Switzerland. DOI: 10.1007/978-3-031-66623-0_5

Kayyali, M. (2025 a). The Impact of Personalized Learning on Student Engagement and Achievement in STEAM. In *Integrating Personalized Learning Methods Into STEAM Education* (pp. 51–78). IGI Global Scientific Publishing. DOI: 10.4018/979-8-3693-7718-5.ch003

Kedi, W. E., Ejimuda, C., Idemudia, C., & Ijomah, T. I. (2024). AI Chatbot integration in SME marketing platforms: Improving customer interaction and service efficiency. *International Journal of Management & Entrepreneurship Research*, *6*(7), 2332–2341. DOI: 10.51594/ijmer.v6i7.1327

Kellogg, S. P. (2021). The Mountain in the Machine: Optimization and the Landscapes of Machine Learning. *Culture Machine*, , 20.

Kemp, J. (2023). Child-centred design for educational platforms. *Child Data Protection Review*, *1*(1), 10–30.

Kerr, M. (2020). AI hallucinations and education: Identifying false outputs. *Educational Technology Insights*, *4*(2), 39–57.

Khine, M. S. (2024). Using AI for adaptive learning and adaptive assessment. In *Artificial Intelligence in Education: A Machine-Generated Literature Overview* (pp. 341–466). Springer Nature Singapore. DOI: 10.1007/978-981-97-9350-1_3

Kimmons, R., & Hall, C. (2020). Professional learning and development for educational technology integration: The role of teacher learning communities. *Journal of Research on Technology in Education*, *52*(3), 309–326. DOI: 10.1080/15391523.2020.1729387

King, P., & Kitchener, R. (2024). Ethical reasoning in AI education. *Journal of Moral Education*, *53*(2), 145–166.

Kobets, V., & Kozlovskyi, K. (2022). Application of chat bots for personalized financial advice. *Herald of Advanced Information Technology*, *5*(3), 229–242. DOI: 10.15276/hait.05.2022.18

Koç, M., Liu, X., & Wachira, P. (2015). Assessment strategies in online and blended learning. *Journal of Digital Learning*, *29*(4), 201–216.

Koedinger, K. R., & Corbett, A. (2006). *Cognitive tutors: Technology bringing learning sciences to the classroom*. 61–77.

Koedinger, K. R., Anderson, J. R., Hadley, W. H., & Mark, M. A. (1997). Intelligent tutoring goes to school in the big city. *International Journal of Artificial Intelligence in Education*, *8*, 30–43.

Kolluru, V., Mungara, S., & Chintakunta, A. N. (2018). Adaptive learning systems: Harnessing AI for customized educational experiences. *International Journal of Computer Science and Information Technologies*, *6*(3), 13–26. DOI: 10.5121/ijcsity.2018.6302

Kooli, C. (2023). Chatbots in education and research: A critical examination of ethical implications and solutions. *Sustainability (Basel)*, *15*(7), 5614. DOI: 10.3390/su15075614

Korda, D. R., Dapaah, E. O., & Akolgo, E. A. (2024). The Role of AI Chatbots in Education: A Review. *Academy Journal of Science and Engineering*, *18*(1), 79–87.

Kort, B., Reilly, R., & Picard, R. W. (2002). An affective model of interplay between emotions and learning: reengineering educational pedagogy-building a learning companion. *Proceedings IEEE International Conference on Advanced Learning Technologies*.

Kostadimas, D., Kasapakis, V., & Kotis, K. (2025). A Systematic Review on the Combination of VR, IoT and AI Technologies, and Their Integration in Applications. *Future Internet*, *17*(4), 163. DOI: 10.3390/fi17040163

Koumpouros, Y. (2024). Revealing the true potential and prospects of augmented reality in education. *Smart Learning Environments*, *11*(1), 2. Advance online publication. DOI: 10.1186/s40561-023-00288-0

Kozlowski, D. (2023). Avoiding overregulation while promoting innovation. *Regulation & Education*, *3*(1), 29–48.

Kuhail, M. A., Alturki, N., Alramlawi, S., & Alhejori, K. (2023). Interacting with educational chatbots: A systematic review. *Education and Information Technologies*, *28*(1), 973–1018. DOI: 10.1007/s10639-022-11177-3

Kuh, G. D., Kinzie, J., Schuh, J. H., & Whitt, E. J. (2011). *Student success in college: Creating conditions that matter*. John Wiley & Sons.

Kumar, D. (2024). Ai-driven automation in administrative processes: Enhancing efficiency and accuracy. *International Journal of Engineering Science and Humanities, 14*(Special1), 256–265. DOI: 10.62904/qg004437

Kumar, A., & Das, S. (2023). Local content integration in edtech. *Education & Culture Journal, 16*(3), 213–236.

Kumar, A., Krishnamurthi, R., Bhatia, S., Kaushik, K., Ahuja, N. J., Nayyar, A., & Masud, M. (2021). Blended learning tools and practices: A comprehensive analysis. *IEEE Access : Practical Innovations, Open Solutions*, *9*, 85151–85197. DOI: 10.1109/ACCESS.2021.3085844

Kumar, J. A. (2021). Educational chatbots for project-based learning: Investigating learning outcomes for a team-based design course. *International Journal of Educational Technology in Higher Education*, *18*(1), 65. DOI: 10.1186/s41239-021-00302-w PMID: 34926790

Kumar, S., & Jain, M. (2024). Mobile-first AI tools for low-bandwidth settings. *International Journal of Mobile Learning*, *13*(1), 1–22.

Kumar, S., Rao, P., Singhania, S., Verma, S., & Kheterpal, M. (2024). Will artificial intelligence drive the advancements in higher education? A tri-phased exploration. *Technological Forecasting and Social Change*, *201*, 123258. DOI: 10.1016/j.techfore.2024.123258

Kushwaha, U. (2024). 17 EMPOWERING EVERY ABILITY: PERSONALIZED LEARNING PATHS IN FUTURE-SPECIAL EDUCATION. Future of Special Education in India, 217.

Kvale, S., & Brinkmann, S. (2009). *Interviews: Learning the craft of qualitative research interviewing*. sage.

Labadze, L., Grigolia, M., & Machaidze, L. (2023). Role of AI chatbots in education: Systematic literature review. *International Journal of Educational Technology in Higher Education*, *20*(1), 56. DOI: 10.1186/s41239-023-00426-1

Lam, H. (2024). Personalisation algorithms and student motivation. *Journal of the Learning Sciences*, *33*(1), 77–99.

Lechuga, C. G., & Doroudi, S. (2023). Three algorithms for grouping students: A bridge between personalized tutoring system data and classroom pedagogy. *International Journal of Artificial Intelligence in Education, 33*(4), 843–884. DOI: 10.1007/s40593-022-00309-y

Lee, G. G., Mun, S., Shin, M. K., & Zhai, X. (2023). *Collaborative learning with artificial intelligence speakers (CLAIS): Pre-service elementary science teachers' responses to the prototype*. arXiv preprint arXiv:2401.05400.

Lee, H. Y., Chen, P. H., Wang, W. S., Huang, Y. M., & Wu, T. T. (2024). Empowering ChatGPT with guidance mechanism in blended learning: Effect of self-regulated learning, higher-order thinking skills, and knowledge construction. *International Journal of Educational Technology in Higher Education, 21*(1), 16. DOI: 10.1186/s41239-024-00447-4

Lee, J., & Park, S. (2023). Real-time monitoring for policy evaluation. *Education Policy Analytics, 6*(2), 88–110.

Lekota, N., & Mthembu, S. (2023). Funding inclusive technologies in schools. *South African Journal of Education Technology, 5*(2), 44–63.

Leong, W. Y. (2025, March). Enhancing academic integrity in e-exams through AI-powered proctoring. In *2025 IEEE International Conference on Educational Technology (ICET)* (pp. 10–15). IEEE.

Liang, A. R. (2021). Examining the factors of experiential learning and teaching style: A case study of a hospitality and tourism program. *Journal of Hospitality, Leisure, Sport and Tourism Education, 29*, 100332. DOI: 10.1016/j.jhlste.2021.100332

Liang, H., Hwang, G., Hsu, T., & Yeh, J. (2024). Effect of an AI-based chatbot on students' learning performance in alternate reality game-based museum learning. *British Journal of Educational Technology, 55*(5), 2315–2338. DOI: 10.1111/bjet.13448

Liao, C. H., & Wu, J. Y. (2022). Deploying multimodal learning analytics models to explore the impact of digital distraction and peer learning on student performance. *Computers & Education, 190*, 104599. DOI: 10.1016/j.compedu.2022.104599

Li, C. T., & Hou, H. T. (2024). Remote Blended Game-Based Learning: Integrating Synchronous Game-Based Learning with Asynchronous Inquiry-Based Learning. *Journal of Science Education and Technology, 33*(5), 746–758. DOI: 10.1007/s10956-024-10118-8

Lien, A. K., Randem, L. M., Taralrud, H. P. F., & Edalati, M. (2022). Implementing a Chatbot So-lution for Learning Management System. *arXiv*, arXiv:2206.13187. [**Google Scholar**]

Li, L. (2022). Students' isolation challenges in blended EFL learning during covid-19: How can social presence and interaction help develop sense of community? *Psychology Research and Behavior Management, 2022*, 3117–3131. DOI: 10.2147/PRBM.S388317 PMID: 36317089

Lima, C., & Torres, P. (2021). University-school partnerships for AI literacy. *Higher Education & Community Engagement, 12*(4), 211–234.

Lima, D., & Souza, R. (2021). LabAI Educação: Piloting blended AI curricula. *Brazilian Educational Research Review, 7*(3), 150–173.

Limniou, M., & Smith, M. (2010). Teachers' and students' perspectives on teaching and learning through virtual learning environments. *European Journal of Engineering Education, 35*(6), 645–653. DOI: 10.1080/03043797.2010.505279

Lin, C. J., & Mubarok, H. (2021). Learning analytics for investigating the mind map-guided AI chatbot approach in an EFL flipped speaking classroom. *Journal of Educational Technology & Society, 24*(4), 16–35.

Lin, C.-C., Huang, A. Y. Q., & Lu, O. H. T. (2023). Artificial intelligence in intelligent tutoring systems toward sustainable education: A systematic review. *Smart Learning Environments, 10*(1), 41. DOI: 10.1186/s40561-023-00260-y

Li, S., & Wang, W. (2022). Effect of blended learning on student performance in K-12 settings: A meta-analysis. *Journal of Computer Assisted Learning, 38*(5), 1254–1272. DOI: 10.1111/jcal.12696

Liu, C.-C., Lin, Y.-Y., Lo, F.-y., Chang, C.-H., & Lin, H.-M. (2025). From readers to players: Exploring student engagement in a gamified metaverse and its effect on reading interest. *Education and Information Technologies, 30*(1), 421–447. DOI: 10.1007/s10639-024-13068-1

Livingstone, S. (2021). Media literacy and digital citizenship in schools. *Journal of Medical Education, 18*(2), 98–117.

Li, Y. F., Guan, J. Q., Wang, X. F., Chen, Q., & Hwang, G. J. (2024). Examining students' self-regulated learning processes and performance in an immersive virtual environment. *Journal of Computer Assisted Learning, 40*(6), 2948–2963. DOI: 10.1111/jcal.13047

Li, Y., Zhou, X., Yin, H. B., & Chiu, T. K. (2025). Design language learning with artificial intelligence (AI) chatbots based on activity theory from a systematic review. *Smart Learning Environments*, *12*(1), 24. DOI: 10.1186/s40561-025-00379-0

Lo, C. K. (2023). What is the impact of ChatGPT on education? A rapid review of the literature. [Google Scholar] [CrossRef]. *Education Sciences*, *13*(4), 410. DOI: 10.3390/educsci13040410

Lodhavia, J., Jain, V., Gupta, A., Prabhu, H., & Pandit, A. (2020, July). User-profiling based e-learning system using question adaptation. In *2020 Second International Conference on Inventive Research in Computing Applications (ICIRCA)* (pp. 723–728). IEEE. DOI: 10.1109/ICIRCA48905.2020.9183068

Lomer, S., & Palmer, E. (2021). 'I didn't know this was actually stuff that could help us, with actually learning': Student perceptions of Active Blended Learning. *Teaching in Higher Education*, *28*(4), 679–698. DOI: 10.1080/13562517.2020.1852202

Lopes, J., & Andrade, M. (2023). EducaAI and regional rollouts: An impact study. *Journal of Educational Technology & Society*, *26*(1), 77–100.

Lopez, P., & Valdés, R. (2023). Asynchronous supports in blended models. *Journal of Distance Education*, *14*(2), 59–78.

Luckin, R. (2017). Towards artificial intelligence-based assessment systems. *Nature Human Behaviour, 1*(3), 0028.

Luckin, R., & Holmes, W. (2016). Intelligence unleashed: An argument for AI in education.

Luckin, R., & Holmes, W. (2023). A pedagogical perspective on AI in classrooms. Cambridge Education Press.

Luckin, R., Cukurova, M., Kent, C., & Du Boulay, B. (2022). Empowering educators to be AI-ready. *Computers and Education: Artificial Intelligence*, *3*, 100076.

Luckin, R., Holmes, W., Griffiths, M., & Forcier, L. B. (2016). *Intelligence unleashed: An argument for AI in education*. Pearson Education.

Lui, A. L., Not, C., & Wong, G. K. (2023). Theory-based learning design with immersive virtual reality in science education: A systematic review. *Journal of Science Education and Technology*, *32*(3), 390–432. DOI: 10.1007/s10956-023-10035-2

Maas, M. J., & Hughes, J. M. (2020). Virtual, augmented and mixed reality in K–12 education: A review of the literature. *Technology, Pedagogy and Education*, *29*(2), 231–249. DOI: 10.1080/1475939X.2020.1737210

Maghaydah, S., Al-Emran, M., Maheshwari, P., & Al-Sharafi, M. A. (2024). Factors affecting metaverse adoption in education: A systematic review, adoption framework, and future research agenda. *Heliyon, 10*(7), e28602. DOI: 10.1016/j.heliyon.2024.e28602 PMID: 38576548

Maity, S., & Deroy, A. (2024). Human-Centric eXplainable AI in Education. *arXiv preprint arXiv:2410.19822*. DOI: 10.35542/osf.io/k5u9b

Makarenko, O., Borysenko, O., Horokhivska, T., Kozub, V., & Yaremenko, D. (2024). Embracing artificial intelligence in education: Shaping the learning path for future professionals. Multidisciplinary Science Journal, 6.

Mak, B., Lau, C., & Wong, A. (2017). Effects of experiential learning on students: An ecotourism service-learning course. *Journal of Teaching in Travel & Tourism*, •••, 1–16. DOI: 10.1080/15313220.2017.1285265

Makransky, G., & Lilleholt, L. (2018). A structural equation modeling investigation of the emotional value of immersive virtual reality in education. *Educational Technology Research and Development, 66*(5), 1141–1164. DOI: 10.1007/s11423-018-9581-2

Mallik, S., & Gangopadhyay, A. (2023). Proactive and reactive engagement of artificial intelligence methods for education: A review. *Frontiers in Artificial Intelligence, 6*, 1151391. DOI: 10.3389/frai.2023.1151391 PMID: 37215064

Margulieux, L. E., McCracken, W. M., & Catrambone, R. (2016). A design for synthesis of asynchronous online and face-to-face learning environments. *Educational Technology Research and Development, 64*(4), 969–988.

Mariam, G., Adil, L., & Zakaria, B. (2024). The integration of artificial intelligence (ai) into education systems and its impact on the governance of higher education institutions. *International Journal of Professional Business Review: Int. J. Prof. Bus. Rev., 9*(12), 13.

Mariyono, D., & Nur Alif Hd, A. (2025). AI's role in transforming learning environments: A review of collaborative approaches and innovations. *Quality Education for All, 2*(1), 265–288. DOI: 10.1108/QEA-08-2024-0071

Marshall, S. J. (2018). *Shaping the university of the future*. Springer., DOI: 10.1007/978-981-10-7620-6

Martins, A., & Lima, B. (2020). Iterative policymaking and education sandboxes. *Innovation in Public Policy, 5*(1), 21–42.

Martins, A., & Lima, B. (2021). Teacher feedback loops in AI pilots. *Journal of Educational Experimentation, 9*(2), 66–90.

Matthews, G., Cumings, R., De Los Santos, E. P., Feng, I. Y., & Mouloua, S. A. (2025). A new era for stress research: Supporting user performance and experience in the digital age. *Ergonomics*, *68*(6), 913–946. DOI: 10.1080/00140139.2024.2425953 PMID: 39520089

Maumbe, K. (2014). Teaching and Learning in Recreation and Tourism: A comparison of three instructional methods. *Journal of Teaching in Travel & Tourism*, *14*(4), 365–385. DOI: 10.1080/15313220.2014.955305

Mayaka, M., & Akama, J. S. (2006). Systems approach to tourism training and education: The Kenyan case study. *Tourism Management*, *28*(1), 298–306. DOI: 10.1016/j.tourman.2005.12.023

Mayer, R. E. (2011). Multimedia learning and games. In Tobias, S., & Fletcher, J. D. (Eds.), *Computer games and instruction* (pp. 281–308). IAP.

Mayer, R. E., & Moreno, R. (2003). Nine ways to reduce cognitive load in multimedia learning. *Educational Psychologist*, *38*(1), 43–52. DOI: 10.1207/S15326985EP3801_6

McGrath, C., Farazouli, A., & Cerratto-Pargman, T. (2024). Generative AI chatbots in higher education: A review of an emerging research area. *Higher Education*, •••, 1–17.

McMurtry, A. (2024). Learning theory and interdisciplinarity: reframing learning in terms of evolving coherences rather than "true" representations or correspondences. In *Handbook of Interdisciplinary Teaching and Administration* (pp. 13–24). Edward Elgar Publishing. DOI: 10.4337/9781035309870.00009

McStay, A. (2023). The metaverse: Surveillant physics, virtual realist governance, and the missing commons. *Philosophy & Technology*, *36*(1), 13. DOI: 10.1007/s13347-023-00613-y

McTear, M. (2022). *Conversational ai: Dialogue systems, conversational agents, and chatbots*. Springer Nature.

Medeiros, F., & Almeida, G. (2019). Open-source pilots for rural schooling. *Rural Education Innovation*, *3*(1), 22–44.

Mehrabi, N., Morstatter, F., Saxena, N., Lerman, K., & Galstyan, A. (2021). A Survey on Bias and Fairness in Machine Learning. *ACM Computing Surveys*, *54*(6), 1–35. DOI: 10.1145/3457607

Mehta, S., & Rao, V. (2023). Co-creation for scalable education reforms. *Public Policy & Education*, *10*(3), 210–233.

Memon, F. N., & Memon, S. N. (2025). *Digital Divide and Equity in Education: Bridging Gaps to Ensure Inclusive Learning Impact of Digitalization on Education and Social Sustainability*. IGI Global.

Menon, P., & Patel, S. (2024). Procurement practices for ethically aligned AI. *Public Administration & Technology*, *11*(1), 88–107.

Metaverse, I. (2025). Exploring the Future of Education: Integrating Metaverse and AI Tools to Enhance Learning Experiences.

Mhlanga, E. (2023). Blended learning success factors in Africa. *African Journal of Educational Technology*, *5*(2), 30–52.

Michael, J., McMichael, J., & Vrugtman, J. (2014, March). Machine learning for continuous formative assessment. In *Proceedings of the 4th International Conference on Learning Analytics and Knowledge* (pp. 250–254). ACM.

Mínguez, C., Martínez-Hernández, C., & Yubero, C. (2021). Higher education and the sustainable tourism pedagogy: Are tourism students ready to lead change in the post pandemic era? *Journal of Hospitality, Leisure, Sport and Tourism Education*, *29*, 100329. DOI: 10.1016/j.jhlste.2021.100329

Mishra, P., & Koehler, M. J. (2006). Technological pedagogical content knowledge: A framework for teacher knowledge. *Teachers College Record*, *108*(6), 1017–1054. DOI: 10.1111/j.1467-9620.2006.00684.x

Mitani, H., Honda, Y., Narita, K., Nakamura, Y., Morishita, S., Kondo, S., & Higaki, T. (2025). Effectiveness of a virtual reality-based interventional radiology simulator for medical student education. *Japanese Journal of Radiology*, *43*(8), 1–7. DOI: 10.1007/s11604-025-01771-z PMID: 40156739

Mitra, U., & Rehman, S. U. (2025) a Integrating AI/ML With Wearable Devices for Monitoring Student Mental Health. In *Wearable Devices and Smart Technology for Educational Teaching Assistance* (pp. 257-284). IGI Global Scientific Publishing.

Mitra, U., & Rehman, S. U. (2025) b. Significance of AI/ML Wearable Technologies for Education and Teaching. In *Wearable Devices and Smart Technology for Educational Teaching Assistance* (pp. 1-26). IGI Global Scientific Publishing.

Mitra, S., & Rajan, P. (2024). Accessible AI features for learners with disabilities. *Disability and Education Journal*, *6*(1), 14–36.

Moallem, M. (2015). The impact of synchronous and asynchronous communication tools on learner self-regulation, social presence, immediacy, intimacy and satisfaction in collaborative online learning. *The Online Journal of Distance Education and e-Learning : TOJDEL, 3*(3), 55–77.

Mohanty, B. S., Shaikh, Z. H., Mahapatra, D. M., Ratnakaranm, S., & Manikeswari, D. (2025). Wearable technologies in education: Advantages, limitations, and technical difficulties. In *Wearable devices and smart technology for educational teaching assistance* (pp. 309–330). IGI Global Scientific Publishing.

Morrison, G. R., Ross, S. J., Morrison, J. R., & Kalman, H. K. (2019). *Designing effective instruction* (8th ed.). John Wiley & Sons.

Moyo, T., & Banda, L. (2024). Edtech adoption and teacher identity. *Teaching & Learning in Africa, 7*(1), 78–98.

Mukherjee & Sharma (2023). Extending data protection laws to education: Options for low-capacity governments. *Legal Review of Educational Policy, 1*(1), 1-18.

Mukherjee, D., & Sen, A. (2022). NLP and local dialects in edtech. *Comparative Education Review, 3*(2), 44–66.

Müller, C., & Mildenberger, T. Facilitating flexible learning by replacing classroom time with an online learning environment: A systematic review of blended learning in higher education, Educational Research Review, Volume 34, 2021, 100394, ISSN 1747-938X, DOI: 10.1016/j.edurev.2021.100394

Mwangi, P., & Karanja, T. (2023). Case study: Kenya's Digital Literacy Programme. *East African Education Review, 6*(2), 102–126.

Naik, I., Naik, D., & Naik, N. (2023, September). Demystifying the working, types, benefits and limitations of chatbots. In *UK Workshop on Computational Intelligence* (pp. 558-566). Cham: Springer Nature Switzerland.

Narayanan, R., & Luo, H. (2024). Evaluating Squirrel AI and Century Tech in STEM. *Journal of Adaptive Learning Systems, 11*(1), 12–34.

Nascimento, F. (2023). Hybrid classroom outcomes from Brazil pilots. *Educational Field Trials, 2*(1), 45–72.

Navarro, L. (2022). Community-based digital inclusion programs. *Community Education Research, 8*(3), 181–203.

Ncube, T., & Hlongwane, S. (2023). Embedding ethical AI in procurement: Practical steps. *Public Procurement & Ethics, 4*(2), 60–84.

Neophytou, R., Liasidou, S., Pipyros, K., & Christofi, A. (2025). Artificial intelligence driven adaptive learning methods in sustainable tourism education. *Worldwide Hospitality and Tourism Themes*, *17*(1), 120–131. Advance online publication. DOI: 10.1108/WHATT-12-2024-0308

Neto, A. J. M., & Fernandes, M. A. (2019, July). Chatbot and conversational analysis to promote collaborative learning in distance education. In 2019 IEEE 19th International Conference on Advanced Learning Technologies (ICALT) (Vol. 2161, pp. 324-326). IEEE.

Ng, D. T. K., Lee, M., Tan, R. J. Y., Hu, X., Downie, J. S., & Chu, S. K. W. (2022). A review of AI teaching and learning from 2000 to 2020. *Education and Information Technologies*. Advance online publication. DOI: 10.1007/s10639-022-11491-w

Nguyen, H., & Liu, J. (2023). Professional development models for AI literacy. *International Journal of Teacher Education*, *14*(2), 101–123.

Nguyen, Q. H., Nguyen, M. H., & Nguyen, T. T. (2022). AI-based Online Exam Proctoring: Techniques, Challenges, and Future Directions. *IEEE Access : Practical Innovations, Open Solutions*, *10*, 123456–123472. DOI: 10.1109/ACCESS.2022.3156789

Nguyen, Q. N., Sidorova, A., & Torres, R. (2022). User interactions with chatbot interfaces vs. Menu-based interfaces: An empirical study. *Computers in Human Behavior*, *128*, 107093. DOI: 10.1016/j.chb.2021.107093

Nicol, D. J., & Macfarlane-Dick, D. (2006). Formative assessment and self-regulated learning: A model and seven principles of good feedback practice. *Studies in Higher Education*, *31*(2), 199–218. DOI: 10.1080/03075070600572090

Niloy, A. C., Hafiz, R., Hossain, B. M. T., Gulmeher, F., Sultana, N., Islam, K. F., Bushra, F., Islam, S., Hoque, S. I., Rahman, M. A., & Kabir, S. (2024). AI chatbots: A disguised enemy for academic integrity? *International Journal of Educational Research Open*, *7*, 100396. DOI: 10.1016/j.ijedro.2024.100396

Nunes, K., Gagné, A., Laliberté, N., & Rawle, F. (2023). Evidence-informed Practices for Fostering Self-regulated and Resilient Learners. In Pandemic Pedagogy: Preparedness in Uncertain Times (pp. 49-71). Emerald Publishing Limited. DOI: 10.1108/S2055-364120230000049004

Nuong Deri, M., Singh, A., Zaazie, P., & Anandene, D. (2024). Leveraging Artificial Intelligence in Higher Educational Institutions: A Comprehensive Overview. *Education and Law Review*, (30). Advance online publication. DOI: 10.1344/REYD2024.30.45777

Nyathi, P., & Zondi, S. (2023). Smart Classroom pilot: South Africa case study. *South African Educational Journal*, *12*(2), 135–158.

O'Brien, K. (2023). Adaptive systems and diagnosing knowledge gaps. *Journal of Adaptive Instruction*, *9*(4), 212–236.

Obi, C., & Nnaji, M. (2023). Cybersecurity norms for learning platforms. *African Journal of Cyber Policy*, *2*(1), 20–41.

Ocak, M. A. (2011). Why are faculty members not teaching blended courses? Insights from faculty members. *Computers & Education*, *56*(3), 689–699. DOI: 10.1016/j.compedu.2010.10.011

Ododo, E. P., Iniobong, U. B., Udoessien, A. I., Ukpe, I. U., & James, O. D. (2024). Artificial intelligence in the classroom: Perceived challenges to vocational education student retention and critical thinking in tertiary institutions. *American Journal of Interdisciplinary Innovative Research*, *6*(9), 30–39. DOI: 10.37547/tajiir/Volume06Issue09-05

OECD. (2021). OECD skills outlook 2021: Learning for life. OECD Publishing. https://www.oecd.org/content/dam/oecd/en/publications/reports/2021/06/oecd-skills-outlook-2021_6f4da936/0ae365b4-en.pdf

Ofori, G., & Asare, R. (2023). AI4Ed Ghana: Training teachers in AI literacy. *Ghana Education Review*, *7*(1), 64–86.

Ogunsakin, R. E. (2024). The impact of artificial intelligence on personalized learning experiences. *Journal of Computer Assisted Learning*, *40*(1), 99–113.

Oh, H. J., Kim, J., Chang, J. J., Park, N., & Lee, S. (2023). Social benefits of living in the metaverse: The relationships among social presence, supportive interaction, social self-efficacy, and feelings of loneliness. *Computers in Human Behavior*, *139*, 107498. DOI: 10.1016/j.chb.2022.107498

Okonkwo, C. W., & Ade-Ibijola, A. (2021a). Chatbots applications in education: A systematic review. *Computers and Education: Artificial Intelligence, 2*, 100033.

Okonkwo, C. W., & Ade-Ibijola, A. (2021b). Evaluating the ethical implications of using chatbot systems in higher education. *digiTAL, 2021*, 68.

Oliveira, D. (2020). Stopping harmful deployments: When to retire edtech. *Technology & Education Ethics*, *1*(1), 40–62.

Onu, P., Pradhan, A., & Mbohwa, C. (2024). Potential to use metaverse for future teaching and learning. *Education and Information Technologies*, *29*(7), 8893–8924. DOI: 10.1007/s10639-023-12167-9

Onyango, A., & Akinyi, B. (2024). Policy instruments for blended AI learning in East Africa. *Education Policy in Practice*, *4*(1), 52–76.

Orynbay, L., Razakhova, B., Peer, P., Meden, B., & Emeršič, Ž. (2024). Recent advances in synthesis and interaction of speech, text, and vision. *Electronics (Basel)*, *13*(9), 1726. DOI: 10.3390/electronics13091726

Otieno & Wekesa (2024). Localised curricular materials and AI. *Kenyan Journal of Curriculum Studies, 2*(1), 10-31.

Ouyang, F., Zheng, L., & Jiao, P. (2022). Artificial intelligence in online higher education: A systematic review of empirical research from 2011–2020. *Education and Information Technologies*, *27*(10), 7893–7925. DOI: 10.1007/s10639-022-10925-9

Owan, V. J., Abang, K. B., Idika, D. O., Etta, E. O., & Bassey, B. A. (2023). Exploring the potential of artificial intelligence tools in educational measurement and assessment. *Eurasia Journal of Mathematics, Science and Technology Education*, *19*(8), em2307. DOI: 10.29333/ejmste/13428

Pachoulas, G., Christopoulos, A., & Stylios, C. (2024). *A Conceptual Framework for Educational Metaverse.* Paper presented at the 2024 2nd International Conference on Intelligent Metaverse Technologies & Applications (iMETA). DOI: 10.1109/iMETA62882.2024.10807878

Pane, J. F., Steiner, E. D., Baird, M. D., & Hamilton, L. S. (2017). *Informing progress: Insights on personalized learning implementation and effects*. RAND Corporation. DOI: 10.7249/RR2042

Papakostas, C., Troussas, C., & Sgouropoulou, C. (2024). Review of the Literature on AI-Enhanced Augmented Reality in Education. In *Cognitive technologies* (pp. 13–50). DOI: 10.1007/978-3-031-52005-1_2

Pardo, A., Jovanovic, J., Dawson, S., Gašević, D., & Mirriahi, N. (2019). Using learning analytics to scale the provision of personalised feedback. *British Journal of Educational Technology*, *50*(1), 128–138. DOI: 10.1111/bjet.12592

Park, Y., & Doo, M. Y. (2024). Role of AI in blended learning: A systematic literature review. *International Review of Research in Open and Distance Learning*, *25*(1), 164–196. DOI: 10.19173/irrodl.v25i1.7566

Patel, R. (2022). Mapping AI competencies into national curricula. *Curriculum & Instruction Journal*, *10*(3), 128–149.

Patra, N., & Kumar, S. (2024). Device availability and maintenance for blended learning. *Journal of Educational Infrastructure*, *2*(1), 45–68.

Patton, M. Q. (2014). *Qualitative research & evaluation methods: Integrating theory and practice*. Sage publications.

Paul, R., & Elder, L. (2017). Critical thinking: Concepts and tools (3rd ed.). Foundation for Critical Thinking.

Paul, J. S., Farhath, O., & Selvan, M. P. (2024, April). AI-based proctoring system – A review. In *2024 International Conference on Inventive Computation Technologies (ICICT)* (pp. 1–5). IEEE.

Pavlidou, I., Dragicevic, N., & Tsui, E. (2021). A multi-dimensional hybrid learning environment for business education: A knowledge dynamics perspective. *Sustainability (Basel)*, *13*(7), 3889. DOI: 10.3390/su13073889

Pelau, C., Dabija, D. C., & Ene, I. (2021). What makes an AI device human-like? The role of interaction quality, empathy and perceived psychological anthropomorphic characteristics in the acceptance of artificial intelligence in the service industry. *Computers in Human Behavior*, *122*, 106855. DOI: 10.1016/j.chb.2021.106855

Pellas, N., Mystakidis, S., & Christopoulos, A. (2021). A systematic literature review on the user experience design for game-based interventions via 3D virtual worlds in K-12 education. *Multimodal Technologies and Interaction*, *5*(6), 28. DOI: 10.3390/mti5060028

Pellicelli, A. C. (2024). Challenges and risks of AI in education. In *Proceedings of EDULEARN24* (pp. 233–242). DOI: 10.21125/edulearn.2024.1767

Pereira & Costa. (2018). AI sandboxes: regulatory experimentation and lessons. *Policy & Tech Review, 2*(1), 1-28.

Pereira & Martinez. (2023). AI tutoring and blended delivery in Uruguay. *Latin American Journal of Educational Technologies, 5*(2), 77-95.

Pereira, A. (2021). Intelligent tutoring systems in Brazilian public schools. *Journal of Intelligent Systems in Education, 14*(3), 155–179.

Pérez, J., & Santiago, M. (2023). Regional collaboration for AI policy: Brazil-India initiatives. *South-South Cooperation Journal, 1*(1), 28–50.

Perkins, M. (2023). Academic Integrity considerations of AI Large Language Models in the post-pandemic era: ChatGPT and beyond. *Journal of University Teaching & Learning Practice*, *20*(2). Advance online publication. DOI: 10.53761/1.20.02.07

Persing, I., Ng, V., & Adams, R. (2019). Modeling discourse moves for assessing argument quality in student essays. *Transactions of the Association for Computational Linguistics*, *7*, 507–521. DOI: 10.1162/tacl_a_00295

Peters, J., & Adebayo, O. (2023). Co-designing AI curricula with communities. *Global Curriculum Journal*, *9*(2), 99–121.

Phillips, A., Pane, J. F., Reumann-Moore, R., & Shenbanjo, O. (2020). Implementing an adaptive intelligent tutoring system as an instructional supplement. *Educational Technology Research and Development*, *68*(3), 1409–1437. DOI: 10.1007/s11423-020-09745-w

Picard, R. W. (1999). Affective computing for hci. In *HCI (1)* (pp. 829–833).

Poiroux, J. (2024, October). Disengagement through Algorithms: How Traditional Organizations Aim for Experts' Satisfaction. In Proceedings of the AAAI/ACM Conference on AI, Ethics, and Society (Vol. 7, pp. 1145-1156).

Pokryszko-Dragan, A., Marschollek, K., Nowakowska-Kotas, M., & Aitken, G. (2021). What can we learn from the online learning experiences of medical students in Poland during the SARS-CoV-2 pandemic? *BMC Medical Education*, *21*(1), 450. DOI: 10.1186/s12909-021-02884-5 PMID: 34445982

Poole, D. L., & Mackworth, A. K. (2010). *Artificial Intelligence: Foundations of computational agents*. Cambridge University Press. DOI: 10.1017/CBO9780511794797

Popenici, S. A. D., & Kerr, S. (2017). Exploring the impact of artificial intelligence on teaching and learning in higher education. *Research and Practice in Technology Enhanced Learning*, *12*(1), 1–13. DOI: 10.1186/s41039-017-0062-8 PMID: 30595727

Popham, W. J. (2001). *The truth about testing: An educator's call to action*. ASCD.

Prabhakaran, A., Mahamadu, A., Booth, C. A., & Manu, P. (2025). Applications of immersive technology in architecture, engineering and construction. In *Routledge eBooks*. DOI: 10.1201/9781032662909

Rachmad, Y. E. (2022). Adaptive Learning Theory.

Radu, I. (2014). Augmented reality in education: A meta-review and cross-media analysis. *Personal and Ubiquitous Computing*, *18*(6), 1533–1543. DOI: 10.1007/s00779-013-0747-y

Raes, A. (2022). Exploring student and teacher experiences in hybrid learning environments: Does presence matter? *Postdigital Science and Education*, *4*(1), 138–159. DOI: 10.1007/s42438-021-00274-0 PMID: 40477740

Rahaman, S. U., Abdul, M. J., & Patchipulusu, S. (2023). AI-DRIVEN EMPATHY IN UX DESIGN: ENHANCING PERSONALIZATION AND USER EXPERIENCE THROUGH PREDICTIVE ANALYTICS. [IJCET]. *Technology*, *14*(2), 255–268.

Rahman, . (2023). AI communication tools for multilingual policy outreach. *International Journal of Government Communication*, *6*(1), 14–36.

Rahman, A. (2022). Education continuity in crises: AI and blended solutions. *Disaster & Education*, *1*(1), 55–78.

Rahsepar Meadi, M., Bernstein, J. S., Batelaan, N., van Balkom, A. J., & Metselaar, S. (2024). Does a lack of emotions make chatbots unfit to be psychotherapists? *Bioethics*, *38*(6), 503–510. DOI: 10.1111/bioe.13299 PMID: 38735049

Raj, S., Sharma, S., & Dutt, D. (2024). Digital Disruption: 'Transforming Tourism Education for the 21st Century.' In *Emerald Publishing Limited eBooks* (pp. 137–145). DOI: 10.1108/978-1-83608-704-520241010

Rajkumar & Fernandez. (2023). Speech-to-text tools for learners with impairments. *Assistive Education Technologies, 3*(2), 108-129.

Raj, P., & Das, S. (2024). Ensuring AI does not widen educational gaps. *Development & Education*, *3*(1), 22–45.

Ramos & Teixeira. (2023). Digital divide metrics and policy responses. *Global Education Metrics, 7*(2), 88-109.

Rane, N. L. (2024). Education 4.0 and 5.0: integrating Artificial Intelligence (AI) for personalized and adaptive learning. *Journal of Artificial Intelligence and Robotics*. DOI: 10.61577/jaiar.2024.100006

Rasheed, R. A., Kamsin, A., & Abdullah, N. A. (2020). Challenges in the online component of blended learning: A systematic review. *Computers & Education*, *144*, 103701. DOI: 10.1016/j.compedu.2019.103701

Ravichandran, K. (2024). Identifying Learning Difficulties at an Early Stage in Education with the Help of Artificial Intelligence Models and Predictive Analytics.

Ray, K. S., Mahapatra, D. M., Rout, B. L., & Shaikh, Z. H. (2026). E-Learning for Sustainability Education in Corporate World: An Appraisal From Stakeholder Engagement Perspective. In E. Hans & A. Hans (Eds.), Harnessing E-Learning to Create a Sustainable Future (pp. 75–118). IGI Global Scientific Publishing.

Reardon, S. F. (2018). The widening academic achievement gap between the rich and the poor. In *Social stratification* (pp. 536–550). Routledge.

Reigeluth, C. M. (1999). The elaboration theory: Guidance for scope and sequence decisions. In Reigeluth, C. M. (Ed.), *Instructional-design theories and models* (Vol. 2, pp. 425–453). Lawrence Erlbaum Associates.

Reiser, R. A. (2001). A history of instructional design and technology: Part I: A history of instructional media. *Educational Technology Research and Development*, *49*(1), 53–64. DOI: 10.1007/BF02504506

Rekha, K., Gopal, K., Satheeskumar, D., Anand, U. A., Doss, D. S. S., & Elayaperumal, S. (2024). *Ai-Powered Personalized Learning System Design: Student Engagement and Performance Tracking System.* Paper presented at the 2024 4th International Conference on Advance Computing and Innovative Technologies in Engineering (ICACITE). DOI: 10.1109/ICACITE60783.2024.10617155

Reyes & Torres. (2024). Incentivising public-private partnerships for infrastructure. *Journal of Public Policy & Technology, 8*(1), 101-126.

Ribeiro, . (2021). LabAI Educação: Pilots and outcomes. *Brazilian Journal of Educational Experiments*, *5*(2), 77–101.

Roblyer, M. D., & Doering, A. H. (2007). *Integrating educational technology into teaching* (5th ed.). Pearson.

Rocha & Almeida. (2023). EDUCA-AI program evaluation: Accessibility outcomes. *Brazilian Assistive Technology Review*, *4*(1), 30–54.

Rocha & Silva. (2021). Ethics in AI deployments: Lessons from pilots. *Ethics & Education Technology, 2*(1), 67-90.

Rodríguez & Campos. (2023). Podcasts as educational media: Uruguay case study. *Media Pedagogy Journal*, *4*(2), 77–96.

Rodríguez & Fernández. (2023). Plan Ceibal and blended learning: Integration and impact. *Uruguay Education Review*, *2*(1), 12–39.

Rodway, P., & Schepman, A. (2023). The impact of adopting AI educational technologies on projected course satisfaction in university students. *Computers and Education: Artificial Intelligence*, *5*, 100150. DOI: 10.1016/j.caeai.2023.100150

Røe, Y., Rowe, M., Ødegaard, N. B., & Lie, A. (2022). Blended learning in higher education: A review of the literature. *Technology, Pedagogy and Education*, *31*(1), 1–18.

Rose, R. M., Smith, A., Johnson, K., & Glick, D. (2023). Ensuring equitable access in online and blended learning. In *Online, blended, and distance education in schools* (pp. 71–83). Routledge. DOI: 10.4324/9781003446194-9

Rossett, A., Douglis, F., & Frazee, R. V. (2003). Strategies for building blended learning. *Learning Circuits*, *4*(7), 1–9.

Rotherham, A. J., & Willingham, D. (2009). 21st century. *Educational Leadership, 67*(1), 16–21.

Ruano-Borbalan, J. C. (2025). The transformative impact of artificial intelligence on higher education: A critical reflection on current trends and futures directions. International Journal of Chinese Education, 14(1), 2212585X251319364.

Rubio-Tamayo, J., Barrio, M. G., & García, F. G. (2017). Immersive Environments and Virtual Reality: Systematic review and advances in communication, interaction and simulation. *Multimodal Technologies and Interaction, 1*(4), 21. DOI: 10.3390/mti1040021

Ruhanen, L., Axelsen, M., & Bowles, L. (2020). Engaging students through authentic learning: Connecting with international tourism partners. *Journal of Hospitality, Leisure, Sport and Tourism Education, 29*, 100291. DOI: 10.1016/j.jhlste.2020.100291

Russell, S. J., & Norvig, P. (2016). *Artificial intelligence: A modern approach.* Pearson.

Russell, S., & Norvig, P. (2024). *Artificial intelligence: A modern approach, global edition 5Yr subscription* (4th ed.). Pearson Education.

Ryan, R. M., & Deci, E. L. (2000). Intrinsic and extrinsic motivations: Classic definitions and new directions. *Contemporary Educational Psychology, 25*(1), 54–67. DOI: 10.1006/ceps.1999.1020 PMID: 10620381

Saçak, B., Bozkurt, A., & Wagner, E. (2022). Learning design versus instructional design: A bibliometric study through data visualization approaches. *Education Sciences, 12*(11), 752. DOI: 10.3390/educsci12110752

Sadler, D. R. (1989). Formative assessment and the design of instructional systems. *Instructional Science, 18*(2), 119–144. DOI: 10.1007/BF00117714

Safikhani, S., Keller, S., Schweiger, G., & Pirker, J. (2022). Immersive virtual reality for extending the potential of building information modeling in architecture, engineering, and construction sector: Systematic review. *International Journal of Digital Earth, 15*(1), 503–526. DOI: 10.1080/17538947.2022.2038291

Saifi, A. G. (2024). Pedagogy and AI in Education. In *Advances in Educational Technologies and Instructional Design* (pp. 136–156). IGI Global. DOI: 10.4018/979-8-3693-6397-3.ch006

Sajja, R., Sermet, Y., Cwiertny, D., & Demir, I. (2023). Platform-independent and curriculum-oriented intelligent assistant for higher education. *International Journal of Educational Technology in Higher Education, 20*(1), 42. Advance online publication. DOI: 10.1186/s41239-023-00412-7

Sajja, R., Sermet, Y., & Demir, I. (2025). End-to-end deployment of the educational AI hub for personalized learning and engagement: A case study on environmental science education. *IEEE Access : Practical Innovations, Open Solutions, 13*, 55169–55186. DOI: 10.1109/ACCESS.2025.3554222

Samsonovich, A. V. (2020). Socially emotional brain-inspired cognitive architecture framework for artificial intelligence. *Cognitive Systems Research, 60*, 57–76. DOI: 10.1016/j.cogsys.2019.12.002

Santos & Lima. (2021). Low-bandwidth solutions for rural classrooms. *Rural Education Technology, 1*(2), 10-29.

Santos & Rodríguez. (2023). Digital citizenship delivered through mixed modalities. *Journal of Online Pedagogies, 6*(1), 34-56.

Santos, A. (2020). Digital inclusion and Plan Ceibal. *Synthesis.*

Santoso & Wulandari. (2024). Merdeka Belajar reform and localized AI curricula. *Indonesian Education Policy Review, 3*(1), 103-129.

Saputra, I., Astuti, M., Sayuti, M., & Kusumastuti, D. (2023). Integration of artificial intelligence in education: Opportunities, challenges, threats and obstacles. A literature review. *The Indonesian Journal of Computer Science, 12*(4). Advance online publication. DOI: 10.33022/ijcs.v12i4.3266

Saputra, I., Kurniawan, A., Yanita, M., Putri, E. Y., & Mahniza, M. (2024). The evolution of educational assessment: How artificial intelligence is shaping the trends and future of learning evaluation. *The Indonesian Journal of Computer Science, 13*(6), 112–128. DOI: 10.33022/ijcs.v13i6.4465

Sareen, S., & Mandal, S. (2024). Challenges of blended learning in higher education across global north-south: A systematic and integrative literature review. *Social Sciences & Humanities Open, 10*, 101011. DOI: 10.1016/j.ssaho.2024.101011

Sari, H. E., Tumanggor, B., & Efron, D. (2024). Improving educational outcomes through adaptive learning systems using AI. *International Transactions on Artificial Intelligence, 3*(1), 21–31. DOI: 10.33050/italic.v3i1.647

Sarnato, A. Z., Sari, W. D., Rahmawati, S. T., Hidayat, R., & Patry, H. (2024). The evolution of E-learning platforms: From U-learning to AI-driven adaptive learning systems. *Journal of Social Science Utilizing Technology*, *2*(2), 289–300. DOI: 10.70177/jssut.v2i2.1131

Savastano, M., Biclesanu, I., Anagnoste, S., Laviola, F., & Cucari, N. (2024). Enterprise chatbots in managers' perception: A strategic framework to implement successful chatbot applications for business decisions. *Management Decision*. Advance online publication. DOI: 10.1108/MD-10-2023-1967

Saxena, M. K., & Bajotra, V. (2024). Potential of artificial intelligence in education and ethical issues. *Far Western Journal of Education*, *1*(1), 1–18. DOI: 10.3126/fwje.v1i1.68773

Schank, R. C., Fano, A., Bell, B., & Jona, M. (1994). The design of goal-based scenarios. *Journal of the Learning Sciences*, *3*(4), 305–345. DOI: 10.1207/s15327809jls0304_2

Segal, A. (2022). When the student is the 'problem'and the teacher is not the solution: Teacher professional identity in an era of accountability and personalized instruction. *Learning, Culture and Social Interaction*, *32*, 100597. DOI: 10.1016/j.lcsi.2021.100597

Seitz, L. (2024). Artificial empathy in healthcare chatbots: Does it feel authentic? *Computers in Human Behavior: Artificial Humans*, *2*(1), 100067. DOI: 10.1016/j.chbah.2024.100067

Selwyn, N. (2019). *Should robots replace teachers?: AI and the future of education*. John Wiley & Sons.

Shafa, A. A. (2024). Implementasi Learning Management System dalam meningkatkan efektivitas pembelajaran. *Jurnal Teknologi Pendidikan*, *1*(4), 8–8. DOI: 10.47134/jtp.v1i4.658

Shaikh, Z. H., Irfan, M., Nomran, N. M., Ratnakaram, S. P., Abey, J., & Anto, M. L. (2025). Measuring Vital Sign: A Case Study of India's Emerging Wearable Technology (EzeCheck) for Mass Screening and Health Monitoring. In Ul Rehman, S. (Ed.), *Wearable Devices and Smart Technology for Educational Teaching Assistance* (pp. 285–308). IGI Global Scientific Publishing., DOI: 10.4018/979-8-3693-7817-5.ch011

Shaikh, Z. H., Irfan, M., Vemavarapu, K. R., Sadayan, S., Hawaldar, I. T., & Rehman, S. U. (2024). Assessing the Effectiveness of Learning Outcomes: In Achieving Quality Education at Higher Learning Institutions in Bahrain. In Naim, A., Saklani, A., Khan, S., & Malik, P. (Eds.), *Evaluating Global Accreditation Standards for Higher Education* (pp. 50–65). IGI Global Scientific Publishing., DOI: 10.4018/979-8-3693-1698-6.ch004

Sharma, M., & Singh, A. (2024a). Embracing Technological Innovation: A Review of Hi-Tech Services in Hospitality Industry. *Evergreen, 11*(4), 2818–2830. DOI: 10.5109/7326926

Sharma, R., & Singh, A. (2024). Use of Digital Technology in Improving Quality Education: A Global Perspectives and Trends. In Nadda, V., Tyagi, P., Moniz Vieira, R., & Tyagi, P. (Eds.), *Implementing Sustainable Development Goals in the Service Sector* (pp. 14–26). IGI Global., DOI: 10.4018/979-8-3693-2065-5.ch002

Sharples, M., de Roock, R., Ferguson, R., Gaved, M., Herodotou, C., Koh, E., . . . Wong, L. H. (2016). Innovating pedagogy 2016: Open University innovation report 5. Institute of Educational Technology, The Open University. https://oro.open.ac.uk/48153/

Sheldon, P. J., Fesenmaier, D. R., & Tribe, J. (2011). The Tourism Education Futures Initiative (TEFI): Activating Change in Tourism Education. *Journal of Teaching in Travel & Tourism, 11*(1), 2–23. DOI: 10.1080/15313220.2011.548728

Shepard, L. A. (2000). The role of assessment in a learning culture. *Educational Researcher, 29*(7), 4–14. DOI: 10.3102/0013189X029007004

Shermis, M. D., & Burstein, J. (Eds.). (2013). *Handbook of automated essay evaluation: Current applications and new directions*. Routledge. DOI: 10.4324/9780203122761

Shoaib, M., Sayed, N., Singh, J., Shafi, J., Khan, S., & Ali, F. (2024). AI student success predictor: Enhancing personalized learning in campus management systems. *Computers in Human Behavior, 158*, 108301. DOI: 10.1016/j.chb.2024.108301

Siemens, G. (2004). Connectivism: A learning theory for the digital age. Elearnspace. https://www.elearnspace.org/Articles/connectivism.htm

Siemens, G. (2013). Learning analytics: The emergence of a discipline. *The American Behavioral Scientist, 57*(10), 1380–1400. DOI: 10.1177/0002764213498851

Silva, . (2019). Industry-university co-creation and product feedback loops. *Innovation in Learning, 6*(1), 44–67.

Silva, . (2023). EDUCA-AI accessibility report. *Assistive Technology & Society*, *7*(1), 11–32.

Silva, A., Oliveira, B., & Batista, C. (2022). Inclusive edtech design in Paraná. *British Journal of Educational Technology*, *8*(3), 211–235.

Silva, E., & Lima, F. (2020). Removing bias from educational datasets. *Data Ethics Journal*, *1*(1), 12–34.

Singh & Menon. (2024). Extending cybersecurity standards to schools. *Journal of School Safety & Security, 4*(1), 33-56.

Singh, A. (2022). Conceptual framework on Smart Learning Environment- An Indian perspective. *Journal of Education and Law*, (25). Advance online publication. DOI: 10.1344/REYD2022.25.36706

Singh, A. (2024). Impact of E-learning on Student Motivation in Higher Education Institutions: An Indian Perspective. *Journal of Education and Law*, (29). Advance online publication. DOI: 10.1344/REYD2024.29.43214

Singh, A., & Hassan, S. C. (2024). Identifying the skill gap in the workplace and their challenges in hospitality and tourism organisations. In *Contemporary challenges in social science management: Skills gaps and shortages in the labour market* (pp. 101–114). Emerald Publishing Limited.

Singh, A., & Iyer, S. (2023). Culturally responsive algorithmic design. *Cultural Education Review*, *5*(2), 89–112.

Singh, K., Goel, N., Gupta, B., & Bansal, D. (2023). Emotion prediction through facial recognition using machine learning: a survey. In *In2023 International Conference on Computer Communication and Informatics (ICCCI)* (pp. 1–5). IEEE. DOI: 10.1109/ICCCI56745.2023.10128348

Singh, M. (2024). Exploring the possibilities to implement metaverse in higher education institutions of India. *Education and Information Technologies*, *29*(15), 20715–20728. DOI: 10.1007/s10639-024-12691-2

Sinha & Patel. (2024). Teacher onboarding to blended AI systems. *Teacher Development Quarterly, 10*(2), 59-82.

Slade, S., & Prinsloo, P. (2013). Learning analytics: Ethical issues and dilemmas. *The American Behavioral Scientist*, *57*(10), 1510–1529. DOI: 10.1177/0002764213479366

Snehalatha, M. (2024). AI and OpenAI in education: Unveiling the future of learning and teaching. In *Enhancing Higher Education and Research With OpenAI Models* (pp. 176–205). IGI Global Scientific Publishing.

Sousa, . (2021). Evaluating regional digital inclusion programs. *Regional Policy Review, 11*(2), 70–92.

Souza & Santos. (2020). Iterative pilot assessment: Methods and indicators. *Program Evaluation in Education, 3*(1), 44-66.

Spurava, G., & Kotilainen, S. (2023). Digital literacy as a pathway to professional development in the algorithm-driven world. *Nordic Journal of Digital Literacy, 18*(1), 48–59. DOI: 10.18261/njdl.18.1.5

Starkey & Tapscott. (2020). Preparing youth for digital futures. *Future Skills Journal, 2*(1), 18-40.

Stiggins, R. (2005). From formative assessment to assessment for learning: A path to success in standards-based schools. *Phi Delta Kappan, 87*(4), 324–328. DOI: 10.1177/003172170508700414

Strekalova-Hughes, E., Nash, K. T., Schmer, B., & Caldwell, K. (2021). Meeting the needs of all cultureless learners: Culture discourse and quality assumptions in personalized learning research. *Review of Research in Education, 45*(1), 372–407. DOI: 10.3102/0091732X20985081

Strielkowski, W., Grebennikova, V., Lisovskiy, A., Rakhimova, G., & Vasileva, T. (2025). AI-driven adaptive learning for sustainable educational transformation. *Sustainable Development (Bradford), 33*(2), 1921–1947. DOI: 10.1002/sd.3221

Sugimoto, C. R., & Larivière, V. (2018). *Measuring research: What everyone needs to know*. Oxford University Press. DOI: 10.1093/wentk/9780190640118.001.0001

Suh, A., & Prophet, J. (2018). The state of immersive technology research: A literature analysis. *Computers in Human Behavior, 86*, 77–90. DOI: 10.1016/j.chb.2018.04.019

Šumak, B., López-De-Ipiña, D., Dziabenko, O., Correia, S. D., De Carvalho, L. M., Lopes, S., Şimşek, İ., Can, T., & Kline, D. I. (2024). *Pušnik M. AI-Based Education Tools for Enabling Inclusive Education: Challenges and Benefits. In2024 47th MIPRO ICT and Electronics Convention (MIPRO)*. IEEE.

Sumathy, V., & Navamani, G. (2024). AI-Driven Personalized Learning: Enhancing Student Success through Adaptive Technologies. *Library of Progress-Library Science, Information Technology & Computer, 44*(3).

Suntharalingam, H. (2024). Enhancing digital learning outcomes through the application of artificial intelligence: A comprehensive review. *International Journal of Innovative Science and Research Technology, 9*(4), 718–727. DOI: 10.38124/ijisrt/IJISRT24APR530

Suryawinata, B. A. (2021). Immersive technology as a tool for sustainable architecture. *IOP Conference Series. Earth and Environmental Science*, *794*(1), 012185. DOI: 10.1088/1755-1315/794/1/012185

Suta, P., Lan, X., Wu, B., Mongkolnam, P., & Chan, J. H. (2020). An overview of machine learning in chatbots. *International Journal of Mechanical Engineering and Robotics Research*, *9*(4), 502–510. DOI: 10.18178/ijmerr.9.4.502-510

Su, Y., Lin, Y., & Lai, C. (2023). Collaborating with ChatGPT in argumentative writing classrooms. *Assessing Writing*, *57*, 100752. DOI: 10.1016/j.asw.2023.100752

Sweller, J. (1988). Cognitive load during problem solving: Effects on learning. *Cognitive Science*, *12*(2), 257–285. DOI: 10.1207/s15516709cog1202_4

Tack, A., & Piech, C. (2022). The AI teacher test: Measuring the pedagogical ability of Blender and GPT-3 in educational dialogues. In *arXiv [cs.CL]*. https://arxiv.org/abs/2205.07540

Tammets, K., & Ley, T. (2023). Integrating AI tools in teacher professional learning: a conceptual model and illustrative case. *Frontiers in artificial intelligence*, *6*, 1255089.

Tan & Ng. (2021). Equity through blended learning: Comparative perspectives. *Asia Pacific Education Review, 22*(4), 345-367.

Tan, L. Y., Hu, S., Yeo, D. J., & Cheong, K. H. (2025). Artificial Intelligence-Enabled Adaptive Learning Platforms: A Review. *Computers and Education: Artificial Intelligence*, 100429.

Tapalova, O., & Zhiyenbayeva, N. (2022). Artificial intelligence in education: AIEd for personalised learning pathways. *Electronic Journal of e-Learning*, *20*(5), 639–653. DOI: 10.34190/ejel.20.5.2597

Tariq, M. U. (2024). Navigating the personalization pathway: Implementing adaptive learning technologies in higher education. In *Adaptive Learning Technologies for Higher Education* (pp. 265–291). IGI Global. DOI: 10.4018/979-8-3693-3641-0.ch012

Tavares, . (2020). Lessons from classroom pilots: Data collection and ethics. *Journal of Field Education Research*, *6*(3), 123–144.

Temme, M. (2017). Algorithms and transparency in view of the new general data protection regulation. *Eur. Data Prot. L. Rev.*, *3*(4), 473–485. DOI: 10.21552/edpl/2017/4/9

Thakur & Jain. (2024). Monitoring & evaluation frameworks for AI in schools. *Policy Monitoring Journal, 2*(1), 55-78.

Thomas, N. J., Baral, R., Crocco, O. S., & Mohanan, S. (2023). A framework for gamification in the metaverse era: How designers envision gameful experience. *Technological Forecasting and Social Change, 193*, 122544. DOI: 10.1016/j.techfore.2023.122544

Thompson, N., & Mcgill, T. J. (2012). Affective tutoring systems: Enhancing e-learning with the emotional awareness of a human tutor. [IJICTE]. *International Journal of Information and Communication Technology Education*, *8*(4), 75–89. DOI: 10.4018/jicte.2012100107

Thuy, P. B., & Tien, P. D. (2024). AI-Powered administration: The role of intelligent tutoring systems in education. *International journal of religion*, *5*(10), 4560-4569.

Tiwari & Sharma. (2023). Transnational sharing of AI policy models. *International Journal of Policy Exchange, 1*(1), 29-51.

Tlili, A., Huang, R., Shehata, B., Liu, D., Zhao, J., Metwally, A. H. S., Wang, H., Denden, M., Bozkurt, A., Lee, L.-H., Beyoglu, D., Altinay, F., Sharma, R. C., Altinay, Z., Li, Z., Liu, J., Ahmad, F., Hu, Y., Salha, S., & Burgos, D. (2022). Is Metaverse in education a blessing or a curse: A combined content and bibliometric analysis. *Smart Learning Environments*, *9*(1), 1–31. DOI: 10.1186/s40561-022-00205-x PMID: 40477962

Troussas, C., Krouska, A., & Sgouropoulou, C. (2020). Collaboration and fuzzy-modeled personalization for mobile game-based learning in higher education. *Computers & Education, 144*, 103698. DOI: 10.1016/j.compedu.2019.103698

Tsegaye & Mohammed. (2024). Local content requirements for inclusive edtech. *Journal of Education & Development, 9*(1), 12-34.

Tulasi, L., & Rao, C. S. (2023). Integration of AI-technologies into ELT: A brief study. *Journal for Research Scholars and Professionals of English Language Teaching*, *7*(38). Advance online publication. DOI: 10.54850/jrspelt.7.38.003

Uddin & Rahman. (2023). Sandbox governance for educational innovations. *Governance & Innovation, 4*(2), 101-122.

UNESCO. (2021). *Recommendation on the Ethics of Artificial Intelligence*. UNESCO.

UNESCO. (2023). Ethical foundations for AI in education: Guidance and tools. UNESCO.

UNESCO. (2023). *Guidance for generative AI in education and research.* United Nations Educational, Scientific and Cultural Organization. https://www.unesco.org/en/articles/guidance-generative-ai-education-and-research

Vaghela, V. S., & Parsana, D. F. (2024). *Teaching and Learning: Fostering Student Engagement.* Critical Thinking, and Lifelong Learning Skills.

van der Stap, N., van den Bogaart, T., Rahimi, E., & Versendaal, J. (2024). Fostering online interaction in blended learning through social presence and convergence: A systematic literature review. *Journal of Computer Assisted Learning*, *40*(4), 1712–1726. DOI: 10.1111/jcal.12981

Van Rooij, E. C., Jansen, E. P., & van de Grift, W. J. (2018). First-year university students' academic success: The importance of academic adjustment. *European Journal of Psychology of Education*, *33*(4), 749–767. DOI: 10.1007/s10212-017-0347-8

VanLehn, K. (2011). The relative effectiveness of human tutoring, intelligent tutoring systems, and other tutoring systems. *Educational Psychologist*, *46*(4), 197–221. DOI: 10.1080/00461520.2011.611369

Vargas & Nascimento. (2022). Pedagogical inclusivity in national digital programmes. *Education & Society, 9*(3), 145-167.

Vaughan, N. (2007). Perspectives on blended learning in higher education. [Association for the Advancement of Computing in Education] [AACE]. *International Journal on E-Learning*, *6*(1), 81–94.

Verma & Choudhury. (2023). Teacher certification for AI-enabled blended learning. *Teacher Education Policy Review, 7*(2), 88-105.

Viberg, O., & Grönlund, Å. (2024). Exploring teachers' (future) digital assessment practices in higher education: Instrument and model development. *British Journal of Educational Technology*, *55*(3), 1–19. DOI: 10.1111/bjet.13462

Villegas-Ch, W. E., García-Ortiz, J., & Sánchez-Viteri, S. (2023). Identification of emotions from facial gestures in a teaching environment with the use of machine learning techniques. *IEEE Access*, *11*, 38010-38022.

Villegas-Ch, W., García-Ortiz, J., & Sánchez-Viteri, S. (2024). Educational advances in the metaverse: Boosting learning through virtual and augmented reality and artificial intelligence. *IEEE Access : Practical Innovations, Open Solutions*, *12*, 59093–59112. DOI: 10.1109/ACCESS.2024.3393776

Vygotsky, L. S. (1980). Mind in Society. *Mind & Society*. Advance online publication. DOI: 10.2307/j.ctvjf9vz4

Vygotsky, L. S., & Cole, M. (1978). *Mind in society: Development of higher psychological processes*. Harvard University Press.

Waladi, C., Sefian, M. L., & Khaldi, M. (2023). Kolb's learning styles: Implementation and integration in an adaptive e-learning system. In *Handbook of Research on Scripting, Media Coverage, and Implementation of E-Learning Training in LMS Platforms* (pp. 398–413). IGI Global.

Walkington, C., & Bernacki, M. (2014). Personalized learning in mathematics for adolescent learners. *Journal of Research on Technology in Education*, *46*(4), 327–351.

Wang, M., Yu, H., Bell, Z., & Chu, X. (2022). Constructing an edu-metaverse ecosystem: A new and innovative framework. *IEEE Transactions on Learning Technologies*, *15*(6), 685–696. DOI: 10.1109/TLT.2022.3210828

Wang, S., Wang, F., Zhu, Z., Wang, J., Tran, T., & Du, Z. (2024). Artificial intelligence in education: A systematic literature review. *Expert Systems with Applications*, *252*, 124167. DOI: 10.1016/j.eswa.2024.124167

Wang, S., & Zhang, H. (2024). Digital capabilities and metaverse entrepreneurial performance: Role of entrepreneurial orientation. *Journal of Innovation & Knowledge*, *9*(4), 100617. DOI: 10.1016/j.jik.2024.100617

Weller, . (2024). Algorithmic oversight in school systems. *Education Policy & Technology*, *12*(1), 1–25.

Wellings, J., & Levine, M. H. (2009). *The digital promise: Transforming learning with innovative uses of technology*. Paper presented at the New York: Joan Ganz Cooney Center at Sesame Workshop.

Whiteside, A. L., & Dikkers, A. G. (2016). Leveraging the social presence model: A decade of research on emotion in online and blended learning. In Tettegah, S. Y., & McCreery, M. P. (Eds.), *Emotions, technology, and learning* (pp. 225–241). DOI: 10.1016/B978-0-12-800649-8.00013-4

Wieczorek, M., Hosseini, M., & Gordijn, B. (2025). Unpacking the ethics of using AI in primary and secondary education: A systematic literature review. *AI and Ethics*, *5*(5), 1–19. DOI: 10.1007/s43681-025-00770-0 PMID: 40959538

Wiedbusch, M. D., Kite, V., Yang, X., Park, S., Chi, M., Taub, M., & Azevedo, R. (2021). *A theoretical and evidence-based conceptual design of metadash: An intelligent teacher dashboard to support teachers' decision making and students' self-regulated learning*. Paper presented at the Frontiers in education. DOI: 10.3389/feduc.2021.570229

Wiliam, D. (2011). What is assessment for learning? *Studies in Educational Evaluation*, *37*(1), 3–14. DOI: 10.1016/j.stueduc.2011.03.001

Williamson, B., & Eynon, R. (2020). Historical threads, missing links, and future directions in AI in education. *Learning, Media and Technology*, *45*(3), 223–235. DOI: 10.1080/17439884.2020.1798995

Winkler, R., & Söllner, M. (2018, July). Unleashing the potential of chatbots in education: A state-of-the-art analysis. In *Academy of management proceedings* (Vol. 2018, No. 1, p. 15903). Briarcliff Manor, NY 10510: Academy of Management. DOI: 10.5465/AMBPP.2018.15903abstract

Woolf, B. P. (2010). *Building intelligent interactive tutors: Student-centered strategies for revolutionizing e-learning*. Morgan Kaufmann.

World Economic Forum. (2023). The future of jobs report 2023. https://www3.weforum.org/docs/WEF_Future_of_Jobs_2023.pdf

Wu, W.-H., Wu, Y.-C. J., Chen, C.-Y., Kao, H.-Y., Lin, C.-H., & Huang, S.-H. (2012). Review of trends from mobile learning studies: A meta-analysis. *Computers & Education*, *59*(2), 817–827. DOI: 10.1016/j.compedu.2012.03.016

Wu, Y. (2023). Integrating generative AI in education: How ChatGPT brings challenges for future learning and teaching. *Journal of Advanced Research in Education*, *2*(4), 6–10. DOI: 10.56397/JARE.2023.07.02

Xu, W., & Ouyang, F. (2022). The application of AI technologies in STEM education: A systematic review from 2011 to 2021. *International Journal of STEM Education*, *9*(1), 59. DOI: 10.1186/s40594-022-00377-5

Yacef, K. (2002, December). Intelligent teaching assistant systems. In *International Conference on Computers in Education (ICCE)* (pp. 136–140). IEEE. DOI: 10.1109/CIE.2002.1185885

Yadav, S. (2024). Artificial Intelligence (AI) Integration in Higher Education: Navigating Opportunities and Ethical Frontiers in Education with Advanced Technologies. In *Impact of artificial intelligence on society* (pp. 43–59). Chapman and Hall/CRC.

Yang, L., & Li, H. (2023). Advances in AI-Based Automated Scoring and Proctoring Systems: Enhancing Assessment Validity and Integrity in Online Education. *Computers & Education*, *189*, 104620. DOI: 10.1016/j.compedu.2022.104620

Yang, W., Fang, M., Xu, J., Zhang, X., & Pan, Y. (2024). Exploring the mediating role of different aspects of learning motivation between metaverse learning experiences and gamification. *Electronics (Basel)*, *13*(7), 1297. DOI: 10.3390/electronics13071297

Yeganeh, L. N., Fenty, N. S., Chen, Y., Simpson, A., & Hatami, M. (2025). The Future of Education: A Multi-Layered Metaverse Classroom Model for Immersive and Inclusive Learning. *Future Internet, 17*(2), 63. DOI: 10.3390/fi17020063

Yekollu, R. K., Bhimraj Ghuge, T., Biradar, S., & Haldikar, S. (2024). *Farook Mohideen Abdul Kader O. AI-driven personalized learning paths: Enhancing education through adaptive systems. InInternational Conference on Smart data intelligence.* Springer Nature.

Yekollu, R. K., Bhimraj Ghuge, T., Sunil Biradar, S., Haldikar, S. V., & Farook Mohideen Abdul Kader, O. (2024, February). AI-driven personalized learning paths: Enhancing education through adaptive systems. In *International Conference on Smart data intelligence* (pp. 507-517). Singapore: Springer Nature Singapore. DOI: 10.1007/978-981-97-3191-6_38

Yenduri, G., Kaluri, R., Rajput, D. S., Lakshmanna, K., Gadekallu, T. R., Mahmud, M., & Brown, D. J. (2023). From assistive technologies to metaverse—Technologies in inclusive higher education for students with specific learning difficulties: A review. *IEEE Access : Practical Innovations, Open Solutions, 11*, 64907–64927. DOI: 10.1109/ACCESS.2023.3289496

Yingsoon, G. Y., Chua, N. A., Suyan, Z., Yiming, C., Haiyan, Z., & Xiaoyao, T. (2025). *Empowering Digital Citizens: Navigating AI Ethics, Engagement, and Privacy in the Era of Advanced Education Digital Citizenship and the Future of AI Engagement, Ethics, and Privacy*. IGI Global Scientific Publishing. DOI: 10.4018/979-8-3693-9015-3.ch003

Yin, J., Goh, T. T., Yang, B., & Xiaobin, Y. (2021). Conversation technology with micro-learning: The impact of chatbot-based learning on students' learning motivation and performance. *Journal of Educational Computing Research, 59*(1), 154–177. DOI: 10.1177/0735633120952067

Yu, J., & Couldry, N. (2022). Education as a domain of natural data extraction: Analysing corporate discourse about educational tracking. *Information Communication and Society, 25*(1), 127–144. DOI: 10.1080/1369118X.2020.1764604

Yuvasri, J., Senbagavalli, M., Rahul, R., & Saravana Kumar, C. S. (2025, March). Automated subjective answer evaluation using GenAI and NLP by enhancing accuracy, fairness, and feedback in education. In *2025 International Conference on Intelligent Computing and Control Systems (ICICCS)* (pp. 648–654). IEEE.

Zainuddin, Z., Chu, S. K. W., & Perera, C. J. (2024a). *Gamification in Education Gamification in A Flipped Classroom: Pedagogical Methods and Best Practices.* Springer. DOI: 10.1007/978-981-97-2219-8

Zakaria, A. L. J., Anas, B. O. U. A. Y. A. D., & Oucamah, C. M. M. (2022). Intelligent system for personalised interventions and early drop-out prediction in MOOCs. *International Journal of Advanced Computer Science and Applications, 13*(9). Advance online publication. DOI: 10.14569/IJACSA.2022.0130983

Zawacki-Richter, O. (2023). The state of AI in higher education: A systematic review. *Educational Technology Research and Development, 71*(5), 1–24.

Zawacki-Richter, O., Marín, V. I., Bond, M., & Gouverneur, F. (2019). Systematic review of research on artificial intelligence applications in higher education – Where are the educators? *International Journal of Educational Technology in Higher Education, 16*(1), 1–27. DOI: 10.1186/s41239-019-0171-0

Zhang & Wang. (2020). Urban-rural disparities in digital education. *Journal of Comparative Education, 40*(2), 88-112.

Zhang. (2023). Digital literacy and youth preparedness. *Youth Education Journal, 6*(1), 50-72.

Zhang, L., Jiang, Q., Xiong, W., & Zhao, W. (2024). Effects of ChatGPT-Based Human–Computer Dialogic Interaction Programming Activities on Student Engagement. *Journal of Educational Computing Research*, 07356331251333874.

Zheldibayeva, R. (2025). The impact of AI and peer feedback on research writing skills: a study using the CGScholar platform among Kazakhstani scholars. *arXiv preprint arXiv:2503.05820.*

Zhou & Raj. (2023). Connectivity challenges and policy responses. *Telecommunications & Education, 7*(2), 99-121.

Zimmerman, B. J. (2002). Becoming a self-regulated learner. *Theory into Practice, 41*(2), 64–70. DOI: 10.1207/s15430421tip4102_2

Zohuri, B., & Mossavar-Rahmani, F. (2024). Revolutionizing education: The dynamic synergy of personalized learning and artificial intelligence. *International Journal of Advanced Engineering and Management Research, 9*(1), 143–153. DOI: 10.51505/ijaemr.2024.9111

Zou, Y., Kuek, F., Feng, W., & Cheng, X. (2025). *Digital learning in the 21st century: trends, challenges, and innovations in technology integration.* Paper presented at the Frontiers in Education.

Zulkifli, . (2024). MyDigitalEducator: Teacher upskilling program evaluation. *Malaysia Education Review, 5*(1), 28–54.

Zupic, I., & Čater, T. (2015). Bibliometric methods in management and organization. *Organizational Research Methods, 18*(3), 429–472. DOI: 10.1177/1094428114562629

About the Contributors

Shafiq Ul Rehman is an experienced educator and professional consultant with a background in curriculum development and educational technology. With over 10 years in the field, Dr. Shafiq has worked with various educational institutions to implement sustainable practices and innovative teaching strategies. Dr. Shafiq received his Ph.D. degree from Universiti Sains Malaysia (USM), Malaysia, in 2017. He was a Postdoctoral Research Fellow at Singapore University of Technology and Design (SUTD), Singapore, from 2017 to 2020. He is currently Acting Dean, College of Information Technology and Chairman Department of Computer Science, Kingdom University, Bahrain. He is also an Assistant Professor with research interests in cybersecurity, artificial intelligence, and the latest emerging IT technologies. He lectures in various Computer Science and IT courses, including developing curriculum and courseware in tandem with current technology trends. He has authored and coauthored more than 50 peer reviewed publications, published in journals, conference proceedings, and book chapters. He supervises Ph.D., postgraduate, and undergraduate students. He also gives talks and training on cybersecurity, artificial intelligence, and the latest emerging IT technologies at various organizations, conferences, seminars, and workshops.

***

Amira Saif, a PhD in Instructional Technology from Universiti Sains Malaysia, specializes in human computer interaction within Computer Science. She holds a Master's in IT and Management from Taiz University and Delft University of Technology. Her areas of research interest include PBL, online learning environments, critical thinking, and technology-enhanced learning in programming education. She is also interested in the application of artificial intelligence, data analytics, and technology applications for special education.

Hanan Aldowah is currently a senior lecturer at Universiti Sains Malaysia (USM), where she has earned both a Ph.D. and a Master's degree in Instructional Technology and Multimedia. Aldowah possesses a comprehensive educational background. This is further enriched by a Bachelor's in computer science, offering a versatile skill set honed through practical experience and academic achievements. Her extensive expertise spans diverse domains, including Artificial Intelligence (AI), Machine Learning (ML), Data Analytics, Business Analytics, Data Management, Data Mining, and Sentiment Analysis, Information Systems, Technology adoption, Digital Transformation, and Organizational behavior; Advanced Data Analytics and Decision-Making Techniques across Business and Management, Human Computer Interaction (HCI), Virtual and Augmented Reality, Metaverse Applications, and Internet of Things (IoT). Aldowah holds a keen interest in online learning, E-learning, educational technology, and the application of emerging technologies such as AI, IoT, ML, and sentiment analysis to enhance various sectors, including management, education, computer education, and engineering education. Driven by a commitment to contribute to experiential education research and develop robust evaluation strategies. Aldowah's impactful research operates at the intersection of Computer Science and educational technology.

Wajdi Ben Rejeb is a Senior Lecturer in Business Strategy at Lincoln International Business School, University of Lincoln, UK. He teaches business strategy, strategic management, project management, entrepreneurship, and innovation. He holds a PhD in Management from the University of Tunis El Manar, Tunisia. He has over 20 years of experience in academia including research, lecturing and management experience. His research fields cover topics in relation with corporate governance, strategic management, corporate social responsibility and stakeholder management. His research interests include examining and understanding board processes, roles and behavior, and their relationship to strategic organizational outcomes.

Sarra Berraies is a Doctor of Management (Higher Institute of Management of Tunis, University of Tunis). She is an associate professor in the Higher Institute of Management of Tunis, University of Tunis and member of the Research 'Applied Research in Business, relationships and Economics' and the Tunisian Association for strategic intelligence, University of Tunis. Her research interests include knowledge management, learning, leadership, strategy, innovation, organizational behaviour, digital marketing, organizational performance, and governance. She published extensively in indexed academic journals and participated in several international conferences.

Saad Darwish is a director of Entrepreneurship Center and Acting Head of Community Engagement and Continuing Education Unit, College of Business Administration, Kingdom University, Bahrain

Srabani Priyadarsini Dash is an Assistant Professor and researcher affiliated with Maa manikeswari University, Bhawanipatna odisha. With a strong background in Computer Applications, she has contributed to the field through her teaching, research, and academic publications.Her research areas include Computer Networking, Cyber Security, Soft Computing, and Data Mining. She is known for her insightful analyses and innovative approaches in these areas. Srabani Priyadarsini Dash actively engages in curriculum development and student mentoring. She regularly participates in national and international seminars and workshops to stay updated with the latest advancements in her field and share her knowledge. She is deeply committed to promoting inclusive education and interdisciplinary research. Her work reflects a balanced integration of theoretical knowledge and practical relevance, addressing issues pertinent to the region and beyond. Through her research in Computer Networking, Cyber Security, Soft Computing, Data Mining, and programming languages like Python, C, C++, and Java, Srabani aims to contribute to the development of robust and secure computing solutions that can benefit society.

Shaji Joseph did his graduation and postgraduation in Sociology from Pune University (SPPU) and PhD in Management from Symbiosis International University in 2020. Currently, he is an associate professor at Symbiosis International Deemed University Pune. His area of expertise is in sustainability standards and reporting, Human resources management, and corporate governance and ethics. His research interests include sustainable development, ethical leadership, leadership assessment, and human resources management. Dr Shaji Joseph can be reached at shaji@scit.edu

Bünyami Kayali graduated from Erzincan University, Faculty of Education, Department of Mathematics Education in 2008. Between 2018 and 2022, he completed his doctorate at Atatürk University in Computer and Instructional Technologies Education. From 2008 to 2021, he taught at various institutions affiliated with the Ministry of National Education. Currently, he is employed as an Assistant Professor at Bayburt University, Department of Computer Technologies. His areas of research interest are Distance Education, Instructional Technology, and Artificial Intelligence.

Mustafa Kayyali is an ardent advocate for excellence in higher education, driven by a relentless pursuit of quality, recognition, and innovation. Their journey in academia started with a Master's in Quality Management and Evaluation in Higher Education from Universitat Oberta de Catalunya, followed by a Ph.D. in Quality

Management from Azteca University. These academic pursuits have laid a strong foundation for their expertise in Accreditation, Quality Assurance, and Higher Education Rankings. As an entrepreneur, researcher, translator, and publisher, they are deeply involved in various facets of the academic world. Their diverse interests encompass Management, Translation, Interpretation, and Academic consulting, contributing to a well-rounded understanding of the industry. Throughout their career, they have made significant contributions to academic literature, with more than 40 published papers and 30 book chapters to my name. Additionally, they take pride in having translated 6 books, bridging language gaps, and promoting knowledge exchange on a global scale. They are committed to fostering positive change in higher education and contributing to its continuous improvement.

Benu Kesar did her Master's in Business Administration (MBA) from NMIMS Mumbai and is pursuing her PhD from Symbiosis International (Deemed University) Pune. Dr. Kesar's research interests lie at the intersection of technology, communication, and societal impact, focusing on how digital platforms are reshaping human interaction and influencing organizational strategies. Dr. Benu Kesar can be reached at drbenukesar@gmail.com.

Dev Kesar is an Analyst at a Finance firm, where he contributes to data-driven financial strategies and technology solutions. He holds a B.Tech in Computer Science and Engineering from VIT Chennai. His interests lie at the intersection of finance, analytics, and emerging technologies.Dev Kesar can be reached at devkesar4210@ gmail.com

Durga Madhab Mahapatra is an Associate Professor in the Department of Commerce at North-Eastern Hill University (NEHU), Shillong, India. With a distinguished academic career spanning over two decades, Dr. Mahapatra has made significant contributions to the fields of commerce, business strategy, and socio-economic development. He holds a Ph.D. in Commerce and has developed a strong research portfolio that bridges theory and practice, particularly in the areas of marketing management, consumer behaviour, rural entrepreneurship, and sustainable development. Dr. Mahapatra is widely recognised for his interdisciplinary approach and has published extensively in national and international peer-reviewed journals. His current research interests include digital transformation in commerce, tribal entrepreneurship, inclusive business models, and the socio-economic dynamics of the North-Eastern region of India. He has also actively participated in national conferences and UGC-sponsored seminars and has contributed chapters to edited volumes on contemporary issues in commerce and development. An advocate for community-based research and academic outreach, Dr. Mahapatra frequently collaborates with NGOs and government agencies to promote grassroots entrepreneurship and capacity-building initiatives. He is committed to advancing indigenous knowledge systems and fostering educational excellence in underserved regions.

Sakshi Mann is an Assistant Professor of Human Resource Management at Indira Institute of Management, Pune. With a Ph.D. in HR and over 11 years of combined industry and academic experience, she brings a practical edge to her teaching. Her expertise spans Organizational Behavior, Recruitment & Selection, Employee Engagement, and Leadership. Having managed HR operations across various organizations, she seamlessly integrates real-world insights into academia. Passionate about research, she explores contemporary HR challenges to contribute valuable insights to the field. Committed to bridging academia and industry, Dr. Mann fosters critical thinking and practical application, equipping students for the evolving HR landscape.

Shikha Mann is an academician, Certified MBTI Coach, internationally certified TIFF Provider, Enneagram Coach, Certified SII coach, Motivational Speaker, Leadership Coach, Organizational Culture Consultant and Corporate Trainer. She is associated with Indira School of Business Studies PGDM, Pune as Deputy Director. She completed her Ph.D. from Symbiosis International (Deemed University) in Organizational Behaviour. She is an academician, trainer and a consultant. She was conferred upon the award of "40under40 education leaders by Business World Education in 2024" and "Best Faculty on Human Resource" in Pune Education Leadership Awards 2019. She has been involved as Assessor in Development centre and Assessment centres for various renowned MNCs. She has set up HR processes for start-ups. She has done succession planning for many organizations in Pharmaceuticals and manufacturing domain. She has worked with senior management of various organizations and has been involved in developing leadership. She regularly provides trainings on areas such as Team Building, Business Communication, Presentation Skills, Stress management, Leadership, Motivation and Body Language. She has conducted various workshops for many MNCs and B Schools on topics such as Employability Skills, Personality Development, Be the Best version of Yourself, Know your Potential, Explore the "real you". She has been invited as a guest speaker in many national and state level conferences. She has teaching experience of 9 years, she has written many research papers in national and international journals. Her subject expertise include Organizational Behaviour, HRM, Psychometric Tests, Compensation & Benefits, Performance Management System, SHRM, Industrial Relations, Learning & Development, Talent Management and OD

Shreeansh Mishra is an Assistant Professor, Department of Tourism & Hospitality Management, Central University of Tamil Nadu, Tamil Nadu, India

Rohit Kumar Rawat is an Assistant Professor at the School of Management Studies, Rajiv Gandhi National Aviation University. He holds a Ph.D. in Economics from the School of Economics, University of Hyderabad. His academic interests lie at the intersection of development economics, labour markets, and urban transitions, with a growing specialisation in aviation and managerial economics. He has significant research experience in Micro and Macro Economics, Econometrics, and Large-scale survey data analyses. Mr. Rawat is keen on interdisciplinary collaborations, especially those involving Aviation economics, Employment, Survey data, Gig economy, farmer-producer organisation, Rural non-farm economy and Informal sector. He has presented his work at various international conferences in India and abroad. He has contributed to academic workshops and policy-focused seminars. At RGNAU, Mr. Rawat teaches Aviation Economics and Managerial Economics courses. His current research interests include the economics of the aviation sector, workforce development in air transport, and regional connectivity in India.

K. S. Shibani Shankar Ray is an Assistant Professor at Rajiv Gandhi National Aviation University, Fursatganj, Amethi. He is a scholar-practitioner at the intersection of strategy, policy, and behavioural science. With an MBA from IIM Indore and a doctoral research in Marketing Management, his research explores heuristics in strategic decision-making, stakeholder engagement in sustainability, and digital health systems. He has taught across premier institutions and delivered flagship programs on women's financial leadership and rural entrepreneurship. Shibani has worked with various renowned corporate houses, bringing rich field insights into his classrooms and publications. His writing appears in Empirical Economics Letters, Technology in Society, and IGI Global volumes on AI, blended learning, and sustainable e-commerce. A recipient of multiple national awards, Shibani combines academic rigour with on-ground impact, driven by a commitment to inclusive development and transformative pedagogy.

Zakir Shaikh is an Assistant Professor, Department of Accounting and Finance, School of Business Administration, Kingdom University, Bahrain. Prior to this, he worked more than 28 years in commercial and academic industry. He has published numerous articles in referred journals and presented many papers in various conferences, both local and abroad in the different area of Accounting, management and Islamic Banking and Finance. He has also participated in a variety of seminars, forums, workshops and international conferences. He obtained his Ph.D.

(Islamic Banking and Finance) from India in 2018. His doctoral thesis explored the entrepreneurial phenomenon from an Islamic perspective and argued for profit and loss sharing (PLS) contracts as viable alternatives to conventional interest-based financing instruments. He holds Master degree in Commerce, Business Administration & Finance and Control. He is a member of AAA, Chartered Institute of Islamic Finance Professionals (CIIF), Malaysia; Indian Accounting Association; Orissa Commerce Association, India and associated with Accounting & Auditing Organization for Islamic Financial Institution (AAOIFI), Bahrain

Amrik Singh is working as Professor in the School of Hotel Management and Tourism at Lovely Professional University, Punjab, India. He obtained his Ph.D. degree in Hotel Management from Kurukshetra University, Kurukshetra. He started his academic career at Lovely Professional University, Punjab, India in the year 2007. He has published more than 40 research papers in UGC and peer-reviewed and Scopus/Web of Science) journals. He has published 12 patents and 01 patent has been granted in the inter-disciplinary domain. Dr. Amrik Singh participated and acted as a resource person in various national and international conferences, seminars, research workshops, and industry talks. His area of research interest is accommodation management, ergonomics, green practices, human resource management in hospitality, waste management, AR VR in hospitality, etc. He is currently guiding 8Ph.D. scholars and 2 Ph.D. scholars have been awarded Ph.D.

Mehmet Yavuz is a faculty member at Bingöl University, located in the Eastern Anatolia Region of Türkiye. He currently serves in the Faculty of Economics and Administrative Sciences, Department of Management Information Systems, Distance Education Application and Research Center, and Digital Transformation and Software Offices. He focuses on teaching and research in the areas of distance education, educational technologies, digital transformation, and artificial intelligence. His academic work primarily focuses on innovative teaching methods. He actively contributes to national and international academic networks and aims to promote knowledge production and community engagement through research and collaboration.

Index

A

B

C

D

E

F

G

H

I

L

M

P

S

T

www.ingramcontent.com/pod-product-compliance
Lightning Source LLC
LaVergne TN
LVHW060006031026
849161LV00025B/1524
* 9 7 9 8 3 3 7 3 3 8 1 5 6 *